509

BEYOND
CONTAINMENT

WILLIAM HENRY CHAMBERLIN

BEYOND CONTAINMENT

HENRY REGNERY COMPANY

Chicago   *1953*

Introduction

Although the cold war between the communist empire ruled from Moscow and the loose coalition of free nations headed by the United States is of urgent concern to every American, the causes and background of this struggle are imperfectly understood. This is partly because the Soviet Government has tried to veil its policies in mystery and has shut off its empire, so far as possible, from outside observation. Another reason for misunderstanding of Soviet psychology and intentions is the impatience of the average American with theory and his frequent failure to realize that ideas can be weapons.

The present book is an attempt to sketch the history and interpret the causes of the cold war. The conclusions are based on the author's experiences and impressions during twelve years of residence in the Soviet Union as a journalist; on Soviet newspapers and periodicals; on talks with Soviet and East European refugees in America and Europe; and on the memoirs of statesmen who are able to describe at first hand the evolution of Soviet-Western relations during and since the war. I have found especially informative and illuminating *The Second World War,* by Winston Churchill; *Roosevelt and Hopkins,* by Robert E. Sherwood, and the memoirs and papers of James F. Byrnes, Arthur Vandenberg, James A. Forrestal, Lucius Clay and Walter Bedell Smith.

At a time when, following the death of Stalin, new maneuvers and zigzags in Soviet foreign policy are taking place, I believe the emphasis on the permanent factors in Soviet communist theory and practice which have produced the cold war will prove timely. I should like to express appreciation to the editors of *The Wall Street Journal, The Freeman, The New Leader, Human Events* and *The Russian Review* for permission to include in the book some material which has appeared in these publications.

WILLIAM HENRY CHAMBERLIN

Cambridge, Massachusetts
May 15, 1953

CONTENTS

BEYOND
CONTAINMENT

Chapter I ～ USA–USSR:

The Great Confrontation

There are, at the present time, two great nations in the world which seem to tend toward the same end, although they started from different points; I allude to the Russians and the Americans. . . . The Anglo-American relies upon personal interest to accomplish his ends, and gives free scope to the unguided exertions and commonsense of the citizen; the Russian centers all the authority of society in a single arm; the principal instrument of the former is freedom, of the latter servitude. Their starting point is different and their courses are not the same; yet each of them seems to be marked out by the will of heaven to sway the destinies of half the globe.*

There are few examples of prophetic insight more conspicuously vindicated by the course of events. When de Tocqueville wrote (1835–1840) the young American Republic counted for little in European politics. Russia was already a great power. But later in the century Great Britain and France did not hesitate to invade Russia during the Crimean War—an unthinkable military venture for Great Britain and France today.

But there were elements of fundamental strength in the future of the United States and of Russia which the keen observer de Tocqueville took into account in making his predic-

* Alexis de Tocqueville, *Democracy in America* (Oxford, 1947), pp. 242–43.

tion. Both countries possessed, for the needs of growing populations, untapped resources of continental scope. Russia could expand eastward to the Pacific, as America could expand westward to the Pacific without encountering serious opposition. In the Russian Far East, as in the American Far West, there was only a sparse settlement of primitive tribesmen.

Neither Russia nor the United States felt any economic pressure to build up overseas empires which might in time become restive and break away. Both held already in their possession vast stretches of land which awaited migration and development. A thoughtful and farsighted observer could foresee the time when both America and Russia could engage in enterprises of internal development beyond the possibilities of the comparatively small and crowded European countries.

Moreover each country symbolized an idea, carried to an extreme conclusion. The United States represented a new example of social equality and individual opportunity, within a framework of free institutions, protected by a system of checks and balances against excessive concentration of government power. In Russia, in our own time as in de Tocqueville's, all the authority of society is indeed centered in a single arm. Stalin was a far more potent ruler than Nicholas I, because he added to the unlimited political authority of the Tsars complete control of the national economy. Two sharply opposed principles of human action were at work.

More than a century elapsed after the American Revolution before America and Russia came face to face in the arena of world politics. At first there was extremely little contact, political or commercial. Twenty-six years passed after the conclusion of peace with England in 1783 before diplomatic relations were established between the American Republic and the Russian Empire. There was a lapse of sixteen years between the setting up of the Soviet Government in November, 1917, and the establishment of American-Soviet diplomatic relations.

There is no real similarity between these cases, however.

Tsarist Russia had no grievances against republican America, whereas United States recognition of the Soviet regime was delayed by Soviet international subversive propaganda, repudiation of Russian debts to the United States and confiscation of American property.

Indeed differences in political ideology played a minor role in the ups and downs of American-Russian relations before 1917. It would have been preposterous to carry on propaganda in America for the Tsarist system of government and American influence in Russia was too slight to cause the Tsarist Government any concern. Russian revolutionaries drew their inspiration from Marx and other continental socialist thinkers, not from Jefferson and Lincoln.

Tsar Alexander I, who had imbibed some liberal theories from a French tutor, La Harpe, treated the first American Ambassador to Russia, Thomas Jefferson, with conspicuous graciousness. There was some friendly correspondence between the Tsar and Thomas Jefferson, who sent the autocrat of all the Russias some books dealing with the American Constitution.

An element that made for American-Russian agreement in the early nineteenth century was a common distrust of the pretensions of British sea power. On the other hand there was some fear of Russia as a possible competitor in the Pacific Northwest. Russia owned Alaska and there was a small Russian settlement for a time at Fort Ross, about fifty miles north of San Francisco. There were disputes over sealing and fishing rights in the North Pacific.

There was also some apprehension that the Holy Alliance, a union of European sovereigns dedicated to the preservation of the status quo, might intervene against the newly established republics of South America. Alexander I, who turned into a reactionary mystic in the later years of his reign, was an enthusiastic promoter of the Holy Alliance.

The Monroe Doctrine, announced as a unilateral declaration of United States policy, but with the concurrence of Great

Britain, was aimed at Russia more than at any other power. The proclamation of this Doctrine, which committed the United States to oppose any new colonization of the American continent by a European power or the restoration of Spanish authority in South America, was preceded by a note, emphasizing these points, addressed to the Russian Government.

These clouds in early American-Russian relations cleared away. The Holy Alliance proved to be an empty threat. Russia made no serious effort to push the development of Alaska or to establish settlements further to the South. There was almost a honeymoon atmosphere in American-Russian relations during the Civil War. Alexander II created a favorable impression on Northern opinion by liberating the serfs in 1861, shortly before Lincoln's Emancipation Proclamation. The Tsar firmly opposed any suggestion of being drawn into European action favorable to the Confederacy. There was nothing sentimental about this Russian policy.

The Tsar, like his predecessors, saw in a strong United States an offset to the power of Great Britain, Russia's principal enemy throughout the nineteenth century. However, Russia's friendship was warmly appreciated at a time when there was still danger that Great Britain and France might recognize the Confederacy.

There was special enthusiasm when Russian warships visited the ports of New York and San Francisco in the autumn of 1863. The reason for this visit to the possible shelter of neutral ports was Russian fear that a new Crimean War might be in prospect because of British and French resentment against the suppression of the Polish uprising in 1863. This was not generally realized at the time. The visit of the Russian fleet was warmly welcomed as a friendly gesture to the Northern cause. This incident inspired a couplet written by Oliver Wendell Holmes when the Russian Grand Duke Alexis visited the United States in 1871:

Bleak are our shores with the blasts of December,
Fettered and dull is the rivulet's flow;
Throbbing and warm are the hearts that remember
Who was our friend when the world was our foe.

A possible source of Russian-American friction was removed when Alaska was sold to the United States for 7,200,000 dollars in 1867. In view of the strategic importance of Alaska in the air age it is amusing to recall that the Russian Government wanted to get rid of this territory at almost any price, while there was strong United States opposition to "Seward's Folly" in acquiring what was considered a frozen wasteland.

The commercial significance of Alaska for Russia had declined and the Russian Government feared that the region would be indefensible in the event of a war with Great Britain. A factor that helped to win Congressional approval of the transaction was the feeling that the Russian attitude of goodwill during the Civil War deserved a friendly response.

Later in the century new clouds appeared upon the horizon of American-Russian relations. The tyrannical nature of the Tsarist regime, obscured by the liberation of the serfs and other liberal measures in the first years of the reign of Alexander II, was more generally realized. There were more political refugees from Russia whose stories gained a hearing. Liberals like Professor Paul Milyukov and picturesque revolutionaries like Mme. Breshko-Breshkovskaya, "the Grandmother of the Russian Revolution," made a sympathetic impression on American liberal opinion. George Kennan, publicist and great-uncle of the American diplomat of the same name who served for a short time as Ambassador to the Soviet Union, gave a vivid picture of the hardships of exiled prisoners in Siberia.

There was a substantial emigration of Russian Jews to the United States between 1880 and 1910. This quickened American consciousness of anti-Semitic discrimination in Russia. Such incidents as the pogrom, or anti-Jewish riot, in Kishinev in 1903, in which some fifty persons were killed and several hundred wounded, aroused horror and indignation in the United States and western European countries. Diplomatic friction was generated because the Russian authorities often refused to validate the passports of former Russian Jews who had become American citizens. This dispute led to the termination of the American-Russian commercial treaty in 1911.

There were also clashes of American and Russian interests in the Far East, the part of the world where the two countries came into most direct contact. As early as 1855 Humphrey Marshall, United States commissioner to China, was so alarmed at the possibility that the Chinese Government might pass under Russian control that he wrote to Secretary of State Marcy:

> I think that almost any sacrifice should be made by the United States to keep Russia from spreading her Pacific boundary and to avoid her coming directly to interference in Chinese domestic affairs.

More of Mr. Marshall's insight might have been useful in the State Department almost a century later, when Soviet Russia achieved what Tsarist diplomacy had scarcely dreamed of: complete political domination of China.

While Great Britain and France employed mainly naval power to open up China to communication with the West, the Russian approach to China was on a basis of overland expansion. By 1860 Russia had taken over what had formerly been Chinese territory north of the Amur and east of the Ussuri rivers. After joining with Germany and France in imposing a veto on Japanese acquisition of South Manchuria after the Sino-Japanese War of 1894–95 Russia obtained from China both a lease of strategic points in this territory and the right to build a railway across North Manchuria, with a southern spur to Dalny (Dairen), at the southern tip of Manchuria.

Secretary of State John Hay's attempts in 1899–1900 to obtain international recognition for his so-called Open Door policy for China (a policy of nondiscrimination in commercial matters) met a chilly and evasive reaction in St. Petersburg.

Neither Hay nor President Theodore Roosevelt cherished a favorable opinion of Russian reliability in international transactions.

"Russia's vows are as false as dicers' oaths when treachery is possible," Hay exclaimed on one occasion. During the Russo-Japanese War Roosevelt wrote to his friend, the British diplomat, Sir Cecil Spring-Rice:

> Russia for a number of years has treated the United States as badly as she had treated England, and almost as badly as she has treated Japan. Her diplomatists lied to us with brazen and contemptuous effrontery and showed with cynical indifference their intention to organize China against our interest.

When war broke out between Russia and Japan in 1904 American sympathy, like British, was generally on the side of Japan. However, the unexpected speed and completeness of the Japanese victories on land and sea produced a change of atmosphere in Washington. Despite his frequent impulsiveness in speech, Theodore Roosevelt possessed the classical diplomat's sense of the desirability of maintaining a balance of power. He realized that complete predominance of Japan in the Far East might be just as injurious to American interests as the Russian domination that would have followed the crushing of Japan. The peace treaty between Russia and Japan, concluded with American mediation at Portsmouth, New Hampshire, was favorable to Japan, but left Russia a substantial power in the Orient.

Japan took over the Russian concessions and sphere of influence in South Manchuria and received the southern half of the island of Sakhalin, north of the northernmost of the Japanese chain of islands, Hokkaido. After the end of the war there was a rapprochement between St. Petersburg and Tokyo. Russia and Japan both opposed a proposal of the American Secretary of State, Philander C. Knox, which would have paved the way for American investment in Manchurian railway development.

An effect of the First World War was the elimination of American-Russian tension in the Orient. Russian exertions were concentrated in Europe and Russia was fighting on the side which enjoyed most sympathy in the United States.

However, Tsarist Russia was a somewhat embarrassing partner in what was represented as a struggle for freedom and democracy. The fall of the autocracy on March 12, 1917, was generally welcomed in the United States. President Wilson, in his message to Congress requesting a declaration of war against Germany, singled out the new Russia for an especially favorable reference:

> Russia was known by those who have known it best to have been always democratic at heart. . . . The autocracy that had long crowned the summit of her political structure, long as it had stood and terrible as was the reality of its power, was not in fact Russian in origin, character or purpose; and now it has been shaken off and the great, generous Russian people have been added in all their native majesty and might to the forces that are fighting for freedom in the world for justice and for peace. Here is a fit partner for a League of Honor.

However appropriate this passage may have been as an opening blast of wartime propaganda, it was scarcely worthy of Wilson's scholarship as historian and political scientist. The Romanov dynasty which had ruled for three centuries was thoroughly Russian in origin and carried on a very old Russian tradition of absolute rule which was soon to be intensified under a revolutionary dictatorship. There was little in the Russian historical experience, in Russian social conditions, in the Russian cast of thought to suggest that a western conception of democracy, with safeguards for individual liberties, would spring up on Russian soil.

One of the first results of the collapse of the imperial rule was the disintegration of the huge Russian army as an effective fighting force. By November it was possible for the Bolsheviks, the extremist wing of the Russian Social Democratic Party, under the leadership of Vladimir Ilyitch Lenin, to overthrow the weak Provisional Government and set up a Republic of

Soviets, based on the principle of the dictatorship of the proletariat and committed to an attitude of implacable hostility
against the "capitalist" world.

American judgment of Russia, a small minority of communist sympathizers excepted, changed sharply in a negative direction. There was bitterness over Russia's abandonment of the
common cause against Germany. The view gained currency
that the Bolshevik leaders were mere hired German agents.
This was a false conception, although it may well be that Lenin
and his associates, with the unscrupulousness of fanatics, took
other aid from the German Government besides free transportation across German territory from Switzerland to Russia. But
their fundamental ambition was to destroy all "capitalist" and
"imperialist" governments, the German included.

In the summer of 1918 Wilson rather reluctantly allowed
himself to be persuaded into taking part in military intervention against the Soviet regime at two points, Archangel, Russia's
chief Arctic port, and Vladivostok, in the Far East. The original
purpose of this intervention was to safeguard military stores
which had been shipped to these ports against possible seizure
by the Germans, who had imposed the unfavorable peace of
Brest-Litovsk on the Soviet regime and were believed at that
time to be in a position to impose their will throughout Russia.
Fighting with Soviet troops was on a very small scale and American troops were withdrawn from Archangel in 1919. American
intervention in Siberia was favorable, rather than otherwise,
in its effect on Soviet interests. The American expeditionary
force served as a check on the ambitions of Japan, which had
sent a much larger army into Siberia, and fought very little
with the local Soviet sympathizers.

The reasons for the prolonged period of absence of diplo-
matic relations between the United States and the new Soviet
Government were set forth in a diplomatic communication by
Secretary of State Bainbridge Colby in August, 1920:

We cannot recognize, hold official relations with or give friendly reception to the agents of a government which is determined and bound to conspire against our institutions; whose diplomats will be the agents of dangerous revolt; whose spokesmen say that they sign agreements with no intention of keeping them.

Subsequent American official declarations laid down three conditions for recognition. These were compensation for American property nationalized by the Soviet regime, recognition of the war debt which had been contracted by the Provisional Government and cessation of propaganda directed from Moscow against American institutions. The American Government refused to recognize the validity of the distinction which Soviet spokesmen tried to establish between the activities of the Soviet Government and those of the Communist International, or Comintern.

Although American policy in the postwar years was uncompromising as regards diplomatic recognition, it was consistently favorable to Russian national interests. American pressure, exercised at the Washington Conference of 1922 and on other occasions, was a factor in bringing about Japanese evacuation of Vladivostok and the fall of the dependent Russian administration which had been maintained with Japanese aid in Eastern Siberia. America favored the Russian as against the Polish viewpoint regarding the proper frontier between these two states. United States recognition of the new Baltic states, Latvia, Lithuania and Estonia, came late, long after the Soviet Government itself had acknowledged their independence. Whether this policy, apparently based on a vague hope that some day somehow a strong friendly Russia would emerge, was wise seems questionable, in view of the subsequent course of events. It certainly earned no dividends of goodwill from the Soviet Government.

Paradoxical as it may seem, the period when there were no formal relations between the two governments was the time of freest contact of Americans with Soviet life. Travel and residence in Russia were easier and journalistic activity, although always subject to censorship, was much freer than has been the case in recent years. Some thousands of American engineers and technicians, as individuals on contracts with the Soviet Government and as employees of construction firms, helped the first big upsurge toward industrialization in Russia after 1929.

The change of the party in power in America after the election of Franklin D. Roosevelt in 1932 set the stage for the establishment of American-Soviet relations. Probably the soundest reason for this step was the desirability of having some means of regular communication with a regime which occupied an important place in the politics of Europe and of Asia. It had long been clear that the withholding of American recognition would not cause the Soviet regime to fall.

Some of the other arguments which were advanced for recognition proved invalid. Alluring visions of great trade opportunities soon vanished. There was no visible increase in American-Russian goodwill. Indeed restrictions on freedom of activity for Americans, as for other foreigners, were intensified.

Nor was there any satisfactory settlement, from the American standpoint, of the issues which had delayed recognition. During the negotiations which preceded the resumption of relations Soviet Foreign Commissar Maxim Litvinov, on behalf of his government, undertook "not to permit the formation or residence on its territory of any organization or group . . . which has as an aim the overthrow or the preparation for the overthrow of, or bringing about by force of a change in the political or social order of the whole or any part of the United States, its territories or possessions."

If words have any meaning this pledge called for the suppression in Moscow of the activities of the Comintern. However, this organization continued to exist for ten years after the pledge was given and held a congress in Moscow in 1935, where American communists delivered reports on their revolutionary activities in the United States. Although Litvinov had held out hopes on this subject in the preliminary negotiations, the Soviet Government refused to make any settlement of American property and debt claims, except in return for a new loan, which the United States was unwilling to give.

So the hopes of an era of American-Soviet good feeling were not realized. Secretary Hull might have recalled Secretary Hay's phrase about Russian vows being "as false as dicers' oaths" when he composed a note of protest about the congress of the Comintern.

During the thirties Soviet conditions became to some extent a football of internal politics in the United States, with American conservatives taking a negative view, while New Dealers were apt to be apologetic, if not positively enthusiastic for the new order in Russia. In the main American public opinion was sceptical, if not hostile. Communist hostility to religion was unpopular. And, despite severe Soviet censorship, which weakened the impact of these events on the consciousness and conscience of the outside world, some inkling of such grim Soviet developments as the "liquidation of the kulaks as a class," the forced-labor camps, the great famine of 1932–33 and the ruthless purge of the Communist Party itself did leak out.

However, a section of American leftist intellectuals remained obstinate enthusiasts for the bright new day of planned economy and full employment which, as they conceived, had dawned in Russia. Seldom if ever have individuals who prided themselves on rationality and humanity been so impervious to evidence or so indifferent to mass inhumanity. A regular sequel to every new mass execution in Moscow was a manifesto, signed by scores of leftwing intellectuals and glorifying the executions as a new triumph of socialism and democracy.

Even in leftist circles, however, Soviet prestige declined heavily when the Stalin-Hitler Pact of August 21, 1939, an obvious curtain-raiser for a new war, was announced. The pretense of being an uncompromising enemy of fascism had been dropped.

The brutal partition of Poland with the Nazis was another blow to Soviet prestige. The British cartoonist David Low, a good barometer of liberal opinion, published one of his most vivid sketches, showing Stalin and Hitler shaking hands over the corpse of Poland and greeting each other ironically as "the scum of the earth" and "the bloody assassin of the workers."

The unprovoked Soviet invasion of Finland on November 30, 1939, caused President Roosevelt to utter words of strong condemnation when he addressed members of the communist-infiltrated American Youth Congress, who hissed and booed him for his remarks:

> The Soviet Union is run by a dictatorship as absolute as any dictatorship in the world. It has allied itself with another dictatorship, and it has invaded a neighbor so infinitesimally small that it could do no conceivable harm to the Soviet Union.

Unfortunately the clear insight which President Roosevelt showed on this occasion exercised no visible influence upon America's wartime policy. There was apparently no consideration in Administration circles for the possibility that a Kilkenny Cats' fight of dictatorships, in which Nazism and communism might have been expected to weaken, if not destroy each other, would be preferable to all-out alliance with one of these "absolute dictatorships," with all the moral and political disadvantages which this might be expected to involve.

Hitler's attack in June, 1941, did not change in the slightest degree the character of the Soviet Government as an absolute tyranny, obsessed with a theory of eternal conflict with the non-communist world. But American public opinion, influenced and manipulated by official and unofficial Administration spokesmen, indulged in an orgy of self-delusion about the nature and purposes of Soviet communism which is intellectually humiliating in retrospect and which was disastrous to American national interests.

Vice-President Henry A. Wallace led the chorus. The following citations from a speech which he delivered in Madison Square Garden on November 8, 1942, give a fair picture of the spirit which prevailed in that time of folly:

> Russia, perceiving some of the abuses of excessive political democracy, has placed strong emphasis on economic democracy. . . . Russia has probably gone farther than any other nation in the world in practising ethnic democracy. . . . When Lenin and Stalin gave them [the Russian people] the opportunity they changed in twenty years from a nation which was 90% illiterate to a nation of which nearly 90% are able to read and write. . . . The American and Russian people can and will throw their influence on the side of building a new democracy which will be the hope of the world.

As often happens in Mr. Wallace's oratory, definitions are conspicuously absent. Is "economic democracy," for instance, an accurate characterization of a system in which there are no free trade unions and in which millions of people are compelled to work under inhuman conditions in forced labor camps? "Ethnic democracy" finds rather curious expression in laws liquidating whole national communities in the Soviet Union and in Soviet legislation which makes it impossible for Soviet citizens to marry foreigners. The figures of pre-war illiteracy and of Soviet literacy are both substantially exaggerated.

Mr. Wallace was not the only voice in the wartime pro-Soviet chorus. The Council of American-Soviet Friendship, later placed on the Attorney-General's subversive list, was then a popular and respectable forum. The late Harold Ickes, then Secretary of the Interior, told the Council, at a meeting on November 8, 1943:

> The truth is that, despite the vicious Hitlerisms of Hearst and of the Patterson-McCormick newspaper axis * there are many

* This has been and to a certain extent still is a very familiar controversial device of pro-Soviet propaganda: to represent criticism of communism as an outgrowth of fascist sympathy. Fascists, in their days of

things of which the Soviet Union has reason to be proud. In certain respects we could do well to learn from Russia, yes, even to imitate Russia . . . I do not see what possible cause for an embroilment there could be between the United States and the Soviet Union after the present war.

A still more ecstatic note was struck by Senator Elbert D. Thomas, of Utah, who contributed the following eulogy to the communist partyline magazine *New Masses* of June 22, 1943:

In the future, when we make an estimate of Soviet leadership, we will see that it is based upon the finest of democratic principles, the cultivation and development of the people by providing proper education, proper health, proper hospitalization, and proper social opportunities.

Another character witness for the Soviet regime was Joseph E. Davies, former Soviet Ambassador to the Soviet Union, who told an audience in Chicago in February, 1942: "By the testimony of performance and in my opinion the word of honor of the Soviet Government is as safe as the Bible." Mr. Davies also thought up an ingenious explanation of the Soviet purges. They were a liquidation of a traitorous "fifth column." This explanation failed to explain why the Soviet Union, if its "fifth column" had been exterminated, furnished far more recruits for the German armed forces than all the other invaded countries put together.

With so many prominent figures joining in this adulation, it is not surprising that the average American, no specialist in foreign affairs, was badly deceived about the nature and purposes of the Soviet regime. In this climate of public opinion it was easy to pass off the sacrifices of moral principle and American political interest at Yalta as a great diplomatic success.

But this one-sided American-Soviet honeymoon (there was no corresponding enthusiasm for the United States in the disci-

power, were similarly inclined to disparage critics as "communists." Both assumptions are, of course, completely false.

plined Soviet press) did not last very long. The Second World War brought to final accomplishment de Tocqueville's prophecy of a supreme confrontation of Russia and America and the confrontation, despite much American wishful thinking to the contrary, was not and could not have been of a peaceful and friendly character.

The cushions that had formerly softened direct American-Russian contact disappeared. Every continental European nation, except a few minor neutrals, was shattered and overrun by the power of Nazi Germany. Germany itself finally crumbled in the wreckage of total defeat. Great Britain, technically a victor, emerged from the war gravely impoverished and weakened, no longer able or willing to apply those principles of free trade and keen competition on which its nineteenth century prosperity was based. Much of Britain's former wealth, in the shape of overseas investments, was consumed in the crucible of the war. The anti-colonial revolt in Asia destroyed or impaired some former sources of British wealth.

The destruction of German military power in Europe and of the Japanese Empire in Asia left big power vacuums, which the Soviet Union was quick to fill. The late Jan Christian Smuts, Prime Minister of South Africa, and one of the more profound thinkers among Commonwealth statesmen, clearly foresaw the shape of things to come. In a speech delivered toward the end of 1943, which attracted much less attention than it deserved, Smuts summed up the situation with clear-sighted realism:

> Russia is the new colossus on the European continent. What the after-effects of that will be no one can say. We can but recognize that this is a new fact to reckon with, and we must reckon with it coldly and objectively. With the others [Germany, France and Italy] down and out and herself the mistress of the continent, her power will not only be great on that account, but will be still greater because the Japanese Empire will have gone the way of all flesh. Therefore any check or balance that might have arisen in the East will have disappeared. You will have Russia

in a position which no country has ever occupied in the history of Europe.

Smuts proved as true a prophet as de Tocqueville. Stalin after the war achieved conquests, direct and indirect, which far surpassed the accomplishments of the most imperialist of his Tsarist predecessors. Alexander I played an important part in defeating Napoleon and in arranging the subsequent European peace settlement. But Russian troops at that time did not remain in the heart of Europe, quartered in such old European capitals as Berlin and Vienna. There was no Russian territorial expansion to compare with the reduction of Poland, Rumania, Czechoslovakia, Hungary, Bulgaria, Albania and East Germany to the status of Soviet frontier provinces. There was no Russian fifth column, working to undermine the independence of the countries which were still independent.

The great confrontation of Russia and America because of the collapse or decline of the powers which formerly stood between these two giants of the twentieth century soon revealed its consequences: bitter rivalry and antagonism. The United Nations soon became the Divided Nations. The allies in the war against Germany became the opponents in a cold war that was no longer so cold after fighting began in Korea in 1950.

There is no common Soviet-American territorial frontier. But the two powers face each with military, economic, diplomatic and propaganda weapons deployed along a global frontier that runs from the Arctic area of Northern Norway, along the demarcation line in sundered Germany and Austria, along the frontiers of Yugoslavia, Greece and Turkey, through the fermenting Near and Middle East, to the steaming rice paddies of Indo-China and the bleak hills of Korea.

The two nations, of which the instrument of the one is freedom, of the other servitude, both stand at the peak of their power in the middle of the twentieth century. Their dispute,

incomparably the most important issue in contemporary politics, is most difficult to resolve, because it is not rooted in
some specific controversy about territory or trade which could
be compromised. But the four basic causes of the cold war are
of the intangible character where compromise is scarcely possible. They are:

(1) The conviction of irrepressible conflict. It is an article
of dogmatic faith with Soviet leaders, set forth repeatedly in
the writings of Lenin and Stalin, that a last decisive struggle
between the communist and noncommunist worlds is inevitable. Before this final struggle comes there may be temporary truces and adjustments, but never any genuine peace.

(2) The persistent bad faith of the Soviet Government, the
product of communist contempt for abstract morality. Soviet
diplomatic history is a long record of broken promises, repudiated treaties, engagements that were entered into voluntarily and then disregarded. Here are a few examples of this
consistent Soviet disregard for obligations.

The Soviet Government, on its own initiative, concluded
treaties of non-aggression and neutrality with its five western
neighbors, Poland, Finland, Latvia, Lithuania and Estonia.
(The treaty with Lithuania was concluded in 1926 and twice
extended. The treaties with the other four nations were concluded in 1932 and extended for ten years in 1934.) All these
pacts were torn up like scraps of paper at the first convenient
opportunity, as part of Stalin's deal with Hitler in 1939.
Latvia, Lithuania, Estonia and large parts of Poland and Finland were annexed by the Soviet Union.

The Soviet Government at Yalta pledged itself to the principle that "free and unfettered elections" should be held in
Poland. Stalin also agreed that the liberated peoples of eastern and southeastern Europe should create "democratic institutions of their own choice." But Polish elections have been
fraudulent farces and small communist minorities have imposed a common pattern of one-party dictatorship on all coun-

tries and areas within the sphere of Soviet military control. The only exception to this rule is the small Soviet zone in Austria.

The Soviet Government signed the "Big Three" Potsdam Agreement of August 2, 1945, which contains the following provisions:

> All democratic political parties with rights of assembly and of public discussion shall be allowed and encouraged throughout Germany.
>
> Subject to the necessity for maintaining military security, freedom of speech, press and religion shall be permitted. . . .
>
> During the period of occupation Germany shall be treated as a single economic unit.

All these provisions have been systematically nullified or infringed in the Soviet Zone of Germany.

(3) The Iron Curtain. This expression may have become a cliché through repeated use; but it is an eminently correct figure of speech. No great power in history has approached the record of the Soviet Government in methodically isolating its subjects from normal contacts with foreigners. The relaxation of tension, the abatement of mutual fear and suspicion which might come from free and frank intercourse between Russians and foreigners is deliberately made impossible by Soviet policy.

(4) The Fifth Column. This, like the Iron Curtain, is something formidably new and without precedent: a great power to which millions of people outside its frontiers feel a sense of fanatical allegiance. To reconcile normally friendly relations with foreign governments with leadership of a world revolutionary movement which aims to destroy these governments is as impossible as to square the circle.

Soviet official repudiation of responsibility for the activities of the Comintern and for the closely coordinated activities of foreign communist parties since the formal self-dissolution of the Comintern is not convincing. For the last quarter of a century Stalin has been the undisputed master of the Soviet

Government. And there is the testimony of D. Manuilsky, a prominent Russian official in the Comintern, that "not one important document of big international significance was issued by the Comintern without the most active participation of Comrade Stalin in its composition." *

Another consideration disposes of the fiction that the Soviet Government has not been fully responsible for every act of conspiracy and insurrection planned by the Communist International. The Soviet authorities have always maintained the closest control over all foreign activities on Soviet soil. The few foreign correspondents in Moscow have not been allowed to organize a press club. It is absurd to suppose that an organization like the Comintern, with its farflung international ramifications, would have been permitted to exist for five minutes in the Soviet Union if the Soviet Government had not fully controlled and approved its activities.

The great confrontation of the United States and the Soviet Union is much more than a rivalry of two great powers. It is the conflict, the irrepressible conflict, between two diametrically opposed national ideas, accurately described by de Tocqueville as freedom and servitude.

The American Republic was historically fortunate in being able to develop and grow strong in population and resources without any serious threat from without. America's one great war during the nineteenth century was the internal struggle between North and South. Such familiar features of life in Europe as large standing armies, conscription, heavy taxation for military purposes, were unknown until very recent times. This freedom from fear of external attack was very favorable to the smooth working of free institutions. It helped to implant in the American character the spirit of individual self-reliance that does not flourish in a militarized society.

* This statement is to be found in *Stalin,* a publication issued by the Soviet State Publishing Company, p. 93.

The medieval Russian state, on the other hand, was located in a vast plain, with no natural frontiers. It grew up and expanded in an atmosphere of almost continuous war. The first Russian principalities were swamped by the tide of the Tartar conquest. As the Muscovite Tsars became more powerful they expanded their frontiers in a long series of wars with Turks and Tartars, Poles, Lithuanians and Swedes. Ultimately Russia became a strong force in European politics. Russian troops temporarily occupied Berlin during the Seven Years' War (1756–1763). The stubborn courage of the Russian armies and the rigors of the Russian winter started Napoleon on the road to decline and fall. Both under the Tsars and under the Soviets Russia maintained a huge military establishment.

Absence or presence of outside military pressure is not the only reason why Russia and America, as they grew into world powers, developed differing sets of values, especially in the matter of individual freedom.

Autocracy, absolute power of the Tsar, was the distinctive principle of Russian political life. Its origins were oriental and semi-oriental. Russian ideas of government were largely derived from the absolutist Byzantine Empire, from which Russia accepted Christianity, and from the Tartar Khans who were overlords for two centuries. Russia remained almost entirely outside the influence of three movements which, in various ways, fostered the growth of individual judgment: the Renaissance, the Protestant Reformation, and the French Revolution. Russian autocracy stood like an immovable rock while most of Europe was evolving toward constitutional regimes, with limitations on the power of the sovereign.

There was some development of local self-government in Russia in the second half of the nineteenth century. A parliament, the Duma, elected on a limited franchise and invested with limited power, was set up in Russia after the 1905 Revolution. But in the main, apart from a minority of western intellectuals, the Russian conception of government power was something far removed, vast, unlimited, beyond effective check or control.

Westernized Russian liberals and radicals and foreigners who admired Russian achievement in literature and the arts and found Russians, as individuals, congenial looked hopefully to the coming of a revolution that would sweep away tyranny and release the energies of the Russian people. The revolution came, but the tyranny over the minds and bodies of men only became more intense. This is evident from comparative figures on executions and the numbers of political prisoners in slave labor camps, under the Tsars and under the Soviets.

This was a profoundly tragic development, especially for the civilized and humane pre-Bolshevik Russian intellectuals, who counted among their number an extremely high proportion of the finest human beings who could be found anywhere in the world. But the carrying on by the Soviet regime of the methods of rule practiced not by the more modern Tsars, but by Ivan the Terrible, however disappointing, is not surprising, if two facts are taken into consideration. First, there was the poverty, ignorance, sometimes downright illiteracy and inexperience in self-government of the Russian masses. Second, very few Russian revolutionaries were true liberals.

If one studies Russian revolutionary literature, one finds very little emphasis on assuring the rights of the individual, on protecting the individual against the state. The emphasis is almost invariably on the realization of some kind of social utopia. The aspiration of the typical Russian revolutionary is not to curb the power of the state, but to capture that power and use it to force people, if necessary, to conform to some ambitious blueprint of social reorganization that is supposedly guarantied, in some future, to produce a millennium of virtue and happiness.

The founders of the American Republic were equally far removed in their political thinking from the models of Tartar Khans and Byzantine Emperors and from such revolutionary fantasies as Lenin's theory that absolute freedom would ultimately be realized as the consequence of a "temporary" period of "proletarian dictatorship." Jefferson, Adams, Madison and Hamilton were among the best-read men of their time. The Federalist Papers are full of historical analogies drawn from the experience of the Carthage Senate, the Achaean League, the Archons of Athens, the League of Cambray. Their study of history convinced them that there were other dangers to liberty besides oldfashioned royal absolutism. A mob could be a tyrant, as well as a monarch. The "people's tribune" of today is often the dictator of tomorrow.

These founders of the American Republic believed that the best means of assuring "life, liberty and the pursuit of happiness" was to create a government of limited and divided powers. Lord Acton had not pronounced his famous dictum: "All power tends to corrupt and absolute power corrupts absolutely." But the American Constitution is written in the spirit of Acton.

This charter of American liberty sets up three branches of government, co-equal, with separate and specific powers and functions. The Constitution bristles with "Thou Shalt Nots," directed against possible abuses of power, whether by the Executive, by Congress or by the Judiciary.

> Congress shall make *no* law respecting an establishment of religion, or prohibiting the free exercise thereof, or abridging the freedom of speech, or of the press.
> Excessive bail shall *not* be required, nor excessive fines imposed, nor cruel and unusual punishments inflicted.
> The right of the people to be secure in their persons, houses, papers and effects against unreasonable searches or seizures shall *not* be violated. [Italics supplied]

In these and many other provisions of the Constitution one sees a reflection of the conviction of Locke, Montesquieu and other liberal philosophers: that government power, if it is not to turn into tyranny, requires constant and specific curbs. An admirable expression of the philosophy of the Founding Fathers may be found in this sentence of No. 47 of the Federalist Papers, written by Madison:

> The accumulation of all powers, legislative, executive and judiciary, in the same hands, whether of one, a few or many, and whether hereditary, self-appointed or elective, may justly be pronounced the very definition of tyranny.

How completely opposed and contrasted is the Soviet conception of the state as an instrument for the suppression of one class by another! The best expression of this is Lenin's absolutist formula: *

"While the state exists there is no freedom. When there is freedom there will be no state."

Lenin also refers to the state as a machine or cudgel with which the ruling class crushes other classes.

It is profoundly instructive to read and compare the American and Soviet Constitutions. The former is conceived in terms of natural rights which the state may not touch. The latter is full of promises of material benefits which an all-powerful state will bestow on obedient citizens. Very characteristic of the spirit of the Soviet Constitution is the wording of Article 125:

> In accordance with the interests of the working people, and in order to strengthen the socialist system, the citizens of the USSR are guaranteed by law:
> (a) Freedom of speech.
> (b) Freedom of the press.
> (c) Freedom of assembly and meetings.
> (d) Freedom of street processions and demonstrations.
> These rights of citizens are insured by placing at the disposal of the working people and their organizations printing shops, supplies of paper, public buildings, the streets, means of communication and other material requisites for the exercise of these rights.

* V. I. Lenin, *The State and Revolution* (International Publishers), p. 79.

On paper this might suggest a paradise for such libertarians as John Stuart Mill: freedom of speech and expression, with free publishing facilities thrown in. What turns these assurances into mockery is that the government, providing the facilities, also decides what use is to be made of them. Soviet civil liberties in practice amount to this: that the citizen may read what the government wants him to read, say publicly what the government thinks he should say and demonstrate for what the government thinks he should demonstrate for.

How much surer as a guaranty of genuine freedom of expression of varied viewpoints is the simple negative injunction in the American Constitution, instructing the government to leave freedom of speech and press unhampered.

The richest, most powerful and populous nation of the New World, the largest, most powerful and populous nation of the Old World have come to maturity as world powers at the same time. The Second World War has left as its political legacy a two-power world. More than a rivalry of two nations is involved. There is an opposition of two camps.

One of these camps is represented by the huge Soviet empire, resting with one flank on the satellite countries of Eastern Europe, with the other on Red China. The United States has become the leader, magnet and rallying point for a much looser coalition of noncommunist powers. Some countries, especially in Asia, are outside these two camps and neutral for all practical purposes. But they are not sufficiently powerful to represent a balancing third force.

The ascendancy of the United States and the Soviet Union may pass in time, as other great powers have declined throughout the course of history. But for the near future the leadership of these two nations, "marked out by the will of Heaven to sway the destinies of half the globe," seems solidly assured.

Only in the United States and in the Soviet Union are to be found all the elements necessary for sustaining very long the effort and sacrifice of modern war: population, resources, space, industrial and technological development, vast stockpiles of modern weapons. At the present time the strength of the United States and of the Soviet Union is in precarious balance. Should either of these leviathans be greatly weakened the scales of world power would tilt swiftly and heavily in favor of the other.

All-out war between the two camps divided by the barricade of the Iron Curtain is not inevitable. Both sides are conscious of the tremendous losses and risks involved in a final, irrevocable resort to arms. But true peace is also impossible, unless there is some almost miraculous internal change in the Soviet Union. Barring some such change, strife and tension, struggle with all means short of all-out war, seems to be the destiny of the greater part of the human race in the second half of the twentieth century. The Great Confrontation is here.

And, regardless of whether the United States and the Soviet Union ever become involved in direct all-out military conflict, this Great Confrontation has already assumed many aspects of an irrepressible conflict, politically and economically, diplomatically and morally.

Chapter II ⤳ From Appeasement to Containment

Much the most unsatisfactory phase of American–Russian relations during the entire history of contact between the two countries was the policy of appeasing the Soviet dictatorship which was pursued during the war and for some months after the end of the war. As will be shown in the following chapter, almost all America's more serious international difficulties have their roots in this policy, which reached a supreme and disastrous climax at the Yalta Conference in February, 1945. It is largely because of this policy that the Soviet Union, a mighty power within its frontiers of 1939, has swelled into a gigantic empire, disposing of the manpower and resources of one third of the human race.

It is the very existence of this empire that imposes on the United States military and financial sacrifices which would have seemed fantastic before the late war. The appeasement of one totalitarian despotism is all the more inexcusable because it occurred during a great war which was being fought on the theory that the appeasement of a similar regime was morally indefensible and politically useless. Appeasement may be defined as the onesided abandonment of the independence and vital interests of weaker peoples in the hope of buying off or placating a persistent aggressor.

There are several recognizable causes of the policy of giving Stalin everything he asked for which reached its culmination at Yalta and went into bankruptcy soon afterwards. The personal attitude of President Roosevelt was perhaps the most important. Roosevelt condemned communism on some occasions and his own very empirical political and economic philosophy, so far as it existed as a coherent body of thought, was far removed from the dogmas of Karl Marx.

But Roosevelt never seems to have taken the trouble to acquire any precise knowledge of Soviet communism in theory and practise. He once remarked to his Secretary of Labor, Frances Perkins: "I don't understand the Russians; I don't know what makes them tick." And when a formerly favored adviser, William C. Bullitt, who had served as Ambassador in Moscow and in Paris, laid before the President a memorandum setting forth the reasons why the policy of appeasement would fail Roosevelt replied, according to Bullitt:

> Bill, I don't dispute your facts; they are accurate. I don't dispute the logic of your reasoning. I just have a hunch that Stalin is not that kind of a man. Harry [Hopkins] says he isn't and that he doesn't want anything but security for his country. And I think that if I give him everything I possibly can and ask for nothing in return, noblesse oblige, he won't try to annex anything and will work with me for a world of democracy and peace.

There is even an indirect White House admission that appeasement was an accurate description of the policy which was being followed. A Washington journalist, Forrest Davis, described Roosevelt's Russian policy as follows in an article published in *The Saturday Evening Post* in May, 1943:

> The core of his [Roosevelt's] policy has been the reassurance of Stalin. . . . Suppose that Stalin, in spite of all concessions, should prove unappeasable. . . .
> Roosevelt, gambling for stakes as enormous as any statesman ever played for, has been betting that the Soviet Union needs peace and is willing to pay for it by collaborating with the West.

This article was submitted in advance of publication for White House endorsement. There was no objection to the significant word, "unappeasable."

It cannot be plausibly suggested that Roosevelt had not been warned by past experience that Stalin's word was worthless. The breach of faith in connection with the permission of communist anti-American propaganda on Soviet territory has been described in the preceding chapter. The Soviet–Nazi deal of 1939 and the violation of the Soviet nonaggression pacts with Poland, Finland, Latvia, Lithuania and Estonia were events of recent occurrence. There were many American, as well as British experiences in dealing with the Soviet Union during the war which would justify Churchill's remark about "our new ally [the Soviet Union], surly, snarly, grasping and so recently indifferent to our survival." *

But Roosevelt seemed incapable of learning from experience. In his dealings with Stalin he was always ready to trade substance for shadow, a solid political or strategic advantage or a moral principle for a paper promise. There were factors besides Roosevelt's personal attitude which made for the appeasement policy. Some of America's military leaders, notably General George C. Marshall, thought of the war in too narrowly military terms and took no account of the political desirability of setting up some postwar check and balance against Soviet domination in the Eurasian continent. American public opinion, stimulated, to be sure, by the Administration, went on an emotional pro-Soviet binge of wishful thinking. Communist agents and sympathizers and fellow-travelers in high places made their contribution.

But, because of Roosevelt's highly personal conduct of foreign affairs the primary responsibility for the appeasement policy was his. All the overtures for meetings came from him, not from Stalin. It was always Stalin who set the place of meet-

* Winston Churchill, *The Second World War* (Houghton Mifflin Company), III, 452.

ing. Sometimes the President's efforts to woo the communist dictator assumed ridiculous and undignified forms. At Teheran, for instance, Roosevelt felt that he had won a great diplomatic triumph when, by some labored teasing of Churchill, he coaxed Stalin into a guffaw of laughter.* In the atmosphere of that time keeping Stalin in a good humor was considered more important than keeping faith with Poland and the principles of the Atlantic Charter.

Apologists for Roosevelt and Yalta like to represent the policy of appeasement as something inevitable and predestined. But there were feasible alternatives. A firm political Anglo-American front, for instance, would almost certainly have been an effective barrier against Soviet expansionist demands. But Roosevelt was obsessed with the idea that the British Empire would represent a greater threat to international peace and security after the war than the Soviet Union. There was also an element of personal vanity in his belief that he could charm Stalin into international good behavior. As early as March, 1942, he expressed to Churchill the conviction that he could handle Stalin personally better than either the State Department or the British Foreign Office.†

So, instead of concerting with Churchill a line of joint diplomatic action calculated to vindicate the self-determination clauses of the Atlantic Charter and to preserve some balance of power in continental Europe, Roosevelt at the first "Big Three" conference in Teheran made a point of dissociating himself from Churchill and trying the effect of his personal charm on the Soviet dictator.‡ Stalin, a man of shrewd percep-

* Cf. Frances Perkins, *The Roosevelt I Knew* (Viking), pp. 70–71.

† Churchill, *op. cit.,* IV, 201.

‡ On the eve of the Teheran Conference Roosevelt showed the same attitude of dissociating himself from close relations with Great Britain when he at first rejected Churchill's desire for American-British staff talks in Cairo. Roosevelt felt it would be a "terrible mistake" if Stalin felt that America and Great Britain were "ganging up" on him. (Churchill, *op. cit.,* V, 319.)

tion and infinite guile, was quick to take advantage of what he perhaps privately called a "rift in the capitalist world." He played back to Roosevelt by proposing that the American President act as chairman at all sessions of the conference. Then he invited Roosevelt to move from the American to the Soviet Embassy, on the ground that a plot to assassinate him had been discovered.

Feeling himself somewhat deserted by Roosevelt, Churchill at Teheran took his flier in appeasement. He took the initiative in raising the question of handing over Polish territory to the Soviet Union. Churchill proposed that the three heads of governments, without Polish participation, should formulate a policy which they could recommend to the Poles and advise them to accept.

Churchill and Eden, who was also at Teheran, proposed that Poland should take German territory in the West as compensation for the large section of Polish territory which the Soviet Union wished to annex in the East. Churchill took some match sticks to illustrate how Poland could be "moved" westward. This, according to Churchill, pleased Stalin,* as well it might. Here was an abandonment of Poland's unanswerable moral case for territorial integrity by one of Poland's principal supposed allies.

It is hard to recognize the Churchill who denounced the sacrifice of Czechoslovakia at Munich, the heroic Churchill of the dark days of Britain, in the appeasing Churchill of Teheran. Yet there can be no doubt as to the facts, as these are established by Churchill's own testimony.†

Churchill shares with Roosevelt the responsibility for throwing the Poles, who had fought against overwhelming odds since the beginning of the war, to the Soviet wolves. But the American President's share of the responsibility is greater. He represented the greater concentration of power. When Roosevelt

* Churchill, *op. cit.*, V, 362.
† Cf. Churchill, *op. cit.*, V, 361–62, 396–97.

was clearly aiming at some kind of bilateral understanding with Stalin, Churchill had some reason to feel that he had no alternative except to follow suit. Neither the American nor the British venture in appeasement led to good results for either country. Roosevelt perhaps died too soon to realize the full measure of his failure. Churchill seemed to be feeling doubt as to whether the sacrifice of Poland and other concessions to Stalin had paid off when he struck a note of thoughtful warning in a broadcast of May 13, 1945, after complete military victory had been won on the European continent:

> On the continent of Europe we have yet to make sure that the simple and honorable purposes for which we entered the war are not brushed aside or overlooked in the months following our success and that the words "freedom," "democracy" and "liberation" are not distorted from their true meaning as we have understood them. There would be little use in punishing the Hitlerites for their crimes, if law and justice did not rule, and if totalitarian or police governments were to take the place of the German invaders.

Churchill's final awakening to the danger and futility of trying to appease aggressive communism in Europe found expression in his vigorous and eloquent speech in Fulton, Missouri, a year later.

Roosevelt's insensitiveness to the danger of communist infiltration was reflected in his reaction to a communication from Adolf Berle, security officer in the State Department at the time of the outbreak of the war in Europe, about a group of communists working in various departments of the government. This communication was based on the firsthand testimony of Whittaker Chambers. Roosevelt, "in expurgated language," told Berle to "go jump in the lake." *

This combined attitude of indifference to subversive activity at home and of making every effort to placate Stalin in foreign policy naturally had its effect on American government

* Cf. Whittaker Chambers, *Witness* (Random House), p. 470.

departments and on American public opinion. The men in the foreign service who frankly voiced their opinions about the nature and designs of the Soviet regime were passed over for promotion and shifted to inconspicuous posts. Those who were less scrupulous hastened to conform to the Roosevelt-Hopkins line of unlimited trust in Stalin's peaceful and benevolent intentions.

Communist spy rings flourished in Washington with little let or hindrance.* Pro-Soviet sympathy was a help, not a handicap in obtaining employment in strategic wartime agencies. The old typical American left-wing attitude of the 30's, refusal to face the unpleasant facts of life in the Soviet Union, was revived on a much larger scale, and with the full encouragement of the government.

Stalin's wartime cooperation was restricted to unloading western ships with lend-lease supplies. Acknowledgments of the eleven billion dollars worth of American aid and the smaller shipments from Canada and Great Britain were few and grudging. There was no public revision of the orthodox communist theory of fundamental, irreconcilable conflict of interest with the noncommunist world. But American public opinion, always inclined to be mercurial in foreign affairs, went to extremes of pro-Soviet enthusiasm.

One supposedly authoritative commentator offered the assurance that the alliance of the United States, the Soviet Union, Great Britain and China was as durable as the Rock of Ages. A radio voice, much listened to in those years, specialized in the cultivation of a guilt complex in regard to previous western attitudes toward the Soviet regime. Russia, so ran the argument, had been misunderstood and wronged and therefore had

---

* Full and corroborating details about communist espionage before and during the war may be found in *Witness,* by Whittaker Chambers, *This Deception,* by Hede Massing (Duell, Sloan and Pearce), *Out of Bondage,* by Elizabeth Bentley (Devin-Adair), and *Seeds of Treason,* by Ralph de Toledano and Victor Lasky (Funk and Wagnalls).

a special right to coddling and conciliation. The insignificant and ineffective foreign military intervention in Russia after the First World War was played up, without mention of an avowed communist policy which both antedated and outlasted this intervention: overthrow of all noncommunist governments.

The double standard of moral bookkeeping which had become so fashionable in "liberal" circles during the 30's worked in favor of the appeasement policy during the war. It is remarkable how many individuals who possessed tender consciences about Franco and Chiang Kai-shek were completely insensitive to the grave moral and political dangers of all-out alliance with Stalin. Even before Hitler's attack on Russia Soviet crimes had enjoyed rather good public relations in the United States and had not sunk into public consciousness like the acts of cruelty and aggression associated with German Nazis and Japanese militarists.

There were no audible protests among American "liberal" groups, habitually vocal about wrongdoing in foreign lands, when the Soviet Government starved millions of peasants to death, sent millions more to slave labor camps, ruthlessly persecuted all forms of religious faith and unloosed a political terror, during the purges of the 30's, that had no parallel, even in Russian history, since the days of Ivan the Terrible. Indeed there was often the unseemly spectacle of professed progressives and humanitarians signing manifestoes of approval for each new public slaughter of Stalin's real or supposed rivals on charges that were palpable inventions and frame ups.

Strict Soviet censorship, of course, helped to muffle the impact of Soviet tyranny abroad, because it made information slow, fragmentary and sometimes indirect. Absence of contact between the victims of this tyranny and the outside world also helps to explain, although it does not justify, this double moral bookkeeping.

Many Jews and other fugitives from Nazi persecution were permitted to leave Germany or escaped abroad. Germany was accessible to foreign visitors, who could hear of and sometimes witness incidents of brutality or discrimination. The glamorous broadcasts of Mme. Chiang Kai-shek, American missionaries in China and Chinese students and other visitors in America kept public opinion well posted on Japanese misdeeds. But the victims of Soviet terror were unknown and therefore unreal. Very few Soviet citizens before the war escaped from the closely guarded frontiers of their country.

Russian kulaks did not have relatives or friends in New York and Chicago. If a prominent Catholic prelate or Protestant minister was insulted or arrested by the Nazis there was swift reaction in church circles abroad. But the many Russian Orthodox priests who were sent to concentration camps after their churches were closed had no international connections, no means of calling attention to what was happening.

The same kind of fuzz curtain concealed from most Americans the Soviet record in the war years. Outside of Polish-American circles little was published or known about the deportation of a million and a quarter people from Eastern Poland under Soviet conditions. The Katyn massacre was uncritically ascribed to the Germans, although Poles who examined this question closely in the Soviet Union and abroad were unanimous in their belief that the fifteen thousand Polish officer prisoners who disappeared in the Soviet Union (the bodies of only a minority were found in the Katyn Forest) could only have met death at the hands of their Russian captors.

American public opinion was not properly briefed morally for the Yalta meeting of Roosevelt, Churchill and Stalin, which was to outline the general terms of peace settlement. There was much discussion, in public forums and in university and church circles, of the necessity for basing a just and durable peace on the Atlantic Charter and the Four Freedoms. But there was a tendency, perhaps unconscious, to shy away from applying these principles to boundaries in Eastern Europe.

One could search the files of the American serious magazines of this period without finding recognition of the impending tragedy of Poland, faced with the prospect of defeat in victory, threatened by a new form of foreign oppression after fighting for years against another. There was no appreciation of the fact that handing over any people to Soviet rule was an offense against humanity and civilization. Too often the argument was heard that we must "get along with Russia," with the implication that the proper means to achieve this end was to give the Soviet Government everything it asked for.

Morally, politically and militarily the Yalta Conference of February 4–11, 1945, was held under unfavorable conditions. The Soviet armies had recently launched a successful offensive. The memory of what proved to be the last German offensive, in the Ardennes region, was still fresh. The speed with which Germany would crumble before Eisenhower's offensive in the spring was not anticipated. Singularly faulty intelligence work had conveyed the impression that Japan still possessed large and effective forces in Manchuria.

The two leading figures in the American delegation, Roosevelt and Hopkins, were in very poor health and were committed by past attitudes to the policy of trusting Stalin and hoping for the best. The newly appointed Secretary of State, Edward R. Stettinius, possessed no visible qualifications for this office except an impressive shock of white hair, an adulatory attitude toward Roosevelt and a naive faith that all international problems could be solved by a determined application of goodwill and optimism.

A measure of the political judgment of Mr. Stettinius is furnished by his expression of opinion, four years after Yalta, that the Soviet Union at this conference made greater concessions than the United States, and that Yalta was an American diplomatic triumph.*

In his record of the Yalta proceedings Mr. Stettinius is effusive in his praise of one of his subordinates whose name inspires little confidence in most American minds today. Alger Hiss, according to Stettinius, "performed brilliantly" at Yalta, as in the Dumbarton Oaks conversations where preliminary details of the United Nations organization were worked out, at the San Francisco conference and the first meeting of the UN Assembly.† When Roosevelt asked Stettinius to get a lawyer to consult with him on the Polish boundary statement Stettinius promptly called for this "brilliant performer." ‡

Of the other members of the American delegation only two, Averell Harriman, Ambassador to the Soviet Union, and Charles E. Bohlen, assistant to the Secretary of State and a Russian language expert who acted as translator, possessed a background of Soviet experience. There is nothing in the records of the conference to indicate that either Harriman or Bohlen did anything to avert moral and diplomatic debacle. Years later Harriman and Bohlen, nominated Ambassador to the Soviet Union by the Eisenhower Administration, were stubbornly maintaining that nothing was wrong with the Yalta Agreement except Soviet nonobservance of its provisions.

The principal decisions at Yalta, some revealed in a communiqué after the end of the meeting, some kept secret for a year or longer, dealt with the following subjects.

Poland. It was agreed that the eastern frontier of Poland should follow substantially the so-called Curzon Line, with minor digressions in favor of Poland. This was a ratification, for Stalin, of the spoils of his pact with Hitler. Poland was to receive accessions of German territory not precisely specified.

The existing Provisional Government of Poland was to be

---

* Edward R. Stettinius, *Roosevelt and the Russians* (Doubleday), p. 295.
† *Ibid.,* p. 31.
‡ *Ibid.,* p. 270.

reorganized on a broader democratic basis, "with the inclusion of democratic leaders from Poland itself and from Poles abroad." The new government was to be called the Polish Provisional Government of National Unity and was to receive diplomatic recognition from the Big Three powers. This government was to be pledged to "the holding of free and unfettered elections as soon as possible on the basis of universal suffrage and secret ballot."

Germany. "We are determined to disarm and disband all German armed forces, break up for all time the German General Staff, remove or destroy all German military equipment, eliminate or control all German industry that could be used for military production, bring all war criminals to swift and just punishment and exact reparation in kind for the destruction wrought by the Germans; wipe out the Nazi Party, Nazi laws, organizations and institutions, etc." It was specified in the protocol of the conference that German labor might be used as a source of "reparations." A commission with American, Soviet and British representatives was set up to study the question of dismemberment of Germany.

The Far East. According to an agreement that was kept strictly secret at the time and that was published a year later, on February 11, 1946, the Soviet Union promised to enter the war against Japan "two or three months after Germany has surrendered and the war in Europe has terminated" on the following conditions:

That the status quo in Outer Mongolia be preserved. (Outer Mongolia, nominally a part of China, had been a Soviet protected state since 1921.)

That the southern part of Sakhalin with adjacent islands be returned to the Soviet Union.

That the commercial port of Dairen be internationalized, "the pre-eminent interests of the Soviet Union in this port being safeguarded, and the lease of Port Arthur as a naval base of the Soviet Union restored."

That the Chinese Eastern Railway and South Manchuria Railway (the principal railways of Manchuria) be operated by a joint Soviet-Chinese company, "it being understood that the pre-eminent interests of the Soviet Union shall be safeguarded and that China shall retain full sovereignty in Manchuria.

"That the Kurile Islands shall be handed over to the Soviet Union."

Declaration on Liberated Europe. There was to be mutual agreement between the three powers to concert their policies "in assisting the peoples of the former Axis satellite states of Europe to solve by democratic means their pressing political and economic problems." Interim government authorities were to be formed "broadly representative of all democratic elements in the population and pledged to the earliest possible establishment through free elections of governments responsive to the will of the people."

It was agreed that a conference to prepare the Charter of the United Nations should meet in San Francisco in April and that two of the affiliated Soviet Republics, the Ukraine and Byelorussia, should have individual seats in the UN Assembly. An agreement on Yugoslavia substantially confirmed the establishment of Tito's dictatorship, with one or two facesaving reservations, which, in practice, proved quite meaningless.

A separate important compact at Yalta, signed by Major General John R. Deane, chief of the United States military mission in Moscow, and Major General A. A. Gryzlov, on behalf of the Soviet Government, provided that all Soviet citizens liberated by the United States and all United States citizens liberated by the Soviet Union should be segregated from enemy war prisoners and maintained in separate camps until they had been handed over to their respective military authorities.

Here, in brief summary, is the factual content of the Yalta agreements. What is their moral and political significance?

First, the principle of self-determination for all peoples, emphasized in the first three clauses of the Atlantic Charter, was clearly scrapped, although professions of respect for the principles of the Atlantic Charter are sprinkled through the Yalta Declaration. The Soviet annexation of Eastern Poland, of Koenigsberg and part of East Prussia and the Polish authorized seizure of ethnic German territory were clearly against the will of the vast majority of the peoples concerned. There was no pretense in any of these changes of an honestly conducted plebiscite. These decisions created millions of homeless, embittered refugees and drew frontier lines that were unjust and unnatural and a very probable cause of future conflicts.

Second, the independence and territorial integrity of Poland were sacrificed. The legitimate Polish government in London, composed of representatives of all the leading political parties in pre-war Poland, was thrown over. A made-in-Moscow, communist dominated government which had come to Poland in the wake of the Red Army, received the prestige of promised diplomatic recognition by the western powers. (In actual practice the "enlargement" of this government by the addition of Poles in Poland and abroad made no change in its domination by Moscow puppets.)

The Polish government in London was not a phantom. It had the undivided allegiance of hundreds of thousands of Poles who were fighting for the allied cause in the West, on land, on sea and in the air. It guided one of the most effective underground resistance movements in Europe.

It should not have been difficult to foresee how the pledges of "free unfettered elections" would work out, with Soviet-trained communists in charge of the police, the Red Army in occupation of the country and no safeguards for honest voting, such as the presence of foreign inspectors and American and British troop units, to counterbalance the effect of the Red Army. The effect of this abandonment of Poland was certain to be profound throughout Eastern Europe. For of all the countries in this area Poland had much the strongest legal and moral claim to American and British support. Polish resistance to

Hitler's aggression had been the original occasion of the war. Poland had concluded an alliance with Great Britain on the eve of the outbreak of hostilities.

The treatment of Poland at Yalta offers a remarkably close parallel with the treatment of Czechoslovakia at Munich in 1938. If one substitutes Poland for Czechoslovakia, Stalin for Hitler, Roosevelt and Churchill for Daladier and Chamberlain the likeness is complete. Publicists of the Left showed (and sometimes still show) the same complacency about Yalta that some publicists of the Right displayed about Munich. There were the same distorted and irrelevant arguments to justify a shabby and dishonorable transaction, about Sudeten Germans in Czechoslovakia and Ukrainians in Eastern Poland. There was the same eagerness to find excuses for the rapacious dictator and there was the same impatient distaste with the protests of the victim against being murdered.

Harry Hopkins who, next to Roosevelt, bears the principal American responsibility for the Great Betrayal which reached its climax at Yalta, brushed the moral issue off with the remark: "The Poles are like the Irish. They are never satisfied with anything anyhow." And a junior diplomatic official in the United States told the Polish Ambassador that the Polish problem had to be settled because it had become "an intolerable headache"! *

Like Munich, Yalta must be set down as a dismal failure, practically as well as morally. For Hitler was not satiated by his acquisitions at Munich and Stalin was not appeased at Yalta. The human and industrial resources of Czechoslovakia became an asset for the Nazi war machine. Poland also, under its communist rulers, is being organized systematically against the West.

Third, the Yalta Agreement, besides foreshadowing the enslavement of tens of millions of people in Eastern Europe, rep-

* Jan Ciechanowski, *Defeat in Victory* (Doubleday), pp. 383–84.

resented, in two of its features, the endorsement by the United States of the principle of human slavery. One of these features was the recognition that German labor could be used as a source of reparations. This gave implied American sanction to the retention of large numbers of German war prisoners, years after the end of hostilities, as forced laborers in the Soviet Union, Great Britain and France. And the agreement that Soviet citizens who were found in the western zones of occupation should be handed over to the Soviet authorities amounted, for the many Soviet refugees who did not wish to return, to the enactment of a fugitive slave law.

Fourth, the secret clauses of the Yalta Agreement which offered Stalin extensive territorial and economic concessions in the Far East as the price of Soviet participation in the war against Japan were immoral, unnecessary and unwise. These secret clauses were immoral because they gave away effective control of Manchuria, the most industrialized part of China, without consulting with or even informing the Chinese Government, an ally since Pearl Harbor. They were unnecessary because Stalin would almost certainly have entered the war without any bribe.

Moreover, it was a case of paying Stalin a second time for something he had already agreed to do, presumably in consideration of lend-lease aid and the second front, without any bribe. When Cordell Hull visited Moscow in October, 1943, Stalin proposed to enter the war against Japan after the defeat of Germany. According to Hull, this offer was unsolicited and had no strings attached to it.*

Stalin repeated this promise at Teheran. But Roosevelt, without waiting for a request, suggested that the Soviet Union should have access to the key Manchurian port of Dairen.† Finding Roosevelt so eager to anticipate his wishes, Stalin began to raise his price.

* *The Memoirs of Cordell Hull* (Macmillan), p. 1310.
† Robert Sherwood, *Roosevelt and Hopkins* (Harper's), p. 792.

During Churchill's visit to Moscow in October, 1944, the Soviet dictator consented to take the offensive against Japan three months after the defeat of Germany, but on two conditions. The United States was to build up reserve lend-lease supplies for the operation and the "political aspects of Russian participation" were to be clarified.*

It was typical of the Soviet attitude toward obligations that, although there were repeated promises of bases for the American air force in Eastern Siberia, no such bases were ever made available. The United States, however, continued unusual efforts to build up the Soviet military reserve stocks in Eastern Siberia.†

Finally, the invitation to the Soviet Union to take over the Kurile Islands, South Sakhalin and an economic stranglehold on Manchuria was unwise, from the standpoint of American national interests. To increase what was already a prospective formidable predominance of Soviet strength in the Far East after the war by giving the Soviet Union take-off points for threatening Japan (South Sakhalin and the Kuriles) and economic domination of Manchuria was not a demonstration of farsighted statesmanship.

Even now Yalta has its defenders. They are to be found mainly among the unreserved admirers of Franklin D. Roosevelt's foreign policy and among those who, because of wartime association with the Administration, feel that their personal prestige is bound up with the vindication of this conference. Their four principal arguments are:

(1) That Yalta gave Stalin nothing that he was not in a position to take, or had not taken, anyway.

(2) That there was moral value in obtaining such Soviet promises as "free unfettered elections in Poland" and "democratic processes" in the "liberated countries."

* John R. Deane, *The Strange Alliance* (Viking), p. 247.
† *Ibid.*, p. 254.

(3) That the Yalta concessions were necessary to keep the Soviet Union in the war against Germany and to bring about Soviet intervention in the war against Japan.

(4) That the only alternative to the Yalta Agreement was the politically impossible one of going to war with the Soviet Union.

The first of these arguments misses the political and moral heart of the Yalta issue. The question was not what Stalin might have taken by military force in Eastern Europe and the Far East, but what he could take with the approval of the western powers. The difference is extremely important. In the case of Poland, for instance, it would have been far more difficult to maintain a Soviet satellite regime if this regime had not received the endorsement of the western powers. Nor was there anything inevitable about the Soviet domination of Manchuria and North Korea. It is a reasonable assumption that a peace treaty could have been concluded with Japan months before the end of the war if there had been enough farsighted statesmanship to propose the same terms which were finally signed in San Francisco in 1951. Had this been done before the Soviet Government was able to intervene in the Far Eastern war the Korean-Manchurian door could have been bolted against Soviet intrusion.

Argument two seems to be on a par with praising a man as a financial genius because he accepted a number of bad checks from a fraudulent bankrupt. The Yalta promises were not the first international obligations on which Stalin defaulted.

The third argument is based on the assumption that Stalin's own interests did not prompt him to seek to deliver a knockout blow against the two powers which were the greatest potential checks against his ambitions, in Europe and in Asia, Germany and Japan. There was no reason to bribe him to continue a war in Europe or to start a war in Asia so clearly prompted by his own sense of interest.

Was there an alternative to the appeasement of Yalta, besides war? Of course there was. Suppose the United States and Great Britain before Yalta and at Yalta had committed themselves to a firm, uncompromising declaration that they would neither use the war as a means of territorial gain themselves nor recognize any annexations carried out by other powers in violation of the principles of the Atlantic Charter. The Soviet frontiers of 1939 (frontiers with which the Soviet Government before the war often expressed itself as entirely satisfied) and not one square foot of Polish, Latvian, Estonian, Lithuanian, Finnish, Rumanian, German, Chinese or Japanese territory beyond these frontiers would have been acknowledged as legal and valid.

Behind such a declaration would have stood the mightiest concentration of sea and air power the world had ever seen, a highly mechanized army and an American war economy capable of almost unlimited further achievement. On the other side would have been a Soviet Union devastated by invasion and bled white in manpower, dependent in the final drive to victory on American trucks, field telephones, canned food and other lend-lease supplies.

Moreover, at the time of Yalta the hope of a genuine liberation from Nazi tyranny was still high in Poland and other countries of central and eastern Europe. Except in Czechoslovakia the communist parties in these lands were tiny minority groups, with no appreciable popular following. So hated was the very name communist in Poland that the revived Polish Communist Party, which had been written off as a bad fifth column investment by Moscow in the late thirties, tried to conceal its real nature by calling itself the Workers' Party.

In view of these circumstances, in view of Stalin's habitual caution in foreign affairs, the Soviet dictator might well have renounced his designs of conquest and been satisfied with the preservation of his original realm. And if Stalin had taken a tough and negative attitude the date of the cold war would have been advanced,—very much to the advantage of the West. For at the time of Yalta the power relation was less favorable to the Soviet Union than it became later, when the Soviet Union repaired its war damage, crushed all semblance of open dissent in the satellite countries and swung China against the West. It was not the least of the sins of Yalta that it helped to blind American and British public opinion to the threat of Soviet expansion and contributed to the mood of recklessly hasty demobilization as soon as the shooting war with the Axis was over. There was no corresponding demobilization on the Soviet side.

Yalta should not be regarded as an isolated accident or a piece of black magic. It was a consequence, as well as a cause, a consequence of the dryrot of appeasement which was already well advanced at the time of the Teheran Conference, if not earlier. But Yalta will be remembered as the climax of a gravely mistaken course in foreign affairs. It was the supreme example of giving Stalin an unlimited diplomatic blank check, of deserting friends and favoring enemies in the vain hope of appeasing a regime which, by its nature and philosophy, is unappeasable.

At first the news of Yalta was greeted with enthusiasm in the United States—another parallel with the joy which Munich aroused in Great Britain and France. There was little notice of the many suicides of Polish soldiers from eastern Poland who had been deprived of home and country by the decisions of foreign statesmen.

Raymond Gram Swing, then an influential news commentator, declared: "No more appropriate news could be conceived to celebrate the birthday of Abraham Lincoln." For William L. Shirer Yalta was "a landmark in human history." Harry Hopkins thought the first great victory had been won for the whole civilized human race.* *The Philadelphia Record* found Yalta "the greatest United Nations victory of the war" and *Time* prematurely asserted: "All doubts about the Big Three's ability to cooperate in peace as well as in war seem now to have been swept away."

* Sherwood, *op. cit.*, p. 870.

But the Yalta honeymoon was of brief duration. There was almost daily contradiction of the promise of free unfettered elections in Poland by acts of violence and oppression against noncommunist political groups. The promise about concerted Big Three action in the "liberated countries" was disregarded less than a month after the Yalta Agreement was signed. Andrei Vishinsky, then deputy Foreign Minister, went to Bucharest and bullied the King into dismissing the Cabinet of General Radescu and appointing a new government headed by a communist collaborator, Petru Groza. Roosevelt himself, on the eve of his death, seems to have felt that appeasement had reached its limit. Roosevelt replied with unusual sharpness when Stalin sent him a message asserting that political negotiations were in progress between the allied military authorities and the German commander on the Italian front, General von Kesselring. There had been an agreement, according to Stalin, that Germany would receive easier peace terms if von Kesselring would open up the front and permit the American army to advance. Considering how scrupulously Roosevelt had avoided any suggestion of separate negotiations or dealings, even with anti-Nazi groups in Germany, how he had stuck to his "Unconditional Surrender" formula, he had reason to feel resentment when faced with such wild and baseless charges.

The most striking example of Soviet determination to crush Polish liberty was the arrest and transportation to Moscow for trial of sixteen Polish underground leaders who had come out of hiding on the "word of honor" of a Soviet security officer that their freedom would be respected. All were put through the usual forms of torture, all but one pleaded guilty and were sentenced to various terms of imprisonment.*

* For a firsthand account of the intolerable pressures of sleeplessness, hunger, exhaustion and abuse employed to extort confessions, see *Invitation to Moscow*, by Z. Stypulkowski (Thames and Hudson, London). Mr. Stypulkowski, a young man in good physical condition when he was arrested, held out against forms of torment, systematically applied over long

The shift in American policy from appeasement to resistance or "containment" occurred too late to save Poland. The United States Government recognized the Soviet satellite government in Poland in July, 1945. The election held in Poland in January, 1947, almost two years after the Yalta Agreement, was preceded and accompanied by so much violence, intimidation and fraud that it offered no indication as to the political desires of the Polish people. Stanislaw Mikolajczyk, leader of the Polish Peasant Party and a former Prime Minister in the Polish government-in-exile, joined the new regime in Warsaw and was given the post of Minister of Agriculture. From the beginning his real position was that of a prisoner or hostage and he finally escaped death or imprisonment by fleeing from the country.

It is difficult to fix the precise date when appeasement gave way to resistance in American policy toward the Soviet Union. The spirit of Yalta was carried over into the last meeting of the Big Three, in Potsdam in July–August, 1945. Stalin got his way on all important points in return for assurances that were never kept, such as the promises that Germany would be treated as an economic unit and that democratic parties would be encouraged in Germany. From the beginning of the occupation the Soviet Zone in Germany has been sealed off from the rest of the country and treated as a colony to be exploited for the exclusive benefit of the Soviet Union. And no genuine opposition political parties have been tolerated there.

Stalin at Potsdam obtained a promise of American and British support for the annexation by the Soviet Union of the city of Koenigsberg and part of East Prussia. Western sanction was also given for the expulsion of all Germans and persons of German ethnic origin from Poland and other East European countries and for the confiscation for Soviet benefit of German assets in Soviet occupied countries. An arbitrary interpretation of

periods of time, which break the health and spirit of most Soviet political prisoners before they are produced in court.

this concession helped the Soviet Union to get a tight grip on the national economies of Rumania and Hungary and to exploit Austrian oil wells and other assets. Finally, the United States, although Japan was clearly on the verge of collapse, repeated at Potsdam its invitation to the Soviet Union to enter the war in the Far East and share in the spoils of victory.

The first sign that the United States had reached the end of making one-sided concessions was given at the conference of the Foreign Ministers of the "Big Five" powers (the United States, Soviet Union, Great Britain, France and China) in London in September, 1945. This conference ended in a deadlock, with Soviet Foreign Minister Molotov stiff and unaccommodating and the United States unwilling to grant diplomatic recognition to tyrannical and unrepresentative governments set up with the support of the Red Army in Rumania and Bulgaria. There were deadlocks on other issues, such as the occupation of Japan and the number of countries entitled to be represented in peace treaty negotiations.

At this conference Molotov showed strong aversion to limiting the armies of the former German satellite states which had passed into the Soviet sphere of influence. He was also uninterested in a proposal of the American Secretary of State, James F. Byrnes, for a four-power twenty-five-year treaty to insure the demilitarization of Germany. From the beginning the Soviet Government looked at every new country brought under communist rule as a source of auxiliary military strength.

Byrnes, who was slow to recognize the uncompromising nature of the force in Moscow with which he had to reckon, tried to break the ice which had formed over Soviet-Western relations by taking the initiative for a new meeting of Foreign Ministers in Moscow in December. Here there was some lapse into one-sided concessions. American recognition was extended to Rumania and Bulgaria on very inadequate and deceptive assurances that free institutions were being established. There was no settlement of the serious issue posed by the unwillingness of the Soviet Government to fulfill its treaty obligation to withdraw troops from Iran within six months after the end of the war.

The American attitude became consistently stiffer during the first months of 1946. Secretary Byrnes used what was then unfamiliar strong language about Soviet–American relations when he said, in a speech at the Overseas Press Club, in the latter part of February, 1946:

> It is not enough for nations to declare that they do not want war. Hitler said that . . . To banish war, nations must refrain from doing the things that lead to war. . . . The Charter [of the United Nations] forbids aggression and we cannot allow aggression to be accomplished by coercion or pressure or by subterfuges such as political infiltration. . . . We will not and we cannot stand aloof if force or the threat of force is used contrary to the purposes and principles of the Charter.

Only a year had passed since the high point of appeasement was reached at Yalta. But the climate of opinion had changed. The transition from appeasement to resistance was under way. Senator Arthur Vandenberg provided bipartisan reinforcement for Byrnes in a speech which he delivered in the Senate along the same lines about the same time.

This change was caused by several factors. The Soviet purpose of crushing out any semblance of liberty in countries occupied by the Red Army was becoming increasingly clear. A storm was blowing up in Iran, whence Soviet troops were finally grudgingly withdrawn after a severe crisis in the United Nations. Stalin had delivered a speech in Moscow in February, 1946, with an ominous implication:

> The war began in reality as the inevitable result of the development of the world economic and political forces on the basis of monopoly capitalism. The First World War began as a result of the first crisis in the development of the capitalist world economy. The Second World War originated as a result of the second crisis.

The obvious deduction from this speech was that Stalin, as a Marxist, believed in a third crisis—and a third world war.

President Truman broke away from the appeasement policy of his predecessor and placed the power and prestige of his office behind a policy of fairly consistent resistance to Soviet expansion. This was easier because of the attitude of bipartisan support in foreign policy adopted by most Republicans. The Republicans were in the majority in both Houses of Congress between the elections of 1946 and 1948. Such important steps as the inauguration of aid to Greece and Turkey and the first appropriations for economic aid to Europe could only have been passed with the aid of Republican votes.

There is a noteworthy contrast between the Republican attitude toward the Roosevelt Administration, in its road to war from 1939 until 1941, and the Republican reaction to President Truman's conduct of what began to be called the cold war with the Soviet Union. A majority of Republican votes was cast against military conscription, against lend-lease, against the arming of United States merchant ships, against all measures which seemed to portend more active American intervention in the war. Republican criticism of Truman, on the other hand, has been directed not against his reaction to the Soviet challenge, but against certain failures in the waging of the cold war, especially in the Far East.

This may be interpreted as a turning away from so-called isolationism. But it may also be defended as an intelligent shift of judgment in response to a changed world situation. It is arguable (the proposition can never be proved or disproved because the course was not followed) that if the Roosevelt Administration had emphasized determination to remain aloof from the impending war, instead of stressing rhetorical moral indignation in its public statements, British and French policy would have been influenced in the same direction.

The result might have been a war limited to the dictatorships, from which the United States and Western Europe could have stood aside. Hitler was not the only tyrant bent on aggression, as is now painfully evident. And a clash of totalitarian tyrannies in which the free nations would have remained neutral might have led to a desirable result: the all-around weakening of the totalitarian part of the world.

No such possibility existed after the Second World War. There was one and only one significant totalitarian power, despite the occasional leftist tilting at windmills in Spain, Argentina and even in disarmed West Germany. This was the Soviet empire. The United States, as the only other strong power emerging from the war, was face to face with the challenge of this expanding empire. The balance of power had been destroyed in Europe and in Asia. There was no possibility of playing off one strong alien dictatorship against another.

These facts of international life were not understood as promptly and as clearly as they should have been. But there was a fairly general subconscious appreciation of these new realities, and this made for a rather remarkable measure of unity between our two main parties in foreign policy. There was some fuzzy confusion during the transition from appeasement to resistance. But the elections of 1948 and 1952 revealed a public opinion solid and united about the necessity of opposing the Soviet threat.

Opposition to this policy of resistance was voiced by the American Communists, a negligible and dwindling minority, and by the Progressive Party. The latter organization nominated former Vice-President Henry A. Wallace as its presidential candidate in 1948. Wallace had been dropped from the Truman Cabinet after delivering a speech in Madison Square Garden in September, 1946, in which he denounced British imperialism as a threat to peace and suggested a division of the world into American and Soviet political spheres of influence. This would have meant the abandonment by the United States of all opposition to the consolidation by the Kremlin of its East

European satellites. The effect of this speech on public opinion abroad was enhanced because President Truman naïvely endorsed its contents, apparently after a hasty reading. Forced to choose between accepting the resignation of Secretary Byrnes and dismissing Wallace from the Cabinet, he chose the second alternative.

The foreign policy planks of the Progressive Party platform bore a remarkable similarity to those of the Communist Party. This is evident from the following citations.

COMMUNIST PLATFORM

Fight for peace by checking and defeating the Truman Doctrine and the Marshall Plan.

Withdrawal of all American military aid and personnel from Greece, China and Turkey, and an end to American military and naval pressure in the Mediterranean area, as well as a halt to the militarization of Latin America.

Resist the militarization of the United States; oppose universal military training, conscription and the colossal war budgets.

PROGRESSIVE PLATFORM

We demand the repudiation of the Truman Doctrine. We demand the repudiation of the Marshall Plan.

We demand . . . an end to military and economic intervention in support of reactionary and fascist regimes in China, Greece, Turkey, the Middle East and Latin America. . . . We demand the abandonment of the inter-American military program.

The Progressive Party calls for the repeal of the peacetime draft and the rejection of universal military training.

It was with this program, so very similar in phrasing and spirit to that of the Communist Party, that the Progressive Party went to the polls in two presidential elections. Henry Wallace in 1948 received 1,157,172 votes, as against over 47 million cast for the three other principal candidates, President Truman, Governor Thomas E. Dewey and J. Strom Thurmond, of the States Rights Party. Vincent Hallinan, Progressive candidate in 1952, received about 140,000 votes, in a total vote of over 61 million.

An individual who contributed much to the change in American policy was James Forrestal, Assistant Secretary and later Secretary of the Navy in the Roosevelt Administration and Secretary of Defense under President Truman. When Forrestal, after a nervous breakdown caused by overwork and aggravated by the scurrilous abuse of cheap gossip columnists, took his own life in 1949, his country lost a farsighted statesman and a passionate patriot. Forrestal had never been enamored of appeasement. As early as September 2, 1944, he was writing to a friend, with a characteristic mixture of keenness and bluntness: *

> I find that whenever any American suggests that we act in accordance with the needs of our own security he is called a goddamned fascist and imperialist, while if Uncle Joe [Stalin] suggests that he needs the Baltic Provinces, half of Poland, all of Bessarabia and access to the Mediterranean, all hands agree that he is a fine, frank, candid and generally delightful fellow who is very easy to deal with because he is so explicit in what he wants.

In the uncertain and confused atmosphere of transition in 1945–46 Forrestal was a tower of strength. When Secretary Byrnes remarked that one of the difficulties after Roosevelt's death was that Stalin did not like Truman, Forrestal was quick with the retort that Truman was the first one who had ever said "No" to anything Stalin asked.†

Forrestal was in a position where he could often translate his ideas into action. He was closely associated with two decisions which helped to project American naval and air power into Europe as a counterweight to Soviet land power. One of these was the permanent stationing of an American fleet in the Mediterranean in 1946. The other was the decision, after the communist coup d'état in Czechoslovakia and the Soviet block-

* *The Forrestal Diaries* (Viking), p. 14.
† *Ibid.*, p. 318.

ade of West Berlin in 1948, to station longrange American bombers at British bases.

This second decision was taken, of course, in full cooperation with the British Government. It may be noted, incidentally, that Prime Minister Clement Attlee and Foreign Minister Ernest Bevin showed considerable moral courage in disregarding deeprooted Labor Party traditions of pacifism and sentimental pro-Soviet sympathy and leading Great Britain, side by side with the United States, on the road to resistance. There was a grave divergence of policy later, when Great Britain recognized the communist regime in China and failed to annul this step even after Red China went to war with Great Britain, along with other members of the United Nations. But in the first phases of the cold war British policy vis-à-vis Moscow was closely aligned with America's.

Forrestal was well in advance of the Administration and perhaps of American public opinion generally in recognizing the necessity, in America's own interest, of letting the Germans and the Japanese earn their national livelihood again. Occupation policy in Germany, and to a smaller extent in Japan, in the first years after the war, was warped by a mixture of revengeful destructionism and misguided idealism. Most extreme expression of the first trait was the notorious Morgenthau Plan and a similar, if slightly milder Pauley Plan was devised for Japan. While these extreme proposals were not carried out, German and Japanese recovery was hampered and delayed by many punitive regulations, which were gradually dropped as more constructive attitudes began to prevail in 1948.

Misguided idealism took the form of a missionary attitude, of trying to impose on the Germans and the Japanese American ways and habits which were not congenial to their habits and psychology. There was an attempt to teach the Japanese square dancing and to turn German secondary schools into replicas of American high schools. More serious were the attempts to break up efficient existing forms of business under the general slogan

of "decartelization." Forrestal had no sympathy with these attitudes and his correspondence is full of vigorous denunciations
of the tendency to impose socialist formulas on the defeated
countries.

1947 was the year when the new policy of resistance hardened
into the pattern of the cold war. An important date is March
12, when President Truman went to Congress with a request
for 400 million dollars for aid to Greece and Turkey. Both
countries were targets of a Soviet thrust aimed at reaching the
Mediterranean. Both had been direct objects of aggression.

A Soviet note in August, 1946, proposed that the Soviet
Union should take over the defense of the Dardanelles. Articles
in the controlled Soviet press demanded the cession to the
Soviet Union of the Turkish frontier regions of Kars and
Ardaghan. This area, with a mixed Armenian-Turkish population, belonged to Russia before the First World War and was
taken over by Turkey during the period of revolutionary confusion and civil war. The population is now solidly Turkish.
The Turks, with some assurance of American backing, stood
firm against both Soviet demands, acceptance of which would
have reduced Turkey to the status of a vassal state. The Soviet
demands were not pushed to the point of conflict and there was
no internal fifth column on which Soviet agents could work.

There was a more complicated situation in Greece, where
communist guerrilla bands were terrorizing the northern part
of the country. When pursued by government troops they took
refuge in neighboring communist countries, Yugoslavia (Tito
had not yet broken with Moscow), Bulgaria and Albania.
Greece was economically prostrate after war losses and devastation. Great Britain had traditionally been a guardian of peace
and order in the eastern Mediterranean. In the nineteenth century Great Britain had fought one war and risked others to
keep the Russians out of Constantinople. But Britain, impoverished by the war, was further weakened by the economic consequences of a tremendous storm which raged during the

winter of 1946–47, stopping transportation, paralyzing industrial production, causing havoc among the country's livestock. The British Government felt unable to carry the burden of helping Greece to resist communist pressure.

Truman faced the dilemma of leaving Greece and Turkey to their fate or stepping into the vacuum created by the British withdrawal. He chose the second course and asked for the appropriation for economic and military aid for Greece and Turkey, most of it for Greece. The avowed purpose of this appropriation was "to support free peoples who are resisting attempted subjugation." Another broad statement in the President's message clearly summed up the American and western case in the cold war:

> Totalitarian regimes imposed on free peoples, by direct or indirect aggression, undermine the foundations of international peace and hence the security of the United States.

In this aid to Greece and Turkey one may find the germ both of the alliances and security pacts in which the United States became a partner and of the Marshall Plan. This scheme for large scale American subsidization of the economic recovery of Western Europe was foreshadowed in a speech delivered by General George C. Marshall, as Secretary of State, at Harvard University on June 5, 1947.

Two Soviet-Western conferences on Germany, one held in Moscow in the spring of 1947, the other in London in December of that year, ended in futile deadlock. Among the causes of breakdown were large Soviet reparation demands, the Soviet desire to obtain a grip on the rich Ruhr industrial area and the impossibility of reconciling Soviet with Western definitions of democracy.

New aggressive moves from the communist side were a revolutionary general strike in France in 1947, put down with considerable difficulty, and the formation, on October 5, 1947, of the Cominform (Communist Information Bureau) as a succes-

sor to the self-dissolved Comintern. The Cominform was composed of representatives of the communist parties of the Soviet
Union, Poland, Rumania, Czechoslovakia, Hungary, Yugoslavia (which withdrew after Tito's breach with Moscow in
1948), Bulgaria, France and Italy. Its avowed primary purpose
was to fight American imperialism.

So the lines in the cold war were clarified and more precisely
drawn. It became clear that what was happening was not a
series of accidental misunderstandings, but a struggle of two
worlds, two differing political, economic and moral systems.

Two questions are sometimes asked in connection with the
cold war. Could not the United Nations have prevented this
struggle? And is there not a possibility to create peace through
mutual agreement for the control and limitation of armaments?
The answer to both questions, I think, is in the negative.

The ability of the United Nations to keep the peace was ab-
surdly exaggerated in much advance propaganda for that organization emanating from official and unofficial sources in the
United States. One wellmeaning religious group put out the
slogan: "You can save the peace with a three cent stamp." The
idea was that if Americans would write to their Senators urging
ratification of the UN Charter peace would be assured. The
Charter was ratified; but the problem of peace was unfortunately not so easily solved.

The UN Charter grants a privileged position, with permanent representation on the Security Council and the right of
veto on any action, to five principal members: the United
States, the Soviet Union, Great Britain, France and China.
Under the Charter, therefore, the United Nations could stop
a war only in a contingency so unlikely as to be virtually impossible. This would be war started in defiance of the will of
the five Charter members. But such a war is scarcely conceivable, in view of the overwhelming force which the five great
powers could bring to bear, if they were in agreement.

Against the kind of conflict most likely to arise, a conflict, direct or indirect, between the great powers themselves, the Charter offers no remedy whatever. There are no provisions for compulsory arbitration of disputes. There is not even a definition of aggression, to serve as the basis of a judicial ruling.

The UN has never possessed police power in its own right. The Charter contemplates a UN force, to be placed at the disposal of the nine-member Security Council. But this force never materialized. It would be fantastic to imagine American and Soviet military units operating in trustful harmony in such a force.

UN action on many issues, the Greek civil war, the unification of Korea, the admission of new members, has been paralyzed by the Soviet veto, which had been used more than fifty times by the end of 1952. Even the moral value of debates and resolutions in the General Assembly, where the veto does not operate, was limited by the strict control of information in the countries behind the iron curtain and by the indifference of communist governments to foreign public opinion.

Efforts to revitalize the United Nations (a most unhappily and ironically named organization, incidentally) have met with little success. As a result of the absence of the Soviet representative, the Security Council was able to sanction action against the invasion of South Korea without a veto. But the Korean experience has not been encouraging for those who saw in collective action by "peaceloving" nations an effective shield against aggression. Only the United States made a substantial contribution to the struggle. And some of the UN members not only gave little or no help, but used all their diplomatic influence to obstruct and hamper American plans for bringing the war to a victorious conclusion.*

Secretary of State Acheson tried to plug the big hole in the structure of collective security represented by the veto power possessed by members of the Security Council. His design was to transfer the right to act to the Assembly, in the probable

* This subject is treated in more detail in Chapter V.

event that a veto deadlock should develop in the Council. The Assembly, following American initiative, adopted in November, 1950, a "Uniting for Peace" resolution. Its most important provision was that, if the Security Council should be prevented by the veto from taking action to maintain international peace and security, the General Assembly should consider the matter and make recommendations to its members, including the use of force.

The legality of this resolution is open to doubt. It represents a substantial alteration in the Charter, which vests executive power in the Security Council. Under Article 108 of the UN Charter, amendments shall come into force only if ratified by all the permanent members. The Soviet Union, which attaches great importance to the right of veto, could not be expected to accept the "Uniting for Peace" resolution.

More practical than the question of what UN members may have a theoretical right to do, under the "Uniting for Peace" resolution is the question what they would have the will to do, in the event of a supreme emergency. Here the Korean experience offers little encouragement. The United Nations may have limited value as an arena of discussion, a "town meeting of the world." But it is unrealistic to treat this organization of proved impotence as "the cornerstone of American foreign policy."

The UN Charter is workable and makes political sense only on an assumption that has long been disproved, namely that the Soviet Union would be a cooperative, conciliatory partner in a world association of nations committed to settling their differences by peaceful procedures. Proposals to breathe life into it by revising the Charter, by eliminating the veto power, by excluding the Soviet Union from membership are not promising. The United States, in all probability, would not be willing to forego the veto in all circumstances. The Charter provides no means of expelling a member and many noncommunist countries would hesitate to quit the existing organization and set up a rival body.

Quite fantastic and outside the realm of serious consideration in any predictable future are the various schemes for setting up a world government. A world government, by definition, would have to include the Soviet empire, which now embraces almost one third of the population of the globe. But the Soviet Government has uniformly and consistently rejected far smaller renunciations of national sovereignty than the most limited type of world government would entail. Its vetoes have paralyzed many UN experiments in international action. It has boycotted the special agencies set up by the United Nations. It has consistently refused, in disputes with other nations, to accept the procedure of arbitration or of submission to some impartial judicial authority.

There are other schisms among nations which would make world government impracticable, even if the great schism represented by the communist empire did not exist. Is it possible to conceive of a form of world authority that would satisfy French and Moroccan nationalists, Israel and the Arab states, the white minority and the black majority in South Africa? Would the United States be willing to accept the authority of a world parliament in which it would be outvoted on a population basis by China and India? Would oriental countries be willing to accept any system of voting that would weight the scales in favor of the West?

Americans would be well advised to forget utopian dreams and adjust themselves to the hard realities of the present tense and difficult period in international relations. One of the most important of these realities is that United States security depends first on America's own strength, military, diplomatic and economic, second, on alliances which may be concluded with European and Asiatic powers on a basis of mutual interest, mutual risk and reasonable equality of sacrifice and third, if at all, on anything that may be expected from the United Nations.

The late Senator Vandenberg had words of wise comment for

the argument that the United States has been unnecessarily "by-passing" the United Nations. Greece, wrote the Senator, could have "collapsed fifty times before the UN could ever hope to handle a situation of this nature." *

Another suggested approach to peace has been through agreed limitation of armaments. This is one of the ideals of the Atlantic Charter, which affirms the belief that "all of the nations of the world, for realistic as well as spiritual reasons, must come to the abandonment of the use of force."

The new destructive force of atomic energy, revealed by the bombs which were dropped on Hiroshima and Nagasaki, furnished a stimulus for plans looking to the control of atomic energy and elimination of atomic weapons. By resolution of the UN General Assembly of January 24, 1946, an Atomic Energy Commission was set up and authorized to prepare proposals for international exchange of scientific information for peaceful ends, and looking to "the elimination of national armaments of atomic weapons and of all other major weapons adaptable to mass destruction" and "effective safeguards by way of inspection and other means to protect complying states against the hazards of violations and evasions."

American proposals on this subject were crystallized in a report prepared by Dean Acheson, then Assistant Secretary of State, and David Lilienthal, head of the TVA and published on March 16, 1946. This called for the creation of a UN Atomic Development Authority, which should own all the world's uranium and thorium mines, together with laboratories and plants using fissionable materials, and should conduct all future atomic research, with a view to utilizing atomic power for peaceful purposes and preventing the manufacture of atomic weapons. Bernard Baruch presented these proposals in the Atomic Energy Commission on June 16, along with a provision that there should be no Security Council veto in matters affecting violation of the proposed convention.

* *The Private Papers of Senator Vandenberg* (Houghton Mifflin), p. 341.

The Soviet representative, Andrei Gromyko, suggested as an alternative a treaty which would forbid the production and use of atomic weapons and provide for the destruction of all stockpiles within three months. According to the Soviet proposal there was to be a UN committee to recommend measures of inspection and control. But Baruch's condition of eliminating the veto was not accepted.

Between these schemes there was a wide chasm, which has remained unbridged. There was every reason to expect that the Soviet Government would not accept what has come to be known as the Baruch Plan. Both the proposal to submit Soviet and all other atomic resources to international operation and inspection and the demand for the abolition of the veto were alien to the Soviet mentality of jealously guarded secrecy. The Soviet suggestion that the United States should strip itself of atomic weapons and trust its security to Soviet good faith naturally found little favor except among extreme fellow-travelers and absolute pacifists.

A similar deadlock has prevailed in regard to other forms of arms limitation. Soviet representatives in the United Nations have repeated several times a proposal for a one third cut in all armed forces and have emphasized the desirability of destroying the American atomic stockpile. A one third cut in ground forces would have left the Soviet Union and its satellites in a position of clear superiority, because there was no parallel in the Soviet Union for the hasty demobilization in the United States and Great Britain. Moreover, the Soviet Government has armed its satellites to the teeth, while the United States has lagged badly in the race for armed auxiliaries. The Soviet Government has been vague and cool in regard to possibilities of continuous and effective inspection, to see that the terms of an arms limitation convention were being carried out.

The American Government, in agreement with Great Britain and France, laid before the United Nations in the autumn of 1951 a plan for the "regulation, limitation and balanced reduction" of armed forces and armaments. This was to start with an arms census, a progressive disclosure and verification of the armed forces at the disposal of every country. It was also proposed that the Atomic Energy Commission and the Commission for Conventional Armaments should be merged in a single Disarmament Commission.

Vishinsky's acid comment was that he could not sleep for laughing when he was informed of this plan. As an alternative he repeated old Soviet proposals and added new ones, including denunciation of the North Atlantic Pact, calling of a world disarmament congress and a peace pact among the five great powers. This last suggestion has been a stock item in international communist propaganda. What such a pact could add to the obligations which nations have already assumed under the UN Charter is not clear.

It is not surprising that virtually no progress has been achieved in arms limitation in the atmosphere of the cold war. For armaments are a consequence, not a primary cause of international hostility and distrust. Past experience indicates that arms limitation agreements, given bad will on one or both sides, can always be evaded. In the event of goodwill such agreements are superfluous.

Nothing in the Soviet record would justify the western powers in beating their swords into ploughshares on an assumption of Soviet goodwill and good faith. Even if the Soviet representatives had been less intransigent on the question of inspection, there are two characteristics of the Soviet Union which would make the effectiveness of any such inspection within Soviet borders difficult and perhaps impossible.

First, Soviet terrorist methods of rule and the absence of free expression would make it improbable that a UN commission would receive any help from Soviet citizens in detecting violations of an arms limitation convention. Second, much of the vast area of the Soviet Union, especially in the Asiatic parts of the country, is imperfectly known and has been inaccessible to foreigners for many years. Therefore the political and geographical possibilities of concealing key atomic and other arms plants are far greater in the Soviet Union than in the United States, or any western country.

So, over a testing period of years, no attempt to solve the issues at stake in the cold war has led to practical results. The cold war has slashed a new frontier line across the heart of Europe. And in the Far East, in Korea and Indo-China, the war became lukewarm, if not hot.

Chapter III ~ Can We Escape from Victory?

There is profound historical irony in the fact that America's security, perhaps its survival as an independent world power, depends on its ability to escape from the consequences of its complete military victory in the Second World War. That victory has proved a trap, deadlier than the one which the Chinese communists tried to close on the Marines in the wild hills of North Korea. Never in history has a great war been fought for such illusory and self-deceptive ends. Never has retribution for pursuing illusion, not realism, in foreign policy been so swift and stern.

The full irony of the victory in 1945 can be established by a very simple test. How would an American be regarded today if he should advocate the destruction of all German and Japanese heavy industry, the complete and permanent disarmament of Germany and Japan, the transfer of Formosa to the government now in control of China, the handing back of political refugees from the Soviet Union? He would be regarded, and with good reason, as a very bad "security risk," as a conscious or unconscious agent of the Kremlin.

Yet President Roosevelt, as the responsible director of American foreign policy, committed himself to every one of the above-mentioned objectives, and to others which were equally detrimental to long range American interests. It is significant that it is always communists (and die-hard apologists for Roosevelt) who like to appeal to the memory of Teheran, Yalta and Potsdam. Earl Browder, when he was the authoritative spokesman for the American Communist Party, wrote in his book, *Teheran:*

> The greatness of Roosevelt, Churchill and Stalin at Teheran was shown in the fact that they all operated on the higher level of statesmanship, which searches for and finds the common interest which can be advanced by joint action, without any suspicion arising that one is trying to gain advantage at the expense of the other.

The Soviet Government was appealing to the supposed authority of the Potsdam Agreement long after the western powers had abandoned its ruthless and economically unworkable provisions.

The failure of military victory to assure American security or enduring peace is most vividly illustrated by the course of events in the Far East. The war in that part of the world was fought on the theory that here was a clearcut issue between a villainous Japan and a virtuous China, with the Soviet Union as a desirable, trustworthy potential ally, to be wooed and bribed into taking part in hostilities against Japan. Eliminate the villain, so ran the argument, and America and all the peoples of the Orient would live happily ever afterward.

Over one hundred and thirty thousand casualties in Korea have already paid for this sadly oversimplified view of the Far Eastern situation. The most important result of the war in the Pacific has been the emergence in China of a communist dictatorship, implacably hostile to this country and closely associated with the Soviet empire.

Our war against Japan made political sense only on the assumption that a friendly and reasonably strong China would be in a position to fill the power vacuum which would be created by the destruction of the Japanese Empire. The bankruptcy of the Roosevelt-Hull Far Eastern policy received final confirmation when the Chinese communist representative, Wu Hsiu-chuan, addressing the United Nations, almost on the anniversary of Pearl Harbor, hurled at the United States a speech more threatening and vituperative than the Japanese declaration of war. Deeds followed words, as the Chinese Red armies poured across the Yalu River and drove back the UN forces in Korea. We received very up-to-date proof of the wisdom of George Washington's warning against "excessive partiality for one foreign country and excessive dislike of another."

Our thinking on the Far East had been dominated by the dogma that China was our sure and tried friend, Japan our predestined enemy. Now we have received a costly lesson in the changeability of national sentiments. It is not adequate or convincing to argue that the communist conquest of China was an unforeseeable danger. There was much evidence in diplomatic and private reports of the weakness of the Chinese nationalist government after it was driven into the remote interior of China and of the gains which the communists were making as a result of the breakdown of normal administration in regions invaded but not effectively occupied by the Japanese.

Nor was there any excuse for not foreseeing the peril of Soviet ascendancy in the Far East. It was by a narrow margin that Soviet communist agents, headed by the astute Michael Borodin, failed to capture control of the Chinese nationalist movement in 1927. And at that time Soviet military power was insignificant, compared with what it was certain to be after the Second World War.

One of America's ablest, most erudite and realistic diplomats in the Orient, John Van Antwerp MacMurray, former Ambassador to China, raised a voice of prophetic warning in a memorandum composed in 1935 and hence not exposed to the reproach of being written with hindsight. Remarking that the United States was set on a course which was likely to lead to

war with Japan, Mr. MacMurray pointed out that victory in
such a war promised no positive fruits.

> Even the elimination of Japan, if it were possible, would be no
> blessing to the Far East or to the world. It would merely create
> a new set of stresses, and substitute for Japan the USSR as the
> successor to Imperial Russia as a contestant (and at least an
> equally unscrupulous and dangerous one) for the mastery of the
> East. *Nobody except perhaps Russia would gain from our vic-
> tory in such a war.**

For more than half a century Far Eastern politics has re-
volved around a triangle composed of the three nations on the
spot: Japan, China and Russia. The latter, alone among European powers, enjoys land access to China across one of the longest frontiers in the world. Russia is consequently able to de-
ploy large armies in this area without the use of sea power.
And for the last thirty-five years the new revolutionary creed of
communism has served as an instrument of Russian expansion
in China and in other Asiatic countries.

Japan, until its recent crushing defeat, was a strong military
and naval power, with additional sources of national strength
in the disciplined, hard-working nature of its people and their
ability to learn the industrial, as well as the military lessons
of the West.

China possesses the weight of the largest national population
in the world, the memory of past imperial splendors and, in
recent years, the dynamism of a ruling revolutionary faith.

A sensible regard for America's interests in the Far East
would have demanded that some balance be maintained between these three powers, that no one of them should be allowed to become markedly stronger or weaker than the other
two. And it should have been axiomatic to utilize all our diplomatic resources against the formation among these powers of
a combination hostile to the United States.

* Cited in George F. Kennan, *American Diplomacy, 1900–1950* (University of Chicago Press), pp. 51–52.

America's involvement in the Far Eastern war was often defended on the ground that an unchecked Japan, master of China's manpower and resources, would have been a threat to American security. But this hypothetical danger (it is very doubtful whether Japan could ever have organized China effectively) seems very pale by comparison with the real danger which we face as one of the many ironical consequences of victory. This is the huge continental bloc of the Soviet Union and China, welded together by a common faith which includes as one of its main articles fanatical hatred of western individualist civilization.

Certainly the situation which the United States faced in the Orient after the communist seizure of China was far more threatening than anything that might have come out of a compromise agreement with the Japanese Prime Minister, Prince Konoye, before Pearl Harbor. Such a compromise would have involved Japanese renunciation of some of its more far-reaching acquisitions in China, but would have left the Japanese Empire a strong power in East Asia, in possession of Korea, Formosa, Manchuria and some strategic and economic toeholds in China Proper.

In retrospect this looks like a very attractive prospect, by comparison with the hostile leviathan which confronts us now. It seems that what we fought for is the dubious and very costly privilege of replacing Japan as the power holding the line against Chinese communism and Soviet imperialism. A Japanese army on the Yalu, or, better yet, on the Amur would have saved the American lives that have been lost in Korea. When Japan had sole responsibility for the Korea-Manchuria area the United States was not obliged to lose one soldier or spend one dollar in difficult political salvage operations in that part of the world.

The peace treaty concluded with Japan in September, 1951, was a forward step and a constructive achievement of American diplomacy. It represented a sincere attempt to transform Japan from a defeated enemy into a prospective friendly ally. It is certainly better to repair a blunder than to persist in it indefinitely. But it is better still not to make the blunder in the first place.

For it is no simple easy matter to induce a defeated and disarmed enemy to rearm. We are learning this in Japan, as in Germany. Such aspects of the early phase of the occupation as the trials of so-called war criminals and the imposition on Japan of a constitution which specifically renounces the right to make war have made it more difficult for the Japanese to achieve the psychological transition from the status of a protected occupied country to that of an independent state, responsible for its own defense. Opposition to rearmament in Japan is voiced by various groups, by embittered, frustrated nationalists, by businessmen afraid of high taxes, by intellectuals who are reluctant to face up to the realities of a cold war in which a country in Japan's position could not hope to remain neutral, and, of course, by open or secret communist sympathizers.

China has been solidly organized against us and millions of Chinese communist troops, armed by Moscow, have been thrown into the balance against us. Japan is at present unable, and may be unable over a long period, to resume its normal role as a great power, capable of checkmating by its own strength expansionist Soviet and Chinese designs. It is against this discouraging background that the war in Korea dragged on. The United States is trying to escape from the disastrous consequences of victory by making an unprecedented effort, in terms of military manpower and money, in the Far East. Success still hangs in the balance.

There is a similar ironical situation in Europe. Two principal avowed objectives of Roosevelt's policy toward Germany during the war were "unconditional surrender," to be followed by complete disarmament, and the destruction of German heavy industry, as spelled out in the Morgenthau Plan, some features of which were carried over into the Potsdam Agreement and the first allied decree about the level of industry which was to be permitted in Germany.

The Morgenthau Plan was mainly the handiwork of one of Morgenthau's chief assistants in the Treasury, Harry Dexter White. The latter, before his sudden death, had been identified as a communist sympathizer and a source of information for communist spy rings by Whittaker Chambers and Elizabeth Bentley. There has been singularly little inquiry into the origins of the Morgenthau Plan. A Congressional inquiry might throw more light on the validity of the suspicion that White's strong communist sympathies were a factor in the concoction of a scheme admirably calculated to push the Germans into the arms of Stalin.

In Germany, as in the Far East, the retreat from victory was soon under way. By 1948 the United States had come around to the view, accepted more slowly and grudgingly by Great Britain and France, that Germany should be given the opportunity to revive economically. The vindictive and unprecedented strangulation of the German economy contemplated by the Morgenthau Plan and realized, in milder degree, during the first years of the occupation, was put aside. Progress, to be sure, was slow and halting and there were inconsistencies, such as the continuance of dismantling of German industries as late as 1949. But the general trend was away from the kind of victory that had been envisaged at Yalta and Potsdam.

By 1950, only five years after the conclusion of the Carthaginian preliminary peace settlement which was supposed to wipe out German armed forces forever, the cold war had advanced so far that the United States came out for the rearmament of West Germany. The only tenable criticism of this action was that it came too late. The Soviet Union did not lose a moment in arming the countries in its camp, including East Germany.

The failure as late as 1953 to get beyond words in bringing Germany into a West European defense scheme with the rights, obligations and risks of an equal partner is a tragedy for the anticommunist cause for which responsibility is divided between the Americans, the French, the British and the Germans themselves.

This failure to realize one of the essential prerequisites of winning the cold war, the enlistment of full German military cooperation, is due in no small degree to the necessity for escaping from the consequences and attitudes of victory in World War II. Hangovers and vestiges of the "conqueror" and "Hate Germany" psychology were incompatible with the new policy of enlisting Germany as an ally.

Much of Chancellor Adenauer's difficulty in obtaining ratification of the European Defense Community treaty may be ascribed to the imposition on Germany, as on Japan, of a "pacifist" constitution, which did not specifically recognize the right of the German government to raise defense forces. Long after the cold war had begun there was a systematic attempt to destroy all German "war potential," including even air raid shelters. As late as 1951 a German official at Bonn, in conversation with the writer, pointed out a curious inconsistency. Negotiations for a German defense contribution had been under way for months. Yet an inter-allied Military Security Board was functioning with the avowed purpose of making Germany militarily impotent.

The spectacle of German generals serving long sentences as "war criminals" is not an encouragement to Germans to put on uniforms again in alliance with the western powers. Indeed another of the fruits of victory, the trial of vanquished by victors, however gratifying it may have been to wartime passions of hatred, revenge and self-righteousness, seems in retrospect a colossal blunder, morally, legally and politically.

Unquestionably acts of horrible brutality, some of which could scarcely even be regarded as acts of war (the bestialities in concentration camps and the wholesale killing of Jews, noncombatants, women and children) were committed by the Nazi tyrants in Germany. Had stern and swift sentences been meted out by courts-martial for such crimes there would have been little ground for protest.

But the organization of the Nuernberg and other war crimes tribunals and the conduct of the prosecutions suffered from several grave defects. Many diplomats and businessmen were tried and sentenced on extremely flimsy evidence. In some cases it could fairly be said that they were punished because they did not commit suicide by rebelling against the Nazi Government and its orders. A very serious precedent was set when the principle was laid down that a military officer or civilian official could not invoke the orders of superior authorities as a justification for his actions.

The Soviet Government could invoke this precedent to "try" and execute every captured German officer in a war against the West which, according to Soviet propaganda, would, of course, be started by the West. Threats of this kind have already been made by German communists against the leaders of the Bonn Government.

There was little pretense of objectivity or impartiality in the "victors' justice" (to borrow the phrase of the British publicist, Montgomery Belgion) which was meted out after the Second World War. As is shown in another chapter, there is overwhelming circumstantial evidence that the Soviet authorities massacred some fifteen thousand Polish officer war prisoners, some in the Katyn Forest, others in unknown places of execution. But the judges at Nuernberg almost literally ran away from the evidence which the Polish General Wladyslaw Anders, the Swiss professor of medical pathology François Naville (who had visited the scene of the massacre soon after the bodies were discovered) and other competent witnesses were prepared to give.

The war crimes trials set a precedent which had best be forgotten. They represent another product of the victory from which America must escape if it is to stand a good chance of winning the cold war.

It has also been necessary to make a speedy retreat from one of the basic principles of the United Nations Charter, so widely hailed as a glorious fruit of victory. This is the exclusive power to deal with threats to world peace vested in the Security Council of the United Nations, where the five permanent members, the United States, the Soviet Union, Great Britain, France and China, possess the right of veto. The most ambitious practical move in the direction of checking Soviet expansion has been the conclusion of the North Atlantic Pact. And it is not easy to square this alliance with the wording of the UN Charter. Articles 51 and 52 of the Charter are sometimes invoked in defense of the alliance.

Article 51 affirms that "nothing in the present Charter shall impair the inherent right of individual or collective self-defense if an armed attack occurs against a member of the United Nations, until the Security Council has taken the measures necessary to maintain international peace and security." Article 52 authorizes "regional arrangements or agencies for dealing with such matters relating to the maintenance of international peace and security as are appropriate for regional action."

However, a closer study of the Charter shows that these are, legalistically, rather weak reeds on which to lean. For Article 51 stipulates that measures taken in the exercise of the right of self-defense shall be immediately communicated to the Security Council. And Article 54 provides that "the Security Council shall at all time be kept fully informed of activities undertaken or in contemplation under regional arrangements or by regional agencies for the maintenance of international peace and security."

Now it would be ridiculous to imagine the NATO communicating its military plans to the Security Council, with its Soviet representative. It would be equally fantastic to imagine the military plans agreed on between the Soviet Union and

China, or between the Soviet Union and its satellite states being made available to the Council. Instead of trying to twist or ignore the wording of the Charter it would be more honest and realistic to recognize that the whole pattern of UN organization is futile and unworkable in a situation when the main permanent threat to peace comes from one of the permanent members of the Security Council. The United Nations Charter should be written off as another fruit of victory gone sour.

The tangled confusion about the disposition of Formosa represents another attempt to escape from a mistaken wartime decision. Roosevelt, Churchill and Chiang Kai-shek signed their names to a moralistic declaration at Cairo in 1943 to the effect that "all the territories Japan has stolen from the Chinese, such as Manchuria, Formosa and the Pescadores, shall be restored to the Republic of China."

Like most wartime declarations, this was far from being a full and accurate statement of the facts. Neither Manchuria nor Formosa was a closely integrated part of China. Both benefited strikingly economically from Japanese administration and industrial development, and this brought at least some incidental benefits to the local populations.

This writer visited South China and Formosa in quick succession in 1937. As regards hygiene and sanitation, freedom from banditry and piracy, transportation facilities and general well-being, Formosa made a far superior impression. For the sake of consistency with the Atlantic Charter there should have been at least an affirmation of the right of the Formosan people to be consulted about their fate after the war.

But Truman and Acheson took the Cairo Declaration so seriously (although it was never submitted to the Senate as a treaty and consequently had no binding force) that for a long period of time they were prepared to have America stand aside passively and let this strategically and economically important island fall into the hands of the Chinese communists. This in spite of the fact that General MacArthur's expressed opinion about the importance of Formosa to American defense in the Pacific was subsequently confirmed by General Marshall and Secretary Acheson himself.

This subject of Formosa led to one of the most striking of the many contradictions and shifts of position which undermined American confidence in the State Department during Mr. Acheson's term of office.

On December 23, 1949, when abandonment of Formosa to the Reds was the clear intention of the American Government, State Department information officers abroad received the following instructions in how to react in the event that the island should fall:

> Formosa, politically, geographically and strategically, is part of China, in no way especially distinguished or important. . . .
> Formosa has no special military significance.
> Avoid: References which would indicate important strategic significance or that the island is a political entity.

But Secretary Acheson gave very different testimony to the Congressional investigating committee at the time of the Mac-Arthur hearings, in the spring of 1951:

> First of all, it was understood and agreed that Formosa had strategic significance, so far as the United States was concerned.
> The second point was that this strategic importance related to keeping Formosa out of the hands of a power which would be hostile to the United States.

If these points were true in 1951 they were just as true when the instructions to the State Department officials to deny the importance of Formosa were sent out in December, 1949.

A Yalta decision which has been a stumblingblock in subsequent efforts to enlist the aid of Soviet political refugees abroad in political and psychological warfare against the Kremlin was the agreement to hand over to the Soviet authorities Soviet citizens who might be found in the western zones of occupation. The bad effect of this decision was twofold. First, it led to the execution of many of the most prominent and influential anti-communists among the refugees. Second, it left in the minds of those refugees who escaped repatriation a sense of fear and grievance and doubt as to America's political capacity. As in so many other cases, the victory decisions of World War II are an albatross around our necks in trying to formulate a strategy suitable for winning the cold war.

This point finds another illustration in the hostile attitude toward Spain which prevailed for some years after the end of the Second World War. Spain from the beginning was excluded from the United Nations and, for a time, from the UN special agencies. The United Nations recommended for a time the withdrawal of ambassadors of member states from Madrid. Spain received no allotment of Marshall Plan aid and has been kept out of NATO military planning.

For this discrimination there never was any sound basis in morals or expediency. Had it been a condition of membership in the United Nations that political and civil liberties be maintained, Spain under Franco would certainly have been subject to exclusion. A United Nations comprehensive enough to include Stalin's Soviet Union and its satellite states, Poland and Czechoslovakia, together with the ex-satellite, Yugoslavia, still a communist dictatorship, had no reason to exclude Spain under the authoritarian rule of General Franco. From the standpoint of American national interest and security, the only sound basis for carrying on foreign policy, Franco's dictatorship is certainly preferable to any "people's democracy" of the Polish, Rumanian, Bulgarian, Czechoslovak, Hungarian or Chinese type.

Franco has not maltreated or arbitrarily arrested American citizens. He represents no conceivable threat to American safety. He has been resolutely and consistently anticommunist. He disposes of a substantial, if poorly equipped army and he occupies a geographical position of great strategic value, especially from the standpoint of air power, behind the strong rampart of the Pyrenees Mountains.

Yet American foreign policy has been so imprisoned by the false "'popular front" values and judgments of the war years that the original attitude of aloof hostility toward Franco Spain was given up slowly and reluctantly, in response to military and political imperatives. Now it has become official American policy to bargain realistically and unsentimentally with Franco for air and naval bases in exchange for military and economic aid. Another retreat from the mistakes of victory has been executed.

What has been necessary since the end of the war is much more than the correction of a few excesses or minor blunders of our victory policies. Run down the list of subjects on which there have been fundamental shifts of policy: the disarmament and general treatment of Germany and Japan, the trials of "war criminals," the assumption that Formosa had to be returned to communist China, the organization of the United Nations, the cold-shouldering of Spain, the handing back of anticommunist refugees.

Every one of the original American attitudes on these subjects, and every major decision of allied policy at Yalta and Potsdam must now be recognized as a bad security risk. A familiar argument in defense or extenuation of these blunders is the familiar excuse of the man who accidentally shoots his best friend: "I didn't know it was loaded."

But our present plight is not the result of any particular cunning and deception on the part of our enemies in the Kremlin. The communist design for world conquest through world subversion (backed when necessary by Soviet military power) is one of the most open conspiracies in history.

How much stronger and safer America's position in world affairs would be if the men in charge of its foreign policy during the thirties and the forties had believed Stalin, when he pronounced the dogma:

"It is, therefore, the essential task of the victorious revolution in one country to develop and support the revolution in others."

Or William Z. Foster, when he told a Congressional investigating committee, with a frankness which communists do not always show:

> When a communist heads the government of the United States (and that day will come just as surely as the sun rises) that government will be not a capitalist government, but a Soviet government, and behind this government will stand the Red Army to enforce the dictatorship of the proletariat.

Or Mao Tse-tung when he declared on July 1, 1949:

> To sit on the fence is impossible; a third road does not exist . . . Not only in China, but also in the world, without exception, one either leans to the side of imperialism or to the side of socialism. Neutrality is a mere camouflage and a third road does not exist.

But during the war and after the war the men in policy-making positions in Washington, with a few honorable exceptions, preferred to hug illusions, compounded of ignorance and wishful thinking. Maybe Lenin and Stalin did not mean what they wrote and said so often. Maybe Stalin was a well-meaning man, hampered by an obstreperous Politburo. Maybe the Chinese communists were not really communists at all. Maybe . . .

The brutal shock of Korea helped to dispel these illusions to the point of stimulating a genuine American rearmament effort. The revision of the disastrous decisions of victory, which pointed so obviously to defeat in the cold war with the Soviet Union was speeded up. But will there be time to repair the tremendous follies of Teheran, Yalta and Potsdam? Can we accomplish quickly enough in many parts of the world what the wise old Greeks said was impossible, even for the gods: to make the past as if it had never been?

Quite apart from questions of internal policy, it is unfortunate that a break in the continuity of American political leadership occurred only after the election of 1952. The same men who bore much of the responsibility for the decisions which turned military victory into political defeat continued, in many cases, to shape policy.

Mr. Dean Acheson was no Paul Revere sounding an alarm against the future designs of the Kremlin during the war years. Quite the contrary, as the following bit of testimony from one of his State Department colleagues, Mr. A. A. Berle, and other evidence would show. Referring to the situation in 1944 Mr. Berle said:

> I felt that the Russians were not going to be sympathetic and cooperative. I was pressing for a pretty clean showdown when our position was strongest. The opposite group in the State Department was largely the men—Mr. Acheson's group, of course—with Mr. Hiss as a principal assistant in the matter. . . . I got trimmed in that fight and, as a result, went to Brazil and that ended my diplomatic career.

As late as November, 1945, when Soviet bad faith and bad will had been fully manifested, Mr. Acheson appeared on the platform with such familiar figures at communist-front meetings as the "Red Dean" of Canterbury and Paul Robeson, under the auspices of an organization which was subsequently placed on the Attorney-General's subversive list, the Council of American-Soviet Friendship. Acheson assured the audience that there was no reason to suppose that the vital interests of the American and Soviet peoples would clash anywhere in the world and he endorsed the idea of "friendly governments" along the Soviet borders. Stalin had already given abundant proof of his definition of a "friendly" government, one that was completely subservient.

The Daily Worker, communist organ, referred to Acheson in June, 1945, as "one of the most forward-looking men in the State Department." And Mr. Acheson's claim to the confidence of his countrymen would be stronger if he had been quicker to turn his back on Alger Hiss and slower to turn his back on Chiang Kai-shek.

General George C. Marshall, like Acheson, was an extremely influential figure in the Truman Administration, as Secretary of State and later as Secretary of Defense. During the war he enjoyed a reputation as a superb military technician, a master of logistics. But he bears and shares the responsibility for many grave political misjudgments.

Marshall's influence on the big wartime political decisions was very considerable. At no time does he seem to have shown any appreciation of the necessity of holding Soviet expansion in check after the end of the war. He made the twin errors of underestimating Japanese power before Pearl Harbor and over-estimating Japanese power in the last months of the war. This second error contributed to the Yalta decision to bribe Stalin, at China's expense, to invade Manchuria and Korea,—first cause of our present troubles in the Far East.

Marshall seems to have endorsed and to have been closely identified with a memorandum which Harry Hopkins brought to the first Quebec Conference, in the summer of 1943, and which may be considered a classic of political bad judgment.* It predicted Russian domination of Europe after the war and seemed to accept this prospect as something natural, if not desirable. It also called for the enlistment of the Soviet Union as an ally against Japan,—a course that was followed, with the lamentable results that are now visible. His mission to China in 1945–1946 was an unmitigated and disastrous failure.

No doubt Acheson and Marshall shifted their views considerably as the pattern of Soviet aggression became more clear-cut and formidable with every new year. Both men deserve credit for building up Western Europe economically and Acheson in his last years of office seems to have swung around to fairly vigorous advocacy of German rearmament.

* See Robert E. Sherwood, *Roosevelt and Hopkins* (Harper's), pp. 748–49.

But neither Marshall nor Acheson grasped the global nature of the struggle against communism. Both failed badly on the test of China. Both, like many other figures influential in the Truman Administration, were to some extent the prisoners of past mistakes.

Averell Harriman was one of the Men of Yalta. Philip Jessup was closely identified with the Institute of Pacific Relations at a time when that organization was under the predominant influence of the pro-Soviet triumvirate, Owen Lattimore, Edward C. Carter and Frederick Vanderbilt Field. One could cite many other examples.

Acheson and Harriman defended the Yalta Agreement during the MacArthur hearings and on other occasions. It seems difficult to reconcile principled opposition to aggressive communist imperialism with the defense of a pact which gave Stalin the keys to Eastern Europe and to East Asia.

By 1952 American foreign policy was running down like an old and rusty clock. It had settled into a tired posture of defensive containment. It was short on ideas, short on understanding of the nature and methods of the enemy, short on fighting will to win the cold war.

American public opinion sensed this condition and the election of 1952 was a mandate for a change in foreign as well as in domestic affairs. If the new foreign policy was to be successful a clean break with Yalta, Potsdam and everything for which these conferences stood, a clean break with the prejudices and emotional involvements of the wartime years was essential.

It was necessary to savor the full irony of a military victory that brought not peace and stability but a new struggle with a new enemy who was stronger because of many mistaken wartime decisions. Escaping from victory had become almost a condition of American national survival.

Chapter IV ~ The Struggle for Europe

The end of the Second World War and the beginning of the cold war saw Europe sundered into two sections, which tended to grow farther and farther away from each other. A new frontier developed, coinciding in the main with the lines held by the western and Soviet armies at the end of the fighting.

Without any historical or ethnic justification this frontier cut Germany almost in half, leaving the more industrialized and populous part of the country with about fifty million people in the three western zones of occupation, while Eastern Germany, with some eighteen million inhabitants remained under Soviet control. The city of Berlin itself, surrounded by the Soviet Zone, was divided, the western sectors maintaining a regime of free elections and individualist economics under the protection of allied troops while East Berlin became the capital of the "German Democratic Republic," a Soviet dependency organized along totalitarian lines.

Little Austria was also divided into zones of occupation. But the split was not so serious as in Germany because the authority of the Austrian Government extended to the entire country. There was no attempt, as in Germany, to set up a separate communist regime in the Soviet Zone of Austria. The normal communist vote in all-Austrian elections has been a negligible minority, about 5 per cent.

On one side of the frontier, marked on the Soviet side by barbed wire and close patrol activity, scene of periodic hostile clashes on the ground and in the air, developed, with American political, military and financial support, a loose association of nations with free political and economic institutions. On the other side, under Moscow controls, the nations of Eastern Europe were transformed into outlying provinces of the Soviet empire, ruled by local communist cliques which were subject to frequent purges and into exploited economic colonies of the Soviet empire.

Methods of exploitation included an enormous amount of organized and unorganized looting as the Red Army swarmed over eastern and central Europe, the setting up of joint stock companies, with Soviet control, to develop natural resources, the exaction of large sums in reparations from East Germany and states which were formerly Axis satellites and a policy of pricing Soviet goods high and satellite goods low in compulsory trade relations. The amount of plunder obtained by the Soviet Union from its colonial possessions has been estimated as high as twenty or thirty billion dollars.*

It is an amusing commentary on communist propaganda about American "monopoly capitalist exploitation" of Western Europe that the United States has paid at least as much in subsidies of various kinds to the nations of Western Europe since the war. The "capitalist" United States gives; the "socialist" Soviet Union takes.

Communication and trade between these sundered halves of Europe have become increasingly difficult. The imprisonment, following torture and extorted confession, of the American

* This is the estimate of David Dallin, following a detailed survey of the various means of economic exploitation employed by the Soviet Union in the foreign countries and areas under its control. See *The New Soviet Empire* (Yale University Press), pp. 20–24.

businessman Robert Vogeler in Hungary, the similar fate of William Oatis, last independent newspaper correspondent in Czechoslovakia, the forcing down of an American airplane over Hungary and the virtual holding for ransom of its crew members were acts not calculated to encourage commercial and cultural contacts.

There was only one important change in this iron curtain frontier. Immediately after the war it seemed that Marshal Josip Broz Tito, communist dictator of Yugoslavia, had been one of the worst British and American political investments during the war. (Tito had been a special protegé of Churchill.) Tito pursued a strongly pro-Soviet and anti-western policy. Unarmed American planes were shot down over Yugoslavia in 1946 and there were continual incidents along the uneasy border where American and British troops faced Yugoslav units near Trieste.

But Tito resented Moscow's overbearing methods of political dictation and economic exploitation. There were no Soviet troops in Yugoslavia and Tito possessed enough personal support in the Yugoslav Communist Party organization and in the armed forces to make a successful break for independence in 1948. Moscow blustered and applied economic sanctions. But Tito was too firmly in the saddle to be upset by intrigue and propaganda, and the Kremlin, up to the spring of 1953, had not undertaken overt military action against its rebellious former vassal.

Tito continued to maintain a collectivist economy at home, although pressure on the peasants to accept the extreme Soviet type of collective farm seems to have gradually relaxed. There was freedom for foreign travel and intercourse and Tito's foreign policy showed a tendency to veer from attempted neutralism to a more definitely pro-western attitude. The treaty of friendship and alliance, concluded between Yugoslavia, Greece and Turkey early in 1953 was a demonstration of how common apprehension of a present common danger could outweigh the memory of former feuds and differences of ideology and political and economic methods.

The promotion of economic reconstruction and the attempt to promote unity were the two principal goals of American cold war strategy in Europe. The United States had made considerable grants for relief and reconstruction purposes immediately after the war. There was a loan of $3\frac{3}{4}$ billion dollars to Great Britain and there were smaller advances to France. Over 70 per cent of the sum, in excess of four billion dollars, spent by UNRRA for the benefit of devastated areas was supplied by the United States. Although the shortsighted vindictiveness of early occupation economic policy delayed the start of Germany's economic recovery, the United States appropriated substantial sums to avert outright starvation.

However, by 1947 it was clear that these piecemeal measures were not sufficient to restore Europe to normal economic health. The war had inflicted on the European economy deep invisible wounds, besides the gashes and scars of direct destruction. Methods of production had sometimes become obsolete. There had been little opportunity to renew equipment, even in undamaged plants. Britain, traditionally a creditor in terms of international investment, had become a heavy net debtor as a result of sales of foreign securities and the piling up of war debts in India, Egypt and other countries. The Netherlands lost much of the former employment and profit opportunities in its rich empire in the East Indies. France, after 1946, found its former Oriental colony, Indo-China, a heavy military and financial liability because of the long, indecisive guerrilla war which broke out there.

Some of Europe's economic troubles were thus consequences of the war. Others were, or should have been, curable by self-help. There was a tendency after the war to look for social and economic salvation in extravagant socialistic schemes, coupled with measures of extreme economic nationalism. Currencies were isolated from the free test of the market by extravagant official fixed overvaluation. Trade was largely on a barter basis, with every country pursuing the mutually self-contradictory aim of trying to sell more than it would buy. The result was a serious contraction in the total amount of trade. There was a prodigious gap, estimated at about 7.5 billion dollars in 1947, between what Europe wished to buy in the dollar area and what Europe could sell in that area.

This was the background of the Marshall Plan, an attempt to revive Europe by a liberal injection of dollars into its anemic economic bloodstream. In its first form this offer of aid was not limited to the friendly countries of Western Europe. As Marshall outlined his scheme at Harvard University, on June 5, 1947, it was "directed not against any country or doctrine, but against hunger, poverty, desperation and chaos."

This was a formula which might appeal to sentimentalists. But its political wisdom was questionable. The Soviet Government could have confronted the United States with a difficult dilemma if it had accepted the proposal—on condition that the Soviet Union and its satellites should receive a large share of the funds. It is doubtful whether Congress would have approved the project on this basis.

However, Soviet Foreign Minister Molotov eliminated this difficulty by walking out of the preliminary conference on the plan and announcing a Soviet attitude of uncompromising opposition. The satellite states were forbidden to have anything to do with the American offer. Most probably fear and dislike of the prospect of American economic influence outweighed, in the minds of the Soviet leaders, the possible advantages of a speedier and easier reconstruction.

The Marshall Plan went into formal effect with the passing of the Economic Co-operation Act of April 3, 1948. When the Economic Co-operation Administration (ECA) terminated operations on December 31, 1951, being replaced by the MSA (Military Security Administration) its expenditure had been about 12.5 billion dollars. Over 11 billion dollars were spent in Europe. The largest recipients of this aid, shortly before the end of ECA operations, were Great Britain (2,706,000,000 dollars), France (2,278,000,000 dollars), Italy (1,228,000,000 dollars), West Germany (1,192,000,000 dollars), Netherlands (958,000,000 dollars).

There are both favorable and unfavorable items in the balance-sheet of this ambitious project. There was a substantial improvement in West European living conditions between 1948 and 1952. People were visibly better fed and better clothed; much war wreckage had been cleared up; transportation facilities were much more abundant; goods were moving more freely across frontiers. This last development was considerably aided by the institution of the EPU (European Payments Union), a scheme initiated and financed by the ECA and designed to make it easier to clear trade balances multilaterally, not bilaterally. Production was above pre-war levels. ECA aid, generally well administered, with some inevitable misjudgments and extravagances and considerable overstaffing of the economic missions which became a feature of every European capital, was among three main causes of this recovery.

A second cause was the irrepressible impulse of human beings, even after such a shattering experience as the late war, to rebuild, to start farms and factories and businesses again. The third cause was a reversion in most European countries to a freer form of economy. It had become almost a dogma during the war and first postwar years that impoverished countries could not "afford" a capitalist, or individualist, economic system.

Experience soon showed that the precise reverse of this proposition was true. Prosperity invariably returned most conspicuously in countries where there was a minimum of rationing, fixing of prices and wages, currency controls and state planning and meddling with economic life. Belgium and Switzerland from the beginning of the reconstruction offered impressive examples of how much energy and efficiency are automatically generated by a competitive economic system, with full emphasis on the profit and incentive motives.

Even more impressive was the economic upsurge in West Germany after the occupation powers scrapped punitive restrictions on German industry, ceased to dismantle German factories and scrapped cumbersome foreign controls on German foreign trade. The soul of this recovery has been Ludwig Erhard, Minister of Economics in the Bonn Government, and a genuine economic liberal, in the proper sense of that much abused term. Erhard outlined his economic creed to me in his office in Bonn in 1951:

> I am for the free market and against state controls and rationing. I am for multilateral trade and against bilateral barter deals. I believe in maximum free exchange of goods, all kinds of goods, between the nations of the world, not in austerity commerce, limited to so-called essentials. I believe these principles are good for Germany, good for Europe, good for the world. Germany under the Nazis, other countries under statist economic regimes, have suffered only harm from autarchy, price-fixing and frozen economies.

Erhard acted as he talks. He made a clean sweep of food rationing, price and wage controls and a multitude of other restrictions, many of these inherited from the Nazis and preserved by the occupation authorities. (It is sometimes forgotten that Nazi is an abbreviation for National Socialist and that such words as bourgeois and capitalist were almost as obnoxious to a fanatical Nazi as to a communist.) Into an economy that had been under strict outside controls for fifteen years Erhard injected the now revolutionary old-fashioned ideas of personal incentive and reliance on the free market.

The results were striking. The cities of West Germany came alive as if by a miracle. Streets that had been barren and desolate began to blossom with stores, restaurants, moving-picture theatres. Heaps of rubble began to disappear and one saw the sights and heard the sounds of energetic new building. Within four years after the free economy had gone into effect West German industrial output had trebled and its foreign trade had increased fourfold. Germany had regained its position as Europe's leading producer of steel and coal. Whole new industries, such as the manufacture of telephones and textile machinery (hitherto concentrated in East Germany) sprang up with amazing rapidity. The new German mark, created out of nothing in 1948, has become one of the soundest European currencies. West Germany, as ruined and bankrupt as a country could be after the end of the war, had become a creditor in its trade relations with many foreign lands.

Of course no economic paradise has been or could have been created. It will be a matter of many years, perhaps of decades, to rebuild all that was destroyed by bombing. In addition to other hardships West Germany had to absorb more than nine million destitute refugees, most of them driven from their homes in the German territory east of the Oder–Neisse line, in the German-speaking Sudeten area of Czechoslovakia and in various countries of eastern and southeastern Europe.

This high figure is constantly swelled by the continued influx of fugitives from East Germany, who were pouring into West Berlin at the rate of over a thousand a day during the first months of 1953. Although the refugees able to work have been remarkably well absorbed (they have to some extent filled the places left by the German war dead) many war widows, children, old people, crippled veterans are living on pitifully small allowances and yet represent a heavy burden on the state resources. Still, taking into full account the widespread poverty that lies beneath the surface prosperity, the German recovery is one of the most striking in Europe. And it is a recovery inseparably associated with the theory and practice of a free economy.

Two things ECA did not accomplish. It did not cure certain fundamental European social and economic maladjustments, which have been aggravated by the war: Italian overpopulation, for instance, French backwardness in efficient distribution and in technical capacity, the lack of a vigorous competitive spirit. And it achieved only the hesitant first steps toward the economic union in which farsighted Europeans of many nationalities see the key to the continent's future well-being.

At a time when the United States and the Soviet Union both enjoy the advantages of big internal free markets, when Great Britain enjoys the trading advantage that derives from the large part of the world which is on a sterling currency basis, Western Europe is cut up into uneconomically small production units. The economies of mass production cannot be realized under such conditions. Europe's relative decline is reflected in the fact that it now produces about one sixth of the world's industrial goods, as against one third in 1913.

Too often one finds in Europe a combination of high costs and low wages. This is not due to lack of enterprise of European industrials, of technical knowledge on the part of European engineers or of skill on the part of European workers. Many European products, Swiss watches and precision machines, German locomotives and cameras, Dutch electric light bulbs, Italian silk and leather goods, French dresses, wines and perfumes, are internationally famous. The two obstacles which have most seriously hampered Europe in world competition are the national economic boundaries and the noncompetitive, cartel mentality which often prevails in European business.

A bold attempt to strike at both these evils and the most positive step yet taken in the direction of European unity is the Coal and Steel Community which has been set up under the so-called Schuman Plan, named after Robert Schuman, the French Foreign Minister who first proposed the scheme. The project is actually the creation of Jean Monnet, a French industrialist who has served his country in various official capacities, and who is a passionate champion of European economic unity.

The Coal and Steel Community, which became a going concern in February, 1953, with headquarters in Luxemburg and

M. Monnet as first president of the High Authority which is the chief executive organ of the Community, is based on the idea of a unified free market of approximately 150 million customers, so far as coal, iron and steel products are concerned. The nations associated in the Community are France, West Germany, Italy, the Netherlands, Belgium and Luxemburg. As between these nations all tariffs, subsidies, quotas, double prices and other hindrances to a free competitive market are supposed to disappear, after a period of gradual adjustment in the interest of the present marginal producers. Output of coal in the six nations was about 240 million tons (about 15 per cent of the world output) in 1952. Output of crude steel products was about 41.5 million tons (about 18 per cent of the world output).

The Coal and Steel Community is governed by a number of institutions with representation of all the participants, and optimists see here the germs of a future working community of European peoples. It is still too soon to know whether the Coal and Steel Community will justify the high hopes of its sponsors, and whether its example will stimulate similar pools in other fields, such as transportation, electrical power and agriculture. The undesirable alternative, if this experiment breaks down and Europe remains fettered to a system of small separate national economies, was vividly pointed out by General Eisenhower, when he spoke on behalf of European unity in London in 1951. The General said:

> Progress has been and is hobbled by a web of customs barriers interlaced with bilateral agreements, multilateral cartels, local shortages and economic monstrosities. . . . Europe . . . is divided by patchwork territorial forces. They pyramid every cost, with middlemen, tariffs, taxes and overhead. Barred, absolutely, are the efficient division of labor and resources and the easy flow of trade.

While the United States entered into close relations with Europe economically through the Marshall Plan, it also con-

cluded an important mutual military obligation in the North
Atlantic Pact, which was signed in Washington on April 4,
1949. This is a regional defensive alliance, with the United
States, Canada, Great Britain, France, Italy, Belgium, the Netherlands, Luxemburg, Denmark, Norway, Iceland and Portugal
as original members. Later Greece and Turkey were admitted,
giving the Pact an Atlantic–Mediterranean character.

Heart of this agreement is Article 5, which stipulates that

> an armed attack against one or more of them [the signatories]
> in Europe or North America shall be considered an attack against
> them all; and consequently . . . each of them, in the exercise of
> the right of individual or collective self-defense recognized in
> Article 51 of the Charter of the UN, will assist the party or
> parties so attacked by taking forthwith, individually and in con-
> cert with the other parties, such action as it deems necessary, in-
> cluding the use of armed force, to restore and maintain the se-
> curity of the North Atlantic area.

The conclusion of the North Atlantic Pact, a kind of American Monroe Doctrine for Europe outside the iron curtain, was
a logical extension of the reasoning which had led to the extension of aid to Greece and Turkey two years earlier. The fall
of Europe to the Soviet empire (the only conceivable source
of aggression in the predictable future) would be at least as
grave a threat to United States security as the fall of South
America, which has long been recognized as an area which the
United States, if necessary, would fight to protect against foreign invasion.

The signing of the North Atlantic Treaty was probably
hastened by two acts of flagrant Soviet aggression, which seemed
to push Europe dangerously close to the brink of war in 1948.
The first of these was the coup d'état of February, 1948, which
transformed Czechoslovakia from a parliamentary state into a
Soviet model one-party dictatorship. After the war Czechoslovakia furnished an example of a noncommunist government
which carried "friendship" with Moscow to the point of com-

plete subservience in foreign affairs. The Communist Party was strongly represented in the coalition government. Czechoslovakia always followed the Soviet lead in the United Nations.

Czechoslovakia obediently renounced partnership in the Marshall Plan at a word from Moscow. But subservience and appeasement were not enough. Moscow would be satisfied with nothing less than the incorporation of Czechoslovakia, with its considerable industrial resources, into the Soviet empire.

The effect of the Czech overturn was to stimulate a lagging instinct for self-defense in Western Europe. Shortly after the coup Great Britain, France and the Benelux states signed a defensive alliance for fifty years in Brussels.

A still graver threat to peace was posed by the Soviet blockade of West Berlin, which began in June, 1948, and lasted for almost a year. The basic cause of this blockade, as the Soviet commandant in Berlin, Marshal Vassily Sokolovsky, frankly admitted in conversation with his three western colleagues * was the hope of the Soviet Government that the western powers could be blackmailed into giving up their plans for the establishment of a German government in the western zones. Such a step was long overdue, especially after two conferences in Moscow and London in 1947 had revealed no basis of agreement with the Soviet Union on German reunification.

West Berlin, an isolated island in the sea of the surrounding Soviet Zone, was a tempting target for Soviet pressure. It was within the power of the Soviet military authorities to shut off all supplies by rail, road and canal. They took this step, after several preliminary threats, on June 24, 1948. The calculation was that, if the western powers could not be forced to give up the restoration of self-government in West Germany, they could be forced out of Berlin by the suffering of the population. Then Berlin might become the capital of a future Sovietized Germany.

* Lucius D. Clay, *Decision in Germany* (Doubleday), p. 371.

But General Lucius D. Clay, American commandant in Berlin, a tough veteran soldier with an engineer's training, proved to be the right man in the right place. There was wavering in Washington; but Clay's messages were consistently firm and courageous, and increasingly confident that Berlin could be supplied, on a siege basis, with the aid of a gigantic airlift. Clay's spirit found most eloquent expression in a message of April 10: *

> We have lost Czechoslovakia. Norway is threatened. We retreat from Berlin. When Berlin falls Western Germany will be next. If we mean . . . to hold Europe against communism we must not budge.

Clay recommended in July that an American armed convoy be sent into the Soviet Zone, with advance notice to the Soviet authorities that it was equipped to make any technical repairs which might be necessary. The need for "repairs" was the transparently fraudulent pretext on which rail and road communication had been stopped. This suggestion was not accepted and the unique experiment of supplying over a long period of time a city of some 2.5 million people by air was undertaken.

Naturally there were severe hardships. Fuel was scarce and electric power was closely rationed. A good deal of "made work" was necessary to take care of the unemployed. Diet was monotonous and uninteresting. But there was no starvation or collapse. By the spring of 1949 the airlift was bringing in 8,000 tons of supplies a month, as much as had previously been brought by rail and road. The counterblockade against shipments of West German steel and coking coal was hurting the industrial development of the Soviet Zone.

The Soviet authorities called off the blockade in May, 1949. The successful defense of West Berlin raised American prestige and probably did more than anything else to bring about cooperation between Americans and Germans on a basis of mu-

* *Ibid.*, p. 361.

tual respect. The superb resistance spirit of the West Berliners was warmly praised by Americans, from General Clay down. The Germans saw that America was willing, at high financial cost and with some loss of life, to keep Berlin as an outpost of freedom. The renaming of the street on which General Clay's headquarters stood as Clay-Allee was an expression of genuine feeling on the part of the Berliners, who were close enough to communist-ruled territory to have no illusions as to what would have been their fate in the event of a Soviet occupation.

The North Atlantic Treaty gave the United States substantial military advantages and also imposed heavy responsibilities. With almost all the powers bordering the Atlantic and the northern shores of the Mediterranean linked in an alliance it became possible for the United States to establish air bases in Great Britain, France, Morocco, Turkey and other countries. These bases are an implied threat of stern and swift reprisal against Soviet military and industrial installations if the Soviet rulers should step over the borderline into all-out war. There is reality behind the assurance which General Curtis F. Lemay, head of the United States Strategic Air Command, gave to the leaders of the NATO forces in March, 1953: * that, in the event of Soviet attack, American atomic power would be delivered to its proper targets at the right time, in the right quantities and in the face of any opposition.

At the same time the range of American military and political commitments has been much extended. An attack on any country in the long sea perimeter from the North Cape to the mountainous eastern frontier of Turkey can no longer be shrugged off as a matter of local concern. However, the unpromising alternative to the North Atlantic Treaty was the prospect that the Soviet Union would pick off the weaker neighbors of its vast empire one by one, by force, threat of force, internal subversion or a combination of all these methods.

* See *The New York Times* of March 14.

Germany is not yet (spring of 1953) a member of NATO (the familiar alphabetical abbreviation for North Atlantic Treaty Organization). But the presence of American, British and French troops in West Germany and West Berlin, together with specific assurances from the western powers to the federal government in Bonn that an attack on Germany would be regarded as an attack on themselves, means that West Germany is included in the European scheme of defense.

A few question marks remain, where reaction to aggression is not assured with absolute precision. One of these is Yugoslavia, which had not in the spring of 1953 applied for admission to NATO. However, western military aid to Yugoslavia has been increasing and Tito has publicly expressed the viewpoint that Yugoslavia could not remain neutral if the Soviet Union should unloose a general war. Should the Soviet Union, through its satellite states, attack Yugoslavia, this might be the spark which would ignite the Third World War, as Serbia touched off the First.

Perhaps the hardest problem to be faced is what should be done in the event of a local communist coup d'état, without visible Soviet military intervention, in Iran or some other unstable country in the Near East. It is impossible to foresee all contingencies. But one consideration is likely to influence American policy. It is no longer realistic to regard a communist revolution, inspired from Moscow, as a purely internal concern of this or that foreign nation. For every such revolution means so many more satellite legions, so many more economic assets added to the Soviet empire and organized against the United States.

Efficient organization of NATO began to assume new urgency after the invasion of South Korea, and especially after the defeat of the UN forces in North Korea in November and December, 1950. The crossing of the 38th Parallel showed that the Soviet Government was prepared, in certain circumstances,

to move armies across frontiers in order to achieve its purposes. This greatly heightened the tension of the cold war.

With West Germany completely disarmed there was a danger of a new Korea in the heart of Europe. The Soviet authorities in East Germany had created a huge police force, stronger
in numbers and arms than the police forces in West Germany.
Still more formidable para-military units, the so-called *Bereit-
schaften* (Alert Squads) were being formed with aircraft and
artillery. And the possibility of a Soviet onslaught on Western
Europe could no longer be ruled out.

These considerations led to a belated recognition, in American military circles, of the desirability of a German contribution to the defense of Europe. In weighing the worth of the
emotional arguments against German rearmament that have
been raised in France, to a lesser extent in Great Britain and
the United States, and also in Germany itself, one fact of over-
riding importance must be kept in mind.

Without German participation there is no prospect (barring
some miracle, on which it would be unwise to rely, such as a
sudden collapse behind the iron curtain or the emergence of
some "wonder weapon" unmatched by the enemy) that Europe
could be defended very long on land. With German participation there would be a fair fighting chance of repulsing such an
invasion, with all sorts of political repercussions in the Soviet
empire (especially in East Germany) as a result. The deterrent
effect on any adventurous schemes in the Kremlin of a European defense set-up will be enormously greater if Germany is
represented in this set-up. Whatever may be their motives the
opponents of German rearmament, French, German, British
and American, should they succeed, are likely to be remembered in history as the gravediggers of European independence,
culture and civilization.

For there was another lesson in the Korean experience, besides the higher temperature of Soviet bellicosity. This is the
inability of air and naval power alone to defend a land area

from being overrun by superior forces. The peripheral type of defense by retaliatory action from American air bases might or might not afford protection to the American continent. But it would be no protection for the Europeans, who would be caught between the two grim prospects of Soviet terrorist occupation and American bombing and maximum destruction of industrial plants and production facilities.

In view of the sufferings under occupation and the ruin and destruction which accompanied liberation, Europeans are entitled to the fullest sympathy when they say that, in the event of another war, they want to be "defended, not liberated." But they deserve no sympathy, indeed they put it almost beyond the power of the United States to render effective assistance when they delay, oppose and sabotage the only project which offers a genuine assurance that Europe can be "defended, not liberated." This is the creation of a strong effective ground defense force, with the largest possible contributions from all countries outside the iron curtain.

Secretary of State Acheson has changed his mind on many subjects. He reversed his position about German rearmament in the summer of 1950. On June 5 he stated as American policy the demilitarization of Germany. By August 30 he had come around to the view that a program for Western Europe which did not include the productive resources and the military manpower of Western Germany as well as France "will not be effective in the longrange political sense." *

The United States began to press for German rearmament at a conference of the three western foreign ministers in September, 1950. French opposition was strong and was voiced with special vigor by Jules Moch, a Jew who had lost his son in the French resistance movement. A compromise formula found expression in a communiqué issued after the meeting. "The re-creation of a German national army would not serve

* Cf. *The Pattern of Responsibility,* edited by McGeorge Bundy (Houghton Mifflin), pp. 116–17.

the best interests of Germany or of Europe," it was stated. It was agreed, however, that West Germany should be allowed to possess "mobile police formations."

This was the beginning of extremely protracted and complicated negotiations between Washington, Paris, London and Bonn. At the end of two and a half years (April, 1953) not one German soldier is in uniform. And, although European defenses have been strengthened in other ways, by the build-up of a unified NATO army under Eisenhower and his successor, General Matthew Ridgway, by the stationing of more American and British divisions in Germany, the prospect of defeating a major Soviet offensive remains dim.

There were two methods of obtaining a German military contribution. The first, and simplest, would have been to accept Germany as a member of NATO and to raise a German national contingent for the international army of Americans, British and continental Europeans which is at the disposal of SHAPE, the headquarters, near Paris, for the defense of Europe.

This suggestion aroused strong opposition in France. The French Prime Minister, M. René Pleven, offered a counterproposal in the winter of 1950–51. This was the formation of a multi-national European army, with contingents from the six states which are members of the Coal and Steel Community. As the plan evolved in discussion there were to be national divisions of French, German, Italian, Belgian and Dutch troops. But the high command would be international. And there would be fusion, at the corps level, of divisions of various nationalities. Sponsors of the project argued that it would yield the advantage of obtaining German troops without the political danger of creating an independent German national army. The EDC (European Defense Community) envisaged under the Pleven project was also advocated as a further step toward European federation and a logical extension to the military field of the economic cooperation proposed in the Coal and Steel Community.

American diplomatic support was placed behind the EDC. On this question Eisenhower and Dulles carried on where Truman and Acheson left off. A treaty establishing the EDC was signed in Paris on May 27, 1952. The Community is to be run by a set of institutions similar to those established for the administration of the Coal and Steel Community, including a Council of Ministers, an Assembly, an Executive Board and a Court of Justice. In all these bodies there is a suggestion of European federation. The ultimate military goal is set at forty standing divisions and 55 in reserve. Of the standing divisions France is to supply 14, Germany 12. The United States and Great Britain declared they would regard any threat to EDC as a threat to their own security. The treaty is to be valid for fifty years.

At the same time, as part of what may be called a package deal, a contractual agreement was signed between the three occupation powers and the German Federal Government, to come into effect simultaneously with the ratification of the EDC. The High Commissioners are to be replaced by Ambassadors and the Federal Republic is to be accepted as an equal partner in the European community. However, the former occupation powers may declare an emergency, if the Federal Republic and the EDC cannot cope with a crisis and may reinforce at will their troops, stationed in Germany.

After the preliminary signature of the treaty a new period of long delay set in, with opposition to ratification both in France and in Germany, for differing reasons. Chancellor Konrad Adenauer, a German patriot who also believed in the ideal of a spiritual, cultural and political European community and who was, of all European statesmen, probably the most clear-sighted about the reality of the Soviet threat, used all his influence to obtain ratification from the Bundestag, or German parliament. He had a small but reliable majority and obtained a favorable vote on the second reading of the bill authorizing ratification in December, 1952. Then there was a delay because of a special obstacle.

It was the contention of the Social Democrats and other opponents of the EDC that a constitutional amendment, which would require a two thirds majority in the Bundestag, was necessary to authorize German participation in the EDC. Much time was lost in maneuvering in an effort to obtain an advance ruling on this point from the German Constitutional Court, equivalent of the United States Supreme Court.

Social Democratic opposition to the EDC was not based on absolute pacifism or pro-communist sympathy. It is an outgrowth partly of opposition to Adenauer, partly of nationalist considerations. Social Democratic contentions are that Germany does not receive full equality under the proposed treaty and that such an alliance with the West would exclude the possibility of reunion with the Germans in the Soviet Zone.

The psychological mood in Germany after the crushing defeat in the last war and the occupation is not enthusiastic for rearming. A popular slogan has been "Ohne uns" (Without us). Almost any West German, if pressed for an answer, would admit that western occupation, especially during the last years, has been far preferable to Soviet rule. But no foreign occupation is popular and, when considerable numbers of foreign troops are located in a thickly settled country, there are inevitable pinpricking incidents that make for friction.

Despite the political criticism of the Social Democrats and the special obstacle represented by the Constitutional Court, German opposition to the EDC seems less unmanageable than French. The Bundestag, lower house of the German parliament, ratified the treaties in March. No French statesman of Adenauer's stature has been driving hard for ratification. As a result of a Cabinet shift in the winter of 1952–53 Robert Schuman, most consistent French advocate of the European idea, left his post as Foreign Minister.

The new Prime Minister, René Mayer, sought to win the

support of the followers of General Charles de Gaulle by proposing a number of "protocols" or amendments calculated to
modify the treaty in a sense favorable to France. The general
purpose of the protocols was to give France more freedom in
disposing of its own armed forces, transferring these from
France to overseas possessions, etc. The French have also been
eager to come to an agreement about the status of the Saar and
to obtain more precise British assurances of support for EDC.

Apart from a strong undercurrent of feeling that the Germans should not be trusted with arms at all, French criticism
has centered on the alleged danger of German domination of
the EDC. This fear is reinforced by the memory of France's
swift downfall in the last war and by the fact that substantial
French regular forces are tied up in remote Indo-China.

General de Gaulle raises the criticism that France, in the
EDC, would lose control of its army and its political destiny.
More realistic than some of his countrymen, he recognizes the
gravity of the Soviet threat and the necessity of German rearming. But he would prefer to see this done through the NATO,
although this was the original American plan, and was rejected
with horror by France.

There are elements of narrow shortsightedness on both sides
of the Franco–German frontier. Some Frenchmen are so obsessed with the memories of 1914–1918 and 1939–1940 that they
conjure up an unreal peril and fail to see a real one. Germany
now has not the strength of Germany under the Kaiser or under
Hitler. It has been bled white in manpower; it has diminished
in size and resources. It is dependent on good economic relations with the West for its very economic existence.

There is no reasonable possibility that any German army
could or would turn against France. The strong American and
British forces which are committed to the defense of Europe
are a guaranty against such a possibility. Nor is there any major
German grievance against France. The Saar problem is capable
of reasonable adjustment. The German population of the Saar

has not been barbarously maltreated and uprooted, like the population of the historic German territory east of the Oder. Germany's lost lands are in the East, not in the West.

There is cloudy, unrealistic thinking in Germany, as well as in France. The widespread German desire, after the defeat, ruin and humiliation of the last war, to stay out of all future hostilities is highly understandable. Incidentally this deep, widespread desire should relieve the French apprehension of a bellicose, aggressive Germany.

But wishful thinking is not a good guide to national action. For obvious political, economic and geographical reasons it is impossible for Germany to contract out of the cold war. It is a populous country with vast industrial potential and it is located squarely in the middle of the vital European sector of the struggle. German neutrality would never be respected in the event of actual fighting. A neutralized and disarmed Germany would collapse at the first totalitarian gust from the East. The Soviet attitude is important in connection with German unification, so attractive in theory, so difficult to achieve in practice.

Soviet propaganda has emphasized German unity and the withdrawal of occupation troops. A conference of Foreign Ministers of the Soviet Union and its satellites, held in Prague in the autumn of 1950, adopted a proposal submitted by Molotov, with the following four main points:

A declaration by the four occupation powers that they would not permit the rearming of Germany or the inclusion of Germany in any aggressive plans.

Removal of the restrictions on the revival of the German peacetime economy, without restoration of war industries.

Immediate conclusion of a German peace treaty and the withdrawal of all foreign troops within a year after the signature of the treaty.

The setting up of an all-German constituent council, with equal representation for East and West Germany. This council would prepare for a provisional government and speak for Germany in peace negotiations.

Nothing came of these proposals, which were clearly designed to produce a Soviet-dominated Germany. A withdrawal of occupation troops, for instance, would have left Soviet troops on the German borders, while American troops would have been evacuated across the Atlantic. Equal representation for East and West Germany would mean that 18 million East Germans would receive as much representation as 50 million West Germans.

The next Soviet move was to propose a conference on the German problem. Representatives of the Soviet Union and the western powers met in Paris and wasted several months in futile bickering, without even being able to agree on an agenda for the proposed conference.

Soviet propaganda, aimed at the Germans, made a new start in a note addressed to the western powers on March 10, 1952. This proposed that Germany should be unified, forbidden to take part in any alliance or combination directed against any of its wartime enemies and permitted to maintain its own armed forces. This last item was a novelty, designed to make German neutrality look somewhat more feasible.

An interchange of notes dragged on for several months and died away inconclusively. The Soviet proposal might have made a strong appeal to West German opinion, if it had not been for one fatal weakness, which was not eliminated in the subsequent notes. This was the failure to offer clear, specific guaranties for genuine freedom of voting in East Germany. Indeed such guaranties could not be given without undoing everything the Soviet authorities have been doing in the way of setting up a totalitarian regime in their occupation zone.

For free voting in East Germany would require much more than an absence of open intimidation at the polls. There would have to be a fairly long interim transition period, during which political prisoners would be released, political parties allowed to resume normal functions, newspapers and periodicals freely published and free institutions and the rule of law restored.

Chancellor Adenauer and his bitter opponents in the Social Democratic Party are agreed that freedom is an indispensable prerequisite of German unity. But the Soviet Government has understandably refused to submit to any freedom tests. For East Germany is probably the most embittered and discontented area in the Soviet empire. This is because the element of Russion subjugation and exploitation has been more obvious here than anywhere else. The Soviet overrunning of East Germany in 1945 was an orgy of wholesale pillage, savage destruction, wholesale murder and rape.

Subsequently the discipline of the Soviet occupation troops improved. Indeed the Soviet authorities seem to be so nervous about the possible effects of free contact between Soviet soldiers and the Germans that they enforce rigid nonfraternization rules and keep the soldiers confined to barracks most of the time. However, there has been systematic organized pillaging of East Germany through reparations levies, through Soviet ownership of many factories and stores, and through removal of much factory equipment and rolling stock to the Soviet Union.

The Soviet occupation has been incomparably more ruthless than the Western. To be sure, occupation armies and bureaucracies have been living at German expense, sometimes with unwarranted luxury, in West Germany. There was pillaging and vandalism in the first years after the war, along with such acts of organized spoliation as the confiscation of German foreign assets and patents and a limited amount of dismantling—although much less than in the Soviet Zone.

But in West Germany there are items on the other side of the balance-sheet. Various forms of postwar American aid to Germany add up to about 3.2 billion dollars—certainly an unprecedented contribution from a victorious to a defeated nation. About half of this sum is supposed to be ultimately repaid; but such repayments are problematical, unless the currency transfer problem is more easily solved in the future than it has been in the past. Moreover, even the wasteful spending of the occupation forces has been a stimulus to some forms of German business and has provided some employment. A further consideration is that, if there had been no western troops in Germany, the Soviet Union would almost certainly have seized the entire country and subjected it to far more thoroughgoing pillage than any that can be charged against the western powers.

In East Germany, on the other hand, it has been a case of all take and no give. There have been no Soviet contributions, direct or indirect, to German well-being. The contrast in standards of living between the two areas is tremendous. The communist newspapers in East Germany are full of dire pictures of unemployment and misery in the West. But the constant stream of refugees, willing to leave homes, property, jobs and try their fortune in the West is not diminished. There is no attempt by the West German authorities to prevent unemployed people from going to the Soviet Zone, where plenty of work is available, especially slave labor in the uranium mines near the frontier of Czechoslovakia. But extremely few have shown any inclination to go.

There is also no comparison between the two areas in terms of personal freedom and security. After several elections in which a surprisingly large anti-communist vote was cast the rulers of East Germany finally clamped down the system of one list of candidates to be voted for. In West Germany political parties, from extreme nationalists to communists, function freely and the votes are honestly counted.

The arbitrary arrests which were carried out in the first phase of western occupation and which in some cases, notably in the questioning of the prisoners accused of killing American prisoners at Malmedy, were followed by interrogations of inexcusable brutality have long ceased. There is no habeas corpus in East Germany and terror there was always far worse than in the western zones. It is estimated that by the end of 1951 almost

160,000 "enemies of the people" and 185,000 "war criminals" had been imprisoned or put to death in East Germany.* This is vastly in excess of any comparable figure for West Germany.

Given the bleak, hungry, desolate atmosphere that has prevailed in East Germany since 1945, it seems reasonable to assume that Soviet control can be maintained only by the totalitarian methods which have been stepped up from year to year, until open political opposition has become as impossible in East Germany as in any Soviet satellite state.

The few foreigners who have legally or illegally entered the Soviet Zone have been impressed by the large numbers of young men in the uniforms of the police and the para-military formations. Any fusion of the two sundered sections of Germany, accompanied by withdrawal of foreign troops, under present circumstances would involve a grave risk of paving the way for a communist seizure of power. Genuine communist sympathizers are certainly a small minority, even in East Germany. But the communists are united and have at their disposal military and police forces far in excess of those at the disposal of the Bonn authorities.

This is another reason why, in Germany's own national interest, the creation of a strong efficient military force in the larger part of the country which remains free should be pushed ahead as rapidly as possible. It is quite unrealistic to imagine that the Soviet Union would hand over East Germany to an unarmed West Germany or that, should this happen, East Germany could be easily and safely absorbed. Once a few West German divisions are in existence, the whole picture will change for the better. Then, at any sign of weakness or confusion in Moscow, or in the event of disturbances in some of the satellite countries, East Germany could conceivably rebel, with its German armed units passing over to the West German side. (There have already been many defections from the commu-

* See Norbert Muhlen, *The Return of Germany* (Regnery), p. 81.

nist-organized police.) But there must first be some organized German force in the West to serve as a magnet and rallying point for any such revolt.

At the time of writing (April, 1953) the struggle for Europe hangs in the balance, with the continent divided by the iron curtain. In Western Europe political stability and economic well-being have increased sufficiently since the war to make successful communist revolt from within almost impossible, although the size of the communist following in France and Italy is disquieting.

On the other side of the iron curtain the Soviet masters of the satellite states have purged and repurged the ruling bureaucracies, have destroyed the last faint semblance of open opposition and have driven these nations fairly far along the road which has already been followed by the Soviet Union. Agriculture and consumers goods industries have been sacrificed to the drive for heavy industries and militarization. The satellite armies have been built up, equipped with new Soviet weapons and closely integrated with the Red Army. How loyal these armies would prove in the test of actual war is one of the most important unanswered and unanswerable questions. From time to time a Polish or a Czech aviator flies to the West or the crew of a Polish ship puts into a free harbor. Such defections should be encouraged by every means available to western intelligence services. For every such flight shakes the confidence of the Kremlin rulers in the reliability of their new subjects and makes them less inclined to risk military adventures.

There is far more reason for discontent in Soviet Europe; but there is far more opportunity to express discontent in Western Europe. And there is a real danger that freedom, if unassociated with realism and responsibility, may fall before well-organized tyranny, as has happened more than once in historical experience. No constitutional court can hold up the rearming of East Germany. If the Kremlin wants a military alliance between Poland and Czechoslovakia that alliance is signed on the dotted line, and without haggling and wrangling extending over years.

America has done much and can and should do more to keep Europe free, to ward off the constant threat of Soviet aggression. But in the end it will be the spirit of the Europeans themselves, and especially of the Germans and the French, that will probably decide the issue. Whether Europe will survive as a great historic centre of Christian civilization, of the rule of law, of individualist culture depends on the will and capacity of Europeans to brace themselves and unite, militarily, economically, politically and spiritually against the new barbarians of the East—barbarians more formidable than their Mongol predecessors because they possess jet planes and tanks and atomic bombs.

Chapter V ⁓ The Struggle for East Asia

East Asia ranks with Europe as one of the two most important theatres of the global struggle against imperialist communist expansion. The challenge in East Asia has been even more forceful and dramatic than the challenge in Europe. Since June, 1950, the United States, with growing military cooperation from the South Koreans and token contributions from a few members of the United Nations, has been engaged in a major war with the North Korean and Chinese communist regimes. American casualties early in 1953 were already about half the figure of the First World War. France has been fighting an exhausting, protracted, indecisive conflict in its former colony, Indo-China, which lies directly south of China. The British have been less seriously involved, but have been compelled to use considerable military and police forces in repressing a savage Chinese communist guerrilla movement (very few Malays have taken part in it) in Malaya, one of the world's principal storehouses of tin and rubber.

In the cold war, as in the Second World War, there have been discussions of the competing claims of the European and Asiatic fronts. In view of the Kremlin's global strategy neither area could be neglected without peril to the other. It is a vital American security consideration that no more European countries should fall under Soviet domination and that the frontier of the present swollen Soviet empire should be not only contained but rolled back as soon as possible.

But Europe could be lost in Asia. The situation in Indo-China is an excellent illustration of the interdependence of the two continents. Because much French military strength is locked up in remote Indo-China the French attitude toward such an essential aspect of European defense as German rearming is nervously negative. (Other considerations enter into the French attitude; but a France able to concentrate its forces more completely in Europe would be less fearful of new German divisions.)

Indo-China is a key region for another reason. Should the Indo-Chinese communist forces under Ho Chi-Minh win a decisive victory in Indo-China such countries of southeastern Asia as Thailand and Burma, perhaps Malaya, would lie open to communist attack. And, if southeast Asia falls, Japan is also likely to fall, or to become an intolerable economic burden on the United States. For Japan, already cut off from former sources of supply in Manchuria and China, must look largely to southeast Asia for rice, for raw materials and for markets for its manufactures. So the war in Indo-China has become part of a much bigger struggle against the communist design for world conquest.

In this struggle a point of no retreat has been reached. The loss of more territory to communism anywhere threatens to produce very disastrous consequences. There are no expendable areas.

The hope that capitalism in the West could be overthrown by inciting revolutions in colonial and dependent countries developed in the first years of the Soviet regime. Lenin's belief that imperialism represents the final stage of capitalist development focussed his attention on the "70% of the inhabitants of the earth" who, as he reckoned, were victims of imperialist exploitation. If the fortress of international capitalism could not be carried by direct attack, by means of "proletarian revolutions" in the West, it might be taken by a flanking operation, by stirring up the peoples of Asia and Africa to revolt. Then, according to communist theory, the European countries would be so impoverished by the loss of profits from colonial possessions that the workers would lose the relatively high standard of living which made them indifferent to the appeal of communism.

"To unite the workers of the West with the peasants of the East in a common struggle against imperialism" became a slogan of the newly organized Communist International. A special appeal to the peoples of the East was launched at a spectacular Congress of Oriental Peoples, held in the old Tartar city of Baku, in the Soviet Union, in September, 1920. At this gathering Gregory Zinoviev, first President of the Comintern, executed for alleged treason in 1935, cried:

> The real revolution will blaze up only when the 800 million people who live in Asia unite with us, when the African continent unites, when we see that hundreds of millions of people are in movement. Now we must kindle a real holy war against the British and French capitalists.

No immediate results followed this colorful meeting, when hundreds of Orientals, most of them in picturesque native costumes, leaped to their feet, waving sabres and revolvers, as they vowed a *jehad*, or holy war, in response to Zinoviev's appeal. Where and how these delegates were recruited is not very clear; but they do not seem to have represented any powerful force in their native countries. The Soviet Union was too weak at that time to risk any foreign military adventures for the promotion of revolution outside its frontiers. Communism was alien to the patriarchal society and religious traditions of the Orient.

However, the Soviet Union almost conquered China without firing a shot in 1926–27. The method was political infiltration. The leader of the modern Chinese nationalist movement, Dr.

Sun Yat-sen, before his death invited Soviet Russians to serve in advisory capacities in the government which he set up in Canton. When this government, in 1926, set out to unify China by overthrowing the feudal warlords who controlled central and northern China, Russians were influential in directing political organization, propaganda, military affairs and finance. The complete inexperience of the Chinese in modern administration made it easy for a small group of foreigners, animated by a common theory and working as a team, to wield influence out of all proportion to their numbers. One may recall the success of a single strongwilled foreigner, the British General Gordon, in turning the tide in favor of the Chinese Imperial regime against the great Taiping rebellion in the nineteenth century.

The influence of Michael Borodin, chief Russian political adviser, was almost unlimited in the high councils of the nationalists. The Soviet General Bluecher, under the pseudonym of Galen,* planned the campaigns of the nationalist armies. Other Soviet advisers were influential in propaganda (a new weapon in Chinese civil war), in forming labor and peasant unions and in other activities. For a time it seemed that China in 1927 would experience not only a political, but a social revolution. Wherever the Kuomintang (nationalist) armies came, life became unpleasant and often unsafe for foreigners and for well-to-do Chinese. The powers of the new unions were sweeping and arbitrary.

But Chiang Kai-shek, leading military figure among the nationalists, who had always distrusted the strong Soviet influence on the Kuomintang, broke definitely with the more radical elements in the nationalist movement and helped to organize a more conservative government in Nanking in April, 1927. After a period of confused intrigue and maneuvering the more

* Bluecher later became commander of the Soviet Far Eastern Army. He was put to death after taking part in a secret military court which condemned eight high-ranking Soviet generals to death in 1937.

leftwing Kuomintang regime in Hankow melted away. Borodin and the other Soviet advisers returned to Moscow.

Shut out of the Kuomintang, which they had attempted to penetrate, the Chinese communists launched a rebel movement of their own. Their attempt to seize Canton by armed uprising in December, 1927, was crushed. For two decades they literally took to the hills. Their leadership came from radical intellectuals, some of them Moscow-trained, who accepted the ideas and discipline of the Comintern. Their rank-and-file soldiers were drawn largely from the poorer peasants who were urged to rob and kill the members of the more well-to-do classes in the villages.

This was especially true during the first years of the communist revolt, when a savage class civil war raged in every district which the communists invaded. Communist tactics became milder after the main base of the movement was transferred from the provinces south of the Yangtze River to northwestern China. In line with the requirements of Soviet foreign policy, the Chinese communists tried to create a united national front against Japan and sought to attract support among the middle classes and the less poor peasants by relaxing their more ruthless practices.

The ultimate aim, the setting up in China of a communist dictatorship with political and economic institutions similar to those of the Soviet Union was never abandoned. The idea, foisted on gullible correspondents and communicated to some American government officials, that they were not really communists at all, but well intentioned Jeffersonian agrarian reformers who hardly knew there was such a place as Moscow was propaganda fiction.

It is one of history's ironies that the success of communism is often promoted by men who have not the slightest sympathy with its cause and by events which are outside the control of communist leaders. Had it not been for the First World War, for example, Lenin would probably have died an obscure exile in Switzerland. The explosive ideas buried in his generally dry writings would have been an object of research for a few specialized scholars. It was the political, economic and moral collapse which the strain of the war brought to Russia that gave Lenin his supreme opportunity.

Had the Orient remained at peace it is probable that Chiang Kai-shek and his associates in the Kuomintang leadership would have coped with the task of giving China a more modern government, along with essential economic and financial reforms. But two forces helped to set the stage for the ultimate victory of the Chinese communists. The first was Japanese militarist expansionism. The second was the failure of American statesmanship to follow a realistic and consistent course in Far Eastern affairs.

The first disturbance in the uneasy status quo in the Orient was Japan's seizure of Manchuria in 1931. Had the Japanese stopped with Manchuria no threat to world peace would have been involved. This large and rich area had never been closely integrated with China. As in Formosa and Korea, the Japanese carried out substantial material improvements. The network of railways was doubled; many new factories were built; big hydroelectric power plants were constructed along the Yalu River. It is doubtful whether the people of Manchuria were worse off under Japanese domination (exercised through a satellite state known as Manchoukuo) than they had been under the arbitrary and inefficient rule of oldfashioned Chinese warlords.

But the Japanese did not stop with Manchoukuo. Local fighting which started at the Marco Polo Bridge, near Peiping, and spread to Shanghai led to largescale, if undeclared war between Japan and China in the summer of 1937. The Japanese won almost all the battles and occupied the principal Chinese cities and lines of communication. But they could not subdue and administer the entire country, even with the aid of satellite Chinese administrations which were set up first in Peiping, later in Nanking. The nationalist government of Chiang Kai-shek withdrew to Chungking, in the deep interior of China, and remained a centre of resistance.

The chaos which prevailed in the large areas of China which were halfway under Japanese occupation was most favorable to the communists. When the local Kuomintang administration fled at the approach of the Japanese, communist guerrillas often stepped into the vacuum. The nationalist armies fought most of the regular campaigns in the war. But the communists, with their long experience in irregular warfare, made the fullest use of their talent for propaganda and organization during the eight years which passed between the outbreak of the war and the collapse of Japan in August, 1945.

Japanese militarism also opened the gates wide for communist and extreme nationalist movements in the large section of southeast Asia that was overrun by the Japanese in the first months after Pearl Harbor. Native populations saw their traditional colonial rulers flee, like the British in Malaya and Burma and the Dutch in Indonesia, or take orders from the Japanese, like the French in Indo-China. The moral effect was tremendous. It is much easier to maintain a colonial administration that has become a tradition than to restore such an administration after it has been overthrown.

There was a Pan-Asian antiwhite streak in Japanese militarist psychology. While Japan exploited southeastern Asia for its own purposes native nationalists were encouraged and placed in positions of nominal authority. It is no accident that the regions of East Asia which fell under Japanese occupation have been the most restless and turbulent since the end of the war.

American policy in the Far East has been impulsive and shortsighted. It was too uncompromising in regard to Japan when the possibility of a reasonable agreement existed, before Pearl Harbor. It was too sweepingly destructionist in postwar plans for Japan and strangely heedless of the threat of enhanced Soviet power. And, after having put all our eggs in the fragile

Chinese nationalist basket, the men in charge of directing our Far Eastern policy showed unwarranted indifference to the consequences of having this basket smashed by the Soviet Chinese fifth column.

The results of America's Far Eastern policy during the last twenty years speak for themselves and reflect little credit on any of its architects, Stimson, Roosevelt, Hull, Truman, Marshall, Acheson. These results are two major wars. The first of these was fought largely to save China from Japan, the second to save Korea and the Japan we had ourselves destroyed as a firstrate military power from China, better armed, better organized, more unified and more hostile to the United States and to the West than at any time in its modern history.

Once the policy of making Japan militarily impotent had been put into effect, the vital importance of keeping China in friendly hands should have been obvious. It required no great gift of foresight to anticipate that a communist seizure of power in China would confront the United States with two very disagreeable alternatives. Either the Far East would be lost to communism and its manpower and resources would be marshalled in the service of the communist empire. Or the United States would have to put forth a great military effort in a remote part of the world for an indefinite length of time.

But no one in high authority in Washington during the postwar years seems to have recognized that, for better or for worse, we were tied to the Chiang Kai-shek regime and that the consequences of Chiang's fall would be much more costly and burdensome to the United States than the effort which might well have assured the stability of the nationalist government and its victory over the communists. To prove this point, one need only count the cost, human and material, of the Korean war and answer the question whether a much smaller sacrifice of blood and treasure in 1946 and 1947 would not have insured a different issue of the Chinese civil war.

That the Chinese nationalist regime suffered from serious faults and weaknesses, from corruption and inefficiency, is undeniable. Some of these were traditional Chinese methods of administration. Some were a consequence of eight years of war fought on Chinese soil.

It required no great perspicacity to point out these weaknesses. What was more needed and what was conspicuously lacking was the perspective to realize that there was no "third force" in China. It was the nationalist regime, with all its faults, or the communists. And the success of the communists would mean an upset, in favor of the Soviet, of the balance of power in the Far East, terrorist methods of rule, far more ruthless than those of the Kuomintang, and a tremendous strain on American military resources.

Some of the early American decisions about China after the war were made in the atmosphere of Yalta, in the dream world where the Soviet Union was considered a reliable "peace-loving" ally and communists were considered suitable partners in a democratic coalition government. The influential publicist Walter Lippmann, for instance, recommended a "united political front" of the Soviet Union, Great Britain and the United States, designed to force a reorganization of the Chinese nationalist government on a "broader democratic basis" by including the communists. "The formula for China is clearly indicated and in principle like that made at Yalta for Poland." * An intelligent student of foreign affairs should have realized in 1945 what almost everyone recognizes now: that this Yalta formula for Poland was a hangman's formula, certain to pave the way for communist dictatorship.

Lippmann's thinking was shared by men in high policy making positions. A memorandum prepared by Secretary of State Byrnes for General Marshall on the eve of his departure on a mission of attempted mediation between the nationalist government and the Chinese communists, who had consider-

* Cited in Freda Utley, *The China Story* (Regnery), p. 151.

ably extended the area under their rule in northwestern and northern China, in December 1945 sets forth this viewpoint:

> We also believe that it [the nationalist government] must be broadened to include the representatives of those large and well organized groups who are now without any voice in the government of China.
>
> This problem is not an easy one. It requires tact and discretion, patience and restraint. It will not be solved by the Chinese leaders themselves. To the extent that our influence is a factor, success will depend upon our capacity to exercise that influence in the light of shifting conditions in such a way as to encourage concessions by the central government, by the so-called communists and by the other factions.

Two assumptions may be seen in this policy-shaping document. One is that the inclusion of communists in the Chinese government was a goal of American policy. The other is the implication in the use of the phrase "so-called communists" that the Chinese Reds were not really communists.

It is not without significance that a sweeping change in State Department personnel dealing with Far Eastern affairs occurred in the summer of 1945. Joseph Clark Grew, veteran career diplomat and staunch anti-communist, was replaced as Under-Secretary of State by Dean Acheson. Eugene Dooman, experienced foreign service officer with special knowledge of Japan, was ousted as chairman of a joint Army-Navy-State Department committee which was helping to frame occupation policy for Japan. Joseph Ballantine retired as Director of the Office of Far Eastern Affairs. Both these offices were assigned to John Carter Vincent, who became one of the chief planners of Far Eastern policy during the next two years.

A panel of the Loyalty Review Board, highest appeal agency in loyalty cases, found "reasonable doubt" as to the loyalty of Vincent on the following grounds: "studied praise of the Chinese communists and equally studied criticism of the Chiang Kai-shek government. . . . Indifference to any evidence that the Chinese communists were affiliated with or controlled by the USSR. . . . Failure . . . to supervise the accuracy or security of State Department documents. . . . Close association with numerous persons who, he had reason to believe, were either communists or communist sympathizers."

The new Secretary of State, Mr. John Foster Dulles, absolved Vincent of disloyalty, but found that his work in dealing with Chinese affairs had not been up to the proper standard of a foreign service and that he could not usefully remain in the diplomatic service. Whether Vincent was lacking in loyalty, as the Loyalty Review Board panel found, or incompetent, as Dulles suggests, he was not a happy selection for a key post in formulating American policy in an important and critical situation.

There is abundant proof of Vincent's policy-shaping influence. He drafted on November 28, 1945, a proposal for action in China which closely resembles in ideas and phrasing President Truman's declaration of China policy and the memorandum prepared by Secretary Byrnes for the guidance of General Marshall.* The hand of Vincent may be found in the generally critical official attitude of the American Government toward the nationalist regime.

General Marshall went to China to seek a political settlement based on a coalition between the nationalist government and the communists. He also attempted to merge the nationalist and communist armed forces into a single national army. The mission was hopeless from the beginning. Experiments in this kind of coalition government, of which there have been a number, have always ended in one of two ways. The communists, as in the countries behind the iron curtain, take all power into their own hands. Or the noncommunists, as in France and Italy, throw the communists out.

The American Government could bring no pressure upon the Chinese communists. It could and did bring pressure on

* See summary of the Report of the Senate Internal Security Subcommittee, pp. 200–201.

Chiang Kai-shek. An embargo was clamped on American shipments of arms to nationalist China from the summer of 1946
until the spring of 1947. Meanwhile the communists were able
to build up stocks of arms from supplies captured from the
Japanese in Manchuria and turned over to the communists for
their use.

The critical attitude of the United States Government toward the nationalist regime found expression in a sharp message which President Truman despatched to Chiang Kai-shek
on August 10, 1946: *

> There is increasing belief that an attempt is being made to
> resort to force, military or secret police, rather than democratic
> processes, to settle major social issues. . . . There is an increas-
> ing awareness, however, that the hopes of the people of China
> are being thwarted by militarists and a small group of political
> reactionaries who are obstructing the general good of the nation
> by failing to understand the liberal trend of the times. The peo-
> ple of the United States view with violent repugnance this state
> of affairs.

It is not surprising to learn that John Carter Vincent was
the man who prepared this document, despatched under Truman's signature.† Unquestionably there were acts of violence,
arbitrariness and repression under Kuomintang rule. However,
it is not easy to understand how a government struggling to
maintain itself against armed revolt and subversive tactics
could dispense with armed force and police methods, unless it
wished to commit suicide.

General Marshall was formally recalled from China on January 6, 1947, and became Secretary of State on the 7th. In a
farewell statement he laid blame for the failure of his mission
largely on "the dominant reactionary group in the govern-

* See *United States Relations with China* (Department of State), p. 652.
This work will be henceforth referred to by the initials *USRC.*
† See *Institute of Pacific Relations: Hearings of Senate Internal Security
Subcommittee,* pp. 2253, 2254.

ment" and saw the best hope in the assumption of leadership by "liberals" in the government.

The Chinese communists lost no time in making clear their hostility to the United States and its aims in China. Foreign Minister Chou En-lai declared that Marshall's mediation aimed at destroying China's freedom and democracy by maintaining the nationalist government, which had "sold out to American imperialism."

After the failure of the Marshall mission the American official attitude toward nationalist China became one of rather malevolent indifference. Dean Acheson, at that time Under-Secretary of State, indulged in an extremely over-optimistic estimate of the situation when he told the House Foreign Affairs Committee on March 20, 1947:

"The Chinese Government is not approaching collapse; it is not threatened with defeat by the communists."

A note of curious confusion was injected into the situation when General Marshall as Secretary of State instructed the Ambassador to China, Dr. Leighton Stuart "to overlook no suitable opportunity to emphasize the pattern of engulfment which has resulted from coalition governments in eastern Europe." *

This might have caused considerable bewilderment to the nationalist authorities. For America's most positive effort in China policy had been to advocate that type of coalition government which was now belatedly recognized as leading to a "pattern of engulfment."

The nationalist military position deteriorated rapidly in 1948, and 1949 was a year of complete collapse. The communist armies overran the mainland and Chiang Kai-shek sought shelter in Formosa. As is shown elsewhere † the Administration was willing to let Formosa fall to the communists. But there was a change of policy after the invasion of South Korea.

* *USRC,* p. 280.
† See Chapter III, pp. 75, 76.

Acheson seems to have seriously considered the recognition of the Chinese communist regime in the last months of 1949. The British Government extended recognition in January, 1950. Straws in the wind indicating the Administration attitude were passivity about Formosa and the predominance of advocates of recognition among participants in a conference of Far Eastern experts held under State Department auspices in the autumn of 1949.

The Chinese communists, however, acted as if they wanted to make recognition impossible. They heaped insult on insult, provocation on provocation. The American consul in Mukden, Angus Ward, was held a virtual prisoner in the consulate and finally arrested, badgered and tormented in an effort to extract a false confession of an imaginary crime. The American assistant consul in Shanghai, Robert Olive, was seized, beaten and tortured into signing such a confession and apology in the summer of 1949. After the communists had seized American government property in Peiping, in defiance of a clear warning, Acheson seems to have given up the cause of recognition as hopeless, for the time being, and ordered the withdrawal of all American diplomatic personnel from that country.

A few instances of outright murder of American missionaries in Chinese custody, and many other cases of arbitrary imprisonment under the foulest conditions, to an accompaniment of insult and torture proved the futility of expecting any resumption of cultural and commercial relations with the communist regime in China on selfrespecting terms. Typical is the experience of Robert Bryan, American lawyer born and educated in China, as described in four magazine articles in *The Saturday Evening Post* in January–February, 1953.

Mr. Acheson himself, who had cold-shouldered the nationalists and given the communists the benefit of every doubt, described the international conduct of their regime as "so low that it would take considerable improvement to raise it to the

general level of barbarism" on November 13, 1951.* Two indisputable facts show that this is not mere abusive name calling. One is the boasting on the Chinese radio that a million
and a half or two million people have been executed under
their rule as "counter-revolutionaries." A frequent form of execution is a mass slaughter, carried out in public, at which children are encouraged to applaud, cheer and sing. It has also
been a practice to try to extort money from Chinese overseas
by threatening relatives with torture or execution.

Was the fall of China to the communists inevitable? This is
Mr. Acheson's contention, in the letter of transmittal of *United
States Relations with China:* †

> The unfortunate but inescapable fact is that the ominous re-
> sult of the civil war in China was beyond the control of the
> government of the United States. Nothing that this country did
> or could have done within the reasonable limits of its capabili-
> ties could have changed that result; nothing that was left un-
> done by this country has contributed to it.

But a program of active help to the nationalist government,
in striking contrast to the do-nothing policy of sulky indifference which prevailed after the Marshall mission, was submitted
to President Truman in September, 1947, by General Albert
C. Wedemeyer. This program was both realistic and prophetic.
Here are some of its principal conclusions: ‡

> Soviet aims in the Far East are diametrically opposed to and
> jeopardize United States interests in China in that their aims
> envisage progressive expansion of Soviet control and dominant
> influence. Realization of their aims in China would threaten
> United States strategic security. Time works to the advantage of
> the Soviet Union.

* See Richard P. Stebbins, *The United States in World Affairs: 1951*
(Harper), p. 385.

† This State Department publication of more than one thouand pages
is a valuable collection of source material on American-Chinese relations,
especially since the war. But its tone is onesided and many of its inter-
pretations of events are highly questionable.

‡ *USRC,* pp. 813, 814.

The Soviet Union, in achieving her aims, is being actively assisted by the Chinese Communist Party, which by its actions and propaganda is proven to be a tool of Soviet foreign policy.

The only working basis on which national Chinese resistance to Soviet aims can be revitalized is through the presently corrupt, reactionary and inefficient Chinese National Government.

In order to preclude defeat by communist forces, it is necessary to give the National Government sufficient and prompt military assistance under the supervision of American advisers in specified military fields.

American military aid to China, ground, sea and air, would, if appropriately supervised, contribute to gradual development of stability in the Far East and lessen the possibility of a communist-dominated China.

Wedemeyer was a general of long wartime experience in China. He was under no illusion as to the faults and weaknesses of the nationalist government. His use of such adjectives as "corrupt, reactionary, inefficient" is evidence on this point. But Wedemeyer grasped a basic political truth which escaped men in higher authority in Washington. This was that America could not afford to take a "plague on both their houses" attitude toward the Chinese situation. Too much was at stake.

No one can say with certainty whether the nationalist regime could have been saved. But America's interest in a friendly China was big enough to warrant a much larger, more serious and consistent effort to ward off the triumph of communism than was actually made. It would be understatement to say that during the critical years 1946–48 no one in the State Department or other key government agencies gave the impression of making much of an effort to stave off the debacle that finally occurred in 1949. The nationalist regime was treated as if it were expendable.

The contention that America did everything in its power to keep China out of communist hands must be measured in the light of what America has already done in Korea. Is it not likely that with a considerably smaller sacrifice in the years when the nationalist armies still held most of China, we could have changed the course of the Chinese civil war and thereby prevented the Korean war from taking place?

One of the most familiar and insidious forms of communist propaganda (insidious because it is calculated to appeal to non-communists who like to think of themselves as liberals and progressives) is to vilify any government that opposes Soviet aggression or that deals firmly with communist subversion at home. Such governments are depicted as reactionary, feudal, corrupt, out of touch with the trend of the times, etc. This technique has been applied again and again,—to the Polish government-in-exile during the war, to the Greek and Turkish governments, to the West German government of Chancellor Konrad Adenauer, to the government of Syngman Rhee in Korea and, most conspicuously and successfully, to Chiang Kai-shek's regime in China.

This kind of attack is more plausible because no government is perfect and truth is mixed with falsehood and exaggeration in the standard indictments of anticommunist regimes. If the situation is to be seen in perspective, however, two questions must be squarely faced:

First, is there a feasible political alternative to the government in question?

Second, would communist dictatorship, with its invariable accompaniment of terrorist repression and violent anti-Americanism, be a desirable improvement, either from the standpoint of the people concerned or from the standpoint of American interest and security?

Not enough Americans asked these questions when American public opinion was subjected to a barrage of publicity, favorable to the Chinese Reds and hostile to Chiang Kai-shek, during and after the war. The best and most completely documented history of how American public opinion was worked on during the years when the fate of China hung in the balance is to be found in the many volumes of testimony relating to the Institute of Pacific Relations, published by the Senate Internal Security Subcommittee, headed by Senator Pat McCarran.

The Institute of Pacific Relations was founded for the desirable purpose of stimulating interest in Pacific studies and creating closer contacts between scholars in the various countries bordering on the Pacific. On this basis it attracted the cooperation of many upright, loyal scholars, publicists and others interested in Far Eastern affairs.

Unfortunately some of its most influential officials developed a strong bias in favor of Soviet and Chinese communism and the activities of the IPR became gravely perverted from their original purpose. One fact shows how heavily this relatively small organization was infiltrated with communist sympathizers and agents. In the concluding volume of its long investigation the Senate Subcommittee lists almost one hundred persons with IPR connections and communist affiliations.* Some of these identifications may be challenged. But in a high proportion of cases the persons mentioned are proved members of the Communist Party, contributors to communist publications, members of "front" organizations which sprang up like mushrooms to paralyze American aid to the nationalist government or members of Soviet spy rings.

And the bias of the Institute was a matter of legitimate public concern. The IPR enjoyed semi-official status as the expert organization in Far Eastern affairs during the war and first postwar years. Men whom it trained were not infrequently given assignments connected with the making of Far Eastern policy. Some served in various capacities in the occupation of Japan.

Owen Lattimore, the most vehemently discussed figure in the Institute, held such responsible public posts as adviser to

* See last volume of *Hearings on the Institute of Pacific Relations,* pp. 151–59.

Chiang Kai-shek in 1941–42, director of the Far Eastern Division of the Office of War Information and member of the Pauley mission to assess reparations from Japan. Lattimore and his sympathizers like to represent him as an objective scholar, slandered by prejudiced and publicity-seeking politicians. In his book, *Ordeal by Slander,* Lattimore poses as not only a disinterested scholar, but as an anticommunist. Yet one can search his fairly prolific writings without finding a passage that adequately describes the cruelty and tyranny of communism or shows appreciation of the disastrous political, military and economic consequences, for the United States, of a communist sweep in Asia. As editor of the official organ of the IPR, *Pacific Affairs,* Lattimore, as a matter of principle, barred contributors who were obnoxious to spokesmen for the Soviet organization which for a time belonged to the loose association of Institutes of Pacific Affairs in various countries. He publicly expressed belief in the credibility of the accusations in the Soviet purge trials of the thirties and saw "democracy" in this savage extermination of Stalin's enemies.

Professing to know little about communism, Lattimore warmly praised books about the Soviet Union by such uncritical enthusiasts as Anna Louise Strong.* Lattimore's "anticommunist" record becomes more curious the more it is looked into. He belonged for some years to the editorial board of *Amerasia,* magazine devoted to Oriental affairs and edited by Philip Jaffe, a man with a long list of communist front affiliations. Even before *Amerasia* closed down in an atmosphere of stolen government documents found in its office and strangely quashed indictments it was not the kind of publication where an opponent of communism would have been likely to seek expression.

In company with Vice-President Henry A. Wallace, John

---

* Professor Richard Walker, of Yale University, has published a detailed analysis of *Pacific Affairs* in "Lattimore and The IPR" (*New Leader,* New York).

Carter Vincent of the State Department and John Hazard, expert in Soviet law, Lattimore visited the town of Magadan, and the Kolyma gold fields, in northeastern Siberia, in 1944. This area is one of the big centres of Soviet slave labor. It has been made notorious, and infamous, by the descriptions of former prisoners, the Russian, Vladimir Petrov, and the Dutch woman, Elinor Lipper.

But Lattimore, the "anticommunist," published in *The National Geographic Magazine* of December, 1944, a most laudatory article about his travel impressions of Eastern Siberia. There was no suggestion that anyone was in Kolyma against his will. Dalstroi, the huge slave labor organization, was euphemistically called "a combination Hudson's Bay Company and TVA." Nikishov, the Simon Legree of the place, was credited with "sensitive interest in art and music and . . . deep sense of civic responsibility."

Lattimore published in 1945 a book entitled *Solution in Asia*. Its spirit is indicated by this descriptive note on the jacket:

> He shows that all the Asiatic peoples are more interested in actual democratic practices, *such as the ones they can see in action across the Russian border,* than they are in the fine theories of the Anglo-Saxon democracies, which come coupled with ruthless imperialism. [Italics supplied]

In this book Lattimore calls for the forcible deposition of the Japanese Emperor. And, according to his own testimony before the McCarran Subcommittee, he "helped quite largely" in drawing up the Pauley Plan, which would have caused a drastic deindustrialization of Japan. If there were two measures well calculated to push the Japanese people into the arms of the communists after the war these were surely the elimination of that great stabilizing symbol, the Emperor, and the destruction of such an essential means of earning their national livelihood as their industrial plants.

The cold war had become fairly warm by 1949; but there was no perceptible change in Lattimore's attitude. In August, 1949, he submitted a memorandum to the State Department, where he was still a prized consultant, urging that the United States dissociate itself from anticommunist regimes in Korea, Formosa and Indo-China, cold-shoulder Japan as a potential ally and "recognize the facts of life in China." This memorandum could be fairly interpreted as a call for complete non-resistance to communism in Asia.

It is in the light of this consistent record, extending over almost two decades, that Lattimore's claims to be an objective scholar and an opponent of communism should be judged. It is also in the light of this record that the judgment of the State Department officials who, at least as late as 1949, were treating Lattimore as a high authority on the Far East should be appraised.

The ex-communist Louis Budenz, in testimony before the Senate Subcommittee, offered the following evaluation of Lattimore's usefulness to the communist cause:

> His [Lattimore's] position from the viewpoint of the Communist Party was a very important one. It was particularly stressed in the Political Bureau [highest Communist Party organ of leadership] that his great value lay in the fact that he could bring the emphasis in support of Soviet policy in language which was non-Soviet. And they consider that a very valuable asset.

The Senate Subcommittee reached the conclusion that "Owen Lattimore was, from some time beginning in the 1930's, a conscious, articulate instrument of the Soviet conspiracy." He was later indicted for perjury on the recommendation of a Washington grand jury, on the ground of discrepancies in his testimony before the Subcommittee.

The case of Owen Lattimore was probably the most publicized and widely investigated. But the process of softening up American public opinion to a point where news of the communist conquest of China would be received with apathy, if not with satisfaction, went on through many channels. The leading book review organs of the country displayed a marked preference, in discussing books on China, for reviewers with the political sympathies of Lattimore and Edgar Snow, a journalist who first came into prominence in China as a eulogist of the Reds. As a natural consequence books which denounced the nationalists and praised the communists were sure of a good introduction to American readers. Books which presented the other side of the case were denounced or neglected.

One more characteristic incident revealed by the McCarran investigation may be noted. One Israel Epstein, characterized by Elizabeth Bentley in her testimony before the Subcommittee as "a member of the Russian secret police in China" and a journalist of some experience there, in 1947 published a book, strongly pro-communist in tone, entitled *The Unfinished Revolution in China.*

Edward Carter, Secretary General of the IPR, took it on himself to see that this book should reach "the right people." He wrote as follows to the publicity director of Little, Brown and Company, publishers of Epstein's book:

> I think it's of the utmost importance that you devise some means of getting it read at an early date, among others, by Secretary of State George Marshall, Senators Vandenberg, Morse and Ives; John Foster Dulles and John Carter Vincent of the State Department. . . . I have another suggestion to make. The book is so full of profound understanding and admiration of the Chinese people that I think it is equally important to find ways and means of getting a wide circulation in China.

Any doubt as to the political sympathies of Mr. Epstein were dispelled when he turned up in communist China, during the Korean war, and contributed to *The Daily Worker* an article full of stereotyped communist abuse of the United States.

There was a close connection between the fall of China and the war in Korea. The position of the anticommunist government which had been formed, with American support, in South Korea became immensely more precarious when the vast bulk of China swung into the Soviet camp. Two grave American blunders, one military, the other political, helped to precipitate the Korean war.

After the surrender of Japan, Korea, a peninsula facing Japan and formerly a part of the Japanese Empire, became, in one respect, an oriental Germany, divided along the line of the 38th Parallel, which was the line of demarcation between the United States and Soviet forces. In the face of many difficulties and obstacles, because very few Koreans had received any training in representative institutions, a formally democratic government developed in South Korea, with its population of some 21 millions.

North Korea, with a population, originally, of about 9 millions, became a standard communist-ruled state, largely directed by Korean communists who had been trained in the Soviet Union or who had served with the Chinese Red Army. Just as in Germany, there was a big movement of refugees away from North Korea into South Korea.

It proved impossible to obtain the unification of Korea, either through direct American–Soviet discussions or through the mediation of the United Nations. The UN Commission appointed to consider the Korean question was never admitted to North Korea. One reason for refusal to admit this Commission was the formidable build-up, by Korean standards, of the North Korean army. As early as 1947 Mr. James F. Byrnes, former American Secretary of State, reported that the Red Army had trained an army of Koreans, estimated to number from 100,000 to 400,000 men.*

The first and most serious American blunder was the failure to create, in South Korea, an army that would have at least matched the North Korean army, man for man, gun for gun, tank for tank. America possessed the resources to do this. And

* See James F. Byrnes, *Speaking Frankly* (Harper), p. 223.

the South Koreans, under the later test of war, proved hard tenacious fighters when they received training and proper equipment.

But, following the setting up of a South Korean Government in August, 1948 (ratified by the United Nations in December, 1948 and recognized diplomatically by the United States on January 1, 1949) the United States withdrew its troops from South Korea in June, 1949, without leaving the South Koreans in a position to defend themselves. North of the 38th Parallel was a powerful army, fitted out with Soviet tanks and modern weapons. South of the 38th Parallel was a lightly armed constabulary, equipped at best for fighting local guerrillas, but no match for the military threat from the North.

This grave military blunder was followed by a political error on the part of Secretary Acheson. In a speech delivered on January 10, 1950, Acheson, who had recently given the Chinese communists a free hand to invade Formosa, defined the "defensive perimeter" of the United States as extending from Japan through the Ryukyu Islands to the Philippines. Korea, like Formosa, was pointedly omitted.

"So far as the military security of other areas in the Pacific is concerned," said Mr. Acheson, "it must be clear that no person can guaranty these areas against military attack."

He then referred to "the commitments of the entire civilized world under the UN, which so far has not proved a weak reed to lean on." This, however, was no offset to the implied American repudiation of intention to defend South Korea. The Kremlin may well have felt that it had received a double invitation to win a cheap and easy victory in Korea. American troops had been withdrawn before any effective South Korean army had been organized. And the American Secretary of State had publicly ruled Korea outside the American "defensive perimeter."

The invasion of South Korea on June 25, 1950, posed a grave dilemma for the Truman Administration. The account-

ing was being presented for a long chain of blunders, beginning with the invitation to the Soviet Union at Yalta to invade
Manchuria and Korea, continuing through the loss of China
and culminating in the failure to make South Korea capable
of self-defense.

It was clear from the first reports of the fighting that only
American intervention would save South Korea from being
overrun within a few weeks at the most. The military odds were
too uneven. The conquest of South Korea would mean the
massacre of every suspected anticommunist in the country and
a profound discrediting both of the United Nations and of the
United States. It would mean, in all probability, the crum-
bling of effective resistance to communism throughout East
Asia and the loss of this entire area, including Japan.

On the other hand the prospective cost of accepting the challenge was heavy. It meant the commitment of large American
forces to a remote part of the world. And behind the North
Korean puppets were two threatening shadows, Red China and
the Soviet Union.

The decision to fight in Korea was right and inevitable,
unless America had been prepared to withdraw from the Far
East altogether and lapse into a hemispheric isolationism which
could create only an illusion of security in an age of swifter-
than-sound airplanes and atomic bombs.

When news of the invasion was received the Security Council, with no veto,* called on the North Korean forces to retire
behind the 38th Parallel. When this request was ignored the
Council recommended that "the members of the UN furnish
such assistance to the Republic of Korea as may be necessary

* The possibility of obtaining a mandate from the Security Council for
action in Korea which would be legal under the UN Charter hinged on
an accidental circumstance. The Soviet representative had been for some
time boycotting the Council as a protest against the nonadmission of the
communist government of China to the United Nations. A Soviet veto in
this case could have been taken for granted.

to repel the armed attack and to restore international peace and security in the area."

President Truman on June 27 ordered American air and sea forces to "give the Korean Government troops cover and support." He also called for the neutralization of Formosa. The American Seventh Fleet was to "prevent any attack on Formosa" and to see that the Chinese nationalists "ceased all air and sea operations against the mainland."

It soon became clear that air and naval support was not enough and United States ground forces were poured into Korea in an unending stream. Apart from the South Korean army, which was gradually built up into a large and effective fighting force, the United States made overwhelmingly the greatest contribution of manpower to the Korean war. There were about a quarter of a million American troops in Korea in 1953. Britain and the Commonwealth nations combined sent the equivalent of about one division. Smaller units were provided by Turkey, Greece, France, the Netherlands, Thailand, the Philippines and a few other UN members. But the majority of the UN members offered only "moral" support, and some did not give even this. Some of the loudest criticism of every move designed to win the war came from nations like India which did not send a man or a gun to the front. As a defense of America's own security the Korean war was a disagreeable necessity. As an experiment in collective security, with every law-abiding nation making a maximum effort to repel and punish aggression, it proved a resounding failure.

The fortune of the war shifted spectacularly during the first year of fighting and then settled into a prolonged stalemate, reminiscent of the trench warfare of the First World War, although with smaller casualties. At first the North Koreans swept down the peninsula until the UN forces were confined to a narrow beachhead around the port of Pusan. The tide turned in September, when a brilliant landing at the port of Inchon, in the rear of the North Korean main forces, led to the rout of their army and the recapture of Seoul, the South Korean capital, and made possible a successful advance into North Korea.

Disaster struck in late November and early December, when Chinese communist armies poured into Korea and drove the UN forces back across the 38th Parallel. Seoul was lost and there was fear of a catastrophic defeat and the forced evacuation of all Korea. Morale in the United Nations sank to an extremely low level. Repeated cease-fire appeals were sent to the Chinese communists and there was strong sentiment in the UN corridors and in some fainthearted circles in the United States for trying to buy peace by sacrificing Formosa and admitting Red China to the United Nations. Had the Chinese communists shown more diplomatic moderation in their military victory they might have split the wobbly and wavering ranks of the UN.

But the Chinese Red demands were so extreme that no agreement was reached. General Matthew Ridgway, who took over the field command in a dark moment of retreat, when his predecessor was killed in an accident, restored the military situation in the spring of 1951. Making effective use of superior firepower, he repulsed several Chinese communist offensives with much slaughter and pushed the fighting line back to and somewhat beyond the 38th Parallel.

American and, to a smaller extent, world public opinion was stirred by a visible cleavage of viewpoint between the Administration in Washington and General Douglas MacArthur, supreme commander of the UN forces during the first nine months of the war. When Red China entered the war in force, late in 1950, General MacArthur proposed the following program of counteraction:

(a) Blockade the coast of China.

(b) Destroy through naval gunfire and air bombardment China's industrial capacity to wage war.

(c) Secure appropriate reinforcements from the nationalist garrison on Formosa.

(d) Release existing restrictions upon the Formosan garrison for diversionary action (possibly leading to counterinvasion) against vulnerable areas of the Chinese mainland.

This program was rejected in Washington on the ground that it would be unacceptable to the UN and would involve undue risk of a general war. The controversy continued to smolder, broke out afresh in the spring and led to MacArthur's dismissal by President Truman on April 10, 1951. MacArthur had eloquently summarized his attitude in a letter to the House Republican leader, Joseph Martin, on March 20:

> It seems strangely difficult for some to realize that here in Asia is where the communist conspirators have elected to make their play for global conquest; that here we fight Europe's war with arms while the diplomats there still fight it with words; that if we lose the war to communism in Asia the fall of Europe is inevitable; win it and Europe would most probably avoid war and yet preserve freedom. As you pointed out, we must win. There is no substitute for victory.

MacArthur's dismissal unloosed a storm of criticism in the United States and led to a full-dress Senate discussion of American strategy and foreign relations, carried on with remarkable frankness. General Omar Bradley, of the Joint Chiefs of Staff, said MacArthur's strategy would "involve us in the wrong war at the wrong place at the wrong time and with the wrong enemy." Acheson called it "a gamble with the essential security of the nation." General Marshall, then Secretary of Defense, asserted that MacArthur "would have us accept the risk of involvement not only in an extension of the war with Red China, but in an all-out war with the Soviet Union."

Some of the passion aroused by MacArthur's dismissal abated when the Soviet delegate in the United Nations, Jacob Malik, in a broadcast delivered in June, 1951, about the time of the anniversary of the outbreak of the war, suggested that "discussion should be started between the belligerents for a cease-fire and an armistice providing for the mutual withdrawal of forces from the 38th Parallel."

This aroused the hope that peace might be in sight. Protracted armistice negotiations were set in motion. Apart from activity in the air, fighting died down to patrol activity and occasional limited attacks as the UN and Chinese and North Korean armies dug into strong fortified positions in difficult mountain country.

But the armistice talks, delayed by one dispute after another, finally bogged down in a stalemate comparable in rigidity with the deadlock on the front. The issue was forcible repatriation of prisoners. A high proportion of the Chinese and North Korean prisoners declared they would resist being sent back to what they considered would be certain death or slavery. The Chinese negotiators, prompted and backed by the Soviet Union in UN discussion, insisted on complete forcible repatriation. The United States, with British backing, in this case, rejected the idea of forcible sending back of unwilling prisoners on grounds both of humanity and of policy. Certainly the sight of prisoners who had surrendered or deserted for political reasons being sent back by force would have destroyed any prospect of success in future political warfare.

A compromise formula on prisoner repatriation offered by India, the eternally unsuccessful would-be mediator, in the UN and accepted by all noncommunist states, was flatly rejected first by the Soviet representative, Andrei Vishinsky, then by the Chinese communists in Peiping. One of the first acts of the new President, Dwight D. Eisenhower, was to lift the ban on Chinese nationalist attacks against the Chinese mainland. Whether this step means much, little or nothing, depends partly on political conditions in China, partly on the amount of naval and air aid which the United States will supply for Chiang Kai-shek and his army of some half million men on Formosa. It is not surprising that very little military aid was sent to

Formosa while Acheson and Marshall, with their inveterate prejudice against the nationalists, were influential in the councils of the Administration.

The issue of the struggle for the Far East, of which the war in Korea is the sharpest expression, is still unclear. The final answer to the question whether America's intervention in Korea was successful or unsuccessful depends on whether this move has given the anticommunist forces in Asia a chance to organize and rally. These forces, in being or in prospect, include the South Koreans, the Japanese, the Chinese nationalists, the anticommunist guerrillas on the Chinese mainland, the Vietnamese who are fighting the communists, and the peoples of the Philippines and Thailand. Neutrality seems the most that can be expected from the weak new states of India, Indonesia and Burma.

The organization of an anticommunist coalition in Asia faces some of the same difficulties that have bedeviled the creation of an effective defense in Europe. Memories of past colonial rule, and of Japanese acts of violence and oppression during the last war, sometimes obscure the necessity for unity against communist expansion.

Some progress has been made. The build-up of the South Korean army, so stupidly neglected before 1950, has advanced to a point where South Korean units hold the larger part of the front. The sane, moderate peace treaty with Japan, negotiated by the present Secretary of State, John Foster Dulles, and signed at San Francisco in September, 1951, ranks as one of the few American acts of constructive statesmanship in the Orient.

There is still a good deal of passive unrealistic neutralism among Japanese intellectuals and in the leftist minority parties. But it seems reasonable to expect that Japan's political leaders will realize increasingly the mutual security interests which bind America and Japan together. America can make a considerable contribution to American-Japanese solidarity by eliminating all vestiges of race and color prejudice in its relations with the Japanese and by providing easier access for Japanese imports to the American market. As Japan regains economic equilibrium and military strength it should furnish a desirable counterweight to Red China in the new Oriental balance of power.

The Korean war has been an alarm bell which has set American military preparation in higher gear. There is little reason to accept the pessimistic theory that Stalin deliberately enticed America into fighting on the double calculation that large American forces would be tied up in a remote part of the world and that America would be driven toward bankruptcy through a costly war. (Incidentally, the alleged statement of Lenin that the best means of undermining America is to destroy its currency is apocryphal and not based on any known passage in Lenin's writings.) Most probably the Kremlin expected a cheap victory with little opposition and only formal notes of protest in 1950.

The United States is much stronger militarily than it would have been had there been no challenge in Korea. And the Soviet rulers are more likely to be impressed by tanks, airplanes and other modern weapons rolling off assembly lines than by the vague and uncertain prospect of seeing America "go bankrupt."

The morale of American troops in Korea, according to almost all observers, has been surprisingly good, considering the frustrating nature of the stalemated fighting. And the biggest of the many "big lies" of communism, that it is a popular spontaneous movement, beloved of the common man, has been exposed by two conspicuous features of the fighting in Korea. First, the tide of refugees, before the war and during the war, has always been overwhelmingly away from, not toward, areas held by the communists. Second, a high percentage of North Korean and Chinese prisoners are bitterly unwilling to return home.

The most disappointing aspect of the Korean war has been

the failure of the UN to mobilize effective resistance to clear and flagrant aggression. What we have seen is not collective security, but flight from responsibility. It has been a UN war, in theory, but a US and South Korean fight, in reality. It was a depressing spectacle to see the UN Assembly delay for months in designating Red China as an aggressor after large Red Chinese armies had invaded Korea and attacked the UN forces there. It has been discouraging to see some countries place petty trade interests above the far greater mutual interest in defeating communist aggression, which, if unchecked, will certainly in time wipe out all Western commercial interests in the Orient.

There have also been failures in the instinct for political warfare on the American side. The issue of repatriation of unwilling prisoners would never have arisen if there had been quiet effective screening of anticommunist from communist prisoners. Then the anticommunist North Koreans could have been absorbed into the South Korean army or allowed to disappear in the South Korean population. The anticommunist Chinese could have been sent to Formosa or to Chinese communities in the countries of southeastern Asia.

Three years of fighting in Korea have taught several lessons. The belief that a land area can be defended by air and naval power alone has been exploded. The implacable hatred which the rulers of Red China feel for this country has been fully expressed in their propaganda charges of germ warfare and other atrocities. The attitude of the prisoners shows that the outward unity which communist China, like every totalitarian state imposes, could be cracked by vigorous psychological warfare, backed by action. The most effective means of cracking this unity would be to stir up an uprising in South China, timed to coincide with a landing in force by the Chinese nationalists.

This would be worth many bloody victories in Korea. For in the long run America cannot singlehanded save either Asia or Europe from communism. The fight against communism in

Asia must be won by Asiatics, as the fight against communism in Europe must be won by Europeans.

During the short interval between the communist conquest of China and the outbreak of war in Korea Mr. Acheson, judging from his speeches, was looking hopefully toward the possibility of Chinese "Titoism," of a breakaway from Moscow by the Chinese communists. A quarrel between the Soviet Union and its largest and most populous satellite would certainly be desirable, from the American standpoint. Such a development cannot be ruled out as impossible.

But no act of the Chinese communists up to the spring of 1953 indicated the likelihood of such a breach. Mao Tse-tung's dependence on the Kremlin is threefold, ideological, economic and military. All the political ideas of the Chinese communists are uncritical copies of Soviet models. The communist rulers of China have done everything in their power to make conditions impossible for western firms and have thereby deliberately increased their economic dependence on Moscow. This general proposition is not affected by the temporary circumstance that communist China may pay inflated prices for contraband war supplies.

Finally, the Chinese could never have sustained a war against the United States without Soviet airplanes, tanks and artillery. Mr. Vishinsky, in a speech in the UN early in 1953, admitted Soviet sales of war material to China, in defiance of a UN resolution prohibiting the sale of strategic materials to Red China by member states. There was no immediate reaction from the UN to this flagrant violation of an obligation by a UN member.

So it would seem reckless to base American policy on the expectation of an imminent breach between Moscow and Peiping. And it would be foolish and dishonorable, a repetition of the disastrous tactics of Yalta, to throw over friends in Asia in the hope of appeasing either the Chinese Reds or the weak uncertain neutrals. It was a grave error to bottle up a potential asset, such as the nationalist army on Formosa, in deference to the feelings of governments which have not put a man or a gun into the front lines in Korea.

In East Asia, as in Europe, a point of no retreat has been reached. A true peace, or at least a tolerable armed truce in the Orient, as in Europe, can only be achieved by firm resolution not to yield one inch of additional territory to communism and to roll back the iron or bamboo curtain wherever and whenever a favorable political opportunity presents itself.

Chapter VI ~ Ten Fallacies About Communism

It was said of the historian Macaulay that his conception of hell would be to hear fiends misstating the facts of history and be unable to correct them. There is similar torment for anyone who is acquainted with Soviet living conditions and communist theory in the fallacies about communism that find a more or less widespread hearing and cloud and obscure American thinking on an issue that may conceivably involve national survival.

To be sure, parroting of Soviet propaganda fiction became less popular and less blatant after the Second World War gave way to the cold war. But the fellow-traveler who made little secret of his communist sympathies and who was always ready with a glib excuse for every questionable aspect of Soviet policy, from slave labor camps to annexations of foreign territory, has been replaced by a different intellectual species, subtler and therefore more plausible. This is the anti-anticommunist, the man who uses up five or ten per cent of his mental and moral ammunition in formally repudiating sympathy with communism and the other ninety or ninety-five per cent in trying to discredit any positive plan for checking the advance of communism at home and abroad.

The anti-anticommunist may be recognized by his addiction to certain propositions which prove, on examination, to be fallacious and misleading. Ten of these "anti-anticommunist" articles of faith and the reasons why they are fallacies are summed up herewith.

(1) *Communism is an idea, and an idea cannot be checked by force.* This is a double fallacy. First, ideas can be and have been stamped out by force—if the force is applied with sufficient ruthlessness over a long enough period. For instance, all traces of Christianity disappeared in North Africa, home of St. Augustine and early stronghold of the Christian faith, after the tide of Mohammedanism swept over this area.

Second, the last thing communism favors or tolerates is free competition in the marketplace of ideas. What always happens immediately after a communist seizure of power is the locking of every door, the closing of every window, the stopping of every loophole, however small, for the expression of ideas contrary to the dogmas of Marx, Lenin and Stalin.

The people in the Soviet Union, in Red China, in the east European satellite states are hermetically sealed off against foreign contacts. So far as rigorous police state controls can achieve this end, they are shut off from every scrap of independent information or opinion.

Nor does communism rely on the peaceful persuasiveness of its ideas as a means of getting and holding power. The history of the spread of communism has nothing in common with the experience of early Christianity, when a new faith, without temporal weapons, conquered a vast empire by filling a moral and spiritual vacuum. Armies marching across frontiers, trained agents of subversion working on projects of espionage, sabotage, strikes, riots and civil war; hard-faced secret police agents rounding up hosts of unfortunate human beings marked for deportation and liquidation: this is the pattern of communist power.

If large numbers of people were voluntarily seeking to renounce private property and organize their lives along communist lines, the process could probably not be stopped by force. Nor, in a free country, would there be any attempt to stop it. There is nothing in free societies to prevent individuals from organizing farms, factories, handicraft cooperatives, even communities on a communist basis. But very few of the many experiments which have been carried out along these lines have proved lasting and successful.

The history of communist success, from Russia in 1917 until China in 1949, is not an example of an unarmed idea winning the hearts and minds of people by its intrinsic justice and moral and spiritual appeal. It is an example of a series of violent seizures of power, leading invariably to the same result: a new revolutionary ruling class imposing its will most ruthlessly upon the masses by what is now a standard combination formula of government behind the iron curtain: unlimited terrorism combined with unlimited propaganda.

(2) *Communism means equal sharing of the fruits of a planned economy and is therefore morally superior to selfish and acquisitive capitalism.* But this leaves out of account the designed inequality under the Soviet economic order. The very word communism is deceptive. It suggests the early Christians sharing their goods in communal living or the idealists of Brook Farm practicing plain living and high thinking.

There is less voluntary sharing in the Soviet Union than in any country in the world. The principle of payment by results, not according to need, is enforced with the utmost rigor. The skilled worker earns more than the unskilled, the engineer more than the skilled worker, the factory manager more than the engineer, and so on through a long hierarchy of higher and lower wage and salary brackets. There is inequality of privilege, as well as inequality of pay. The Soviet ruling elite enjoy a long list of special privileges in access to luxurious vacation resorts, well equipped hospitals, luxury stores.

Communists in "capitalist" countries try to stir up strikes and rebellion against the supposed exploitation of the workers. But, as soon as they come into power, communists promote and organize the most intensive regimentation and speed-up of the workers. Piecework payment is used with an undiluted ruthlessness unknown since the early phase of the capitalist system. The industrial systems in the Soviet Union, Poland, Czechoslovakia and other satellite states function without benefit of the protective devices for the workers which have been built up in the United States and Western Europe.

There are no trade unions independent of government control, there are no opposition political parties. The worker is caught in the grip of a gigantic speed-up machine which he has no means of resisting, except by individual slacking on the job. And this is not a safe resort, under legal systems where the word sabotage is given very broad interpretation.

The gulf in living standards between a member of the Soviet ruling class, rushed in a bullet-proof car between his luxurious villa outside Moscow and his office and a starving slave laborer in the mosquito-haunted pine forests of Northern Russia is far wider than anything that could be found in a free country. It is also noteworthy that no feeling of individual responsibility for relieving poverty exists in communist countries.

The "social conscience" which has been the motive power of many reforms and benevolent activities in the western world, which was active in Russia before the Revolution, has no meaning for the hardboiled bureaucrat of the era of Stalin and Malenkov, bred in a completely materialistic philosophy. To be sure, the general inequality in the Soviet Union at the present time is rationalized and defended by its beneficiaries as a step toward the ultimate goal of a communist society where all will give according to their abilities and receive according to their needs.

But nothing in the Soviet evolution suggests the likelihood that such a society will ever develop. More than thirty-five years have passed since the Bolshevik Revolution took place. There is far more deeprooted inequality in this fourth decade of Soviet rule than there was in the first years of the Soviet regime, when

Lenin's rule that a communist, however high his position, should receive no more than a skilled worker's wage was at least formally observed.

The sympathy that communism has won abroad on the assumption that it means idealistic sharing of the products of common labor has been won under false pretenses. The Soviet cake (in terms of housing, clothes, foodstuffs, consumer goods) is much smaller than the corresponding cake in North America and Western Europe. But it is at least as unequally divided.

(3) *With all its faults communism is not so cruel as Tsarism.* This is a persistent illusion. But it is not justified by ascertainable comparative facts. When Tsar Alexander II was assassinated in 1881 five persons, all revolutionary terrorists whose part in the killing was undisputed, were put to death. When Sergei Kirov, one of Stalin's chief lieutenants, was murdered in 1934, 117 persons, according to Soviet official communiqués, were executed. Of these only thirteen seem to have been even officially charged with complicity in the assassination. The others were "counterrevolutionaries," for whose "liquidation" Kirov's death provided a convenient excuse.

Over 500 persons were slaughtered in Petrograd in 1918, as a reprisal for the wounding of Lenin and the murder of Uritsky, a prominent Soviet official in Petrograd. There is no mass slaughter of this kind, of helpless prisoners without trial, in the history of modern Tsarism.

There is the same comparative picture in the inhuman treatment of prisoners. The subject of Soviet slave labor is discussed in more detail in another chapter. No one knows exactly how many people, during the last quarter of a century, have passed through the enormous grim Soviet slave labor colonies, or how many have died of overwork, malnutrition and general brutality. That the figure runs into millions is not disputed by any serious student of the subject. The number of persons in the hard labor prison camps of Tsarism, which alone might approach Soviet concentration camps in systematic brutality, was

5,790 in 1906 and 32,000, the highest recorded figure, in 1912. Authority for this statement is Andrei Vishinsky, former Soviet prosecutor, Foreign Minister and spokesman in the United Nations.*

One finds the same contrasts in China and in the Soviet satellite states. Everywhere communism has brought not less, but vastly more cruelty in the treatment of the peoples who live under it. The Kuomintang administration in China did not follow the rules of perfect democracy. But no responsible student of China has accused Chiang Kai-shek of killing a million and a half or two million of his political opponents, not in war but in mass executions. These figures are not the inventions of Chinese anticommunists; the Chinese official communist radio boasts of them. Prime Minister Churchill, whose government maintains diplomatic relations with Red China, said at the Lord Mayor's dinner in London, on November 10, 1952: †

> It would be dishonor to send thousands of helpless prisoners of war back by force to be massacred by a Chinese communist government that boasts that it has actually rid itself of two millions of its own people.

Somewhat earlier the leftwing British weekly, *New Statesman and Nation,* consistently critical of American firmness toward Red China and certainly not likely to repeat any unsubstantiated charge against Chinese communist methods of rule, editorially addressed this rather plaintive question to a group of Britons who were departing for a "peace conference" in Peiping:

> They must tell us what the Chinese say about the million and a half "enemies of the people" who, it is apparently admitted, have been executed since the revolution. Were these executions really necessary?

* Vishinsky, *Tyurma kapitalisticheskikh stran* ("The prison of capitalist countries"), pp. 61, 143, cited in Dallin and Nikolaevsky, *Forced Labor in Soviet Russia* (Yale University Press), p. 302.
† See *The New York Times,* November 11, 1952.

Except in Czechoslovakia, there were elements of authoritarianism and dictatorship in the governments of the East European countries which have been taken over by the Soviet Government. Even the worst of these governments, however, did not set up large concentration camps (a typical Soviet political export) or doom whole classes of people to extermination by driving them from their homes and sending them to localities where food and shelter are almost impossible to obtain. This is what has happened to many members of the former middle class in Hungary, Poland, Czechoslovakia and other satellite states.

(4) *The only way to meet the communist challenge is to create a better social and economic order.* This is two false assumptions rolled into one sentence. There is first the preposterous suggestion that communism is winning on its merits, because it offers the peoples under its rule better conditions than they enjoy in noncommunist countries. But an impressive series of informal but convincing plebiscites proves the precise contrary.

Immigration is the sincerest form of flattery. And there has been a tidal wave of movement away from countries and regions under communist rule, as against a negligible trickle of movement toward such areas. More than a year after the end of the war there were over 800,000 registered DPs (displaced persons) in refugee camps maintained by the UNRRA. There were probably as many more hiding out under false papers. Soviet citizens were liable to forced repatriation, and many Russians tried to pass themselves off under various national disguises.

This DP situation was one of the most impressive demonstrations against communism, because it was entirely spontaneous and unorganized. All these refugees, certainly well over a million in number, were from communist-ruled countries. Workers who had been brought to Germany from France and Belgium, the Netherlands and Norway were eager to go home as soon as possible. All those who preferred the bleak life of stateless refugees were fugitives from communism, from the Soviet Union and the Ukraine, from Poland and Yugoslavia, from Latvia, Lithuania and Estonia.

The same situation was repeated in divided Germany. By 1953 at least a million Germans had fled from communist East Germany to capitalist West Germany, in spite of the fact that housing conditions in bombed West Germany are extremely crowded and jobs are not always easy to get. A German official in Bonn estimated in 1951 that this influx was at the rate of about 200,000 a year. It was accelerated in 1953, when 70,000 refugees arrived in West Berlin alone during the first two months.

These East German refugees must, in any case, leave behind them their homes and immovable property; in many cases they run the gauntlet of border guards with orders to shoot to kill. There are no obstacles to the transfer of communist sympathizers from West Germany to East Germany; but movement in this direction is almost non-existent.

Tens of thousands of Czechs fled their country after the communist coup d'état. And one sees the same pattern in Korea, where it has always been the UN retreats, never the communist retreats, that have been clogged and impeded by the throngs of civilian refugees and where a large number of the Red Chinese and North Korean prisoners have stubbornly refused to go home.

The second false assumption is that communism could only be effectively opposed by undertaking some utopian program of social reform. Mr. Aneurin Bevan, leftwing British Labor leader, gives the impression of believing that free dentures and wigs are more effective weapons against communism than tanks, jet airplanes and radar screens. This is dangerous nonsense. An ideal social order without adequate arms in the hands of its defenders would go down very quickly before the onslaught of the mechanized legions of the Red Army. Before June, 1950, the United States appropriated a good deal of money for social and economic benefits in South Korea. The Russians put their money in North Korea into tanks and artillery. It would have been far better for South Korea if the United States had at least matched this Soviet investment.

(5) *If a people doesn't like communism it will quickly throw off the communist yoke.* This is just about as sensible as it would be to say that if an animal didn't like being caught in a steel trap it could walk out. There is no greater illusion about the nature of communism than the assumption that a people once conquered by communists possesses any freedom of choice, any opportunity for peaceful rejection or change, once the juggernaut of organized compulsion and mechanical propaganda has begun to roll.

Indeed there is serious danger that Gresham's Law in economics may be supplemented by a kind of Gresham's Law in politics. The economic law is that bad money drives good money out of circulation. Bad government could conceivably drive out good government, tyranny could oust free institutions, because the terms of competition are not fair.

Italy held a national election in the spring of 1948, shortly after the fall of Czechoslovakia to the communists. Prime Minister de Gasperi made the point during the campaign that, if the communists won, there would be no more free elections, no opportunity for another swing of the pendulum.

And this observation points out one of the disadvantages which free institutions face in the struggle against communist totalitarianism, at least until this totalitarianism is recognized and treated as a criminal conspiracy. Nothing very drastic happens to communists if they lose an election in Italy or France. They are not suppressed or persecuted. They can continue their propaganda, maintain their network of "front" organizations, prepare to exploit new political opportunities. How very different is the fate of anticommunists wherever and whenever communists gain power!

(6) *Communism is a good idea gone wrong.* But "good ideas," like liberty and justice and the rule of law and restraint on the arbitrary power of the state, do not "go wrong." They become the bases on which habits of civilized living rest. It is a fallacy to think of communism as a good system under Lenin which was perverted by Stalin. The cause of every Soviet act of oppression and mass cruelty may be found in the essential points of Lenin's philosophy: the advocacy of the "dictatorship of the proletariat," under the guidance of a revolutionary elite, the insistence that the ultimate end justifies any means of violence and repression, the absence of any protection for the individual against the violence of the state—the absence of any element of absolute moral and spiritual authority, which would place some bounds on man's lust for power and domination.

(7) *To criticize communism places one in the camp of reaction.* This mental attitude, all too common among leftwing sympathizers during the thirties, has wrought tremendous harm. It led to a double standard of morals, to an abdication of reason and conscience in weighing the evidence about what was happening in the Soviet Union. American leftwing publications were rightly severe in their condemnation of Nazi and Fascist outrages and of abuses in America itself, although the latter were sometimes presented in very exaggerated colors.

But it would be instructive to look up the comment, or rather the lack of comment, in these publications on such colossal acts of state organized cruelty as the liquidation of the kulaks as a class, the man-made famine of 1932–33 and the institution of slave labor on a gigantic scale. It seemed that normal human impulses of sympathy with suffering and moral indignation over acts of cruelty and oppression dried up, in many humanitarians, when the frontiers of the Soviet Union were reached. In the fear that criticism of communism would impose the stigma of "reactionary" the fact that the Soviet regime itself represented a gigantic reaction, a going back to some of the darkest practices of the barbarous, semi-Asiatic Muscovite absolutism, was completely overlooked.

A hangover of this identification of communism with "liberalism" and "progressivism" in more recent years has been the marked tendency, in anti-anticommunist circles, to wax indignant not over the many proved cases of communist infiltration and disloyalty, but against the individuals who expose these cases. The abuse that has been heaped on men and women who have atoned for their communist past by telling what they know of the communist conspiracy, the aura of martyrdom that surrounds pro-Soviet apologists—these things indicate an unhealthy climate of moral and intellectual judgment and a sad lack of perspective.

After all, wizards named Hiss and witches named Coplon do exist. And if one looks under enough beds one may find someone answering to the name of Klaus Fuchs.

The tendency of some persons who consider themselves liberals to take a soft, apologetic attitude toward communism is puzzling when one reflects how completely communism, in power, repudiates and stamps out every value of historic liberalism.* This *"trahison des clercs,"* to borrow a phrase which the French writer Julien Benda applied in another connection, may be traced to two causes.

There has been a growing semantic perversion of the once honorable word liberalism. In the United States, although not in Europe, liberalism is often uncritically identified with advocacy of a constant extension of the powers and functions of an all-embracing state. This, of course, is the precise opposite of what the original liberal thinkers, Locke, Montesquieu, Mill, Adam Smith, de Tocqueville, stood for.

Moreover, the reformer is always in danger of developing a

---

* This writer recently heard a professor, well known for his strong communist sympathies, deliver a eulogy on the nonconformist virtues, without showing the slightest appreciation of how impossible the practice of these virtues has become in the countries behind the iron curtain.

perfectionist streak, which leads him to look to the supposed end and forget about the all-important and all-determining means. To a certain type of doctrinaire mind the theory of communism is attractive. If the facts of experience under communist rule do not square with the theory, so much the worse for the facts.

(8) *The Soviet Government only wants security for its country. What it has done in Eastern Europe is comparable with America's Monroe Doctrine.* This word security is very elastic in its interpretation. Every conqueror in history has invoked security, perhaps sincerely, as the justification for every new conquest. A plea of security for a policy which keeps the world in a state of chronic high tension and insecurity is not convincing.

Before the Second World War the Soviet Government never complained that its national frontiers were unjust, or endangered its security. On the contrary, it pressed non-aggression pacts, based upon mutual recognition of the validity and permanence of these boundaries, upon its western neighbors, Poland, Finland, Latvia, Lithuania and Estonia. The value of the Soviet proposal for a peace pact among the five great powers may be judged by the fate of these non-aggression treaties.

Poland was partitioned with Hitler under a secret clause of the Soviet-Nazi Pact of August, 1939. Soviet troops invaded and occupied Eastern Poland after the German offensive had destroyed the main Polish armies. Finland was attacked without provocation on November 30, 1939, and forced to submit to the amputation of about one tenth of its territory. Latvia, Lithuania and Estonia were taken over and annexed by the Soviet Union in the summer of 1940. There was no free voting, no evidence of any popular desire for annexation either in Eastern Poland or in the Baltic States.

Before the Second World War much publicity was given in the Soviet Union to a declaration of Stalin: "We shall not yield an inch of our own soil; we do not want a foot of foreign soil." Stalin did not say: "We do not want a foot of foreign soil, except—Latvia, Lithuania, Estonia, parts of Finland, Eastern Poland, Bessarabia, Northern Bukovina, Carpatho-Ukraine, Koenigsberg and part of East Prussia, South Sakhalin, the Kurile Islands, Port Arthur." But this is the list of territorial annexations during and since the war, a total area of some 200,000 square miles, inhabited by some 24 million people.

The Monroe Doctrine has never been used as a shield or screen for this kind of expansion. The continental frontiers of the United States have been stationary for a century. Even before the Monroe Doctrine was softened and expanded into a multilateral American defense compact there was nothing in the United States record to compare with such acts of Soviet ruthlessness as the mass deportations from Eastern Poland and the Baltic States, the killing of the Polish Socialist leaders, Henryk Ehrlich and Viktor Alter, and the slaughter of fifteen thousand Polish officer war prisoners.

The Soviet conception of security was hit off wittily and accurately by a foreign correspondent in Moscow in 1929 in an interchange with the censor. The Soviet Government at that time was sending troops into Manchuria to force the Chinese to restore the Soviet right of partial ownership of the Chinese Eastern Railway. The censor was insisting that the Soviet operations in Manchuria be described as a "counter-attack." "Oh, yes," retorted the correspondent, "when you take Washington you will still be 'counter-attacking.' "

It is hard to see how the Soviet Union could have been more secure, in the reasonable sense of the word, than it was after the end of the Second World War. Its principal rivals, Germany and Japan, were crushed and disarmed. The United States was engaged in a tumultuous demobilization. American public opinion would certainly have supported the suggestion of Secretary of State Byrnes for a pact among the victorious powers assuring German disarmament for twenty-five or even forty years. There was eager desire throughout the western world for maximum Soviet cooperation. Soviet safety was not remotely threatened from any direction.

But the Kremlin rulers thought in terms not of security but of ultimate world domination. They recklessly squandered the very considerable capital of goodwill which Russian military achievements during the war had built up. By a series of hostile and aggressive actions they convinced even the men in the United States who had advocated most strongly concessions to the Soviet Union during the war that there was no recourse except to accept the challenge of the cold war.

(9) *We got along with the Tsars; why can't we get along with the Soviets?* This question reveals a failure to understand the heart of the irrepressible conflict between the Soviet empire and the noncommunist world. This conflict does not arise because the Soviet Union maintains a one-party system of political rule or turns over to state operation enterprises which in most countries are left to private ownership and operation. The cause lies much deeper, in the commitment of the Soviet leaders to a philosophy of world conquest through subversion and military power which compels them to be continually intriguing and stirring up trouble beyond their own frontiers.

Tsarism was a system with no missionary aims. It could not conceivably have been exported to Western Europe or America. There were never large blocs of deputies in the French and Italian parliaments which looked for inspiration and guidance to the court of the Tsar. There is no recorded case when an American or an Englishman or a Canadian committed treason or espionage out of fanatical sentimental devotion to the Tsar.

In short, Tsarist Russia was a national state, with the limited ambitions of a national state. The Soviet Union is something much more formidable and irreconcilable. It is a huge militarized empire, which has far outgrown the boundaries of Imperial Russia by drawing into its orbit of domination Eastern Europe and China. More than that, Soviet rule is also the head and centre of a gigantic revolutionary conspiracy, with ramifications in almost every country in the world.

Until and unless there is a dissolution of the swollen Soviet empire, until and unless there is a divorce between the Soviet Government and its foreign fifth columns, there can never be peace, as that word was understood before the First World War, or in the first decade after the ending of that war. There can be, at best, a precarious armistice, most probably punctuated by little wars. And the price of maintaining even this twilight zone between war and peace will be constant vigilance and willingness to assume the burdens and sacrifices associated with a high degree of military preparedness.

(10) *Communists deserve the support of progressive idealists because they fight for good causes: social and economic justice, elimination of racial discrimination, peace.* It is true that the communist ultimate aim, the setting up of the absolute dictatorship which prevails wherever communists are in power, is camouflaged behind a façade of attractive sounding ideals. This is why communism is a far more serious subversive threat than nazism ever was or ever could have been.

Nazism was so intertwined with extreme German nationalism and "Nordic" racism that it could not appeal to the vast majority of the world's population. Communism, as a theory, may win the support of men and women of all races and nationalities. That is why the Kremlin has been successful in recruiting volunteer spies and agents in foreign countries.

Communism, like every other political and economic philosophy, should be judged by results, not promises, by what it does, not by what it says. It is important to consider not only what always happens after communist rule is set up, but the true purposes and motives behind the communist campaigns for what seem to be desirable objectives. In labor relations, as innumerable communist tracts and pamphlets and resolutions of authoritative communist congresses show, the objective is not to end industrial strife, but to deepen and aggravate this strife, with violent revolution as the final goal.

The same destructive purpose is evident when communists put on one of their well organized campaigns against a real or alleged case of racial injustice. They are not in the least interested in the victim as a human being; they are only concerned with propaganda capital, with a martyr, if possible.

So, if a Negro is on trial in a Southern state and the communists decide to put on a campaign they will "defend" him in a manner most provocative to Southern sentiment, most likely to injure his chances of acquittal. There is the same characteristic in the communist attempt to build up the conviction of Julius and Ethel Rosenberg for atomic espionage as a "Dreyfus Case," an example of "anti-Semitism."

As it happens, both the prosecutor and the judge, in the Rosenberg case, as well as the defendants, were Jews. There was no taint of religious bigotry or race prejudice in the conduct of the prosecution. The Rosenbergs were convicted not because of their faith or race, but because they had committed the gravest imaginable offense against the security of their countrymen.

The communist design in this affair is obvious. It is to excite anti-Semitism while pretending to deplore it by emphasizing the Jewish origin of the Rosenbergs. This is only one of the more recent of many examples showing that communist agitation on racial issues is designed to aggravate, not to alleviate, prejudice and tension.

The pose of communists as friends and champions of peace is a preposterous hoax. The atmosphere of the typical communist "peace congress" is anything but pacific. The standard communist "peace" speech is a wild abusive tirade against non-communist governments, full of unproved and often palpably absurd charges of atrocities, use of poison gas, germ warfare, etc.

The standard communist "peace" plan is a series of unilateral disarmament moves by the western powers. The true communist attitude toward peace is revealed by the three following indisputable facts.

First, every country under communist control has been put through an intensive process of militarization. While dreamy theorists on the other side of the iron curtain were arguing that the only effective means of resisting communism was to make life soft and easy for everyone the communists were proceeding on a precisely opposite theory, giving guns a maximum priority in all their economic programs and cutting butter to a minimum.

This has been true in every satellite country, in China and, of course, in the Soviet Union itself. Long before there was even a paper project for the rearming of West Germany, paramilitary formations and heavily armed police units appeared in East Germany.

Second, a world in which the vast majority of people certainly yearned for peace after the slaughter and destruction of the last war has been kept in continuous fear and turmoil by acts of violence and aggression instigated or committed by the Kremlin. Among the more conspicuous of these are the civil war in Greece, the terrorist kidnappings in Berlin and Vienna, the blockade of West Berlin, the overthrow of the constitutional government of Czechoslovakia, the invasion of South Korea and the Chinese communist invasion of Korea. Neither of these two last moves could have taken place without full Soviet military support.

Third, communist philosophy, as is shown elsewhere, is committed with dogmatic certainty to the proposition that wars will continue until noncommunist states are destroyed. Given this philosophy, how could the Kremlin conceivably dispense with force and the threat of force?

So it is not necessary to look very far behind the labels to realize that communists are no friends of good causes. Even when it is in communist interest to support something that may be intrinsically right this support is always for wrong ulterior motives.

Here are ten of the most widespread fallacies about communism. They should be studied and understood, because a wrong idea can be as disastrous as a defective tank or airplane. Despite exaggerated catchphrases about "reign of terror" and "black silence of fear" Americans exercise wide freedom in discussing the causes of the cold war and other issues of foreign policy.

It is important that this discussion be based on fact, not fiction, that there should be no rising like trout to bait whenever the Kremlin turns on a deceptive peace offensive. Recognizing fallacies which are the product partly of communist propaganda, partly of ignorance, partly of wishful thinking, is the best guaranty against any relapse into the disastrous errors of wartime appeasement of the Kremlin.

Chapter VII ~ Soviet Communism: A Triple Threat

Soviet communism confronts free countries with a triple threat, with a challenge that calls for response on three levels.

There is the threat of a disintegrating idea which, should it prevail, would destroy all the humanist and individualist values of western civilization, with its Judaeo-Christian and Greco-Roman moral and intellectual values.

There is the threat of a system of organized espionage, sabotage and treason on a scale never known in history.

And there is the threat of a vast empire, already larger than Genghiz Khan's, or Napoleon's, and with an insatiable urge to further expansion.

One hundred and sixty years ago a militant, revolutionary France, with a messianic urge to spread its creed beyond its own borders, offered to Great Britain a challenge very similar to that which the Soviet empire presents to the United States today.

At that time, in 1793, there was a great debate, great both because of the importance of the subject and the stature of the participants, as to what, if anything, should be done to meet this challenge. There is a strangely modern ring about a speech which Prime Minister William Pitt delivered in the House of Commons on February 1, 1793:

> They [the French] will not accept under the name of liberty any model of government but that which is conformable to their

own opinion and ideas and all men must learn from the mouth of their cannon the propagation of their system in every part of the world. . . . They have stated that they would organize every country by a disorganizing principle; and afterwards, they tell you, all this is done by the will of the people. Wherever our [French] armies come revolutions must take place, dictated by the will of the people. And then comes the plain question: What is this will of the people? It is the power of the French.

Substitute Soviet for French and one finds in this passage an excellent analysis of one of the basic issues in the cold war. Edmund Burke, writing to a friend in August, 1793, expressed an idea that seems very modern:

We are at war with a principle and with an example which there is no shutting out by fortresses, or excluding by territorial limits. No lines of demarcation can bound the Jacobin empire. It must be extirpated in the place of its origin, or it will not be confined to that place.

And Charles James Fox, replying to Pitt in the House of Commons struck the note, "You can't fight an idea," popular in some circles in modern times:

If there was any danger from French principles, to go to war without necessity was to fight for their propagation. . . . How was a war to operate in keeping opinions supposed dangerous out of this country? It was not surely meant to beat the French out of their own opinions; and opinions were not like commodities, the importation of which from France war would prevent.

The edge was taken off this debate because France in the summer of 1794 went through an experience for which there has been no exact parallel in the Soviet Union. The extremist revolutionary leader, Robespierre, and his chief lieutenants were overthrown and rushed to the guillotine, to which they had sent so many others. From this time, although the influence of French revolutionary ideas was by no means spent, the struggle between France and Great Britain became more national and less ideological. Even the most ardent English radical, the "fellow-traveler" of the French Revolution in its first phases, could not recognize a liberator in the Emperor Napoleon.

The Soviet communists are very similar to the French Jacobins in such articles of faith as the primacy of politics over economics, the right and obligation of the revolutionary elite to rule the masses for their own good and the necessity for unlimited violence in the present to insure unlimited bliss in the future.* But, perhaps because they lived in an age when mass mediums of communication are far more developed, they learned a secret which was hidden from their Jacobin predecessors. They learned how to perpetuate their own power.

Many attitudes and points of emphasis have changed during the period of Soviet rule. But two foundation stones of this rule, one-party dictatorship and economic collectivism, have become more firmly set than ever. Both these principles enhance very much the power of the ruling group.

Because there never was a healthy reaction against revolutionary tyranny in Russia, followed by a period of moderation and settling down, the Soviet threat to the independence and security of the noncommunist world remains real and sharp. The three aspects of this threat are as follows.

The Threat as Idea. The doctrine of communism, outlined in the works of Marx, Lenin and Stalin, affects in different ways the masters of the Kremlin and communist party members and sympathizers in foreign countries. The Soviet rulers are driven to pursue their policy of constant expansion, pressure and intrigue outside their frontiers by two dynamic forces. There is the conviction of fulfilling a predestined historical mission. And there is the equally powerful urge of fear.

The belief that both war and the final triumph of communist

* There is a brilliant exposition of French Jacobin political ideas in J. L. Talmon, *The Rise of Totalitarian Democracy* (Beacon Press). The numerous parallels with Soviet communist ideology are not explicitly drawn, but are very obvious.

revolution throughout the world is foreordained by infallible laws of social and economic development is clearly expressed in a resolution adopted by the Sixth Congress of the Communist International, in 1928. All these resolutions were prepared under the closest supervision of Stalin.

> With elemental force imperialism exposes and accentuates all the contradictions of capitalist society. It carries class oppression to the utmost limits, intensifies the struggle between capitalist governments, *inevitably* gives rise to worldwide imperialist wars and *inexorably* leads to the world proletarian revolution. [Italics supplied]

Along with this intoxicating sense of riding a historical tide that must finally sweep to victory there is a dynamics of fear. The visible intensity of repression under a communist regime; the numerous armed guards who surround the leaders; the police posts, bloodhounds and land mine fields along the closely guarded frontiers; the armed watchmen in every factory: these are not the signs of a relaxed government, confident of the loyalty of its people. If conditions under communism even remotely approached the picture painted in official propaganda it is hard to understand why so much effort is necessary to detect malcontents and suppress every voice of criticism.

The mere existence of a free society in close proximity to the Soviet frontier is, from the Soviet standpoint, an invitation to disaffection and an intolerable provocation. That is why, barring some unpredictable complete transformation of its nature and psychology, the Soviet regime will never feel safe until the world is brought under communist domination.

The conception of communism which is held by idealistic communist sympathizers abroad, as distinguished from the opportunists and the cynics, is grotesquely at variance with reality. While communism attracts foreign sympathy by professing to oppose racial discrimination the Soviet Government forbids marriages between Soviet citizens and foreigners, liquidates en masse ethnic groups within the Soviet Union which were stigmatized as disloyal during the war (Volga Germans, Crimean Tartars, Kalmyks, North Caucasians) and has flirted with anti-Semitism as an instrument of state policy.

Communism wins foreign converts by promising to abolish poverty. But wherever communism prevails poverty is made more nearly universal. And the communist pose in favor of peace becomes increasingly ridiculous in the light of the bellicose actions of the Soviet Government.

Communists, who, like all fanatics, are masters of the Big Lie, found in western countries audiences passionately eager for a Big Myth, for some new secular creed of salvation that would offer all the solutions to all human and social problems. It is both a disgrace and a psychological puzzle of our time that so many western intellectuals have been willing to sell their birthright of a free liberal humanistic culture for a mess of Marxian messianic pottage.

What a sorry spectacle it has been! Pastors prepared to exalt the "Christianity" of a system which has not only denied and persecuted all forms of religion, but practiced acts of barbarism and genocide matched only by the crimes of the Nazis. Intellectuals going into ecstasies over the "progressive" character of a regime that has made realities out of the grim fantasies of George Orwell's *1984*. Scientists admiring a dictatorship as intolerant of independent scientific thought as the Inquisition was of Galileo. Self-styled friends of human liberty willing to overlook the absence in the Soviet Union of the most elementary rights of man. Pacifists eager to believe the best of a tyranny armed to the teeth.

We know the reality of this spectacle in America and, still more, in Western Europe. The causes are varied and complex. It is customary to equate communism with poverty and lack of opportunity. With some reservations, this is broadly true. Mass support for communism is to be found mainly in countries and among groups living below what would be regarded in North America as the extreme poverty line.

But this correlation between poverty and communism does not always hold good and it breaks down conspicuously in the case of many individual sympathizers with communism, especially in the United States. The communist movement in Italy, for instance, is stronger in the more prosperous industrialized North than it is in the backward destitute South. In France and other European countries it is not always the poorest and least skilled industrial workers who become communist converts. And economic motivation breaks down altogether as an explanation in the case of many well-to-do writers, artists, actors, professors, scientists, even businessmen who have joined communist front organizations.*

Various psychological factors enter into this situation. Sensitiveness to real or imagined racial discrimination is one factor. Dream of a millennial social order is another. A guilt complex about wealth, especially if it is inherited, has made some converts to communism. There is also the belief, more widespread in Europe than in America, that communism is a wave of the future, and that it is safer to swim with this wave.† There is also a kind of intellectual snobbishness that finds expression in the feeling that it is smart and sophisticated to be "open-mindedly" sympathetic with communism and, above all things, not to be an anticommunist.

Some individuals seek escape from personal maladjustments in absorption in the communist faith. And the burden of freedom is too heavy for some individuals to carry. They are at-

---

* A European refugee, after spending some time in the United States remarked that, so far as he could judge, the poor in America were Democrats, the members of the middle class Republicans and the rich—communists. If he had qualified this with the phrase "the rich who take a serious interest in political and social ideas" his statement would be less fantastic than it sounds.

† There is truth as well as wit in the story of the European who, on being asked whether he will join the Americans or the Russians in the event of a war replies: "The Russians, of course. It would be so much pleasanter to be captured by the Americans than by the Russians in the event of defeat."

tracted by a creed which offers dogmatic certainty, which claims to give all the answers, which assigns them tasks and relieves them of the necessity of making decisions of their own. Many ex-communists recall, rather wistfully, even in their time of disillusionment, the sense of purposeful direction which membership in the movement gave them. Dostoevsky, a profound psychologist as well as a great novelist, anticipated and interpreted this mood in his tremendous parable of Christ and the Grand Inquisitor, in *The Brothers Karamazov:* *

"Nothing," says the Inquisitor to Christ, "has ever been more insupportable for a man and a human society than freedom. . . . We have corrected Thy work and have founded it upon *miracle, mystery* and *authority.* And men rejoiced that they were again led like sheep and that the terrible gift that had brought them such suffering was at last lifted from their hearts."

The Threat as Fifth Column. If the world of 1952 were the world of 1912, if there were no great communist empire, eager to create fifth columns for propaganda, infiltration and espionage in every noncommunist country, communism could be left to the play of free competition in the marketplace of ideas. There would be no special cause for concern if a scientist in possession of vital defense secrets or a diplomat in a strategic post favored, on principle, a communist, not an individualist, social and economic order. For at that time there was no communist state to which such a person could have betrayed his secrets.

But the situation in 1952 is entirely different. A communist or a fanatical sympathizer is not just a dissenter whose activities can be left to the operation of the libertarian ideals of Milton and Jefferson. He must be regarded as a potential partner in a tremendous and surprisingly open and overt conspiracy against noncommunist countries in general and the United States in particular.

* *The Brothers Karamazov,* Modern Library edition, pp. 262–66.

It is not surprising that most Americans feel dazed and confused and uncertain how to proceed in the face of this conspiracy. For there has been nothing like it in scale and scope in recorded history. There has never been a case when millions of people were enrolled in parties of which the first and indeed the only consistent principle was blind obedience to the authority of a foreign empire.

The Alger Hisses, the Klaus Fuchses, the Allan Nunn Mays, the Julius Rosenbergs, the Harry Golds, the Bruno Pontecorvos, the many others, detected and undetected, who have been involved in activities directed against the interests of their own countries in the service of Moscow are the product of a combustible combination. The farflung Soviet network of espionage has been very much strengthened by the addiction to communist sympathies among western intellectuals.

Because the communist fifth column threat was new and strange it was met, for many years, with insufficient vigilance and understanding of its gravity. Igor Gouzenko, the Soviet cipher clerk in Ottawa who passed over to the side of freedom was almost sent back to the Soviet Embassy to certain "liquidation" by stupidly incredulous Canadian officials, full of faith in the goodwill of the "Soviet ally."

Some Americans show stubborn unwillingness to believe in the reality of the communist fifth column. They pour out their indignation not against the traitors who furnish information to Soviet spy rings, but against individuals who expose these traitors. Characteristic of this "anti-anticommunist" attitude are two comments published by Mrs. Eleanor Roosevelt in her syndicated newspaper columns of August 16, 1948, and June 8, 1949:

> Anyone knowing either Mr. Currie or Mr. Hiss, who are the two I happen to have known fairly well, would not need any denial on their part to know they are not communists.

> One gets the feeling as one reads the newspaper accounts that Mr. Chambers is on trial and not Mr. Hiss.

The vilification campaign against Whittaker Chambers and Elizabeth Bentley, two former members of Soviet spy rings who broke with communism and denounced their former accomplices, went to extreme lengths. There was every effort to depict them as neurotic, unstable, unworthy of trust or credence. Against this campaign of abuse, carried on by innuendo and by whispering methods as well as in some published comment, one solid and impressive fact stands.

Not one of the many persons named in circumstantial detail in books published by Whittaker Chambers and Elizabeth Bentley has offered satisfactory disproof. The two cases in which libel suits were brought were those of Alger Hiss and William Remington. Neither turned out favorably for the individual concerned. Some of the individuals named later admitted their communist associations. Others suggestively refused to answer the simplest questions for fear of "self-incrimination." There was not even one case of clear, convincing disproof, calculated to shake faith in the general credibility of Chambers and Elizabeth Bentley.

What makes Soviet espionage so formidable and difficult to detect is the ability of Soviet spy rings to recruit foreign agents. The extremely efficient espionage group which Richard Sorge, German communist who passed himself off as a Nazi journalist, organized in Japan, was composed of Japanese and Germans, not of Soviet Russians, who were under the close observation of the Japanese police. The Canadian spy ring, organized by the Soviet military attaché, Col. Nikolai Zabotin, was made up of Canadian citizens. The men who played leading parts in betraying atomic bomb secrets, Klaus Fuchs, Allan Nunn May, Harry Gold, the Rosenbergs, were not Soviet nationals.

This international character of the Soviet fifth column shows that we are not engaged in a simple old-fashioned national power struggle. The Soviet rulers have challenged us to a global international civil war. We shall ignore this challenge at our peril. Pedantic to the point of stupidity is the attitude of those who would have us abstain from any kind of promising propaganda and subversive activity behind the iron curtain or in the Soviet Union itself, if this is possible. It is dangerous folly to fight with one hand tied behind our backs or to observe restraints and conventions which communist states have ignored from the moment of their formation. We are engaged not in a genteel boxing bout conducted according to Marquess of Queensberry rules, but in a barroom brawl. Our tactics must be adjusted accordingly, if defeat is to be averted.

The Threat as Militarized Empire. The third, and most serious aspect of the communist threat is the huge empire, directed from Moscow, which now includes almost one third of the world's population and which stretches from the Baltic to the Pacific Ocean.

This empire includes, with much more territory, one area which the British geo-politician, Sir Halford Mackinder, designated as the "Heartland" of the "World Island." Mackinder conceived the land surface of the globe as a group of islands. Much the largest and most populous of these is what he called the World Island, the adjacent continents of Europe, Asia and Africa.

The American continent, in this view of geography, is a much smaller and more sparsely populated island. And the regions which are usually thought of as islands, Australia, New Zealand, the Philippine and Indonesian archipelagoes, for instance, shrink to very small proportions.

Mackinder, in a book which is a classic of geo-politics and which attracted much more attention abroad than in Great Britain, where it was first published,* emphasized the vast preponderance in manpower of the World Island over the lands of more recent discovery and settlement. Inside this World Island he traced a Heartland, bounded by the Baltic Sea, the navigable middle and lower Danube, Asia Minor, Armenia, Iran, Mongolia and Tibet. This Heartland, according to

* Halford J. Mackinder, *Democratic Ideals and Reality* (Holt).

Mackinder, was invulnerable to sea power, Britain's main reliance for centuries. And he worked out a formula which may
have seemed academic when his book was published after the
First World War but which rings like an alarm bell in the age
of the communist empire:

Who rules East Europe commands the Heartland.

Who rules the Heartland commands the World Island.

Who rules the World Island commands the World.

Mackinder was afraid that Germany, in spite of its defeat,
would rise again and organize the Heartland, building up a
land power capable, in time, of defeating the sea power of the
Anglo-American combination. This threat has now materialized, in the form not of Germany but of the communist empire.

It is easy to imagine how Mackinder would have reacted to
the inherent menace of an empire that, for the first time in
history, has united Russia, China and the countries of eastern
Europe into one gigantic bloc, what he would have thought
of the men of Yalta, who presented Stalin with the keys to the
World Island on a silver platter. Both in Europe and in East
Asia the influence of the western powers has been crowded
back to the narrow coastal fringes of the World Island.

The Soviet empire is formidable in manpower, in natural
resources and in geographical depth. And it is the existence of
this empire that aggravates the threat of communism as a subversive idea and as a school of espionage and treason.

This triple challenge of communism calls for a triple response. The obvious way to fight communism as an idea is to
offer a better, more inspiring and workable idea. Sometimes this
proposition leads to the assumption that communism should
be treated as a "good idea gone wrong," that the only means
of resisting communism is to make far-reaching concessions
to the communist idea of the state as a director of the national
economy and a universal provider.

But practical experience does not bear out this theory that
some kind of socialism is the only effective response to com-

munism. It is the countries that have maintained more individual incentives that have achieved the most striking economic recoveries. The relatively more individualistic United States has been footing the bills for the trade and financial deficits that are often the fruits of socialism.

The best line to hold against communism is the liberty line. The best answer to the quack remedies of the Kremlin is a ringing reaffirmation of the pragmatic value, in terms both of spiritual and material values, of political liberty and economic individualism. The true antithesis of communism would be a rediscovery and revitalization of the basic truths in the thought of Locke and Montesquieu, Burke and de Tocqueville: limited government with divided powers, individual liberties safeguarded by specific laws. Or, in Locke's phrase, life, liberty and property.

There will be much sympathy for the belief set forth in Whittaker Chambers's passionate, eloquent and self-revealing book: * that the basic challenge of communism is the denial of God. It is certainly no accident that the two supreme secular tyrannies of our time, nazism and communism, are atheistic and amoral. The totalitarian ruler is an idol, an earthly god, oblivious of conscience and, in his own conception, beyond the restraint of any law, human or divine. In Nietzsche's phrase he is "beyond good and evil." From the time of the ancient Greeks to Shakespeare's *Macbeth* and Pushkin's *Boris Godunov* the powerful ruler, haunted by remorse, has furnished the stuff of mighty drama. But there is no indication that Hitler or Stalin felt any regret for their indescribable crimes or one pang of sympathy for their innumerable victims.

The totalitarian state recognizes no distinction between what belongs to God and what belongs to Caesar. It claims all as Caesar's portion.

However, it is oversimplification, historically and philosophi-

* Whittaker Chambers, *Witness* (Random House).

cally, to equate a sceptical attitude toward religion with communist sympathy or to assume that only a great religious revival or crusade can defeat communism. It is altogether possible to oppose communism on rational, as well as on spiritual or mystical grounds. Indeed fundamental irrationality is the characteristic of the communists, not of their opponents. It is the communists who make the sweeping dogmatic assertions, some already disproved by experience, others, in their nature, unprovable. It is they who, as soon as they are in power, resort to systematic thought control and suppression of all critical ideas.

It is unfortunately not true that religion, at all times and under all circumstances, has made for the freedom and dignity of the human spirit. Ecclesiastical organizations have been corrupted by the pomp, power and passion of this world. There have been examples, the worst of which happily lie in an era which has passed into remote history, when the spirit of persecuting bigotry has turned official religious institutions into ghastly caricatures of the teaching of Jesus. In the same way the brave hopes and dreams of the great minds and great hearts of the Russian revolutionary movement, of the Kropotkins and Breshkovskayas, are horribly mocked by the standard brutalities of Soviet prisons and concentration camps.

A man without religious faith does not necessarily turn into a power-crazed monster. Many European socialists and radicals have been sceptics or agnostics in matters of religious faith without seeking to create institutions of tyranny and oppression.

It is sometimes argued that communism, with its absolutist, ruthless, purposeful character, can only be successfully opposed by some faith equally absolute in its pretensions, simple, uncompromising and full of mass appeal. If this is a correct analysis, western civilization, of which diversity is one of the main glories, has come on evil days. And it seems unlikely that any such faith can be manufactured synthetically. It is significant that many centuries have passed since a new religion won the faith of millions of followers.

Anticommunist strategy should reckon with diversity of motivation. In the anticommunist house there should be many mansions. In the anticommunist front there must be a place for everyone opposed to the spread of the Moscow empire, even for those who, in the opinion of most Americans, oppose it for the wrong reasons.

There must be a place for the devoutly religious, for the socialist who rejects terror and dictatorship, for the patriot who wishes to vindicate national independence, even for authoritarianism of the Right like Franco's and authoritarianism of the Left like Tito's. A broad coalition including all anticommunist forces is a more sensible and hopeful aim than the launching of a crusade for some vague and probably unattainable goal.

A vigorous campaign of exposure of actual conditions in the Soviet Union and in the satellite states is the most promising answer to the challenge of communism as an idea. This should be a relentless nonstop affair, carried on by the Voice of America, by the various independent radio stations which broadcast to listeners behind the iron curtain, by the refugees of many nationalities who found communism so intolerable that they fled from its rule at any risk and at any cost.

At the same time there should be vigorous affirmation of the close relation between political and economic liberty and individual happiness and well-being. People might be lukewarm about this principle when it was taken for granted before the First World War. There is no excuse for being indifferent after seeing the handiwork of Stalin and Hitler.

The fifth column aspect of the communist threat calls for counteraction on two fronts. Soviet espionage can be detected and defeated only by trained and skilful counter-espionage. As every communist is a potential traitor (he is a bad communist if he is not) and there is a considerable fringe of fellow-travelers whose fanatical sympathy with Moscow makes them distinctly poor "security risks," careful screening of applicants for work in "sensitive" government agencies is not witch-hunting, but a reasonable and necessary security measure.

There is also a constant need for "red-baiting," to use a word which anti-anticommunists like to bring into disrepute. There is no excuse for slander or false or exaggerated accusations, or for the bad habit of calling anyone with whom one may disagree a "communist." Apart from the injustice involved, that sort of thing merely creates a dust cloud of confusion behind which it is easier for communist agents to operate. But when an individual or an organization is acting as a volunteer Voice of Moscow that fact, with supporting evidence, should be pointed out.

Freedom of speech and expression is a two-way proposition, —a point which individuals who tend to wax hysterical over "hysteria" and "red-baiting" are inclined to forget. It is the right of a magazine editor to flirt with pro-Soviet apologetics, for a publishing house to display an affinity for pro-communist books, for a research organization, infiltrated by communist sympathizers, to give a pronounced slant to its published material. It is also the right and the duty of persons who are alert and experienced in the ways of communist propaganda to expose and criticize such manifestations when they occur.

Communism as an idea is best met by the directly contrary idea of integral freedom and maximum liberty for the individual. The communist fifth column threat should be countered, on its overt side, by quick, reasoned exposure of the familiar untruths, half-truths and fallacies of procommunist propaganda. On its covert side it can only be curbed by patient, trained, skilled detective work.

The third element in the communist threat, the military power of the communist empire, with all the possibilities of political pressure and blackmail which this military power creates, can be effectively resisted and defeated only by equal or superior military force. In this connection Americans should immunize themselves against what is perhaps the Number One fallacy about communism: that, as an "idea," it is impervious to military force.

Two historical examples may help to illustrate the distinction between movements that cannot and that can be defeated by physical force. The victory of Christianity over the declining paganism of the Roman Empire was not and probably could not have been stopped by arms, because the early Christians used only spiritual means of persuasion.

But there was a different situation when the Arab Moslems, after conquering and forcibly converting the Near East, North Africa and Spain, entered France in the eighth century and offered the infidels the familiar choice between the sword, the Koran and tribute. Then the element of physical force became all-important. The victory of Charles Martel over the invading Saracens near Tours may have decided the issue whether Europe was to be Christian or Islamic in faith. Had there been an overwhelming impulse among the Christian peoples of that time to accept Mohammedanism no military victory, in the long run, could have arrested the process. But when it was a question of the forcible imposition of an undesired alien faith the military ability to resist was of primary importance.

If it is clearly understood that communism is not a new faith, seeking to conquer the hearts and minds of men by its intrinsic merit, but the armed doctrine of a mighty empire whose rulers maintain and extend their power by the most ruthless violence, there should be less pessimism about the possibility of checking and rolling back the tide of communism. The experience of the last war, properly understood and interpreted, shows that there is nothing invincible about communism. Not only did the Soviet armies sustain severe defeats, but great rifts were revealed in the loyalty, cohesion and morale of the peoples living under Soviet rule. Pessimists who believe that communism is an irresistible wave of the future should consider one impressive contrast.

The Germans raised the equivalent of 25 divisions among

Soviet war prisoners, deserters and inhabitants of occupied Soviet territory. Had the Nazi occupation policy not been so cruel and tyrannical, so tainted with the race superiority theory, the Soviet dictatorship might well have been overthrown with the enthusiastic cooperation of a large number of its first victims, the peoples of the Soviet Union.

But neither the Germans nor the Japanese raised a division, or a regiment, or a company or a platoon among war prisoners who were citizens of free countries. The deep underlying unity that is the product of free institutions proved more reliable as a moral force than the artificial uniformity which is created by terror and propaganda.

In order to defeat the communist threat it is essential to understand its true nature, the three levels on which it operates. Then freedom to criticize will not be confused with freedom to conspire. And an imperialist strategy of terror will not be mistaken for the pervasive intangible power of an ideal.

Chapter VIII ~ "Power That Fills the World with Terror"

The Soviet regime was born in terror and violence and it grew strong enough to spread terror and violence over a large part of the earth. These qualities have become frozen in Soviet methods of rule and have left an indelible stamp on the national characters of the peoples who have fallen under this rule.

Communism has already required probably more human sacrifices than any idea in history. Gladstone's striking phrase about the Neapolitan despotism, "the negation of God erected into a system of government" was spoken too soon. It would have been far more fitting as an epitaph for the Soviet Government.

The list of martyrs under this government is infinitely long and varied. It includes men, women and children of many nationalities. There are innumerable Russians, from the Tsar who, with his wife and children, was slaughtered in a cellar in the summer of 1918, by the typical method of a gangland killing, to the simple barely literate peasants who perished in the famine of 1932–33 or in the concentration camps of Russia's frozen North.

As the Soviet power spread beyond Russia's borders the toll of terror rose to include Poles, Letts, Estonians, Lithuanians, Rumanians, Hungarians, Germans, Austrians. People of these varied nationalities, sometimes bitterly hostile to each other, met in the misery and degradation of the Soviet slave labor camp.

The Red terror that was avowedly practiced during the years of revolution and civil war was grim enough and took far more victims than the corresponding terror against "aristocrats" and "enemies of the people" during the French Revolution. But what is distinctive and ominous about Soviet terror, as compared with French, is its incomparably longer duration. The worst of the French terror was over after a period of some two years, when Robespierre and his associates were guillotined on the Ninth Thermidor. There were no more wholesale proscriptions and mass killings after this event.

But the most tremendous cruelties of the Soviet Government, acts affecting the "life, liberty and pursuit of happiness" of millions of human beings, occurred long after the end of the revolution and civil war, at a time when the excuses which might be advanced for early revolutionary terrorism, civil war, foreign intervention, acts of ruthlessness perpetrated by the "Whites," or counterrevolutionaries, no longer possessed validity. These cruelties were possible because the few self-imposed restraints during the first years of Soviet rule had disappeared as a result of the growing power of the new absolute state.

For example, no prominent communist was executed during the stress and strain of the civil war. There were demotions, falls from favor, assignments to distant posts. But in the main Lenin kept the best abilities of the Party functioning. There was also an unwritten rule that members of socialist parties, such as the Mensheviki (Social Democrats) and the Socialist Revolutionaries should not be summarily executed. This rule was not always observed in the case of rank-and-file members.

But leading members of these parties were permitted to go into political exile abroad.

All these limitations were disregarded in the orgy of terror that raged within the ranks of the Communist Party during the thirties. This terror took the lives of every member of the seven-man Politburo, or highest steering committee of the Communist Party, as it was constituted at the time of Lenin's death, except Stalin himself. Zinoviev, Rykov, Bukharin and Tomsky were shot after public trials in which they confessed to vague and improbable acts of treason, assassination and sabotage. Tomsky committed suicide rather than go through one of these trials. Trotsky, who had been sent out of the country before the policy of wholesale executions of communists went into effect, was murdered in Mexico by a mysterious assassin who was almost certainly an agent of the Soviet political police.

The French historian Taine described the French Revolution as a crocodile, devouring its young. The Soviet "crocodile" was slower in developing its appetite than the French. Retribution for veteran communists who were suspected, rightly or wrongly, of disaffection with Stalin's personal rule came fifteen or twenty years after the revolution and civil war. But this retribution, when it came, was mercilessly thorough.

Soviet top leadership in every field was decimated. Along with the former members of the Politburo the most prominent Soviet diplomats, Vice-Commissars of Foreign Affairs Karakhan and Krestinsky, Ambassadors to Great Britain, France, China and Japan, Sokolnikov, Rakovsky, Bogomolov, Yurenev, were executed or sentenced to long terms of imprisonment. Marshal M. N. Tukhachevsky and seven other generals were shot in 1937 after a secret trial and most of the senior officers who sat in judgment on them soon disappeared.

A high proportion of the seventy-one members of the Communist Party Central Committee vanished and could be described as "missing, presumed dead." Suicides and executions of high Soviet officials became routine news. The purge swept through the non-Russian republics like a prairie fire, and veteran communists were struck down from the swamps of Byelorussia to the deserts and oases of Central Asia. The purge was not confined to political figures; it swept away communist jurists and historians, novelists and playwrights, artists and theatrical producers. Two successive heads of the political police, Yagoda and Yezhov, were put to death after inflicting death sentences on countless others.

The proscription extended to foreign communists. Men and women who had become outlaws and pariahs in their own countries because of their devotion to communism and who had found asylum in the Soviet Union were rounded up, given a firsthand experience of the crowded, filthy Soviet jails and the brutal Soviet police investigation methods and shot or sent to slave labor camps.

Among the leading figures in the Communist International who perished or disappeared during this purge were the Russians Pyatnitsky and Elena Stassova (the latter a veteran woman communist and friend of Lenin), the former leader of the short-lived Hungarian Soviet Republic, Bela Kun, the prominent German communists Remmele and Heinz Neumann, and a number of Polish communists, among them Dombal and Warski.

Three of the many victims of this drive against suspected foreign communists, by rare good fortune, survived prison and concentration camp experiences and were able to tell their stories outside the Soviet Union. One of these was Alexander Weissberg, Austrian communist physicist who had come to the Soviet Union at the invitation of the economic authorities to help in the economic development of the country.

After Weissberg was tortured into signing confessions which he would repudiate as soon as he regained strength the Soviet police decided that he would not make a reliable witness, sure to incriminate himself in a public trial. With a number of other arrested Central European communists he was turned over to the Gestapo.*

One who shared Weissberg's experience was Margarete Buber, wife of the heretical German communist Heinz Neumann, who was shot. She had the unusual experience of living through several years, first in a Soviet, then in a German concentration camp and is an active fighter against communism and any form of dictatorship in Germany today.†

A third foreign victim of the purge who has published her story was Elinor Lipper, a Dutch girl who became a communist while she was a student in Berlin. For this she paid a penalty which would have been unthinkable in her own civilized country. Living in Moscow at the time of the purge she was arrested and spent eleven years in the frozen hell of the slave labor camps of the Kolyma Valley, in Eastern Siberia.‡

No doubt there were strange and ironical meetings in concentration camps between these fallen communists and men and women whom they had themselves destroyed in the days of their power, old officers, middle-class intellectuals, priests, kulaks. There is no means of knowing with certainty how many communists perished in this great purge. But official Soviet statistics show § that almost one million members of the Communist Party and candidates (applicants for membership on probation) were expelled between 1934 and 1939. It would probably be a moderate estimate that half of these were executed or sent to concentration camps.

Another act of extreme ruthlessness, affecting large numbers of people, was the so-called liquidation of the kulaks as a class. First practiced by local authorities without much publicity,

* For Weissberg's full story see his book, *The Accused* (Simon and Schuster).

† Her experiences are set forth in a book, *Under Two Dictatorships* (Dodd Mead).

‡ Elinor Lipper, *Eleven Years in Soviet Prison Camps* (Regnery).

§ Michael Florinsky, *Towards an Understanding of the USSR* (Macmillan), p. 111.

this policy was sanctioned by an official decree in the spring of 1930. What it meant was the complete expropriation of the four or five per cent of the Soviet peasants who earned the name kulak because they were a little richer, or a little less poor, than their neighbors.*

The Soviet Government in 1929 launched a tremendous drive, backed by every resource of administrative pressure and propaganda, to force the peasants to merge their small plots of land in large units, known as collective farms. Most of the peasants were averse to this change. When collective farming was a matter of voluntary choice, up to 1929, not more than two or three per cent of the peasants had adopted this new method of farming. The kulaks, with most to lose and nothing to gain, were naturally strong opponents of the change. So it was decided that they must be liquidated.

All their property was confiscated, even down to women's coats and children's toys. In some cases the dispossessed kulaks were huddled in shanty settlements on the outskirts of villages and permitted to eke out a wretched living on the worst land. More often there was a wholesale round-up of kulak families for transportation to forced labor in northern timber camps, on canals and in new industrial centres.

During the last years of my stay in the Soviet Union (1930–1934) I often saw trainloads of these unfortunates, packed in freight cars with less care than animals would receive in civilized countries, shipped off from their homes to new strange places of forced labor. Large numbers, especially of the old, the sick and the children, died as a result of lack of food and water on the trains and overwork and underfeeding in the camps.

A still larger and more indiscriminate slaughter was the state-organized famine of 1932–33. Starvation conditions prevailed over a large area of southern and southeastern European

* There were about one million kulak families in the Soviet Union.

Russia and also in parts of Russian Central Asia. In three widely separated districts which I visited in the autumn of 1933, one in the normally rich Kuban Valley, one in the eastern and one in the western Ukraine, I found in every village a death rate of at least ten per cent. In one large Ukrainian village, Cherkass, in the Bilaya Tsirkiv district, over six hundred had perished in a population of about two thousand. These were official figures of the local Soviet authorities.

No one who traveled in the affected areas in 1933 could have felt any reasonable doubt about the reality of this famine. Officials in Moscow might blandly assure foreign visitors that there had been no famine at all, just a little hardship and tightening of belts. But local communists on the spot made no effort to conceal what had happened. It would have been impossible to prevent the peasants from talking, when almost every family had its victims to report.

The cause and the responsibility of the famine were clear. The peasants in 1932 had gone on a spontaneous, unorganized strike, partly against collective farming as a system and partly against the systematic extortion to which they were subjected during the First Five Year Plan. They were required to deliver all their produce at low fixed prices. They could not buy a reasonable equivalent in manufactured goods in return, because it was the policy of the government to neglect consumers goods industries and concentrate on building up steel, mining, metallurgy, chemicals and other heavy industries.

The Soviet Government's reply to the strike was organized starvation. The villages were swept clear of reserve foodstuffs by forcible requisitions and the peasants were left to starve. In a similar crisis in 1921–22 the fact of starvation was freely admitted and facilities were provided for the work of the American Relief Administration and other foreign relief agencies. Censorship in 1932–33 prevented any forthright presentations of the situation in foreign newspapers. Foreign correspondents were not permitted to travel in the Ukraine and other famine areas while the disaster was at its height.

It is a sinister and impressive demonstration of tyrannical power when a government can starve several millions of its citizens to death without arousing revolt on any large scale. It is still more sinister and impressive when every voice of audible protest is stilled. One sometimes heard of local communists who were shot for refusing to carry out the food requisitions which the government demanded. But when the Soviet President, Mikhail Kalinin, in the autumn of 1933, told a Congress of Soviets that there had been no famine not one delegate from the Ukraine or the North Caucasus dared to contradict him. This incident, which I personally observed, left an even stronger impression than the fact of the famine itself. It was the absence of protest, even more than the act of cruelty which should have aroused the protest, that showed how completely the minds and souls of the peoples under Soviet rule had been enslaved.

It is not novel for a despotic government to execute enemies. What is new is the ability of the Soviet police to extract degrading and self-incriminating confessions from almost all the individuals who have been brought to public trial. (The great majority of Soviet political prisoners are sent to concentration camps or shot without any kind of public hearing or legal aid.)

How are these confessions obtained? There have been many guesses, including the use of drugs calculated to break down resistance, threats to families and appeals to veteran communists to confess on grounds of party loyalty. However, the testimony of a number of individuals who have been in the clutches of the Soviet political police and were subsequently able to describe their experiences indicates that a scientifically perfected form of torture through sleeplessness, malnutrition and mental and physical exhaustion is the surest means of extracting confessions. Crude "third degree" methods of beating and physical maltreatment are used when the examiners are over-worked and are eager to get confessions quickly. The Ukrainian engineer, Nikolai Prychodko, tells of being kicked and beaten with an oak paling with protruding nails.*

But usually a more refined technique, not calculated to leave traces of physical violence, is employed. According to Soviet prison rules, the prisoner may not lie down and sleep during daytime hours. At night, as soon as he goes to sleep, he is awak-ened and put through endless hours of cross-examination, car-ried on by fresh relays of investigators. This is known as the conveyor method. The torture is enhanced by focussing bright electric lights on the eyeballs of the accused and by forcing him to sit for hours in one position. The Austrian communist engi-neer Weissberg was a man of unusual physical vitality and mental resilience. But after he had been subjected to the con-veyor for six consecutive nights there were strange lights and flashes before his eyes and excruciating agony developed in the groin and the thighs. Complete mental and physical collapse was only a question of time. The examiners increased the pres-sure by shouting the same accusations and questions over and over again, varied by bursts of foulmouthed abuse. Weissberg's defense was to sign a confession when the pain and exhaustion became intolerable. Then he would repudiate the confession and the process would begin again.

There was a General in the Spanish Republican army named Valentin Gonzalez, better known under his pseudonym, El Campesino (The Peasant). He went to the Soviet Union after the victory of Franco. He soon fell from favor because of his independent character and Spanish national feeling. Arrested and accused of all sorts of crimes, such as contact with the British Intelligence, Gonzalez also found enforced sleeplessness the strongest weapon in the hands of his tormentors. The

* Nikolai Prychodko, *One of the Fifteen Million* (Little, Brown), pp. 64–65.

shouted insults, the blows, the abuse meant nothing. Gonzalez thought only of sleep.*

This is also the testimony of Jan Stypulkowski, Polish patriot and lawyer, who went through over 160 interrogations and was one of very few who refused to confess, and of Elinor Lipper, one of the most clear-sighted and factual reporters of the Soviet terror which she experienced. This is her description of the conveyor: †

> The prisoner is not allowed to sleep. Every four hours the examining judges relieve one another. Their sole duty is to keep the prisoner from sleeping. This goes on for days. Again and again the dazed victim is asked to sign the document the examiner has prepared, confessing to his alleged crime. He refuses. His feet and legs swell; he can no longer stand erect.

Here is the corroborating testimony of several individuals, of entirely differing backgrounds, who were examined separately. There is also a high measure of agreement among former Soviet prisoners, even down to small details, as regards vile and crowded prisons and subhuman living conditions in concentration camps.

Margarete Buber ‡ relates how she was thrown into a stinking cell so jammed with half-naked women that they could only lie on their sides, packed like sardines. Vladimir Petrov, Russian student, was one of sixteen in a cell in the Kresti Prison of Leningrad which held a single prisoner under the Tsarist administration.§

Filth and overcrowding in the prisons, bad and insufficient food (sour black bread and watery soup are the principal ingredients) and the torture of the conveyor are calculated to break down the strongest minds and bodies. And the Soviet political police possesses and uses a still grimmer weapon,

* "El Campesino," *Life and Death in Soviet Russia* (Putnam), pp. 152–53.
† Elinor Lipper, *op. cit.*, pp. 40–42.
‡ Margarete Buber, *op. cit.*, p. 32.
§ Vladimir Petrov, *Soviet Gold* (Farrar, Straus), p. 56.

threats, which can easily be put into effect in a land where there is no writ of habeas corpus, to the liberty and life of wife, children and close friends.

The institution of slave labor on a gigantic scale is another main aspect of Soviet terror. At various times and for various reasons the Soviet Government has doomed whole groups of its subjects to extinction. Instead of killing members of such groups quickly and humanely the policy has been to extract from them the maximum of work for the minimum of food.

During the first decade of the Soviet regime confinement in places of exile was mainly for punitive reasons. The most notorious concentration camp was in the Solovetsky Islands, in the White Sea. The number of persons in prison and in concentration camps for political, not criminal reasons was always extremely high, either by western standards or even by those of Tsarist Russia. It was during the first years of the Revolution that the saying became widespread: "Everyone in Russia is, has been or will be in prison." But the output of labor in concentration camps was of slight importance in the Soviet national economy until the early 30's.

Then two developments, occurring at the same time, led to the building of a vast slave labor system, under the direction of the political police. There was a sudden need for additional labor because the Soviet Government was launching a vast program of industrializing the country. And at the same time people were being despatched into exile not as individuals but as whole classes. What more logical, from the viewpoint of the Soviet authorities, than to utilize these "counterrevolutionaries" as a vast reservoir of cheap unskilled hard labor, for which voluntary labor would have been hard to recruit?

The liquidation of the kulaks alone provided many hundreds of thousands of slave laborers. The vast purge of the Communist Party supplied another large batch. Later the ranks of slave laborers were swelled by the citizens of several Soviet Republics and areas which failed to show sufficient patriotic zeal during the war against Germany. (The Volga German, Crimean Tartar, Kalmyk, Chechen-Ingush and Karachaev.) New sources of slave labor recruitment were the mass deportations (affecting between one and two million people) from Eastern Poland and the Baltic States in 1940 and 1941. There were millions of German and hundreds of thousands of Japanese war prisoners and considerable numbers of civilian deportees from occupied countries. Finally, there is a steady flow to the slave labor camps of Soviet citizens who have been arrested and banished, usually without public trial.

There were 175 concentration camps and penal colonies in the Soviet Union in 1951 under the administration of GULAG, an abbreviation of the Russian words *Glavnoye Upravlenye Lagerei* (Main Administration of the Camps). GULAG is a department of the MVD, Ministry of the Interior. Some of these camps are huge sprawling colonies, with hundreds of thousands of inhabitants. Location of these 175 camps has been established on the basis of thousands of affidavits, submitted by Polish soldiers who were released from imprisonment in 1941. Their information is supplemented by testimony from the New York Association of Former Political Prisoners of Soviet Labor Camps and by information gathered by the AFL consultants to the Social and Economic Council of the United Nations.

Although these camps are scattered all over the country, a high proportion are located in the bleak northern regions of European Russia and Siberia. Cold during most of the year is extreme and there are plagues of mosquitoes and other insects during the short summers. The testimony of former inmates of these camps who are free to tell their stories is agreed on the following points.

The prisoners are systematically overworked, often being forced to labor from dawn to dusk, and underfed. They are housed in fetid and filthy barracks and the ordinary criminals are favored by the administration against the "counterrevolutionaries." These common criminals are often of ferocious and degenerate types and offering eloquent living refutation of the idea that communism has uprooted crime. The prisoners receive no clothing suitable for the rough and dangerous work which they are required to perform in mines and forests, often at below freezing temperatures. Discipline and obedience are enforced by the most brutal means, beating, shooting and slow starvation.

Escapes from places of exile and imprisonment under the Tsarist Government were frequent. For several reasons there are few escapes from Soviet slave labor camps. The precautions against flight are ruthless and elaborate. These include electrically charged barbed wire, watchtowers manned by armed guards, bloodhounds trained to hunt down fugitives. Most of the camps are located in desolate, unaccessible parts of the country, where an escaped prisoner would have to wander for many days before he could hope to reach a settlement. Because the penalties for aiding fugitives are very severe, a runaway can count on little help from the sparse local population.

A standard concentration camp menu is outlined by Elinor Lipper: *

> Breakfast . . . Half a herring or 1.75 ounces of salt fish. Sweetened tea. One third of the bread ration. (This ranged from 10.5 ounces for prisoners who were being punished to two pounds for the best overtime workers.)
> Lunch . . . One third of the bread ration. Cabbage leaf soup. One pound of groats.
> Supper . . . One third of the bread ration, cabbage leaf soup, with a few grains of some cereal and a few boiled fish heads floating in it.

This diet would be far below the needs of people in sedentary occupations. It is not surprising that, as Miss Lipper says: "Another frequent cause of death is dystrophic alimentation, that is, starvation."

When Margarete Buber-Neumann was transferred from So-

* Elinor Lipper, *op. cit.,* p. 195.

viet forced labor to the Nazi concentration camp at Ravensbrueck the food was so much better in Ravensbrueck that she
thought some holiday was being celebrated. The Polish lawyer
Jerszy Gliksman tells how in the concentration camp to which
he was sent persons who fulfilled less than 30 per cent of the
assigned work received less than three quarters of a pound of
bread, with watery soup.* After a few days of this semi-starva-
tion they could never muster enough energy to earn any more
bread.

The Russian student Vladimir Petrov, who spent six years in
the concentration camps of the Kolyma gold fields area men-
tions 200 grams (less than half a pound) of bread as a punishment ration and repeats a grim joke. The unfortunates who
had been reduced to physical and mental impotence by this
slow starvation were known as *dokhodyagas,* from the Russian
verb *dokhodit,* to reach or arrive at. The significance of the
name was that these men, who naturally died off rapidly, had
"arrived at" . . . socialism.

The fate of women in what are officially called, perhaps with
unconscious humor, "corrective labor camps" is especially terrible. As Petrov testifies,† they are at the mercy first of the investigators and then of the officials and guards in the camps.
A woman who resists is simply raped without any possibility of
appeal or defense. The fantastic record of sex crimes rolled up
by the Red Army soldiers when they broke into Europe in
1944–45 is a replica of the moral conditions which prevail in
concentration camps.

Of the many millions of human beings who have passed
through these places of confinement a small minority are common criminals. It would be a misleading exaggeration to call
the others, with few exceptions, political prisoners in the sense
of having been active opponents of the Soviet regime. Most of
the prisoners are members of social groups which the Soviet

* Jerszy Gliksman, *Tell the West* (Gresham Press), p. 255.
† Petrov, *op. cit.,* p. 142.

Government wishes to destroy (kulaks, members of minor nationalities of suspected loyalty, remnants of the pre-revolutionary "bourgeoisie," former officials and members of the middle classes from the newly annexed territories in the West, etc.). The concentration camp is also a sanction against slack work in farm and factory and many of its victims are persons who have been denounced for reasons of personal spite in a country where there is no habeas corpus and no remedy for false arrest.

Petrov found among his companions in prison some who had been arrested for singing a satirical song, two boys who had practiced shooting with revolvers and been accused of planning to kill Stalin and a professor whose wife had corresponded with a sister in Latvia. Petrov himself was denounced as a counterrevolutionary by a girl whose affection he did not reciprocate.

Sabotage is a familiar and elastic reason for arrest and assignment to forced labor. When I visited the tractor plant, then in process of construction, in the Ural town of Chelyabinsk two men who were at forced labor told their stories. One was a factory worker who had accidentally broken part of a machine. The other was a peasant who complained at a collective farm meeting that there was not enough to eat.

There is no certain figure for the number of people in concentration camps now or in any given year. Only a few high officials in GULAG know these figures and they are making no public statements. The lowest estimate, by a serious student of the subject, is that of Mr. Naum Jasny, a Russian specialist on Soviet agriculture who is now in this country. On the basis of an analysis, too complicated to summarize, of the Soviet national economic plan for 1941, a copy of which fell into American hands after the war, Mr. Jasny arrives at an estimate of $3\frac{1}{2}$ million slave laborers in 1940. He recognizes that there were additional sources of slave labor after this year: German and Japanese war prisoners, Soviet citizens, repatriated from Germany, who were considered too much infected with admiration for the West, etc.

David Dallin who, in collaboration with Boris Nicolaevsky wrote the most comprehensive study of Soviet slave labor in the English language * offers a higher estimate: 7–12 million. Former Ambassador Walter Bedell Smith believes that the "entire involuntary labor force" is equal to about 8 per cent of the Soviet population, or approximately 15 million. British and American delegates in the UN Social and Economic Council in 1949 and 1950 gave estimates of 8 and 14 million.

There are several reasons why it is impossible to give a precise figure. First, the Soviet Government has never permitted any independent investigation. Moreover, the question arises as to what should be considered slave labor. The severity of the regime and the extent of compulsion vary. Along with the barbed-wire concentration camp there is the penal settlement. I am personally acquainted with a Polish couple of whom the husband was sent to a concentration camp, the wife to a penal settlement.

Persons in penal settlements are compelled to work in local mines or factories. They are not permitted to leave. But they are spared the abuse by armed guards and some of the more cruel punitive features of the concentration camps.

Former Ambassador Smith's high estimate is partly accounted for because he includes among the forced laborers the large numbers of youths of both sexes who are required to enrol every year for industrial training. But their discipline, while strict, is not to be compared with the grim horror of the concentration camp.

Moreover, there is a good deal of fluctuation in the population of the forced labor camps. Many prisoners die; some are released after serving their sentences; there is a continual influx of new victims. Quite probably a figure that would be approximately correct for one year would be too high or too low for another. That slave labor is now one of the basic features of the Soviet economy and represents a coldblooded way of get-

* *Forced Labor in Soviet Russia* (Yale University Press).

ting much of the hardest work done are propositions beyond reasonable doubt or dispute.

The Soviet economic plan for 1941 shows that 14% of the capital construction was to be carried out by slave labor. Prisoners in that year were to produce 12% of the timber, 22.5% of the railroad ties, 40.5% of the chrome ore.* Slave labor is used most extensively in gold production and on big construction enterprises requiring large quantities of unskilled labor, such as the Baltic–White Sea, Moscow–Volga and Volga–Don canals and railway construction in Siberia and elsewhere. Sometimes slave laborers work under segregated conditions not in a separate concentration camp, but in a new construction enterprise. I saw this in several big new plants, then under construction, in the Magnitogorsk iron and steel works, the Chelyabinsk tractor factory and the Berezniki chemical plant, in 1932.

Whatever may be the number of Soviet forced laborers in any one year, it is the unanimous testimony of released and escaped victims that this system represents a revival of human slavery in an extremely cruel form. The number of human beings who, in the last twenty-five years, have been swallowed up, many never to return, in the enormous Arctic wastelands of the Soviet Union, now defiled by scores of these huge slave stockades, far exceeds the number of Negro slaves in the United States when Lincoln issued the Emancipation Proclamation.

And the existence of the Soviet slave laborer is far more miserable than that of the average slave in the ante-bellum South or of the serfs in Russia before Tsar Alexander II decreed the abolition of serfdom in 1861. An individual master might be kind or easygoing; at the worst he was under some restraint because a slave or a serf represented a valuable piece of property.

Both these considerations are non-existent in the Soviet new slavery. Most of the inmates of the camps are regarded as counterrevolutionaries and therefore as the scum of the earth, to be

* See summary of the State Department pamphlet on this subject in *The New York Times* of September 19, 1952.

deliberately degraded and abused as well as exploited. A high death rate is of no consequence because Soviet "justice" can always be depended on to turn up new batches of replacements.

For many years there was little exact knowledge of conditions in Soviet concentration camps. Until the Second World War almost all the prisoners were Soviet citizens. Escapes were infrequent. One of the most spectacular was that of the fisheries expert, Professor Tchernavin, with his wife and son, from the Solovetsky Islands.

What threw a flood of light into the dark recesses of the slave labor camps was the deportation and subsequent release of large numbers of Poles. The deportations took place after the Soviet annexation of Eastern Poland. The release of the Poles followed Hitler's attack on the Soviet Union. Instead of the isolated cases of individual Russians who escaped there is now an enormous literature, describing every detail of the system and largely composed by Poles who experienced deportation and life in the camps and later made their way again to the West.

There is sometimes an attempt, by "anti-anticommunists" or by pedants with no sense of reality to deny or minimize the Soviet restoration of slavery on the ground that no "evidence" is available on the subject from official Soviet sources. This is on a par with refusing to believe that there were atrocities in such places as Dachau and Buchenwald because no affidavits to this effect were furnished by the Propaganda Ministry of Dr. Goebbels.

The balance-sheet of evidence on the Soviet concentration camps and the brutal and utterly arbitrary procedures by which most people are sent to these camps is as follows. On one side is a monumental mass of personal experience testimony from individuals who have been confined in these camps. These witnesses are of varied nationalities and backgrounds. They are Russians and Ukrainians, Poles and Germans, Yugoslavs and

Spaniards. Many have records of previous activity as communists or strong communist sympathizers.

It is simply absurd to suggest that thousands of individuals, most of whom are unknown to each other, would have entered into a gigantic conspiracy to lie and invent brutal and horrible and squalid stories. Naturally some of these former prisoners are better and more reliable observers than others. Not every statement by former inmates of these camps can be accepted, just as some who survived Nazi cruelties might exaggerate this or that individual detail. But in the main there is remarkable agreement as to the basic features of the regime in the camps, even down to such details as the cry, "Davai, Davai," with which the guards drive the prisoners to harder work.

For the defense there is not a word of serious argument. The Soviet authorities have never allowed an independent observer to enter a concentration camp. When pressed with the most specific details as to the location of the camps, the numbers at labor, the conditions of work, Soviet apologists confine themselves to general sweeping denials and vituperation against conditions in noncommunist countries. Not one person who has ever been a prisoner and who was later in a position to testify freely has given a picture short of unrelieved horror.

Such unanimity among the many accusers, such complete default on the part of the defense, can point to only one reasonable verdict in this case of Humanity against the Soviet dictatorship. This verdict is: Guilty as charged.

Until 1939 Soviet terror was mainly restricted to Soviet citizens and to the foreigners, many of them communists, who were caught in the Soviet Union without valid passports or means of appealing to the protection of their governments. Since the Second World War set the stage for Soviet westward expansion terror has spread up to and beyond the new frontier represented by the iron curtain.

Soon after the Soviet occupation of Eastern Poland mass deportations set in. There were wholesale arrests among former officials, intellectuals and members of the middle classes in the cities. Whole village populations, especially when the peasants were Poles, not Ukrainians, were routed out of their homes and rounded up. About a million and a quarter persons were shipped off to Soviet concentration camps and penal settlements.

There were no foreign observers in Eastern Poland at this time. The subsequent wartime propaganda in America, designed to represent the Soviet Union as a gallant champion of freedom and democracy, led to hushing up of the barbarity of these deportations. But the testimony on this subject on the part of the victims is as unanimous and impressive as the similar testimony about conditions in Soviet prisons and concentration camps.

Families were often separated and conditions in the long trains which carried off the Poles to foreign enslavement were unimaginably crowded and filthy. Human beings, men, women, children, old people, invalids, babies, were packed together for days without adequate food, water or sanitary facilities. Thousands of children froze to death.*

The purpose of this mass kidnapping was to eliminate from Eastern Poland all the people who might be expected to oppose annexation by the Soviet Union. The restoration of diplomatic relations between the Soviet Government and the Polish government-in-exile in 1941 made it possible for Polish representatives in Russia to conduct a detailed investigation of the fate of these deportees. They reached the conclusion that, of 1,230,000 persons deported from Eastern Poland, 270,000 perished as a result of executions, maltreatment, neglect and starvation in transportation and in the slave labor camps.†

* See Ann Su Cardwell, *Poland and Russia* (Sheed and Ward), p. 86.
† See Elma Dangerfield, *Beyond the Urals* (League for European Freedom), p. 87. *The Dark Side of the Moon* (Scribner) is a graphic symposium of the narratives of individuals who suffered in these deportations. What is most striking in these impressions is the callous indifference of

I had an opportunity to talk with a Polish young woman, one of 800 peasants deported from a village in Eastern Poland, who finally reached the United States by way of Mexico, with the aid of a Polish-American organization. Her estimate was that of 800 fellow-villagers about 200 died, a rather striking confirmation of the general figure of about 25 per cent mortality as a result of the deportations.

Another unpunished Soviet war crime in connection with Poland was the mass murder of some 15,000 Polish war prisoners, officers who had been captured after the Red Army overran Eastern Poland. All communication between these men, who were held in Soviet prison camps, and their families ceased abruptly in April, 1940.

Had it not been for one circumstance these 15,000 men might have disappeared without leaving any evidence as to their fate—the victims of a "perfect crime." This circumstance was the discovery by the Germans, in the spring of 1943, of several thousand corpses of uniformed Polish officers in the Katyn Forest, near the town of Smolensk, in western Russia. Alert to the propaganda value of a crime against Poles which they had not committed themselves, the Germans made every effort to give publicity to this discovery.

An international commission of European scientists, specialists in pathological medicine, was invited to inspect the scene. Other outsiders, including representatives of Polish organizations and American war prisoners, were invited as witnesses. When the Polish government-in-exile proposed an investigation by the International Red Cross the Soviet Government not only refused but used this invitation as an excuse for breaking off relations with the government-in-exile. After the Germans evacuated the region of Smolensk there was an official Soviet investigation of the affair, which naturally led to the conclusion that the Germans were responsible for the killings.

the Russians, who felt that these foreigners were only suffering something that was quite familiar to them.

No survivor of the massacre, able to give eyewitness testimony, has been found. But the circumstantial evidence that this was a Soviet, not a Nazi crime is overwhelming. This is the conclusion which has been reached by every independent Polish analysis of the available facts.* It is also the verdict of a committee of the United States House of Representatives which carried out a detailed investigation of the Katyn massacre, hearing much testimony on both sides of the Atlantic. The following points are of decisive significance in fixing responsibility.

There is no evidence that communication was received from any of the missing officers after April, 1940. This was fourteen months before the German invasion of Russia.

The fact that there were no survivors is a strong indication that the prisoners were at the mercy of their executioners. It is most improbable that, if the camp had been abandoned during the Soviet retreat, as the Soviet version implies, some of the officers would not have contrived to escape.

In response to repeated urgent inquiries from the Polish Government Stalin, Molotov, Vishinsky and other high officials gave only evasive replies. It was never even suggested as a possibility that the Poles might have fallen into the hands of the Germans. This improbable story was thought up only after the discovery of the bodies made it necessary to offer this explanation.

The Soviet official assertion that the Polish officers had been employed on road work and then had all fallen into the hands of the Germans is highly improbable, even as regards the four or five thousand whose bodies were found in the Katyn Forest. And it offers no explanation of what happened to some ten thousand other war prisoners, who were held in camps near the towns of Ostashkov and Starobielsk. Communication with these men ceased at the same time when all contact with the victims of Katyn was lost. Since no one of the Ostashkov and Starobielsk prisoners was ever seen or heard of after the war it can only be

---

* The best summary of all the circumstances in the case is *The Katyn Wood Murders*, by Joseph Mackiewicz (British Book Centre).

assumed that they were put to death at the same time. And in their case the only possible excutioners were the Soviet jailers.

Another typical instance of Soviet terror was the killing, after a purported secret trial, of the two outstanding leaders of the Polish Jewish Socialist movement, Henryk Ehrlich and Victor Alter. Not content with putting these men to death, the Soviet authorities tried to blacken their memories by accusing them, Jews and veteran Socialists, of carrying on "pro-Nazi propaganda."

A Central European quip after the war was that two things had been bad for communism. The Red Army had seen Europe —and Europe had seen the Red Army. The contrast between what the Red Army soldiers found in Europe in housing, roads, sanitary facilities and general living conditions and what they knew at home and what they had been told about capitalist inferiority created a serious crisis of morale, according to the accounts of a number of Soviet refugees. And the trail of rape, looting and general outrage which the Red Army left in every country it overran was certainly a handicap to local communist propaganda.

Of course every army has its share of bad characters and every invasion is marked by some cases of violence against the civilian population. But what happened when the Red Army poured through Poland and Rumania into East Germany, Hungary and Austria was much more than a normal quota of lapses in discipline. It was a wild orgy of lust, murder, loot and general destruction, such as one might have expected from the hordes of Genghiz Khan. On this point, as on the conditions in concentration camps and the nature of the deportations from Eastern Poland and the Baltic States, eyewitness testimony is strikingly unanimous.

A German publicist, Jurgen Thorwald, collected a number of recollections of men and women who had lived through the last months of the war in Eastern Germany and Berlin. Their stories are a ghastly symposium of wholesale murder, burning, looting and rape, the last often committed on a mass basis and with no attempt at concealment. There were villages where every woman, from the old to young children, was raped, often to death, and the desolation of death settled over whole provinces, notably in Silesia.* The outrages committed during the capture of three Central European capitals, Berlin, Budapest and Vienna, are comparable with what happened in the notorious sack of Rome by the troops of Charles V in 1527. Not even the "proletarian" quarters escaped, because the Red Army soldiers, accustomed to Soviet living conditions, refused to believe that workers could live in comfortable apartments with good furniture.

When I visited Vienna in 1946 Soviet terror had abated and was mainly limited to kidnapping Austrians who were considered politically undesirable. But the memory was fresh and vivid. An ecclesiastic in the office of Cardinal Innitzer estimated that 30,000 women had been raped during the Soviet occupation of the city; a Social Democratic editor estimated the number at 100,000. An Ukrainian woman who had been brought to Austria as a laborer during the German occupation of the Ukraine said that what she saw in Vienna when the Soviet troops entered the city was worse than anything she had seen when the Germans invaded the Ukraine. The wholesale assaults on women, she said, caused her to decide never to return to her native country.

I talked with a Polish woman who had been in Berlin at the time of the Soviet sack of the city. She had not the slightest sentimental sympathy for the Germans. But the memory of sheer horror had remained with her for years. "Those Red Army soldiers were not like human beings; they were like wild beasts bursting out of some forest," she said.

What distinguished the Soviet overrunning of Eastern and

* Jurgen Thorwald, *Flight in the Night* (Pantheon Books).

Central Europe was the mass character of the outrages and the unwillingness or inability of the officers to restrain their men. It is significant that Russian soldiers had often fought in European wars, in the eighteenth and nineteenth centuries, without leaving any such reputation.

Leo Tolstoy was no chauvinist; his description of the Russian troops in Germany and Austria in *War and Peace* may be considered fair and historically accurate. And he shows these troops as no worse disciplined than the other armies of the time. A Swiss publicist remarked to me that the Russian soldiers who fought the French revolutionary armies in Switzerland behaved better than the French, as regards looting. The behavior of Soviet troops on foreign soil must be considered a significant reflection of the kind of individuals who have been formed under communism, with its denial of God and of all absolute principles of religion and morality.

Communist terror quickly infects all countries which are conquered by communism. The belief that there is something peculiarly Russian in the cruelties of Soviet communism, that communism in another country might pursue more civilized methods is disproved by the course of development in the satellite states.

The same lawlessness, the same brutalities, including mass deportations, concentration camps and the systematic torture of political prisoners, are to be found in Poland and Rumania, Hungary and Bulgaria, Czechoslovakia and Albania. Robert Vogeler, American businessman who was arrested in Hungary and forced under threats and long interrogation to sign a false confession, was warned by his examiner what would happen if he should repudiate this confession in open court.

He would be taken to a special hospital where he would be given treatment that would make him very glad to give the answers the prosecutor wanted. This treatment would leave him a cripple for life. Such treatment had been meted out to a Hungarian engineer in the employ of a Swedish firm and had proved entirely effective.*

Other Soviet terrorist methods are faithfully copied in all the satellite states. Independent reporting from this part of the world has long ceased to be possible, as the fate of Associated Press correspondent William Oatis, imprisoned in Czechoslovakia on the always convenient charge of espionage, shows. One of the best edited and best informed European newspapers, the *Neue Zuercher Zeitung,* of Zurich gave up the attempt to maintain correspondents behind the iron curtain because of the undue personal risk to the newspapermen involved.

However, information continues to seep out, through refugees who escape, through letters that sometimes get through, through occasional unguarded admissions in the controlled newspapers. Between 80,000 and 110,000 people were deported from Budapest and the border areas of Hungary in 1951; 40,000 deportations were reported from the larger cities of Poland in the single month of May. Victims of this measure were suspected individuals and members of proscribed classes, former aristocrats, army officers, owners of businesses, however small, members of noncommunist political parties, etc.† More than one million people are estimated to be in slave labor camps in satellite countries.‡

The purge is a Soviet political export, along with the mass deportation and the concentration camp. Many of the prominent early leaders of the satellite regimes have been executed, like Rajk in Hungary and Kostov in Bulgaria; others have been arrested or disappeared from public view, like Ana Pauker and Patrascanu in Rumania and Gomulka in Poland. One of the most spectacular of the satellite purge trials, interesting be-

* See *I Was Stalin's Prisoner,* by Robert A. Vogeler with Leigh White (Harcourt), pp. 192–93.

† See Leland Stowe, *Conquest by Terror* (Random House), p. 89. This is one of the most systematic collections of material from behind the iron curtain.

‡ *Ibid.,* p. 169.

cause of a strong injection of anti-Semitism into the proceedings, led to the conviction of fourteen formerly prominent government and party officials in Czechoslovakia in November, 1952. Rudolf Slansky, former Secretary of the Czechoslovak Communist Party, and Vladimir Clementis, former Czechoslovak Foreign Minister, were among the eleven defendants who were hanged.

It is not reported that any of the defendants denied their guilt, or refused to answer questions for fear of self-incrimination. Eleven of the persons implicated in this trial were Jews and there were many allusions during the trial to "Jewish capitalism," "Jewish bourgeois nationalism," "Zionist conspiracies," and the alleged sinister activities of the Joint Distribution Committee, an American Jewish relief organization which was represented as a tool of the American Intelligence Service. The anti-Jewish trend in Soviet policy became clearer early in 1953, when nine Soviet physicians, six or seven of them Jews, were arrested on charges of having poisoned two prominent Soviet leaders, Stcherbakov and Zhdanov, who had died shortly after the end of the war. The physicians were accused also of attempting to murder Soviet generals. Again alleged instructions from the Joint Distribution Committee were mentioned in the official communiqué about the case. Taking as an excuse the throwing of a bomb into the Soviet Legation in Tel Aviv, the Soviet Government broke relations with the state of Israel.

It is ironical that the Soviet Government, many of whose early leaders were Jews and which has always boasted of its freedom from racial discrimination should have adopted such a familiar weapon of reactionary groups as anti-Jewish agitation. At least a temporary halt in this policy was indicated by the quashing of the proceedings against the doctors after Stalin's death. The proportion of Jews among high Soviet leaders has long been sharply reduced. Many of the prominent victims of the purges of the Communist Party in the 30's were Jews

(Trotsky, Zinoviev, Kamenev, Sokolnikov, Radek, to mention a few); but no open anti-Semitic capital was made out of these trials.

What caused the Soviet Government at least temporarily to assume the propaganda liability which anti-Semitism represents in western countries, to alienate that body of opinion, Jewish and non-Jewish, which felt that there must be something good in the Soviet Union because anti-Semitism was supposed to be a criminal offense there? The following reasons are most plausible:

The state of Israel is an accomplished fact and communist regimes are intolerant of any allegiance to or even sympathy with any centre outside their own frontiers on the part of any of their citizens.

The American Jewish community is the largest and much the richest in the world and any contacts, however innocent, between American Jews and the Jewish communities behind the iron curtain are suspect in Soviet eyes.

An anti-Jewish attitude may be considered a useful ingredient in Soviet designs for stirring up trouble in the Arab world and for winning support from unreconstructed Nazis in Germany.

The anti-Semitic course may be serviceable for convincing Poles, Czechs, Hungarians, Rumanians and other peoples behind the iron curtain that their governments are not being directed from Moscow. For in these countries, as in Russia, a considerable proportion of the few pioneer communists were Jews. To sacrifice these Jews excited no scruples in the minds of the coldblooded politicians in the Kremlin.

It is also very possible that the Jews may be only a pawn in a power struggle inside the Soviet Union, the nature of which is not yet clear.

Whatever the explanation may be, the fact is unmistakable. A revolution which began with unrealizable utopian aspirations for the whole world, and with some Jews who had exchanged the moral teachings of the Prophets for the material-

istic vision of Karl Marx as its tribunes, has evolved into a totalitarian tyranny which can manufacture against Jews and
non-Jews alike accusations as crazily unreal as the old familiar
charge of ritual murder.

Religion has been relentlessly persecuted in the satellite
countries. The Roman Catholic faith has been the object of
special attack, because of its influence in most of the satellite
countries and because it owes obedience to a centre which is
outside the reach of the Soviet political police. The martyrdom
of Cardinal Mindszenty in Hungary, the elimination of his
successor, Archbishop Gross and of Archbishop Beran in Czechoslovakia are typical of a drive to break and demoralize the
Roman Catholic Church.

The Uniat Church (Roman Catholics who practice the Eastern ritual) was wiped out of existence in the Western Ukraine
and most of its ecclesiastics were arrested. In wild and primitive Albania 54 of the 80 Roman Catholic secular clergy are
known to have been killed and 19 are in prison.* Persecution
in Poland has not gone as far as in Hungary and Czechoslovakia because of the wellknown Polish solidarity in Roman
Catholic faith. However, severe harassment has begun. Bishop
Stanislas Adamski, of Kattowice with his coadjutor and auxiliary bishops was arrested in December, 1952. Bishop Adamski
died in prison shortly afterwards, at the age of 78.†

Should communist rule in the satellite states become permanent there is little doubt that religious observance would be
permitted, if at all, only on condition that the churches would
be servile tools in the hands of the atheistic governments. This
is the pattern which has been set in the Soviet Union itself,
where the Orthodox Church is given more outward freedom
than it possessed before the war, but on condition that it take
an active part in every intrigue of Soviet foreign policy.

* See despatch in *The New York Times* of March 8, 1953, which quotes
Fides, a Catholic news agency as the source of this information.

† See Reuter's despatch in *The New York Times* of March 24.

Far Eastern communism shows the same terrorist features. The Chinese communists in 1951 let loose a wave of terror, in the form of mass executions, which equalled the wildest excesses of the French Revolution. A law published on February 21, 1951, and made retroactive, prescribed death as the punishment for a long list of vaguely phrased "crimes," including "contacts with foreign imperialism," "propagation of rumors with counterrevolutionary intent," "giving asylum to an enemy of the people," etc.

From April 30 until September 30, 1951, 1,742 executions were announced in the city of Shanghai. The deputy governor of the Province of Kwangtung, of which Canton is the capital, announced that in this province, between October, 1950, and August, 1951, 28,322 "counterrevolutionaries" were executed.* These figures, and many others of the same purport, are published in Chinese communist newspapers, which try to advertise rather than conceal the dimensions of the terror.

The *China Missionary Bulletin,* a Roman Catholic publication in Hong Kong, estimated in the autumn of 1951 that several hundred thousand people had been put to death. And the leftwing *New Statesman,* of London, a publication certainly not prejudiced against Chinese communism on ideological grounds, stated in the autumn of 1952 that the number of human beings executed by the Chinese communists, according to their own claims, was a million and a half.

Here is the record, necessarily summarized and sketchy, of communist terror in the Soviet Union and throughout the world. It is a record of cruelty and tyranny unmatched in history, whether measured by the number of victims, the length of time over which this regime of terror has extended or the moral degradation imposed alike on those who carry out and those who are subjected to such torture and oppression. It is a

* See article by Robert Guillain, correspondent in the Far East for *Le Monde,* in *Manchester Guardian Weekly,* of November 22, 1951.

measure of the moral and intellectual decay that has eaten into western civilization that a system responsible for such innumerable acts of cruelty should still find its apologists, even its eulogists, in free countries.

Perhaps it is inevitable that Soviet and communist terror should seem far away to Americans. The very number of the victims tends to blunt the feeling of sympathy, even of reality. One vivid story of individual human misery is perhaps better calculated to arouse emotional response than the general knowledge of the fate of millions of anonymous prisoners in Soviet slave labor camps or of the hundreds of thousands of Chinese who have been slaughtered in mass executions.

But we shall remain blind to the communist terror, deaf to the cries of its victims at our peril. This is an age of ominous moral callousness. There is a tendency almost to take for granted acts of mass cruelty which dwarf the Dreyfus and Beilis cases and other lesser crimes that shocked the conscience of a more sensitive time. Now it sometimes seems that murder ceases to be murder, if it is committed on a large enough scale. But that way lies a complete erosion of moral values which is certain to affect disastrously the quality of life and civilization in the western world.

From a purely nationalist standpoint America cannot be indifferent to the implications of the expanding communist empire. Every country that is taken over by Moscow-directed communists means automatically so many more divisions, so many more resources organized against the United States. China offers a vivid object lesson on this point. Oldfashioned conceptions of indifference to the "internal affairs" of foreign countries have become obsolete in this era of global civil war.

Even if the communist empire, built up and cemented by terror, should be "contained" at its present dimensions the consequence would be for America an indefinite continuation of the present burden of armaments, with a prospect of harassing "little wars." Should the expansion of this empire proceed, should further important areas of Europe and Asia be added, America could conceivably find itself outmatched in military potential, especially in manpower, and condemned to experience on its own soil the horror of communist invasion.

For communist hatred of the United States as the strongest champion of political and economic liberty is insatiable and implacable. It is in the light of the permanence of communist terror and of the reality of the communist threat that Americans should judge the necessity for sacrifices required to win the cold war and for measures designed to stamp out Soviet espionage, infiltration and fifth column activities.

Chapter IX ∽ The Weapon of Propaganda

The communist formula of rule, in the Soviet Union, and in countries outside the Soviet Union, may be summed up in a single phrase: unlimited terror plus unlimited propaganda. Under the word propaganda one should also understand intensive organization of the masses.

The subjects of Soviet and communist governments who are not convinced by the propaganda are intimidated by the terror. The combination is formidable. Many, especially of the younger people who know no other system and have no means of comparison, are molded into sincere sympathizers by the tremendous stream of propaganda which plays on them from the cradle to the grave.

Propaganda is also an extremely important adjunct of Soviet foreign policy. The masters of the Kremlin are disciples of the old maxim: *Divide et Impera,* Divide and Rule. Much of their success, first in conquering Russia, later in extending their domination to foreign lands, had been due to their skill in political jujitsu, in taking advantage of the weaknesses and divisions of their opponents. Adroit propaganda is an essential element in this political jujitsu.

When the communists took power in Russia by armed coup d'état in November, 1917, they were a small minority, although at the time they enjoyed the support of mass impulses for ending the war, for seizing the land, for overthrowing the old social order. They held power for years in an atmosphere of terrific suffering, they emerged victorious from a long civil war because they understood how to exploit the differences and antagonisms which existed among the noncommunist majority.

For instance, they promised the peasants "bread and land" and won the support of many peasants in the civil war by holding up the spectre of landlords returning and reclaiming the land which the peasants had seized. But when the Soviet Government was firmly established, with unlimited military and police power at its disposition, individual possession of land was abolished. The peasant's dream of an individual landholding ended in the nightmare of the collective farm, where the peasants all work for one all-powerful landlord, the state.

The communists also promised self-determination to the Ukrainians and other non-Russian peoples of the old Russian Empire. This was calculated to win the political sympathy of these peoples, because the principal anti-Bolshevik leaders, General Denikin and Admiral Kolchak, were straightforward Russian nationalists, unwilling to make concessions, even in words, to the non-Russian peoples.

But the contrast was only in words. The local "bourgeois nationalists" who trusted communist promises of self-determination, were liquidated as soon as circumstances permitted. The pre-revolutionary Great Russian hegemony has been more and more effectively restored in the Soviet Union.

The tactics of sowing dissension in the ranks of the enemy is part of the global strategy pursued by Lenin and Stalin. The purpose is to incite and exacerbate hostility and suspicion between noncommunist nations and between social and economic groups within nations.

The success of Soviet domestic propaganda is enhanced because it is the tightest kind of state monopoly. The measure of thought control which the Soviet regime exercises over its subjects is unique and unmatched. In contrast to the Tsarist regime, the Soviet authorities prescribe not only what may not be said, but what must be said. This distinction is significant. There are always loopholes in a negative censorship, means of writing "between the lines."

But when the state or the ruling party (in the Soviet Union the two are virtually identical) takes over every means of education, information and even recreation the dissenting voice cannot utter even a faint whisper. One could not legally call for the overthrow of the Tsar before the Revolution. But the great Russian authors of the nineteenth century, Tolstoy, Dostoevsky, Turgenev, Gogol, Chekhov, were not required to write eulogies of the Imperial regime. Indeed, in their realistic novels they often convey pictures of human and social relations which are not flattering to that regime.

No such relative freedom of the mind exists in the Soviet Union. It is not enough for the Soviet author to abstain from direct political criticism. He must develop unbounded enthusiasm for the character and achievements of the "new Soviet man." In Stalin's phrase he must be an "engineer of souls."

This state monopoly exists in every field of cultural life. One of the first acts of the Soviet Government was to close and forbid all private schools. From the kindergarten to the university education is under close state control. Press and radio, theatres and moving pictures are all pressed into the service of indoctrination.

What are the principal objects of this indoctrination? High among these objects, until Stalin's death, was the cultivation of an attitude of worshipful adulation of the Soviet dictator. He was represented as a figure of unique wisdom, genius and benevolence, to whom all Soviet citizens and "progressive people" throughout the world owe devotion. The most frequent frontpage Soviet newspaper feature, until March, 1953, was a tribute to Stalin, signed by a group of local officials, by the workers of a factory, the peasants of a collective farm, or some other group, promising to work harder as a proof of their loyalty.

Typical are two communications published on the first page of *Pravda* on October 26, 1951. One, signed by various officials of the Krasnoyarsk district of Siberia, begins and ends as follows:

> We are glad to report to you, dear Josef Vissarionovich, that, thanks to the enormous help which the Party, the Government and you personally, Comrade Stalin, have rendered, the collective farmers, workers of the machine tractor stations and Soviet farms and the agricultural specialists of Krasnoyarsk district, in the unfavorable weather conditions of the last year, raised a good harvest and completely fulfilled the state plan of grain procurements ahead of time, as in past years. . . .
>
> With all our hearts we wish you, our own beloved Josef Vissarionovich, good health and long, long years of life to the joy and fortune of the Soviet people and the toilers of the whole world.

The other message is from the officials of the Kalinin (former Tver) district and is practically a duplicate, except that in this case pride is expressed in deliveries of flax, the principal crop of the region.

One of the main purposes of the one-party Soviet election, if one may judge from the Soviet press, has been to glorify Stalin. *Pravda,* official organ of the Communist Party, on February 18, 1951, day of a national election, predicted with well justified assurance that "the Soviet people will give their votes for the great, their own Stalin" and ends a three column editorial with the slogan:

"Long live the great leader and teacher of the Communist Party and the Soviet people, our own Comrade Stalin."

There was apparently not only unanimous, but plural voting in the Kirov district of Leningrad, where Stalin was the candidate. Not only did every qualified voter in the district turn out, but 29,782 additional voters stormed the ballot-boxes, coming from other parts of the city to enjoy the pleasure of voting for Stalin.

Every Soviet anniversary has been an occasion for outbursts of eulogy of Stalin. *Pravda* on Red Army day, on February 23, 1951, published a very large portrait of Stalin and very small portraits of the Ministers of the Army and Navy, Marshal Vasilievsky and Admiral Yumashev. There was a message from Vasilievsky:

"Long live the inspirer and organizer of the victories of the Soviet Union and its armed forces, our great leader and teacher, the genius commander, Comrade Stalin."

Admiral Yumashev chimed in with an appeal ending:

"Long live our beloved leader and teacher, the great Stalin."

This exaltation of Stalin extends beyond the Soviet frontiers. A Polish newspaper calls him "the leader of the Soviet people, leader of the world camp of peace, leader of progressive humanity." A Bulgarian newspaper displays the headline: "Stalin shows the peoples the way to salvation."

This organized idolatry of Stalin went on for almost a quarter of a century until his death. He was represented as omniscient in every field, from military strategy and economics to philosophy and philology. Standard expressions of adulation were "the great engineer," "the great pilot," "the great architect," "the great master," "the greatest of the great."

The death of Stalin on March 5, 1953, plunged the world into a furore of speculation as to its consequences. Would the gap left by the passing of this personality, built up to an image of almost divine providence, prove a psychological cause of future political crisis? Or would it be possible for the communist machinery of government to continue functioning smoothly and in time, perhaps, to produce a new "infallible" leader? It is too soon to answer this question with certainty.

And, because of the complete blackout of opportunities for independent observation, there may never be a certain answer to another interesting question. How far did this tremendous effort to make out of Stalin a national idol succeed in capturing the minds and hearts of the Soviet peoples? Quite probably many young communists conceived for the image of Stalin in the Kremlin the same vague passionate enthusiasm which Nikolai Rostov in Tolstoy's *War and Peace* feels for Tsar Alexander I.

The adulation of Stalin was a carry-over, in much exaggerated form, of the traditional glorification of the Tsar, just as the preservation of Lenin's embalmed body * was a concession to the Russian tradition of venerating relics. Communists in some cases replaced the traditional ikon corner with a "Lenin corner," filled with pictures and memorials of Lenin.

However, it is doubtful whether the victims of the sweeping Soviet terrorist measures were at heart enthusiastic for Stalin, in life or death; and this is probably also true as regards members of their families and their friends. Perhaps the best commentary on the hopelessness of assessing the real popularity of a dictator is furnished by an anecdote, which I have heard told of Stalin in Moscow, of Hitler in Germany.

The dictator, according to this apocryphal story, goes to a moving picture theatre incognito, in search of recreation. His picture is thrown on the screen and the whole audience stands up applauding furiously. The dictator modestly remains seated, whereupon the man in the next seat leans over and whispers: "A good many of us feel just as you do. But . . . it would be much safer for you to stand up and join in the applause."

It is one of the obligations of the communist party member to be a missionary to the heathen among the noncommunists with whom he works in factory, shop or office. He is supposed to explain the government decisions, according to instructions which he receives from higher party authorities, to explain

* According to Stalin's nephew, Budu Svanidze, Lenin's body began to decompose during the war and was secretly cremated, being replaced by a replica. See Budu Svanidze, *My Uncle Joseph Stalin* (Putnam), pp. 187–89.

why this or that sacrifice is necessary, to keep up with every new trend of Kremlin foreign policy and to denounce whatever "foreign imperialists" may be most in disfavor.

Almost thirty years ago I had an opportunity to see this communist propaganda mill in action. A local communist was addressing a meeting of Ukrainian peasants on the international situation. The Dawes Plan was in the news and a member of the audience asked the speaker: Who is Dawes? The reply was prompt.

"Dawes is the chief bandit who is robbing the German railways."

As the Ukraine during the civil war had been a theatre of operations for many bandits who specialized in train robberies, this image was comprehensible to the peasants, if not strictly accurate. The speaker was a little stumped by another question: "How much profit have the imperialists pumped out of China?" However, he found a way out by declaring: "So much that it would be impossible to count it all."

Propaganda in the first years of the Soviet rule was on a hit-or-miss basis. Now it has been streamlined and organized. A special publication, *Bloknot Agitatora* ("The Agitator's Notebook") offers helpful hints to communist speakers as to what they should say on every imaginable subject, from the machinations of Uncle Sam to some time-saving device in the factory.

Teaching in the schools is designed to condition the minds of the children, from the youngest age groups, to such ideas as the greatness and benevolence of Stalin, the superiority of the Soviet system to every other in the world and the darkness and misery which are supposed to prevail in capitalist countries. I once visited a Soviet school where the pupils were convinced that children in "bourgeois" countries could not go to school unless their parents were rich.

The work of the school is supplemented by two mass youth organizations, the Young Pioneers for younger children and the Union of Communist Youth for young people between the ages of sixteen and twenty-three. Here they become accustomed to marching with banners, singing Soviet songs, repeating Soviet slogans, taking part in civic improvement campaigns, etc. Young Communists are "mobilized" for emergency work in mines, forests and fields and are supposed to be models of industry at their jobs or in their studies.

The aims of Soviet propaganda are clearly reflected in newspapers and periodicals. All opposition newspapers in the Soviet Union disappeared very soon after the establishment of the Soviet Government. There are differences of function among Soviet newspapers, with special organs for the Union of Communist Youth, Red Army, trade-unions, etc. But there is absolute conformity as to the presentation of news and editorial policy. All newspapers are closely coordinated by the press department of the Communist Party Central Committee.

There is a chronic shortage of paper in the Soviet Union. Such leading daily newspapers as *Izvestia* ("News"), voice of the government, and *Pravda* ("Truth"), voice of the Communist Party, are restricted to four large pages. Many features which are believed to attract reader interest in other countries are absent in the Soviet press. One would look in vain for household hints, fashion or society articles, personality stories, literary and musical criticism (except in special publications, such as *Literaturnaya Gazeta*) ("The Literary News"), stock exchange quotations, signed columns of independent opinion, rotogravure supplements and comic strips. There are almost no advertisements, apart from announcements of theatre and radio programs.

On the other hand, in the limited available space much attention is devoted to industrial and agricultural development, to descriptions of new factories and canals. A few random issues of *Pravda* show how the government tries to mold and direct the thinking of the people through the newspapers.

In the issue of August 9, 1951, a two column editorial on the first page describes Soviet policy as animated by a desire for peace. There is a reference to "millionaires who want wars for super-profits" and the "ruling circles of the United States" are accused of trying to unleash such a war. There are also on the front page two adulatory messages to Stalin from local communist bosses in the Ukraine and the North Caucasus, an account of how the harvest is proceeding, some favorable items about developments in "the countries of people's democracy" (the Soviet satellite states) and pictures of seven persons who won the Stalin Prize for various achievements.

The last page is given over to foreign news, headed by a report that "monopolies are robbing the American toilers." The two inside pages contain news reports from within the Soviet Union, with a predominant emphasis on industry and agriculture. There are also a few stray items about events abroad, with special reference to a communist-organized youth festival in East Berlin and to a long article under the title: "Militarization of the economy and robbing of the toilers in the countries of capital."

Neither in this nor in any other issue of *Pravda* is there any intimation that intensive military build-up tends to lower the standard of living in the Soviet Union and in the satellite states.

Pravda of February 6, 1951, includes the following contents. The front page two column editorial is entitled "The Will of the Peaceloving Peoples." This is a diatribe against "American imperialists who feverishly excite war hysteria." There is the standard column about economic progress in "the people's democracies." The rest of the page is devoted to inspirational stories about Soviet sailors who have improved the speed of their cruise, Baku oil workers who are increasing output and a report from Ashkabad, a town on the frontier of Iran, to the effect that "the news that Comrade Stalin has consented to be voted on as a deputy to the Supreme Council of the Turkmenistan Soviet Republic has inspired the workers of Turkmenistan to new productive successes." The longest article on page 4 describes the annual conference of the Society of Anglo-Soviet Friendship in London. The secretary of this Society, one William Wainwright, is quoted as saying that "the press, the British Broadcasting Corporation and other agencies are exploited for the fabrication of lying distortions about life in the Soviet Union and Soviet intentions."

However, the Society had intensified its work. Its members appeared as speakers at 665 public meetings, held in more than 50 cities. 106 Soviet films were shown. Conferences for peace, trade and friendship with the Soviet Union were held in various parts of the country. Wainwright, according to *Pravda,* "exposed the anti-Soviet lies and slanders, circulated by Attlee, Morrison, Morgan Phillips and other leaders of the Labor Party."

One finds no reports in Soviet newspapers of a Society of Soviet-British Friendship, functioning in the Soviet Union and exposing "anti-British lies and slanders."

Another long article on the fourth page is headlined "United States—Country of the Aggressive Dictatorship of Big Monopolistic Capital." There are several shorter news despatches, one datelined "North Korea" and purporting to describe "crimes of the American interventionists." The despatch represents American troops as burning alive, burying alive and inflicting indescribable tortures on "1580 Korean patriots, including many women, children and old men." This is a small item in a gigantic "Hate America" campaign, designed to convince the Soviet peoples that Americans are more barbarous than the Nazis.

A despatch from New York described the execution of seven Negroes in Martinsville, Virginia. There was no indication in the despatch that the Negroes had been tried and convicted of a capital offense.

The small, pocket size *Agitator's Notebook* gives an even more concentrated dose of propaganda than the daily newspapers. The word agitator suggests someone stirring up the "underprivileged" to demand their "privileges," or rights. And the Russian communist "agitator" of pre-revolutionary times played up grievances, stirred up strikes and created as much trouble as possible for the existing order.

But this is not the aim of the Soviet "agitator" today. His job is to uphold the new communist ruling class, to give the workers inspirational talks on the need for better and harder work and to confine his hostile "agitation" to the crimes of foreign imperialists.

An agitator named Grigoriev put to the editors the question: "What is *bizness* (business)?" The reply, published in *Agitator's Notebook No. 18,* for June, 1952, strikes all the familiar chords of anti-American propaganda:

> American billionaires and millionaires profit by the exploitation, ruin and impoverishment of the population of the United States, by the enslavement and systematic robbing of the peoples of other countries, by militarizing the economy, which is exploited to guaranty the highest profit. The toilers of the United States suffer from steady rise in the cost of living, from an unbearable tax burden, from unemployment, hunger and poverty. Even according to colored official data, the average annual income of workers and employees in the United States does not reach 70% of the miserable living minimum.

Agitator Grigoriev is also informed that elections in America are turned into "business," with votes being bought and sold. Banditry is also a flourishing brand of "business" and the briefing on American conditions ends with this blast:

> Even medical aid is turned into business in the United States. It is so expensive as to be inaccessible to the overwhelming majority of the population. Moving pictures, press and radio bring enormous profits to American monopolies. These agencies are exploited to stir up war hysteria, to infect the consciousness of millions of Americans with the poison of chauvinism and militarism, the poison of anti-Soviet slander.

Agitator's Notebook does not concentrate exclusively on anti-American material. It supplies information about industrial building in the Soviet Union and in the satellite states, pleas for economy in raw material in Soviet industries, exhortations for "strict labor discipline," for a model harvest of vegetables and potatoes and an occasional exposition of government policy on some international issue, such as the unification of Germany. There are articles, meant for country communists, about the necessity for strictly observing the collective farm constitution. The desire of the peasants to do as much work as possible on their small individual garden plots and as little work as possible for the collective farm is a constant thorn in the side of the Soviet authorities.

Soviet propaganda has always been anticapitalist. It has tried to persuade the Soviet peoples that they are advancing toward a glorious and happy future and that, even in the present, their hardships are nothing compared with what workers suffer at the hands of "capitalist exploiters." During the twenties and thirties America came off fairly well, among the capitalist nations, in Soviet comment. It was accepted Soviet dogma that, although the American people were still suffering from the oppression of the capitalists, America possessed a modern industrial capacity which the Soviet Union should acquire and use for socialist purposes.

"To overtake and outstrip America" became a widely circulated official slogan during the First Five Year Plan (1929–1933). And this led to the satirical story of a Soviet citizen who came up to a communist leader and put in a timid request: "When we come to America please let me off. I don't want to go any farther."

During the war years, when American lend-lease supplies were pouring into the Soviet Union, an attitude of "correct" formal friendship was prescribed for Soviet publications. There was no parallel in the Soviet Union for the uncritical demonstrations of enthusiasm for the Soviet Union in the United States at that time.

As the cold war became hotter anti-American propaganda became more intense and less discriminating. It was no longer directed merely against "American capitalists." There was a systematic effort to stir up hatred for the entire American people, especially by the repetition of atrocity stories about the behavior of American troops in Korea.

There is also a consistent attempt to represent the United States as a land of wealth for the few and misery for the many. *Agitator's Notebook, No. 2,* for January, 1949, cites the following speech in a Soviet factory:

> Not long ago I read several articles on the life of American workers. Gloomy pictures of capitalist realities appear before one's eyes. Unemployment is increasing constantly in the United States. Wages are being cut and prices are rising and the standard of living of the toilers is deteriorating.

Secure in the knowledge that there will be no criticism and that very few Soviet workers have ever been in the United States, the Soviet propagandists make no attempt to tell a plausibly consistent story. They represent the hapless American worker as suffering simultaneously from the ills of inflation (high cost of living) and deflation (unemployment). The marked improvement in the real wages of industrial workers and the income of the farmers during the decade 1940–1950 is never mentioned, or even hinted at. Wages are always going down, unemployment is always increasing.

Soviet anti-American attacks fall into two categories, pure fantasies and criticisms allegedly based on American sources, which, however, are usually quoted out of context and background. An example of the first category is the Soviet radio report that in New York there is a dog named Toby, who sleeps on a golden bed, attended by a staff of forty-five servants and six lawyers, heir to a fortune of 75 million dollars.

Communist newspapers in the satellite countries several years ago played up a story that the moving picture actor, Buster Crabbe, had been assassinated because of his devotion to the cause of the proletariat and that Gary Cooper and other well-known Hollywood actors had acted as pallbearers. Buster Crabbe's insistence, when the story was called to his attention, that the report of his death had been much exaggerated did not penetrate behind the iron curtain.

A less lurid form of propaganda, probably designed for the Soviet educated classes, is fortified with references to American facts and figures. So the statement is put out that less than one per cent of the United States federal budget is spent on education. There is no mention of the circumstance that education is a state, not a federal responsibility in America.

In recent years two variations in the pattern of Soviet anti-American propaganda may be noted. The former recognition of American superiority in invention and technology is being withdrawn. Now Russians, mostly unknown to history, are being given credit for almost every scientific discovery and invention, from the electric light bulb to the airplane, even including the game of baseball. Incidentally the Russian game, *lapti,* from which baseball was supposedly plagiarized, has more points of resemblance to cricket, but has little real likeness to either of these western sports.

There has also been a crackdown on the would-be fellow-traveler. Before the war some favors were shown to noncommunist Americans who showed consistent sympathy with the Soviet regime. But during the cold war the general rule in Soviet publications has been to attack all Americans who are not authentic party members, even individuals who have bent over backward to give the Soviet Union the benefit of every doubt.

This policy reached an ironical climax in 1949, when Anna Louise Strong, indefatigable apologist and propagandist for the Soviet Union over a period of three decades, was suddenly arrested in Moscow, thrown into the dreaded Lubyanka, scared almost out of her wits (to judge from her own account of the episode) by being put through the usual Soviet prison examination and finally expelled from the Soviet Union as "an American spy." In view of her constant avoidance in her writings of the less pleasant aspects of Soviet life there was an element of poetic justice in this end of her career in Russia.

Soviet propaganda style is self-assured, dogmatic, violent and abusive. Issues are always presented in black and white terms, with no grey areas of doubt. The cold war is waged with full fervor, even in a standard work of reference, such as the *Soviet Encyclopedia*. A new edition of that work contains the following definitions and descriptions, as translated by Mr. Harry Schwartz and published in *The New York Times* of August 5, 1951:

ACHESON, DEAN GOODERHAM . . . Reactionary state official of the United States. . . . One of the chief inspirers of the armed American intervention against the Korean people in June, 1950. Carries on the preparation of war against the Soviet Union.

ASSOCIATED PRESS . . . A United States information agency which is the mouthpiece for the magnates of American financial capital.

AMERICAN FEDERATION OF LABOR . . . American trade-union organization, uniting primarily the trade-union aristocracy and headed by a bought clique of reactionary leaders, the agents of imperialism in the labor movement of the United States.

ABSTRACT ART . . . One of the reflections of the reactionary ideology of the imperialist bourgeoisie, primarily the Americans, directed against realistic and democratic traditions in art.

While excellent presentations of classical Russian and foreign plays are given in the Soviet Union, the theatre, so far as it deals with contemporary life, has been harnessed to the propaganda juggernaut. Before the war the stock theme of the Soviet dramatist was the building of a new factory or power plant or the organization of a collective farm. The villains would be reactionary engineers, kulaks, priests who would try to throw monkey-wrenches into the operation. Their schemes would always be detected in time. And in the end the plant would be set in motion ahead of scheduled time and a foreign engineer (usually an American in those days) would assure the workers that no such speed would be possible in capitalist countries.

Now the anti-American play holds the centre of the Soviet stage. The pioneer in this field was Konstantin Simonov's *The Russian Question,* produced in 1947 and given in hundreds of Soviet theatres. The plot is based on the fate of an American newspaperman who refuses to carry out orders of his reactionary employer to go to Russia and collect material showing that the Soviet Government is plotting war against the United States. There have been many variants on this theme by other Soviet playwrights. The American newspaperman is depicted either as a scoundrel who can be hired to write anything or as a helpless victim in the clutches of the capitalist system. The American Army officer is a fascist sympathizer who does a black market business on the side.

So far as the Soviet police system can insure this, Soviet propaganda at home is exposed to no counterbalancing criticism. Soviet citizens are strictly isolated from contacts with the few foreigners who are permitted to live in the Soviet Union. These foreigners, including diplomats, are kept under conditions of constant police surveillance which are unprecedented in the history of relations between civilized states.

George F. Kennan, one of America's leading foreign service experts, after serving for a few months as Ambassador to the Soviet Union, remarked that, except for actual confinement, the status of foreign diplomats in Moscow reminded him of his internment under the German Nazi regime during the war. The Soviet Government made this remark an occasion for declaring Kennan persona non grata and excluding him from the Soviet Union. Its accuracy, however, is confirmed by the testimony of many other diplomats and journalists.

No foreign noncommunist newspapers may be bought in Moscow. Very few Soviet citizens, only those who are regarded as politically highly reliable, may subscribe for such newspapers or purchase from abroad books and magazines dealing with contemporary politics and economics.

This Soviet insulation is a onesided affair. While every precaution is taken to see that Soviet citizens are not contaminated by any taint of "bourgeois" influence from abroad Soviet propaganda floods the noncommunist world. Radio Moscow beams programs in English and other foreign languages to almost all countries. (The Soviet Government goes to considerable expense and trouble to jam the broadcasts in Russian of the Voice of America and other foreign stations.)

The principal organ of Soviet propaganda abroad is *New Times,* a weekly magazine published in English and several other foreign languages. *New Times* lists some forty main distribution centres in Europe, Asia, the Americas, Africa and Australia. As in the case of propaganda designed for home consumption, *New Times* presents every issue in very black-and-white colors.

Favorite subjects in this publication are the peaceloving aims of Soviet diplomacy, alleged social and economic achievements in the Soviet Union, the satellite states and China and American atrocities in Korea, along with the general decadence of the American system. Typical of the sense of contrast which is constantly hammered in is the following pronouncement in *New Times* on the difference between Soviet and "bourgeois" artistic and literary production:

> A high standard of craftsmanship, vigor, optimism and buoyancy are [sic] typical features of Soviet realist art, which is distinguished for its profound kinship with the people. What a glaring contrast to all this is presented by the sombre spectacle of decadent, morbid bourgeois art, with its disbelief in the human being and its tedious preachment of doom.

It is impossible to say with certainty whether the United States or the Soviet Union spends more money on propaganda abroad. Soviet operations in this and other fields are shrouded in secrecy. But the Soviet Union enjoys one conspicuous advantage. In the foreign communist parties it possesses ready-made channels for aiding and promoting propaganda. These parties themselves sponsor publications which present the Soviet side of every international issue and carry out an enormous amount of pro-Soviet agitation through demonstrations, poster displays, etc.

One of the important instruments of Moscow's international campaign of favorable publicity is the existence, under the direction and influence of the local communist parties, of a multitude of "front" organizations. Formally these are not affiliated with communism. In practice they follow the "party line" faithfully on all important issues. Even in the United States, where the Communist Party is weak, scores of such organizations have been identified and classified as subversive by the Attorney-General's office.

These organizations specialize in the use of such words as "free," "democratic" and "progressive." Some of them, such as the Women's International Democratic Federation and the World Federation of Democratic Youth, claim a total combined membership of more than 150 million. Much the greatest part of this membership is in countries behind the iron curtain and may be considered to a large degree compulsory and nominal.

The larger communist-dominated international organizations hold periodic international demonstrations, such as the "youth festival," sponsored by the World Federation of Democratic Youth, in Berlin in August, 1951. The surest identification tag of a communist front organization is the adoption of resolutions which closely parallel the Soviet Government's proposals in international affairs.

Communist tactics since the war have not set the violent overthrow of existing governments as an immediate aim, although para-military former partisan groups with communist sympathies have been kept up to some extent in Italy and in France. Foreign communist parties have served as advance guards for promoting the ends of Soviet foreign policy; the requirements of the Kremlin always take precedence over the immediate interests of the national communist parties, which are expected to make swift switches at a word or a hint from Moscow. A striking example of this was the scrapping of anti-Nazi agitation, previously a trump card of communist propaganda, as soon as Stalin signed his pact with Hitler in August, 1939. Maurice Thorez, for the French Communist Party, Palmiro Togliatti, for the Italian Communist Party, and other national communist leaders have publicly announced that under no circumstances would they or their followers fight against the Soviet Union. These are advance assurances of treason and fifth column activity if the Red Army should sweep westward in Europe.

International communist propaganda follows a standardized groove. It emphasizes support of peace, anti-Americanism, solidarity with the Soviet Union, Red China and the "people's democracies" of Eastern Europe. The typical communist front resolution calls for denunciation of the North Atlantic Pact, withdrawal of American troops from Europe, Korea and the Far East, denounces the rearming of Germany and Japan and suggests better uses to which funds appropriated for armaments could be put. Communist "pacifism" is strictly unilateral. It demands disarmament only for noncommunist countries.

Communist propaganda is tailored to the needs of individual countries. While French communists were told to harp on the dangers of German rearmament, German communists have been instructed to emphasize the idea that the Soviet Union wants a strong unified Germany, while the western powers wish to divide Germany permanently. The French communist position on German rearmament was somewhat shaken when the Soviet Government itself in 1952 came out in favor of a German national army. But communist parties are taught to consider themselves expendable whenever the higher interests of the Kremlin require a sacrifice.

There has been a strenuous, concerted effort to present Soviet propaganda in the attractive disguise of concern for peace. Following congresses in Stockholm and Warsaw, with communists pulling all the strings, a World Peace Council was set up and held its first congress in Berlin in February, 1951. This body advocated legislation against war propaganda and recommended the setting up of national committees, wherever possible, "to denounce and boycott all publications, schoolbooks, films, radio broadcasts, etc., which contain any incitement to war" and "to launch a great campaign of enlightenment in which thousands of men of goodwill in each country will ceaselessly expose the falsehoods that aid the preparation of war."

This wording seemed designed to appeal to genuine pacifist sentiment. But a full report of the proceedings of the congress clearly reveals its communist background and inspiration. All the speakers took for granted that South Korea and the United States started the fighting in Korea. Said Metropolitan Nikolai, a high dignitary in the Orthodox Church of the Soviet Union:

> From the very first day of their aggression in Korea the American neo-Fascists proceeded systematically and ruthlessly to destroy the Korean nation. The horrible atrocities, the barbaric bombings of peaceful towns and communities, were undertaken for the sole purpose of wiping out the civilian population. Investigation has proved that the American troops are applying Himmler's technique of inhuman torture to the Korean patriots.

This "spiritual" address could have been and may have been copied verbatim from a "Hate America" editorial in the atheistic *Pravda*. Similar anti-American atrocity stories fill a report drawn up by a women's commission which went to North Korea under the auspices of the Women's International Democratic Federation:

> The people of Korea are being subjected by the American occupiers to a merciless and methodical campaign of extermination. In the districts temporarily occupied by American and Syngman Rhee forces, in the period of occupation, hundreds of thousands of civilians, entire families, from old men to little chil-

dren, have been tortured, beaten to death, burned and buried alive. These mass tortures and mass murders surpass the crimes committed by Hitler's Nazis in temporarily occupied Europe.

Although this was supposed to be the report of an international independent commission the Soviet style of invective reporting of the Korean war is copied even down to such a detail as the designation of the South Korean Army as "Syngman Rhee forces."

How effective is communist propaganda, at home and abroad? There can be no sure answer, especially as regards its effect on the peoples of the Soviet Union. For the tests which can be applied to the state of public opinion in a free country are impossible under a dictatorship. There are no free elections, no public opinion polls. No matter how fluent he may be in the Russian language, a foreigner, under present conditions, cannot hope to get on sufficiently intimate terms with enough Soviet citizens to assure himself whether and how far they believe the ideas which are drilled into them by so many agencies at the disposal of the government.

Soviet involvement in the late war provided the only real test of the attitude of the peoples under Soviet rule. The results of this test were somewhat contradictory. Huge Soviet armies fought stubbornly and courageously, engaged and finally defeated the larger part of Hitler's ground forces.

On the other hand, there were massive surrenders of Soviet troops to the Germans in the first months of the war. Far from having "no fifth column," as was loosely stated during the one-sided American–Soviet honeymoon, the Soviet Union provided more recruits for the German armed forces than all the other invaded and occupied countries put together. The unwillingness of hundreds of thousands of former Soviet war prisoners and laborers in Germany and Austria to return home after the end of the war is an indisputable fact, quite unmatched in the experience of citizens of any free country.

There are two extreme views about the mood of the Soviet

peoples. There is the view that they are all enthusiastic for the existing regime. There is the view that discontent is smoldering to such a degree that a few slick experiments in western propaganda could kindle a flame of revolt. These views are probably equally wide of the mark.

It would be a negation of human nature if there were not a good many secretly embittered people because of the tremendous suffering inflicted by Soviet mass terrorist repression. On the other hand the very scale and intensity of this repression make it impossible to maintain in existence any large, well-organized underground movement. There are seeds of disaffection in the Soviet Union, as the last war showed. But these seeds are only likely to sprout if the Soviet dictatorship experiences a severe crisis. This crisis might be a product of several causes: military or diplomatic reverses, some new acute economic distress or a falling out among Stalin's political heirs and successors.

It is easier to weigh and measure the impact of Soviet propaganda in countries outside the iron curtain, where observation is unrestricted. This impact was strongest in the years immediately after the end of the war, when the communists possessed the prestige of having the best organized resistance groups, and wartime destruction and economic chaos created an atmosphere favorable to radical change.

During recent years the communist wave in Europe outside the iron curtain has receded. This is reflected in improved living conditions and in the results of parliamentary and trade-union elections. The communists are still a numerous fifth column in France and Italy. But even in these countries they are no longer able to organize effective political strikes, much less to resort to armed revolt with any prospect of success.

How far the constant repetition, through many channels, of the communist propaganda themes, class division, class war, and the supposed design of the United States to use the peoples of Europe as pawns in aggressive war schemes, has undermined the national unity and social cohesion of the peoples outside the iron curtain cannot be established with certainty. Perhaps only another war would supply a final, convincing answer to this question, as also to the question how much disaffection exists behind the iron curtain.

Chapter X ～ Authority

Unlimited

The Soviet communist system, the most tremendous and formidable tyranny ever erected over the minds and bodies of men, is no sudden historical accident. It is the product of two forces, one very old, the other comparatively new.

The first of these forces is the Tsarist absolutism. The second is the doctrine of Karl Marx, as sharpened and elaborated by the leader of the Bolshevik Revolution, Vladimir Ilyitch Lenin. At first sight Tsarism and communism may seem to be at opposite poles. But no one who is familiar both with Russian history and with Soviet political practice can easily fail to notice the many ironical parallels between the Tsarist and the Soviet states. These parallels become more striking and impressive as one goes farther back into the Russian past, from the somewhat westernized and liberalized administration of the last Tsars to the fullblooded autocracy of Ivan the Terrible, Peter the Great and Nicholas I.

Political absolutism is the common element in Tsarism and Soviet communism. In the empire of the Tsars, as in the Soviet Union, there is no check or limit on the power of the executive. Law is what the Tsar or the dictator says it is. The only views which find expression are those of the government. The individual has no right which the government is bound and required to respect. The Russian Tsar, who after the time of Peter the Great was also head of the Orthodox Church, possessed a semi-divine authority. He was Caesar and Pope in one. Lenin and Stalin and Malenkov, as Marxists, deny that there is any divine authority. The consequences are much the same. There is assumed to be no higher law by which the acts of Tsar or dictator may be judged.

The likenesses between Tsarist rule in the sixteenth, seventeenth and eighteenth centuries and Soviet rule today may be found in great things as in small. The risks of being a Russian subject were and are abnormally great. The figures of executions, imprisonments and sentences of exile were and are abnormally high. If St. Petersburg, the new European capital of which Peter the Great was so proud, was almost literally built on the bones of serfs impressed for forced labor, this same observation is true as regards many of the "industrial giants" of which the Soviet rulers love to boast.

If one reads the *Russian History* of the most brilliant, sensitive and imaginative of Russian historians, V. O. Kluchevsky,* one is impressed again and again by the consciousness that one is reading not only an account of the past, but a prophecy of the future. Kluchevsky died before the Revolution, so that there is not even an unconscious element of satire on Soviet conditions in such passages as the following:

> Espionage became the most encouraged state service; everyone who seemed dangerous or inconvenient was eliminated from society. Many were banished altogether under [the Empress] Anne; more than 20,000 were banished to Siberia; and it is impossible to find a trace of where 5,000 of these were sent.

Kluchevsky was writing of the reign of the Empress Anne, in the first half of the eighteenth century. Multiply his figures

---

* Unfortunately Kluchevsky's historical masterpiece, beautifully written in Russian, is almost unreadable in the only available clumsy and inept English translation.

many, many times and there is a preview of Russia two hundred years later, under the "dictatorship of the proletariat."

Kluchevsky was writing of the Muscovite state of the seventeenth century when, after a long list of invasions, raids, fires, wars and other calamities, he observes:

> Thus developed the Muscovite state. Now we can scarcely understand and still less feel what sacrifices its creation cost the people's welfare, how it pressed upon private existence.

Perhaps this was true for Russia in Kluchevsky's comparatively liberal age. But the more intelligent members of the Soviet generation that experienced revolution, civil war, two great famines, the German invasion and innumerable purges and "liquidations" might well sympathize with their Muscovite ancestors. And Kluchevsky, a scholar with a nineteenth century liberal outlook, composed a suitable epitaph for the future totalitarian society when he wrote of seventeenth century Russia:

"The state swelled and the people shrank."

One should, of course, view the Russian past in terms of conditions which prevailed in other European countries. But foreigners who visited the courts of Ivan the Terrible and other Tsars (there were not many of them; the foreigner, then and now, was an object of profound suspicion) received an impression of an oriental despotism, far exceeding anything they knew in their own countries, strange and shocking. Giles Fletcher, English Ambassador at the time of Ivan the Terrible, observes: "Their method of government is very similar to the Turkish, which they apparently try to imitate. Their government is purely tyrannical; all its activities are directed to the advantage and profit of the Tsar alone, and moreover in the most clear and barbarous fashion." The Austrian Imperial envoy, Baron Sigismund von Herberstein, one of the most widely traveled observers in sixteenth century Russia, reached the conclusion:

It is uncertain whether the roughness of the people demands a tyrant-ruler or whether the people became so rough and cruel as a result of the tyranny of the rulers.

The French Marquis de Custine, who visited Russia in 1839, was profoundly oppressed by the sense of crushing tyranny. And Custine's lively reactions, set down in a long diary, are more than the negative reaction of a conservative Frenchman to the absolutism of Nicholas I. They are an unconscious mirror of what Russia would be a century later under Soviet rule. So he writes:

> The diplomatic corps and westerners in general have always been considered by this government, with its Byzantine spirit, and by Russia as a whole as malevolent and jealous spies.

It is not surprising that Custine's Journals became the favorite reading of American Ambassador Walter Bedell Smith and members of his staff.* Custine sensed in the Russians an inordinate boundless ambition, as a sort of compensation for the oppression which they suffered. "The kneeling slave," as the French observer puts it, "dreams of world domination." The design which Custine attributes to Tsar Nicholas I, of conquering Europe through its own dissensions is remarkably similar to Stalin's last published blueprint on foreign policy, in which he hopefully predicts that war will break out among the capitalist nations, not between the Soviet Union and these nations.

"Russia," writes Custine, "sees Europe as a prey which our dissensions will sooner or later deliver up to her; she foments anarchy among us in the hope of profiting by a corruption she promotes because it is favorable to her views."

"What did man do to God," Custine bursts out, "that He condemned sixty million people to live in Russia?" And the French aristocrat's final conclusion was as emphatic as that of

* Phyllis Penn Kohler, wife of one of the Embassy officials, prepared an abridged translation of the Custine Journals, entitled *Journey for Our Time* (Pellegrini and Cudahy).

many ex-communists who have been "re-educated," to borrow a
favorite communist word, by contact with Soviet realities:

> It is necessary to have lived in this solitude without rest, in
> this prison without leisure, that is called Russia in order to be
> conscious of all the freedom one enjoys in the other countries of
> Europe,—whatever form of government they may have adopted.

Another unconscious prophet of the shape of things in the
Soviet Union was Neill Brown, American Minister to Russia
during the reign of Nicholas I, who reported as follows in a
despatch of January 28, 1852:

> The position of a Minister here is far from being pleasant.
> The opinion prevails that no communication, at least of a pub-
> lic nature, is safe in the post-office, but is opened and inspected
> as a matter of course. Hence those legations that can afford it
> maintain regular couriers and never send anything by mail. The
> opinion also prevails that Ministers are constantly subjected to a
> system of espionage, and that even their servants are made to
> disclose what passed in their households, their conversations, as-
> sociations, etc. . . . Secrecy and mystery characterize everything.
> You will find no two individuals agreeing in the strength of the
> army and navy, in the amount of the public debt, or the annual
> revenue. In my opinion it is not intended by the Government
> that these things should be known.

Ambassador Smith was so impressed by the likeness to conditions which he encountered almost a century after Neill
Brown penned this despatch that he inserted it as a quotation
at the beginning of a chapter of his Russian memoirs entitled
"Foreigners in Moscow." *

The criticism of one of Smith's successors, George Kennan,
has been mentioned in the preceding chapter. There is certainly no precedent in the history of intercourse between civilized nations for the hostile and humiliating treatment which is
meted out to noncommunist foreign diplomats in Moscow.
The foreign diplomat is ostentatiously spied on by agents of

* Walter Bedell Smith, *My Three Years in Moscow* (Lippincott), p. 85.

the political police and followed closely, wherever he may go. He is allowed to travel only in restricted areas, and always under the same kind of surveillance. Apart from a narrow circle of officials designated for association with foreigners he is allowed no Russian friends. A personal friend who spent two years in the American Embassy in Moscow after the war told me that he and his wife never met Russians except at a few official receptions. The penalties for visiting foreign embassies and consorting with foreigners are well known to Soviet citizens. At best unpleasant interrogation by the political police; at worst, a sentence to a concentration camp.

Also quite unprecedented in the legislation of civilized countries is a Soviet decree, issued in June, 1934, which provides that, if any Soviet soldier goes abroad without permission, his close relatives are to be "exiled to remote regions of Siberia for five years," even though they may not have known of his intention to flee. The treatment of members of families as hostages is a notorious feature of Soviet administrative practice; but in this case this principle is formally written into law. The satellite government of Bulgaria went still further, prescribing the death penalty for all Bulgarian citizens living abroad without permission and confinement in concentration camps for their families in a decree of March, 1953.

What are the origins of this Russian absolutism, that makes the country a gigantic prison for its own citizens and for foreign visitors? These origins are both historical and psychological. The Russian state for centuries developed under despotic Byzantine and Tartar influences, almost untouched by the elements of freedom and of check and balance which existed in Western Europe even before the rise of modern parliamentary institutions. And, while generalizations about national character are always dangerous, Russian thought has been conspicuously lacking in the instincts for relativity and moderation. It is impatient of gradualism, intent on some goal of absolute perfection.

The Russians first come into history through their contacts with the Byzantine Empire. These contacts were sometimes friendly, sometimes hostile; toward the end of the tenth century the ruler of Kiev, on the Dnieper, chief city of the early Russian state, accepted Christianity according to the Greek Orthodox rite. This act created a schism of considerable historical importance between Orthodox Russia and Western Europe, solidly Roman Catholic until the time of the Reformation. The Byzantine Empire was an autocracy, a continuation of the later Roman Empire; and this type of government influenced Russia.

The Tartar conquest of Russia, then composed of small warring principalities, in the thirteenth century was another lesson in absolute centralized rule and another factor which deepened the breach between Russian and European civilization during the Middle Ages. The Ukraine, the southern part of European Russia, had been devastated by the Tartar invasion and other wars and the centre of Russian life was transferred to north central Russia, where the princes of Moscow gradually assumed a position of leadership.

Moscow became the seat of the Russian Partiarchate, the religious as well as the political centre of the nation. The early Muscovite princes pursued a cautious and crafty policy, bowing to the Tartar overlordship when it was too strong to be resisted, collecting tribute for the Tartars and sometimes using Tartar aid to subdue and absorb neighboring principalities. A Moscow prince, Dmitry Donskoy, won the first big Russian victory over the Tartars at Kulikovo, near the headwaters of the Don River, in 1380.

The Tartar power declined, partly as a result of internal dissension, and the Muscovite state grew in population, area and prestige. Ivan III (The Great, 1462–1505) unified northern Russia under his rule and married Sofia, niece of the last Emperor of Constantinople. During his reign an enthusiastic monk hailed Moscow as the "Third Rome," which would endure forever. The "Second Rome," Constantinople, had only recently fallen to the Turks.

Ivan III assumed the pomp and ceremonial of an oriental despot. His grandson, Ivan IV (The Terrible, 1533–1584) subdued the Tartars of the Volga Valley and opened the way for Russian penetration and colonization of the vast and largely empty spaces of Siberia. Ivan the Terrible was a savage tyrant, even in an age of cruelty. The number of his victims was only matched by the ingenuity of his tortures. His suspicion of all around him was almost psychotic and suspicion drove him from one massacre or "purge" to another.

One of Ivan's instruments of governing was the *oprichina*, a terrorist police force to which he entrusted almost unlimited power. The *oprichina* was directed especially against the boyars, or old hereditary aristocrats. Their armed agents, on any suspicion of disloyalty, swooped down on the manor-houses of the boyars, killed the men, violated the women and seized the property. The political effect was to weaken very much the power of the hereditary nobility and bring to the front new men, who owed everything to the favor of the Tsar.

Ivan's memory was execrated by Russian liberals before the Revolution. But under Stalin he was elevated to the status of a national hero, a ruler who increased the power and territory of the medieval Russian state. His spirit certainly marches on in many acts of the Soviet regime.

The Muscovite state experienced a major crisis, which almost led to its dissolution during the Troubled Times (1603–1613). The appearance of an impostor, the "false Dimitry," who impersonated the murdered lawful heir to the throne, led to a wave of virtual anarchy, accompanied by widespread peasant revolts and Swedish and Polish intervention. There was a Russian national revival and recovery after this ordeal and Michael Romanov, elected Tsar by a national assembly, became the founder of a dynasty that ruled for three centuries.

The strongest individual personality in this dynasty was

Peter the Great (1689–1725). He was a man of prodigious mental and physical energy and wild ungovernable passions. Like Ivan the Terrible, he had his own son killed. Peter built a new capital in St. Petersburg, on the Neva River near the Baltic Sea, a "window to the West," removed from what he considered the enervating, oriental atmosphere of old Moscow. His first ambition was to introduce European methods of government and industry into Russia.

Peter the Great forced the old-fashioned boyars to shave their beards, acquired the coastline of the Baltic Sea after a long struggle with Sweden, required the younger nobles to accept posts in the government service, launched the first Russian navy, founded an Academy of Science, brought foreign specialists into Russia. Many of these were engaged during the Tsar's highly unconventional trip to Western Europe, where he worked as a laborer in a Dutch shipyard to learn shipbuilding and left the house which was assigned to him in England sadly damaged as a result of the orgies and the unsanitary habits which he and the members of his suite brought with them.

Ministries organized along European lines were introduced in Russia; a Senate replaced the Council of Boyars. But, although Peter gave the old Muscovite edifice a European veneer, he left the principle of autocracy untouched and even strengthened. Kluchevsky's judgment on this innovating Tsar is wise and penetrating:

> His beneficent actions were accomplished with repelling violence. Peter's reform was a struggle with the people, with its sluggishness. . . . He desired that the slave, remaining a slave, should act consciously and freely.

Incompetent or unlucky Tsars were sometimes assassinated or deposed as a result of palace conspiracies. But the principle of autocracy remained unchanged. The individualist forces in the civilization of Western Europe stopped at the Russian frontier. Russia was almost untouched by such movements as the Renaissance, the Reformation and the French Revolution. Its cultural lag was tremendous; until the nineteenth century there is no Russian intellectual figure of international stature.

The free cities, the nobles, the Church all functioned as brakes on the power of the monarch during the European Middle Ages. These brakes were non-existent in Russia. The burgher liberties of Novgorod and Pskov disappeared under the stern rule of Ivan III and Ivan the Terrible. Russia remained a poor, backward, landlocked agricultural country, with few large towns and little foreign trade or association with foreigners. The nobles, although they might own thousands of serfs, were themselves only the first slaves of the Tsar. The Russian Orthodox Church inherited the Byzantine tradition of submission to the temporal power, not the Roman tradition of a Pope empowered to denounce the wrongdoing of kings.

Individual and group liberties in Europe were safeguarded to some extent by charters, laws, customs for which there was no parallel in Russia. There are no records of Russian nobles forcing a Tsar to sign a Great Charter, of a Russian John Hampden, appealing to law in protest against an unjust tax. There is only a story of Asiatic despotism, varied by occasional furious outbursts of anarchy.

Beginning with the sixteenth century Russia became a more and more tightly organized serf state. The free peasants almost disappeared and serfdom became harsher and more universal. Only the wild frontiersmen known as Cossacks escaped the enveloping grip of this system.

In Russian serfdom, as in the European feudal order, there was a vague sense of social contract. The class of gentry, the *pomieschiki,* were supposed to serve the Tsar in war and in government. The peasants, in theory, fulfilled the social obligation of "feeding" and supporting their owners, the landlords.

There may have been some element of necessity in this system for a poor country which was in a state of continuous declared and undeclared war along some of its frontiers. But it bore heavily upon the serfs at the bottom of the social pyramid. A ferment of dissatisfaction was never far below the surface and found expression in the great uprisings led by Stenka Razin in the seventeenth century and by Emilian Pugachev a century later. These Cossacks found a wide response when they called on the peasants to rise against serfdom.

But their disorderly revolts, the two largest among many smaller outbreaks, were crushed by the government troops. Men like Razin and Pugachev had nothing to substitute for the Tsarist state, corrupt, inefficient and tyrannical though it was. Their nearest approach to a political idea was a "good Tsar," who would give the land to the peasants.

There was no repetition of revolts on the scale of the Razin and Pugachev uprisings in the nineteenth century. The military and police forces of the government were stronger and better organized. The Cossacks, an element of unrest in earlier times, had settled down on comfortable land allotments and were the most reliable support of the Tsarist regime. But a different kind of unrest made the nineteenth century important in shaping the final form of the Russian Revolution.

This was the era of Russia's renaissance, of its late coming of age intellectually. It was the era of the mighty Russian poets, Pushkin and Lermontov, of the superb novelists, Tolstoy, Dostoevsky, Turgenev, Gogol, of great composers, Moussorgsky, Tchaikovsky, Borodin, Rimsky-Korsakov, of an awakening in all branches of knowledge and artistic creation. It was also the era when, despite severe official restrictions, the young Russian intelligentsia began to think critically about the existing political and economic shape of society, to dream of revolutionary blueprints for a better future.

There were Russians during this internationally liberal

nineteenth century who were attracted by the ideal of liberty under law, as represented by the constitutional practices of Great Britain, France and the United States. Leading Russian liberals were the political leader and professor, Paul Milyukov, and the famous legal expert, Paul Vinogradov. But, although there was a liberal element among the forces arrayed against autocracy, this was not the strongest element or the one that was destined to prevail when the Romanov dynasty collapsed.

In reading the revolutionary literature of the nineteenth century one is impressed by the slight consideration for guaranties of individual rights, compared with the tremendous absorption in grandiose messianic utopian schemes which, as their authors were firmly convinced, would assure liberty and justice for all. The typical Russian revolutionary was not interested in drawing the fangs of the leviathan represented by the Tsarist state. He wanted to get hold of this leviathan and use it for his own purposes—to make people happy and virtuous, whether they liked it or not.

Western Europeans could discuss radical and revolutionary ideas without driving these ideas to their logical ultimate consequences. Even Marxism, perhaps the most socially explosive theory of the nineteenth century, often worked out, in the practice of the western socialist parties, as little more than an attempt to obtain social legislation favorable to the workers.

But to toss such ideas into the psychological climate of the passionate, repressed Russian intellectuals was like setting a spark to a stick of dynamite. The Russian intellectual was rarely a tolerant sceptic. He would often defend a European idea, however vulnerable on logical grounds, with the passionate intensity of the Russian Old Believers who had a practice of burning themselves alive, rather than submit to the Orthodox Church, which they regarded as having departed from the true faith.

Three marked characteristics of Russian revolutionary thought are repudiation of private property, preference of equality to liberty and a sense of guilt toward the poor and unlettered majority on the part of the educated minority. One of the outstanding revolutionary figures was Michael Bakunin, who, with his philosophy of anarchist communism, disputed the leadership of the First International with Karl Marx. This is Bakunin's program for his Union of Social Democracy:

> The Union declares itself atheistic. It desires the final and complete destruction of classes, the political, social and economic equality of individuals of both sexes; it desires that land, tools of labor and capital of any kind should become the collective property of all society and be utilized only by workers, i.e. agricultural and industrial associations of workers.

N. G. Chernishevsky, influential publicist, strikes the familiar notes of preferring equality to liberty, socialism to constitutional guaranties of individual rights:

> I do not like these gentlemen who say Liberty, Liberty, and do not destroy a social order under which nine tenths of the people are slaves and proletarians. The important thing is not whether there is a Tsar or not, whether there is a constitution or not, but that one class should not suck the blood of another.

One often encounters, in the literature and memoirs of the period, a feeling of mingled guilt, responsibility and pity for the suffering masses. Radischev, whose *Journey from Petersburg to Moscow* is one of the early expressions of social protest, tells how "his soul was wounded by the suffering of humanity."

Marianna, heroine of Turgenev's *Virgin Soil,* a young woman of the upper classes, bursts out:

> It sometimes seems to me that I suffer on behalf of all the oppressed, the poor, the wretched in Russia. . . . No, I do not suffer . . . But I am indignant on their behalf; I rage, so that I am ready to lay down my life for them.

Prince Peter Kropotkin, the kindly philosophical anarchist, felt that he had no right to the joys of scientific research when there were so many social evils to be cured. An expression of this feeling of responsibility was the movement to "go to the people" which developed in the 1870's.

Thousands of educated young men and women, some of them from wealthy homes, went on a kind of revolutionary pilgrimage to the peasant villages. They wanted to serve the peasants as doctors, teachers, nurses, agricultural experts and at the same time to bring them the enlightenment of revolutionary propaganda. From a practical standpoint this movement was not successful. The peasants listened distrustfully to these city strangers and sometimes handed them over to the police.*

Behind this urge to get in touch with the masses was an uneasy sense of alienation. There was much dispute between the schools of thought known as the Slavophiles and the Westerners. The Slavophiles idealized Russia as it was before Peter the Great and preached the necessity of going back to the old faith and customs of the people. The Westerners who were socialists or agrarians, not liberals, felt a necessity for atonement for living in a social order based on exploitation.

Many revolutionaries reached the conclusion that the masses could not be trusted to follow their true interests, even if they were freed from government restraint. The famous critic, Vissarion Belinsky, who became an atheist because he could not see the justice of God in the world, declared that he would be a tyrant on behalf of justice and believed that the people were so stupid that they must be "dragged to happiness."

Peter Tkachev, a disciple of Chernishevsky, was a kind of bridge between the French Jacobins and the Russian Bolsheviks, with their similar, if differently motivated theories of the necessity of revolutionary dictatorship. Tkachev wanted a centralized fighting organization of revolutionaries for the destruction of the old order and a revolutionary dictatorship to insure the building of a new socialist society. He repudiated the possibility of peaceful progress. The transition from the

* Turgenev's novel, *Virgin Soil*, gives a sympathetic picture of the misadventures of these amateur revolutionaries.

old order to the new "requires a certain jump, and everyone must prepare for it." *

Tkachev was passionately concerned for fear capitalism would strike such deep roots in Russia that it could not be destroyed. To avert this he advocated a preventive revolution, to be carried out as quickly as possible. In his own phrase "it was necessary to force consciousness" upon the working class.

Here one has an excellent example of the dualism that pervades much extreme revolutionary thought, not only in Russia, but in France, Germany and other countries. The professed aim of the revolutionary theorist is to take away power and wealth from the few and give these things to the many, to the "people," in French Jacobin phraseology, to "the proletariat," in Russian communist language. But in the revolutionary's mind is a lurking suspicion that the "people" or the "proletariat" will not know how to use power for the right ends. So there must be a revolutionary elite, exercising absolute power, in order to guide the thinking of the masses in the proper direction. The jump from a despotic Tsarism to a despotic rule of the revolutionary elect is not so great, after all.

The man who impressed his stamp upon the Russian Revolution, when it finally came, who shaped more than anyone the form of the Soviet state was Vladimir Ilyitch Ulyanov, who became famous under his revolutionary pseudonym, Lenin.†　Son of a provincial inspector of schools, Lenin was born in the heart of European Russia, in the sleepy town of Simbirsk (now renamed Ulyanovsk) on the Volga. He was a typically Russian revolutionary in the uncritical devotion with which he embraced a theory, in the dedication of his life to the realization of this theory, in the passionate dogmatism which sustained him, as it

* Professor Michael Karpovich, of Harvard University, contributes a scholarly analysis of Tkachev's ideas to the magazine, *Review of Politics* (Notre Dame University), July, 1944.

† Most prominent Russian revolutionaries used one or more pseudonyms as a means of evading the attentions of the police. So Stalin's true name was Djugashvili and Trotsky's Bronstein.

has sustained many religious enthusiasts, in the darkest periods of disappointment and difficulty, in the absolutism of his thinking. For him it was the ultimate communist utopia or nothing. And no price in human sacrifice and suffering seemed too great to pay for the attainment of this goal.

In the field of theory Lenin's mind was not profound or original. It operated always within the limits of the basic tenets of Marx and Engels with a few elaborations suggested by contemporary conditions and some adjustments to the necessities of the Russian situation. Lenin's genius was that of the practical revolutionary, able to transform a doctrine into a living reality.

Lenin started out from the Marxian assumption of inescapable class struggle between a minority of capitalist oppressors and a majority of oppressed proletarians. The capitalist ruling class uses the state as an instrument to insure its own domination over the workers. The supreme task of the proletariat, according to Lenin, is to capture the state, to break up the old machinery of governing and then to organize its own state, a "dictatorship of the proletariat." Lenin conceived the state as "a machine or cudgel" which the ruling class uses in order to crush other classes.

The dictatorship of the proletariat, as Lenin frankly admits,* is not designed to insure individual liberty or to offer safeguards against the arbitrary power of the state. In Lenin's own words: †

> The dictatorship of the proletariat produces a series of restrictions of liberty in the case of the oppressors, exploiters and capitalists. We must crush them in order to free humanity from wage slavery. Their resistance must be broken by force. It is clear that

* By far the best summary of Lenin's basic ideas is the pamphlet, *State and Revolution*, composed on the eve of the Bolshevik Revolution in November, 1917. This is published in an English translation as Vol. 14 in the Little Lenin Library, issued by International Publishers, New York.

† *State and Revolution*, p. 73.

where there is suppression there is also violence; there is no liberty, no democracy.

Lenin's absolutism is expressed still more clearly in the following epigram, based on an idea of Engels: *

"While the state exists there is no freedom. When there is freedom there will be no state."

The dictatorship of the proletariat is not regarded as a permanent condition. Lenin adopts the phrase of Engels that the state will "wither away" as class antagonisms are eliminated by the triumph of socialism. No time is set for this development and Lenin's writings, like those of Marx, are very bare in specific description of what human life will be under socialism. The expropriation of the capitalists, he is convinced, will yield a tremendous development of the productive forces of human society. After an intermediate phase of socialism, when some individual incentives will be necessary and the form of the state will be the dictatorship of the proletariat, the higher final ideal stage of communism will be reached. Then labor will become voluntary, "the first necessity of life." The distinction between mental and physical work will disappear.

Lenin justifies the dictatorship of the proletariat as a necessary transitional stage to the higher order of communism. He also uses the argument that democracy, under capitalism, is false and hypocritical, that it is only for the rich and excludes the poor.

On the other hand, the dictatorship of the proletariat, in Lenin's mind, is "democracy for the poor, democracy for the people." He offers a very simplified view of how production will be organized after the capitalists are ousted: †

> Overthrow the capitalists, crush with the iron hand of the workers the resistance of these exploiters, break the bureaucratic machine of the modern state—and you have before you a mechanism of the highest technical equipment, freed of "parasites,"

* *Ibid.*, p. 79.
† *Ibid.*, 47.

capable of being set into motion by the united workers themselves who hire their technicians, managers, bookkeepers and pay
them *all* as indeed every state "official" with the usual worker's
wage.

Or, as he sums up his position more briefly in another
passage: *

"The whole of society will have become one office and one
factory, with equal work and equal pay."

Lenin also maintained that the suppression of the minority
by the majority, his definition of the dictatorship of the proletariat, would require less bloodshed than the suppression "by
the exploiting minority of the exploited majority," which, according to him, requires "the greatest ferocity and savagery of
suppression" and "seas of blood, through which mankind is
marching in slavery, serfdom and wage labor." †

One of the most important items in Lenin's political creed
is the creation of a strongly disciplined party as a necessary
instrument for leading the proletariat to victory in revolution
and controlling the course of events after revolution. Like
many other fanatics of an idea, he preferred quality to quantity, unquestioning obedience to large numbers. Before the
Revolution, when the Russian Social Democrats of all shades
of opinion were a small and persecuted band, Lenin would
always split the party rather than compromise on what he considered an essential point of doctrine.

Lenin's idea of the elite party, one of the most fateful political conceptions of the twentieth century, was formulated as
early as 1902, when he set forth the following blueprint for
revolutionary victory in his pamphlet, *What Is To Be Done?*:

An organization of revolutionaries must above all and mainly
include people whose profession consists of revolutionary activity. This organization must be not very broad and as conspirative

* *Ibid.*, 84.
† *Ibid.*, 74.

as possible. . . . Give us an organization of revolutionaries and we shall turn Russia upside down.

Lenin's conception was that the proletariat, the industrial wage-workers, should play the leading political role in the socialist state, but under the guidance of a special "vanguard," in the shape of the Communist Party.* In his own words: †
"Marxism educates the vanguard of the proletariat, capable of assuming power and of leading the whole people to socialism, of directing and organizing the new order, of being the teacher, guide and leader of all the toiling and exploited in the task of building up their social life without the bourgeoisie and against the bourgeoisie."

The importance of the single ruling party, governing without check, limit or balance, is of primary importance in communist theory and in Soviet practice. Lenin is reported to have said that there could be any number of parties in Russia, on condition that the Communist Party be in power and all the other parties—in jail. Whether this is a true story or a political joke, it is an accurate statement of the nature of the Soviet regime. Stalin wrote in *Pravda* on November 26, 1936:

> In the Soviet Union there is no basis for the existence of several parties, for the freedom of parties. In the Soviet Union there is a basis only for the Communist Party.

Although Lenin never, so far as is known from his writings, permitted himself a doubt as to the infallibility of Karl Marx, he sometimes interpreted Marx in a fashion calculated to fit in with special Russian conditions. It is a Marxian dogma that socialism can be successfully introduced only after capitalism has reached its highest stage of development. By comparison with the United States, Great Britain and Germany, Russia

* The official change from Bolshevik to Communist took place in 1918. The term *Bolshevik* is derived from the Russian word *bolshinstvo* (majority) and was applied to Lenin's faction among the Social Democrats when they won a majority in a Social Democratic Congress.
† *State and Revolution*, pp. 23–24.

was in an early phase of capitalist development. The majority of the population was composed of peasants.

Lenin's opponents in the Russian Social Democratic Party, the Mensheviki,* reasoned that Russia was not ripe for socialism. The proper task of a socialist party was to work for the overthrow of Tsarism in alliance with middle-class liberals. After this end was accomplished the struggle for socialism should continue within the new framework of free political institutions.

But Lenin recommended another course. He advocated a temporary alliance of the working class with the peasantry and the creation of what he called "the democratic dictatorship of the proletariat and the peasantry." This very phrase, "democratic dictatorship," shows how far Lenin's conception of "democracy" was removed from that of western liberalism. He anticipated a revolution in two stages, which he summed up as follows in his work, *The Proletarian Revolution and the Renegade Kautsky,* published after the Bolshevik Revolution:

> First with the whole of the peasantry against the monarchy, against the landlords, against the medieval regime (and to that extent the revolution remains bourgeois, bourgeois democratic). Then with the poorest peasants, with the semi-proletariat, with all the exploited against capitalism, including the rural rich, the kulaks, the profiteers, and to that extent the revolution becomes socialist.

Lenin added to the general body of Marxist doctrine the theory that imperialism, the rule over colonial lands, represents the highest and final stage of capitalism. In working out this theory he borrowed considerably from the works of the British radical economist, J. A. Hobson, and of Rudolf Hilferding, a German Social Democrat.

He saw imperialism as the last flowering of capitalism, with free competition replaced by monopoly and the capitalist system dependent on the profits which might be extracted from

* So-called from the Russian word *menshinstvo* (minority).

colonies. This led him to the conclusion that the chain of imperialism might be broken in its weakest link, not in the country where capitalism had advanced farthest. It also led him and his associates to concentrate special attention on the possibility of stirring up revolts in colonial countries. Even though these countries might be unripe for socialism, the loss of colonial profits might cause the downfall of capitalism in the imperialist countries.

Lenin is categorical in his belief that there can be no transition to socialism without violence. The state, in his view, is an organ for the suppression of one class by another and cannot be conquered by peaceful means. Leninism also prescribes dogmatic atheism and a complete rejection of absolute morality. He characterized religion as "a kind of spiritual gin in which the slaves of capital drown their human shape and their claims to any decent human life." * Morality merely becomes an adjunct to the class struggle.

> Morality is what serves the destruction of the old exploiters' society and the union of all the toilers around the proletariat, which creates a new society of communists. Communist morality is what serves this struggle . . . We do not believe in eternal morality and we expose the deceit of all legends about morality.†

In his pamphlet, *Left Wing Communism: An Infantile Disorder,* Lenin declares that "we must resort to all sorts of stratagems, maneuvers, illegal methods, evasions and subterfuges only so as to get into the trade-unions, to remain in them and to carry on communist work within them at all costs."

In such a materialistic scheme of values there is no place for honor or mercy or respect for the pledged word. A communist promise, in domestic affairs or in international affairs, is kept just so long as expediency dictates, not a moment longer. There is also no place for consistency, since the rightness or wrongness

* Vol. XI of *Lenin's Selected Works,* New York edition, 1943.
† *Lenin's Collected Works,* Russian edition, XVII, 323–24.

of any attitude on any subject is measured by one standard: Does it advance the triumph of the communist cause?

When the Bolsheviki were struggling for power, in 1917, they emphasized the horrors of war, called for peace and mass desertion of the soldiers from the front. They also denounced any government interference with their incitements to rebellion, claiming unlimited freedom of speech. After they were established in power the death penalty was quickly restored for desertion and all freedom of criticism was suppressed.

The communist would deny the charge of inconsistency with the argument that the supposed interest of the proletariat requires one policy at one time, an entirely changed policy under differing circumstances. This mental attitude, together with the tremendous concentration of power in the hands of the Soviet Government, gives the Soviet Union a maneuvering advantage over free countries where public opinion often has to be brought around slowly and gradually to see the advisability of a shift in policy.

The fallen absolutism of the Tsars in many ways paved the way for communist revolutionary absolutism. It had denied to the Russian people adequate training in self-government. To be sure, the rule of the last Romanovs was more civilized than that of Ivan the Terrible and Peter the Great. The Russian upper and middle classes had been to some extent westernized and humanized. An educated public opinion possessed some means of expression. The half century before the fall of the autocracy witnessed some progressive and liberal developments. Tsar Alexander II abolished serfdom in 1861. The same Tsar created organs of limited local self-government, the *zemstvos*. The revolutionary upsurge of 1905 led to the creation of a Duma, or national parliament, although this body was elected on the basis of a limited franchise and possessed only restricted powers.

Equally significant was the attempt of Prime Minister Peter Stolypin to stimulate an individualist spirit among the Russian peasants. From very old times the Russian peasants lived under a village community system which very much discouraged individual initiative. There were few private farms. The community decided what crops should be planted and assigned to each family its land, usually in strips which were often considerable distances apart. Frequent redivision of the land destroyed the impulse to make permanent improvements.

Even after serfdom was abolished the village community supervision over the land was maintained, since the authorities regarded the *mir,* or peasant council, as a force for order and stability. But when peasant disturbances broke out in the first years of the twentieth century, involving the seizure of landlords' estates and the pillage and burning of many manorhouses, the official attitude changed.

Stolypin introduced legislation designed to appeal to the sense for individual property. The peasant was permitted, if he desired, to leave the village community and set up his own farm. And communities could dissolve themselves by majority vote.

Over one fifth of the peasant households decided to take up individual farming between 1907 and 1915, when the measure was suspended because of the mobilization of vast masses of peasants for the war. Had Stolypin's laws remained in force for a generation or two a new class of well-to-do farmers might have emerged as a strong barrier against extreme socialist schemes. As it was, the Soviet Government had literally to wade through "seas of blood" (Lenin's phrase about capitalism) in order to break the resistance of the peasants who had something to lose to the requisitions in the civil war period and to the imposition of collective farming in the years 1929–1933. But war and revolution cut short the Stolypin experiment. The whole course of Russian history might have been changed if the peasant had been set free from the village commune at the same time when he was freed from serfdom, in 1861.

Lenin was living in poverty and obscurity in exile in Zurich when the fall of the Tsarist regime in March, 1917, gave him his supreme revolutionary opportunity. Returning to Russia with the cooperation of the German Government, which saw in him an agitator who would be successful in demoralizing the Russian army, he proved himself a master of revolutionary strategy and tactics. The well intentioned but weak government of liberals and moderate socialists which had replaced the autocracy could not cope with the mighty forces of revolt, anarchy and general disorder which had been let loose when the traditional symbol of power and authority, the Tsar, disappeared.

Four such forces made possible the seizure of power by the Bolsheviks on November 6–7, 1917, although without Lenin's leadership and the instrument of power which he had forged in his party this seizure of power might never have taken place. There was a gigantic mutiny of the huge armies at the front against military discipline and against the continuation of a war which had cost Russia millions of casualties. There was the nationwide impulse of the peasants to seize the land of the big estates, and to drive away the owners. There was a deepening revolt of the Russian industrial workers, beginning with demands for shorter hours and higher pay, ending in seizures of factories and violent eviction of owners, engineers and foremen. There was a secessionist movement among the non-Russian peoples of the former Empire, Finns, Ukrainians, Georgians, Armenians and the Moslem peoples of the Caucasus and Central Asia.

All these disintegrating forces reduced Russia to such a state of chaotic disorder that the Bolsheviki, with their improvised detachments of sailors, armed workers and rebellious soldiers, were able to oust the Provisional Government and proclaim a Republic of Soviets. Soviets (the Russian word means council) had sprung up more or less spontaneously all over the country after the fall of the Tsar. Their members were elected in factories and military units, with some representation from left-wing political parties, cooperatives and other public organizations.

At first the moderate socialist parties, the Mensheviki and the Socialist Revolutionaries, held the majority in the Soviets. But the rising tide of extremism after an attempt by the Commander-in-Chief, General Kornilov, to restore order and discipline by means of a coup d'état had failed gave the Bolsheviki control of the Soviets in Moscow, Petrograd and other strategic centres. A Constituent Assembly, elected on a basis of universal suffrage, met in January, 1918, but was dissolved by force when the anti-Bolshevik majority refused to accept the entire Bolshevik program.

At first Soviet rule was represented as a form of occupational democracy, with delegates coming directly from the machine or the plough to discuss affairs of state. In practice the Soviets were merely a convenient screen for the dictatorship of the Communist Party, which completely dominated their composition and decisions. All other political parties, including those which professed socialist aims, were eliminated and suppressed. With the adoption of the new Constitution in 1936 the Soviet Union abandoned the practice of using factory or office as the unit of representation. Soviet elections are now held on a geographical basis. As only one list of candidates, carefully handpicked in advance, is presented for popular approval these elections have no significance as a means of expressing public opinion.

So, on the ruins of the Tsarist leviathan arose a new leviathan, the Soviet state, far more unrestrained in its power. The limited concessions to economic individualism and to independent political representative institutions have been wiped out. The methods of the Soviet state suggest Ivan the Terrible and Peter the Great, rather than the rule of the more modern Tsars. And the Soviet Government is much more similar to the fascist regimes of Hitler and Mussolini than to moderate socialist governments, which have existed or exist in Great Britain, Australia, New Zealand and the Scandinavian countries.

An American analogy may convey some idea of the dizzy height of power unlimited occupied by Stalin for a quarter of a century and now by Stalin's political heirs. Suppose that there were only one legal party in the United States and that the leadership of this party concentrated in its hands all the powers now vested by the Constitution in the President, the Congress and the Judiciary, and without any of the restrictions which the American Constitution imposes on the exercise of state power. Suppose that in all the forty-eight states large numbers of people who were merely suspected of disaffection were being worked and starved to death in concentration camps.

Suppose that the same men who directed the government were also in control of every industrial enterprise, every mine, every railway, every store, that all strikes were forbidden, that labor was conscripted whenever this was considered necessary and that wage rates were fixed by the state. Suppose that this small group of men controlled every newspaper and every magazine and dictated what books might be printed, what should be taught in the schools, what should be shown in theatres and movie houses.

This, in brief, is the kind of political and social order which communism has created in the Soviet Union, is creating in the East European satellite states and in China and hopes to create in the entire world. This is the fruit of Lenin's revolutionary absolutist ideas.

There was hopeful expectation among some foreign observers that the Soviet Government, after the first excesses of the Revolution, would become more moderate and liberal. Precisely the reverse has occurred. The concentration of absolute power in the Soviet Union has increased, not diminished with the passing of time. During the first years of Soviet rule there was considerable freedom of discussion in the annual Communist Party

Congresses. Debates were sharp; votes were not always unanimous.

Now the Party Congress has become an infrequent event, with a lapse of thirteen years between the Eighteenth Congress, in 1939, and the Nineteenth, in 1952. No word of criticism has been heard at these Congresses since Stalin consolidated his power; resolutions proposed by the Party leadership are accepted unanimously.

This same trend toward regimentation has almost reached the limits of the possible in the cultural field. The Communist Party Central Committee prescribes what is and is not permissible in literature and the arts, in physics and genetics. The musician is ordered to brighten up his tunes; the satirist to blunt his pencil. In large and important fields of human knowledge, in history, economics, philosophy, memoirs, political science, not one work of creative original thought has been produced under this straitjacket system. Literature and theoretical science have been severely crippled.

To be put to death is only part of the retribution meted out to anyone whom Stalin considered a political enemy. Every trace that such a man existed is carefully expunged from the public records. A journalist, permitted to carry out research in the Soviet central archives in 1936, found that every one of hundreds of photographs of Trotsky had been removed. A documentary film showing the men who carried Lenin's bier in 1924 had been completely altered so as to eliminate the numerous prominent old Bolsheviks who took part in the ceremony, and who were subsequently executed.* What might seem the grim fantasies of George Orwell's *1984* are the commonplace realities of Soviet life.

A trend toward the expansion of individual liberty, such as occurred in Western Europe and North America during the nineteenth century, has its law of momentum. Each new ad-

* See Nikolaus Basseches, *Stalin* (Dutton), p. 8.

vance contains the seeds of further advances. There is an equally inescapable law of momentum when the trend is in the opposite direction. One can observe this in Old Russia, where one decree after another riveted the chains of serfdom more and more tightly until the whole social order became tightly bound, with everyone assigned to some particular task or function, on pain of severe punishment.

There has been an unmistakable similar trend in the New Russia of the Soviets toward a similar bound society, where the individual is deprived not only of political liberty but of what would seem in free countries elementary personal rights.

The Soviet citizen may not travel or live abroad without government permission, which is very rarely given. If he tries to escape he not only risks his own life but exposes members of his family to reprisals.

Like the medieval serf, the Soviet worker is bound to his place of employment. Under a law of June 28, 1940, he may not change his place of employment without permission; the penalty is six months of imprisonment. A law of October 2, 1940, authorizes annual mass mobilization of 800,000 to 1,000,000 youths of both sexes for training in trade, railway and industrial schools. Graduates of these schools "are obliged to work four years continuously in state enterprises, as directed by the Central Labor Reserves Administration." If anyone leaves these training schools he is liable, under the Soviet criminal code of 1948, to a year of confinement in a "labor colony" (reform school).

By a decree of October 19, 1940, the government may transfer workers and their families from one part of the country to another. There has been a steady evolution toward political despotism. The Soviets, vital if disorderly organs of administration in the first months of their existence, have long become mere rubber stamps for registering communist decisions. The "dictatorship of the proletariat" has become a dictatorship over the proletariat. The peasants, promised land and liberty by the Bolshevik agitators of 1917, find themselves in the grip of the new serfdom of the collective farm.

Insecurity is the law of life even for the more favored classes under the Soviet regime. It is an amusing misconception that communism, whatever may be its faults, brings "security." One must go behind the iron curtain to find large numbers of people suffering not from "insecurity" (this would be much too mild a word), but from the abject terror that always prevails where there is no rule of law. If anyone, however highly placed, falls into political disfavor he is likely to find himself undergoing the "conveyor" interrogation method and then shipped off to a concentration camp. No one in the Soviet Union is safe from the terror of the political police, as the highest boyar in the time of Ivan the Terrible might be suddenly despoiled and killed by Ivan's "political police," the *oprichniki*.

Tsarism, long a byword for despotism among the governments of Europe, had been somewhat softened in modern times. But the Bolshevik Revolution, itself the product of a western dogma, Marxism, applied with Asiatic ruthlessness, led to an absolutism exceeding that of the most autocratic Tsars.

The dark forces of the Russian past, unlimited tyranny and serfdom for the masses of the people, proved stronger, when the test of revolution came, than the vision of those liberal educated Russians who dreamed of a Russia where people would not denounce each other and would walk with heads erect, free to act and speak as they chose, unterrorized by secret police. The Russian masses followed, or allowed themselves to be driven, by prophets who claimed the familiar fanatic's right to create a hell in the present for the sake of an imaginary paradise in the future.

The Soviet state, in its present form, represents a sinister fusion of the administrative methods of Ivan the Terrible with modern military weapons and modern technology. Its epitaph was written unconsciously long ago by one of the most learned and gifted of liberal thinkers, Lord Acton:

"All power tends to corrupt. And absolute power corrupts—absolutely."

Chapter XI ～ Objective:

World Domination

What makes Soviet despotism a matter of international concern is its avowed goal of world conquest through a combination of subversive activity and military force. For the first time in history the government of a mighty, populous militarized empire, rich in natural resources, has at its disposal a huge international fifth column, in the shape of the communist parties which exist in almost every country in the world. These parties perform various functions, depending on their size and strength and the political conditions in which they operate. But they are a political and military asset of first importance, an asset which no conqueror in the past has possessed.

Lenin, Stalin, Trotsky and all the leaders of Soviet communism have repeatedly expressed the idea that revolution in Russia would be only the first phase in world revolution, that the Soviet state would never be secure until capitalism was destroyed all over the world. The following is one of the clearest of many formulations of this idea in Lenin's writings: *

> The victorious proletariat of one country, having expropriated the capitalists and organized its own socialist production, would confront the rest of the capitalist world, attract to itself the oppressed classes of other countries, raise revolt among them against

* *Selected Works of Lenin*, V, 141.

the capitalists and, in the event of necessity, come out even with armed forces against the exploiting classes and their states.

Stalin's assertions on this subject are just as positive and categorical as Lenin's. It is an ignorant misunderstanding of the thinking of the two men, fostered by Soviet propaganda, to believe that Stalin's elimination of Trotsky meant that he had renounced the goal of world revolution. The gist of the difference between Trotsky and Stalin was that Trotsky wished to proceed toward this goal more directly and recklessly, while Stalin wished to build up first overwhelming military force and an industry capable of supporting modern war in the Soviet Union.

Stalin fully endorses Lenin's belief that the "victorious proletariat" must do everything in its power to promote revolution in other countries. Among many passages in his writings emphasizing this point one may cite this excerpt: *

> The development and support of revolution in other countries is an essential task of the victorious revolution. Therefore the revolution in the victorious country must regard itself not as a self-sufficient entity, but as an aid, as a means of hastening the victory of the proletariat in other countries.

And there is a remarkably prophetic note in Stalin's analysis of Soviet aims in foreign policy, set forth more than thirty years ago, in *Pravda* of August 28, 1921:

> The tasks of the Party in foreign policy are: (1) To utilize every contradiction and conflict among the surrounding capitalist groups and governments for the purpose of disintegrating imperialism; (2) To spare no pains or means to render assistance to the proletarian revolutions in the West; (3) To take all necessary measures to strengthen the national liberation movements in the East; (4) To strengthen the Red Army.

It would be hard to imagine a more precise blueprint of the foreign policy which Stalin carried on when he became absolute

* Josef Stalin, *Foundations of Leninism* (International Publishers), pp. 45–46.

dictator of the Soviet Union. And what might have been discounted as wishful thinking in 1921 had become far more feasible thirty years later. There could be no comparison between the ragged, hungry Red Army of 1921, armed with obsolete weapons, and the modernized Red Army of 1951, equipped with the latest models of tanks and airplanes. And this makes a substantial difference in the practical aid which Moscow can give to "the national liberation movement in the East" and in the pressure which it can bring on the nations of Western Europe and of the Near and Middle East.

Stalin has broken many promises and treated most of the treaties which he signed as scraps of paper. But he has been true to the four aims which he set forth in the little noted article in 1921. There have been shifts in his tactics, never in his ultimate strategy, and these aims may be considered a legacy in the conduct of foreign affairs which he has handed on to his successors.

Stalin's consistency in his support of revolutionary and subversive activity outside the frontiers of the Soviet Union is confirmed by what is probably his last public address. This was a speech which he delivered at the Nineteenth Congress of the Communist Party, in October, 1952.* A number of prominent foreign communist leaders were present. Here are salient passages in this speech, Stalin's last testament of devotion to world revolution:

> When Comrade Thorez and Comrade Togliatti † declare that their peoples will not fight the peoples of the Soviet Union, . . . that is support for the peaceful aspirations of the Soviet Union.
>
> Naturally our Party cannot remain indebted to the fraternal parties [the foreign communist parties], and it must in its turn render support to them and also to their peoples in their struggle for emancipation. . . . *As we know that is exactly what it is doing.* [Italics supplied]

* Reprinted in the Soviet Publication, *New Times,* No. 42 for 1952.
† Leaders respectively of the French and Italian communist parties.

After declaring that the Soviet Communist Party had received the title, Shock Brigade * of the World Revolutionary and Labor movement, Stalin went on to emphasize the growth of Soviet power since the end of the Second World War and how this growth of power is being used to stimulate world revolution.

> It was very hard, of course, to perform this honorable mission so long as ours was a single and solitary shock brigade, so long as it had to perform the mission of vanguard almost alone. But that was in the past. Today the situation is quite different. Today, when from China and Korea to Czechoslovakia and Hungary new "shock brigades" have appeared in the shape of the People's Democracies, now it has become easier for the Party to fight, yes, and the work is going more merrily.

One of the immediate concerns of the Soviet Government, after coming into power, was to spread the flame of revolution as widely as possible, with no regard for national frontiers. One of the first decrees signed by Stalin, in his capacity as Commissar for Nationalities, calls on the Moslems of Russia to accept the Soviet regime and on the Moslems of the East to "throw off these robbers and enslavers of your countries" (the European powers with colonial possessions in Asia) and to "cast out those who have seized your lands." †

A published Soviet decree of December 24, 1917, places at the disposition of the Commissariat for Foreign Affairs the sum of two million rubles "for aid to the Left internationalist wing of the labor movement of all countries." Such public recording of aid to subversive movements in other countries was soon discontinued and the Soviet Government has taken the position that it has nothing to do with the Communist International or with the activities of the foreign communist parties. But the whole history of the International and such revealing episodes

* A "shock brigade" in the Soviet Union is a special industrial task force, given some especially difficult assignment.
† See *Izvestia*, December 5, 1917.

as Stalin's last speech, cited above, show that this position is quite untenable.

Notice of the holding of the First, founding Congress of the Communist International in 1919 was sent out by the Soviet Commissariat for Foreign Affairs. The Congress was held in Moscow and was addressed by Lenin, Trotsky and other leading members of the Soviet Government. Because of difficulties involved in reaching Moscow (Russia was then isolated by blockade and civil war) attendance at the first Congress was small and not impressive, as regards the groups which were represented.

A Second Congress, also held in Moscow in July–August, 1920, was attended by over 200 delegates, representing thirty-nine countries and five continents. The constitution of the International, framed at this Congress, and the "theses" or resolutions which were also adopted bear the unmistakable stamp of Lenin's mind. What Lenin hoped to forge in the Comintern, as the new organization was often called, was an instrument for achieving on a world scale what the Communist Party had accomplished in Russia: the overthrow of the existing political, economic and social order and its replacement by a world federation of Soviet Republics.

Lenin had always considered numbers unimportant in a revolutionary party, by comparison with discipline and devotion. The twenty-one conditions for admission to the Comintern were so phrased as to make it easier for a camel to pass through the eye of a needle than for a moderate socialist to get into the new revolutionary organization. A number of prominent reformist socialists were singled out by name as ineligible for membership, Hilferding and Kautsky in Germany, Turati and Modigliani in Italy, Jean Longuet in France, Ramsay MacDonald in England, Morris Hillquit in the United States. Parties belonging to the Comintern were required to maintain "iron discipline, with a Party central committee which will be a powerful authoritative organ with wide powers." They were also bound to carry out "systematic purges to clear the party of petty-bourgeois elements."

In other words, every national communist party was to become a copy, in organization, of the Communist Party of the Soviet Union. The conditions of admission, which were made a matter of public record, show that communist parties are not permitted to function as legal organizations within a framework of free institutions. Communist parties are required

> to create everywhere a parallel illegal apparatus, which at the decisive moment should be of assistance to the party to do its duty toward the revolution.
>
> Persistent and systematic propaganda must be carried on in the army, where communist groups should be formed in every military organization. Refusal to carry on or participate in such work should be considered equal to treason to the revolutionary cause and incompatible with affiliation to the Third * International.

Another indication of the role of the Comintern as a school for treason was the fourteenth condition:

> Each party desirous of affiliating with the Comintern should be obliged to render every possible assistance to the Soviet Republics in their struggle against all counterrevolutionary forces.

With the passing of decades and the failure of communist parties to conquer power by their own efforts (with the partial and limited exceptions of China and Yugoslavia) this fifth column aspect of the foreign communist parties became increasingly important.

Besides defining closely the organization of communist parties which were to bring revolution to the world the Second Congress devoted much attention to the strategy of stirring up re-

---

* The Communist International was regarded as the Third. The First came into existence during the lifetime of Karl Marx and foundered in internal dissension. The Second International was composed of socialist parties before the First World War. Lenin felt that the Second International had been hopelessly discredited because of the failure of most socialists to take a revolutionary attitude toward the war.

volt in Asiatic countries which were under European rule or influence. All communist parties were ordered to give aid to "revolutionary liberation movements in colonial lands." There was to be the "closest possible union of the West European communist proletariat with the revolutionary movement of the peasants in the East."

It was recognized that communism was still very weak in oriental countries, that communists could not be expected to take over power directly in the near future. A complex strategy was prescribed for this situation. Communists were to support noncommunist revolutionary organizations, without, however, merging their party identity in these organizations, "preserving the independent character of the proletarian movement, even though it be still in its embryonic state."

This is exactly the strategy which Chinese and Indian communist parties followed in regard to the Kuomintang and the Indian National Congress. There was no immediate fruit from the seeds of revolution which the Comintern tried to sow in the Orient. But a nucleus of leadership was created which proved serviceable when conditions after the Second World War became more favorable to the spread of communism in the Orient.

The use of military force to impose communism on foreign countries or to suppress nationalist movements in the former Russian Empire which wished to break away from communist rule is recognized as desirable and legitimate in many Soviet statements. In theory the right of every nationality in the Russian Empire to "self-determination" was recognized. But Stalin, in a report to the Third Congress of Soviets, in 1918, showed how "self-determination" could be interpreted in such a way as to rob it of all meaning: *

All this points to the necessity of interpreting the principle of self-determination as a right not of the bourgeoisie, but of the

* Cited in E. H. Carr, *The Russian Bolshevik Revolution* (Macmillan), I, 266.

working masses of the given nation. The principle of self-determination must be an instrument in the struggle for socialism and must be subordinated to the principles of socialism.

In other words, the proletariat, a small minority of the population in the predominantly peasant Ukraine and in other non-Russian areas of the old Russian Empire, is to decide the question of national allegiance. And the Communist Party, a minority of this minority, is in communist theory the interpreter of the will of the workers.

To be sure, a more ambiguous formula on the issue of self-determination for non-Russian peoples was adopted at the Eighth Congress of the Communist Party in March, 1919: *

> On the question who is to express the nation's will to secede the Russian Communist Party adopts the class historical viewpoint, taking into consideration the stage of historical development of the given nation: whether it is evolving from medievalism to bourgeois democracy or from bourgeois democracy to Soviet or proletarian democracy, etc.

Lenin was inclined to emphasize the need for caution and for consideration of the national feelings of non-Russian peoples who had suffered oppression or discrimination under Tsarist rule. But in actual practice there was an attempt to impose communism by force wherever the resources at the disposal of the Soviet Government made this feasible.

When, in the summer of 1920, Lenin had a choice between a peace with Poland on favorable territorial terms or continuation of the drive of the Red Army on Warsaw he chose the second course. "We will break the crust of Polish bourgeois resistance," he is reported to have said, "with the bayonets of the Red Army."

That political gamble failed. The Red Army was decisively defeated after reaching the outskirts of Warsaw. Henceforward, and for the next two decades, it became a cardinal principle of

* *Ibid.*, p. 270.

Soviet diplomacy not to become involved in military adventures outside the Soviet frontiers, except where no serious risk was involved, as in beating down the feeble Chinese attempt to reclaim the Chinese Eastern Railway in 1929. But this was purely a matter of expediency, of gaining time until the ravages of civil war were repaired and the foundations of a modern military power were laid. It is noteworthy that war for revolutionary purposes is considered meritorious and desirable by the high priests of the communist faith.

Lenin wrote in 1908: * "The Social Democrats † may even find themselves in the position of having to demand aggressive wars."

And after the Revolution he wrote on the same subject: ‡ "Every war implies violence against nations; but that does not prevent socialists § from being in favor of a revolutionary war."

In a letter to the author, Maxim Gorky, of January 17, 1930, Stalin emphasized an idea which is often encountered in his writings, the desirability of "revolutionary" wars:

> We are not, after all, opposed to *every* war. We are *against* imperialist war because it is counterrevolutionary war. But we are *for* a liberating, anti-imperialist, revolutionary war despite the fact that such a war, as is well known, is not only not devoid of the "horrors of bloodshed," but even abounds in them.

The communist attitude toward war, absolutist and utopian, fanatical and apocalyptic, is summed up with clear finality in this sentence by Lenin: ||

* See Vol. XV, p. 175, in Moscow fourth edition of *Lenin's Collected Works,* 1951.

† Lenin then considered himself a Social Democrat, as the term communist had not come into use.

‡ Fourth edition of *Lenin's Collected Works,* XXVIII, 264.

§ A word used in this case as synonymous with communists.

|| The *War Program of the Proletarian Revolution,* reprinted in the fourth edition of *Lenin's Collected Works,* XXIII, 67.

Only after we overthrow, completely defeat and expropriate the bourgeoisie in the entire world and not only in one country, wars will become impossible.

So Lenin believed that permanent peace would be possible only after a series of international and civil wars, and on the basis of a communist world state. In general cast of thought this is similar to his conviction that full liberty and the "withering away" of the state would be the final consequences of an indefinitely prolonged "dictatorship of the proletariat."

Another official admission that Soviet communist leaders recognize only expediency as a barrier to the spread of communism by force is to be found in a letter addressed by the Central Committee of the Communist Party of the Soviet Union to the Central Committee of the Communist Party of Yugoslavia on May 4, 1948. This was part of a secret polemic which preceded the open breach between Tito's regime and Moscow. Arguing that the French and Italian communist parties had rendered even greater services to the revolutionary cause than the Yugoslav Communist Party, the letter goes on to assert:

> The Soviet Army came to the aid of the Yugoslav people and in this way created conditions which were necessary for the Communist Party of Yugoslavia to achieve power. *Unfortunately the Soviet Army did not and could not render such assistance to the French and Italian Communist Parties.* [Italics supplied]

So there is clear recognition, before the Bolshevik Revolution and after the Bolshevik Revolution, before the Second World War and after the Second World War, of the right and obligation to use the armed force of the Soviet Union and of every communist state for the purpose of overthrowing the governments of noncommunist states. This is a formidable commitment to perpetual war and threat of war.

The Soviet Government issued one of its periodic disclaimers of concern with revolutionary movements abroad in a note addressed to the British Government in February, 1951:

It is necessary to explain that, so long as imperialist oppression exists in the world, there will exist also the liberation movement of the oppressed peoples, irrespective of the will and sympathies of some rulers or others. To accuse the Soviet Government of the existence in different countries of liberation movements caused by the oppression of imperialism is just as absurd as to accuse it of the occurrence in the world of earthquakes or tides.

There is at present no known scientific means by which human beings can produce an earthquake. Political earthquakes are in a different category. There is a science, or an art of inciting and organizing revolution. Two very prolific writers on this subject are Lenin and Stalin.

And some very original "educational institutions" have been set up in Moscow for the purpose of promoting political upheavals. There was a Sun Yat-sen University for the benefit of young Chinese revolutionaries. There was a university for the Toilers of the East, another for the Toilers of the West. Most of the students in the former university were Asiatic citizens of the Soviet Union and were being trained as future Soviet bureaucrats. But there was always a welcome for stray Japanese, Indonesian, Indo-Chinese and Indian communists.

The University for the Toilers of the West was a training school for European and American communists. Its curriculum included, along with indoctrination in the works of Marx, Lenin and Stalin, special training in street fighting and courses in the art of civil war, given by Intelligence officers of the Red Army. As a kind of postgraduate work picked students are given especially secret courses in intelligence work, wire tapping, operation of secret radio stations, passport forgery and kindred subjects.*

Anyone who was in China in 1927 could observe the remarkable number of Soviet Russians in the offices of the Chinese nationalist administration, before Chiang Kai-shek broke with the communists. They were not there as accidental tour-

* See Walter Krivitsky, *In Stalin's Secret Service* (Harper's), pp. 58–59.

ists, or for their health, or for the study of Ming porcelain. They were there to direct the Chinese revolution, if possible, into Soviet channels. The same phenomenon could have been observed in Spain during the civil war in that country. Indeed, Soviet leaders have done so much to touch off political earthquakes in other lands that they might well privately call themselves "Earthquake Producers, Inc."

Leadership of the Soviet Union and of the Comintern was always a close interlocking directorate. In the first years of Soviet rule Lenin and Trotsky took an active part in the deliberations of the International. The presidency of this body was held successively by Gregory Zinoviev and Nikolai Bukharin, both of whom, until their political eclipse,* were members of the powerful Politbureau, highest steering committee of the Communist Party. After the elimination of Bukharin Stalin handed over the direction of the Comintern to some of his lieutenants, such as the Ukrainian Dmitry Manuilsky, always keeping general supervision in his own hands.

Although Stalin could not execute foreign communists or put them in concentration camps (except those who were unlucky enough to have sought refuge in the Soviet Union) he ruled the Comintern as absolutely as he ruled the Soviet Union. A considerable number of once prominent communists outside the Soviet Union have become heretics, and sometimes vigorous anticommunists. Most of the surviving members of the original Executive Committee of the Comintern are now opposed to communism, at least in its Soviet Stalinite version.

But these individual rebels have not taken the masses of rank-and-file party members with them. Only in Yugoslavia has there been a secession of an entire party from Moscow control. This is because Tito was an unchallenged dictator, able to use police power against those communists who were unwilling to follow him in his revolt. But the other non-Russian heretics

* Both were executed in the course of the purge of the Communist Party in the thirties.

of communism have found themselves generals without armies. However eminent in the past, they have declined to the position of leaders of little sects. Nor is there evidence that the Titoist brand of communism has spread widely beyond the frontiers of Yugoslavia.

There are several reasons why attempts to organize communist movements independent of Moscow have failed. Moscow has its special agents and emissaries, well supplied with funds attached to every national communist party and experienced in organizing campaigns of slander and denunciation, even of terrorism, against rebels and dissidents. Moreover, much of the appeal of communism comes from the success of the Russian Revolution, from the idea of being a part of a mighty world movement. And communists are so carefully drilled in the idea that loyalty to the Soviet Union is their highest virtue that they find it difficult to follow a leader who breaks with the Moscow line.

According to the best available estimates there were in 1952 about 24 million communists in the world, some seven million in the Soviet Union, about five million in China. Approximately five million are in lands outside the Soviet empire, the largest parties being in Italy and France, with memberships in the neighborhood of two million and one million respectively.

The formal self-dissolution of the Comintern on May 22, 1943, has in no way altered the status of national communist parties as Soviet fifth columns. The Kremlin did not need the elaborate apparatus of the Comintern to convey its desires to the leaders of the national parties. Dissolution of the Comintern served two immediate purposes. It helped to soften up western public opinion and thereby prepared the ground for the political concessions at Teheran, Yalta and Potsdam. And it helped communists outside of Russia to pose as national patriots and thereby to gain more prestige in the underground resistance movements.

A new instrument for the coordination of communist activity in Europe was the Cominform (Communist Information Bureau), set up at Soviet initiative at a conference in Poland in September, 1947. Representatives of the communist parties of the Soviet Union, Poland, Rumania, Hungary, Bulgaria, Yugoslavia, Czechoslovakia, France and Italy signed a resolution denouncing any division between communist parties as incorrect and harmful. They decided to create in Belgrade an Information Bureau "to organize and exchange experience and, in case of necessity, to coordinate the activities of communist parties on the foundation of mutual agreement." The headquarters of the organization was shifted to Bucharest after Tito's breach with Moscow.

The principal targets of Cominform attack were the United States and the European moderate socialists who were described as "serving as faithful toadies of the imperialists, facilitating by their servile placidity the fulfilment of American capitalist aims and pushing their countries on the road to vassal dependence on the United States."

The formation of the Cominform was probably a reflection of Soviet disappointment with three developments in postwar European politics. These were United States abandonment of Roosevelt's appeasement policy, the tendency of Great Britain, under the Labor Government of Attlee and Bevin, to make a solid front with the United States and the failure, in most cases, of the European communist parties to swallow up the socialists. One exception was in Italy, where the majority of the badly splintered Italian Socialist Party, under Pietro Nenni, has gone hand in hand with the communists.

A volume could easily be filled with instances of the subservience of foreign communist parties to the often changing instructions from Moscow, which shifted in accordance with the requirements of Soviet foreign policy. The record of the American Communist Party may serve as an illustration of this point.

The American communists have proved themselves excellent Soviet patriots. They have kept political time by the Kremlin clock. So long as Maxim Litvinov, Soviet representative in the League of Nations, spoke in the accents of collective security American communists were in the forefront of every movement directed against Germany and Japan. Their views on American foreign policy were vigorously interventionist.

But when the Nazi aggression which they had denounced in anticipation became a reality the communists overnight became isolationists. There was just one reason for this apparently illogical somersault. Stalin had brought off his deal with Hitler. French and British communists were supposed to betray their countries.* Foreign communists were supposed to cry "a plague on both their houses," to denounce the war as "imperialist," but with a special edge in their criticism of Great Britain and France.

American communists followed these instructions to the letter. They denounced lend-lease, the draft, increased appropriations for national defense. Their two favorite slogans, before June 21, 1941, were "The Yanks Are Not Coming" and "The Wall Street-Downing Street Axis." They picketed the White House in the supposed interest of peace. Their motivations were entirely different from those of patriotic Americans who opposed American involvement in the war for reasons of American national interest. They were interested only in Soviet, not in American security.

Communist policy in America was reversed as soon as Germany attacked the Soviet Union. The communists were transformed into super-interventionists. Instead of stirring up strikes in defense plants they endorsed a "no strike" pledge for labor.

* The responsibility of French communist defeatism for the fall of France has been obscured by their subsequent activity in the resistance movement—after Hitler attacked the Soviet Union. The communists possessed considerable influence among the industrial workers. During a trip in France, in the time when the situation on the front was passive, I was impressed by the prevalence of the defeatist mood among the workers.

After the Teheran conference between Roosevelt, Churchill and Stalin, Earl Browder, communist leader who had formerly interpreted the New Deal as an American brand of fascism, forecast a long era of class peace in the United States and proposed to shake hands with J. P. Morgan.

Browder overshot the mark in his enthusiasm and had to pay for this later. For the Kremlin had no idea of maintaining permanently cordial relations with "bourgeois" powers. Soon after the end of the war Jacques Duclos, leading French communist, returned from Moscow and published a violent attack on Browder in *Les Cahiers du Communisme,* French communist monthly.

The effect was electrical and immediate. Duclos' article was reprinted in the American communist newspaper, *The Daily Worker.* From the unchallenged Fuehrer of the Party, Browder was degraded to the status of a pariah. For the third time over a short term of years the American fifth column responded to Moscow wirepulling.

As the cold war became warmer American public opinion belatedly awakened to the realization that the communist party was not a legitimate organization with a program of political and economic change, but a criminal and treasonable conspiracy in the service of a hostile foreign power. Despite outcries about "witch hunting," "hysteria," etc., on both sides of the Atlantic, measures were gradually taken to eliminate communists and communist sympathizers from the public service.

The true ultimate aim of the American communists is set forth with candid clarity in a publication which the Party, for opportunist reasons, has been trying to suppress rather than circulate during recent years. This is *Toward Soviet America,* published in 1932 by William Z. Foster, who became boss of the Party after the deposition of Browder. Foster's blueprint of life in the American Soviet Republic is as follows:

> The American Soviet Government will be organized along the lines of the Russian Soviets. The American Soviet Govern-

ment will join with the other Soviet governments in a world Soviet Union. The American Soviet Government will be the dictatorship of the proletariat. . . . Under the dictatorship of the
proletariat all the capitalist parties, Republican, Democratic,
Progressive, Socialist, etc., will be liquidated, the Communist
Party functioning alone as the party of the toiling masses. Likewise will be dissolved all other organizations that are political
props of the bourgeois rule, including chambers of commerce,
employers' associations, Rotary Clubs, American Legion, YMCA
and such fraternal orders as the Masons, Odd Fellows, Elks,
Knights of Columbus, etc.

There can be no reasonable doubt that a communist American would present just such a picture of terrorist tyranny as
Mr. Foster frankly outlined. For Soviet methods of rule have
proved equally applicable in Asia and in Europe, in China and
in Czechoslovakia. A good knowledge of the basic writings of
Lenin and Stalin would have been a far more instructive guide
to what would happen in China after the communists seized
power than scholarly familiarity with the Confucian classics.
And, despite difference of national background and historical
development in Poland, Rumania, Hungary, Czechoslovakia,
Bulgaria and East Germany, conditions in these countries, near
the end of the first decade of Soviet domination, are remarkably
uniform.

Everywhere all vestiges of political and civil liberty have disappeared. Jails and concentration camps are crowded. Frontiers
are guarded with barbed wire, land mines, armed police and
trained dogs to halt the flight of refugees. State domination of
economic life is complete. A beginning has been made in forcing peasants into collective farms, although the rate of progress in this field varies. Everywhere religion is persecuted, although the intensity of the antireligious drive up to the end of
1952 had been greater in Hungary and Czechoslovakia than in
staunchly Catholic Poland. The trend everywhere is toward the
creation of replicas of the Soviet Union and this is facilitated
by heavy infiltration of Soviet "advisers" and "experts" into

the army and the bureaucracy. The Polish army, for instance, is under the command of a Soviet Marshal, Konstantin Rokossovsky.

Should this trend continue unchecked for another decade some or all of the satellite states may be considered ripe for inclusion in the Soviet Union.

It is significant that the word Russia does not appear in the official title of the Soviet state. The Union of Soviet Socialist Republics is capable of indefinite expansion until it includes the whole world.

Communist parties outside the Soviet Union fall into three categories, with different functions. In the satellite countries communists are the directing hard core of the new ruling bureaucracies. At first there was a pretense, in these countries, of forming coalition governments, with representatives of all "progressive" parties. But real power and the key ministries, especially those dealing with the police, education and propaganda, always remained in the hands of the communists, usually men who had been trained in Moscow. These satellite bureaucracies are kept in order by means of frequent purges of individuals and groups suspected of disloyalty to the Kremlin or otherwise considered expendable.

A different role is prescribed for the communist party in a country where it is not in power, but has acquired a hold on a substantial minority of the population. France and Italy are examples of this situation. The French communists can count on about one fourth of the votes cast in national elections and control the CGT, the principal trade-union organization. The Italian communists are normally supported by about one fifth of the Italian voters; but this proportion rises to about one third if the procommunist Socialists, headed by Pietro Nenni, are included.

For the present communist strategy in France and Italy is not directed toward violent revolution. The odds against the success of any such attempt are strong. The immediate objective is to keep these countries weak, confused and divided, to stir up anti-American feeling, to cultivate pacifist and neutralist sentiment.

A fifth column of French or Italian proportions is an obvious security threat in the event of war. Whether this threat can be countered successfully will depend largely on the vigor and resolution of the men in command of the French and Italian military and police forces if and when the emergency comes.

There remains a third type of country, where the communists are a small minority group, with no prospect of winning enough support at the polls or in the trade-unions to exert much influence politically or economically. Such countries are the United States, Canada, the smaller nations of northern and western Europe. But here also the Kremlin has uses for its fifth columns.

The two principal tasks of communist parties, when they are too weak to influence national politics, are to serve the military interests of the Kremlin by espionage, subversion and infiltration into the state service and to influence public opinion by organizing a host of societies designed to promote a pro-Soviet attitude.

The organization of espionage is one of the major Soviet national industries. No country possesses an espionage network comparable with the Soviet in numbers of agents, in experience, cunning, resourcefulness and complete lack of inhibitions. From 1918, when the first Soviet Ambassador to Germany, Adolf Joffe, was expelled for seeking to promote revolution, until 1952, when Nikolai Skvortsov, high ranking Soviet UN official, was excluded from the United States for attempted espionage, the history of Soviet diplomacy in foreign lands has been marked by a long series of espionage scandals, some of which were not discovered until much damage had been done.

One of the most temporarily successful and one of the most completely exposed cases of Soviet official spying in a friendly and indeed an allied country is the story of the Canadian spy ring, discovered and broken up in 1945. The Soviet military attaché, Col. Nikolai Zabotin (code name Grant), recruited members for this ring among government officials with access to confidential military information and among scientists working on atomic energy and other highly secret research projects. Approach to most of these individuals was through "study groups," organized by the Canadian Labor Progressive Party, a name adopted by the Canadian Communist Party when it was declared illegal.

Among the targets of this espionage group were materials required for the production of the atomic bomb, information about the Canadian atomic research plant at Chalk River, Ontario, a sample of uranium 235, material on Canadian and United States radar, information as to electronic shells used by the American Navy. An especially valuable member of the ring was the British atomic scientist Alan Nunn May, a communist sympathizer who was able to give much valuable information in his field.

This conspiracy was discovered as a result of a remarkable accident. The cipher clerk in the Soviet Embassy in Ottawa, Igor Gouzenko, "chose freedom" in the phrase of another "deserter" from Soviet tyranny, Victor Kravchenko. He was impressed by the contrast between Canadian liberty and the repression and restraint to which he had been accustomed at home. Taking with him a quantity of incriminating messages about the espionage activities, he went to the Canadian authorities.

At first Gouzenko was received with amazed incredulity. It was a time when it was considered improper to speak, hear or think evil of "the Russian ally." But after officials from the Soviet Embassy were caught by the police breaking into Gouzenko's flat, from which he had prudently departed, he got a hearing for his story. His proofs were complete and of eighteen persons arrested twelve were convicted and sentenced to terms of imprisonment by Canadian and British courts. It is probable that clues turned up during the investigation of the Canadian spy case directed attention to Alger Hiss and other Soviet agents in the United States. Gouzenko and his family are now hidden away from vengeance reprisals of Soviet agents, under the guard of the Canadian Royal Mounted Police.

What made the Canadian spy ring a matter of international concern is the ideological fanaticism that made its organization possible. Money inducements played a minor part, although the Soviet organizers, in their usual fashion, insisted on the acceptance of small gifts, with a view to binding the operatives more closely to their cause. In Canada, as elsewhere, participants in Soviet espionage placed loyalty to communism ahead of loyalty to their country.

There has been no American equivalent of Igor Gouzenko, no one in a position to have such full and precise knowledge of all the details of an espionage project. Consequently the available picture of Soviet espionage in the United States is more fragmentary. However, it is now possible to establish beyond doubt that the Soviet Union, through its American fifth column, won considerable successes in espionage and infiltration before the war, during the war and after the war.

One of the most spectacular incidents in the American espionage story was the conviction of Alger Hiss, former high State Department official, on a charge of perjury for denying that he had, before the war, communicated confidential State Department documents to a communist spy group. The principal accuser of Hiss was Whittaker Chambers, former member of the spy group who had broken with communism and made an unsuccessful effort, in 1939, to call the attention of the government to the presence of spies and traitors in important official agencies. Roosevelt's successor, Harry Truman, referred to the accusations against Hiss as a "red herring." But the combined weight of Chambers's testimony, of the corroborating testimony of another former Soviet spy, Hede Massing, of the mute witness, the Hiss typewriter on which the incriminating documents had been typed, and of much circumstantial evidence convinced the jury, on a second trial, that Hiss was guilty.

Because of sympathetic connections in high places, Soviet spies obtained information from the highest government offices during the war years. As Elizabeth Bentley * testifies, there were informants in the Treasury, in the Pentagon, in the OSS † and other strategic places. One Nathan Gregory Silvermaster, described by Elizabeth Bentley as the principal figure in collecting and microfilming material for the use of the communist spy ring with which Miss Bentley was connected, ‡ went from one confidential government post to another, despite adverse reports from the Civil Service Commission and other sources.

That was a time when, grotesque as it may seem now, loyal Americans in some circumstances almost had to go underground. State Department officials with a realistic knowledge of communist subversion were afraid, and not without reason, that their careers would be jeopardized if they were seen in company with writers of strong anticommunist convictions.

Infiltration was even more dangerous to national security than espionage. In war it is far more advantageous to place an agent in a high capacity in the hostile army than it is to receive an ordinary spy's report. Infiltration began in the thirties, when Harold Ware organized his communist group in Washington, with a main centre in the Department of Agriculture and some members working in the Departments of Justice and the Interior and in other government agencies. Among State Department officials involved in the communist conspiracy, according to the testimony of Whittaker Chambers, Hede Massing

* See Elizabeth Bentley, *Out of Bondage* (Devin-Adair), p. 177.

† One of many illustrations of the carelessness of the OSS in employing men for what were presumably top secret assignments was the refusal of a former OSS employee, Maurice Halperin, to tell the Senate Internal Security subcommittee whether he had ever been a member of Elizabeth Bentley's spy ring or whether he had known Alger Hiss.

‡ Silvermaster never sued Miss Bentley for libel. He refused to answer all questions "for fear of self-incrimination."

and others were Noel Field (who later was apparently arrested under mysterious circumstances in Czechoslovakia), Lawrence Duggan, who jumped or fell from a window to his death and Henry Julian Wadleigh, self-confessed accomplice of Hiss.

What Hiss gave to the Soviet spy ring before the war was of negligible importance compared with the service which he could have rendered to the Soviet cause as a high State Department official during and after the war. He was at the Yalta Conference and he played an important part in the discussions of the United Nations Charter and in the San Francisco conference where the Charter was put in final form.

Another conspicuous example of infiltration in high places was Harry Dexter White, an extremely influential individual in the Treasury under Henry Morgenthau Jr. White was America's principal representative at the Bretton Woods conference on international financial reconstruction. He took along to Bretton Woods Nathan Gregory Silvermaster, whose only qualification for participation was his identification with a Soviet spy ring.

White also, according to Elizabeth Bentley, turned over to Soviet agents the plates of American occupation marks, which the Soviet Government was thus able to forge. Most important of all, he was the main architect of the so-called Morgenthau Plan, with its proposals for the destruction of all German heavy industry and mining. Nothing could have been better designed to throw Germany, in sheer despair, into the arms of the Soviet Union. The career and motivations of White, who died suddenly when clouds of suspicion were gathering thickly about him, would be a rewarding subject for a Congressional investigation.

There seems to have been good reason for the boast of the mysterious J. Peters, alias Alexander Stevens, alias Isidor Boorstein, alias Mr. Silver, whose real name was Alexander Goldberger. He was of Hungarian origin and was head of the national underground of the American Communist Party. And he boasted to Whittaker Chambers: * "Even in Germany under the Weimar Republic the Party did not have what we have here."

Communist and pro-Soviet infiltration and influence in connection with Far Eastern policy are discussed in Chapter IV. Another triumph of communist espionage was the enlistment of the German *émigré* scientist, and naturalized British subject, Klaus Fuchs, a man whose brain was unfortunately developed out of all proportion to his mind, or his sense of right and wrong. Fuchs was arrested in Great Britain and sentenced to a term of imprisonment. Of his several American accomplices two, Julius and Ethel Rosenberg, were sentenced to death and Harry Gold, David Greenglass and others received long prison sentences. America was at last beginning to take treason seriously. But the betrayals by Fuchs, Allan Nunn May, the Rosenbergs and others probably speeded up considerably the Soviet timetable of atomic bomb manufacture.

In the face of the innumerable proved cases of Soviet espionage not only in the United States and Great Britain but in Sweden, the Netherlands, Germany and many other countries it is merely silly to dismiss this threat as a product of "hysteria." Nor is the frequently repeated insinuation that ex-communists are unreliable and irresponsible witnesses borne out by the facts.

Whittaker Chambers and Elizabeth Bentley named many individuals as associated in various ways with communist espionage. Only two of these persons brought libel suits, Alger Hiss against Chambers, William Remington against Elizabeth Bentley. Both suits turned out very disastrously for their authors. In this matter of communist fifth column activity, as in the matter of communist slave labor camps, there is a vast amount of corroborative evidence, which only mental laziness or communist bias, conscious or unconscious, can reject.

* *Witness,* p. 33.

Three factors, taken together, make the Soviet fifth column machine the biggest and most formidable in the world. First, there is the historic Russian addiction to spying, which dates from medieval Muscovy and which is intensified by the underground, conspirative tradition of the communists. Second, there is the commitment of a despotic government, in control of vast territory, huge population and unlimited resources, to a program of intrigue and subversion all over the world. It may be argued that all governments resort to espionage to some extent. But no government of a powerful state has endeavored over a long period of time not only to penetrate the military secrets of other countries, but to undermine the political and economic institutions of these countries.

Finally, the attractiveness of communism as a utopian faith has created an army of potential fifth columnists outside the Soviet frontiers—men and women who join and cooperate with Soviet spy rings not for hire but because they believe they are serving a noble cause.

The question is sometimes asked whether Soviet aggressive expansion is a product of old Russian imperialism or of communist revolutionary ambitions. Both forces are at work and the two are sometimes intermeshed. Stalin and Stalin's successors are the heirs of Ivan the Terrible and Peter the Great and Catherine the Great, who added much new territory to the Russian Empire. But they are also the heirs of Lenin, who proclaimed the necessity of world revolution.

Soviet annexations after the Second World War closely correspond with Tsarist ambitions in the First World War. These may be summarized as follows: *

All Polish territories in Germany and Austria were to be absorbed in the Russian Empire.

East Prussia was to be annexed by Russia.

* See David J. Dallin, *Russia and Postwar Europe* (Yale University Press), pp. 168–69.

Eastern Galicia (then a part of Austria-Hungary) was to be transferred to Russia.

A Czech kingdom was to be created under a Russian protectorate.

Turkey was to be ousted from Europe, with Russia receiving most of the Turkish possessions in Europe, including Constantinople.

All these aspirations, except the last, have been realized by Stalin, whether through direct annexation or through the creation of vassal states in Poland and Czechoslovakia. In the Far East also Soviet acquisitions after the war, South Sakhalin, the Kurile Islands, Outer Mongolia,* a privileged status in Manchuria are in line with old Russian imperialist desires.

But the ambitions of Tsarist Russia, although extensive, were not unlimited. Soviet communism aims at a world federation of Soviet Republics. The combination of the old wine of Tsarist imperialist ambition with the new wine of communist revolutionary ambition makes a heady draught.

There is a third element that drives the Soviet regime along the road of direct and indirect aggression. This is the dynamics of fear. Not the fear of foreign armies marching across Soviet frontiers. There is not in being, there is not in prospect, even if optimistic plans for a European army are realized, a land army in Europe or in Asia capable of constituting an offensive threat to the Soviet Union.

What the Soviet rulers fear is something much less tangible. It is the still small voice of freedom. It is the very existence of free societies where the standard of living is much higher than in the Soviet Union. This is why the Soviet Government, safe against land invasion as no Russian government has been in history, feels an irresistible impulse to communize countries within its sphere of control and to sow seeds of class warfare

* Outer Mongolia has actually been under Soviet control since 1921. Formal recognition of this situation occurred after the war.

among peoples who are beyond the reach of immediate communization.

It is doubtful whether Gibbon's *Decline and Fall of the Roman Empire* is favorite reading for the men in the Kremlin. But they would certainly like to create the monopolistic power situation which the great historian describes with such vivid eloquence:

> The empire of the Romans filled the world, and when that empire fell into the hands of a single person the world became a safe and dreary prison for his enemies. . . . To resist was fatal, and it was impossible to fly.

The communist dictators can feel entirely safe only when there are no more free countries to serve as beacons of hope and sanctuaries of refuge for their discontented subjects.

Chapter XII ⟿ Soviet Challenge: American Response

The Soviet challenge of expansion, by direct and indirect aggression, far beyond Russia's ethnic frontiers, demanded an American response of some kind. The first response, appeasement, was a pitiful failure, morally and politically.

The second response was a policy known as containment. This was formulated by George Kennan,* a thoughtful career diplomat with a specialized knowledge of Russian language, history and literature and of Soviet political institutions and communist philosophy. A mind like Kennan's exercised little influence on policy during the war years, when any ignorant amateur with a "hunch" that Stalin's heart was in the right place, found ready audience at the White House.

By 1947 American statesmen were in a sadder and wiser mood about Soviet purposes. An article contributed by Kennan, under the transparent pseudonym, "Mr. X," to the quarterly *Foreign Affairs,* entitled "The Sources of Soviet Conduct," set forth in the following key sentences the basic outline of a new policy, "containment":

> The main element of any United States policy toward the So-
> viet Union must be that of a longterm, patient but firm and vig-

* Kennan served for a time as head of the Policy Planning Staff and as Counsellor of the State Department.

ilant containment of Russian expansive tendencies. . . . Soviet pressure against the free institutions of the Western world is something that can be contained by the adroit and vigilant application of counter-force at a series of constantly shifting geographical and political points, but which cannot be charmed or talked out of existence. . . . The United States has it in its power to increase enormously the strains under which Soviet policy must operate, to force upon the Kremlin a far greater degree of moderation and circumspection than it has had to observe in recent years, and in this way to promote tendencies which must eventually find their outlet in either the break-up or the gradual mellowing of Soviet power.

This new policy came under a crossfire of criticism from two sides. It was argued that United States resources could not check every Soviet move along the vast perimeter of the Soviet empire. The principal spokesman for this type of criticism, Mr. Walter Lippmann, never made clear what was the alternative to containment, what additional areas could safely be abandoned to Soviet conquest.

Containment has been more convincingly criticized from a diametrically opposed standpoint.* Containment, it was argued, was too static. The Soviet empire, including the satellite countries of Eastern Europe and China, would be an intolerable threat to American national security. Mere maintenance of the status quo, with a long period for consolidation, would mean victory for the Soviet grand design of ultimate world conquest. This view was apparently shared by Mr. John Foster Dulles. In a book published before he became Secretary of State Mr. Dulles says: †

> The great danger of war would come if and when Soviet leaders successfully combined Eastern Europe and Asia into a vast political, industrial and military unity and completed the "encirclement" phase of their strategy. They would then be so strong that they might well plan to finish their conquest by war.

* An excellent criticism of passive containment is to be found in James Burnham, *Containment or Liberation?* (John Day).
† See John Foster Dulles, *War or Peace* (Macmillan), p. 251.

President Eisenhower, in a campaign speech before the American Legion in September, 1952, called the long roll of nations and areas of Europe which have been absorbed into the Soviet empire and added: "The American conscience can never know peace until these peoples are restored again to being masters of their own fate."

This seemed to pose a clear issue between liberation and containment as alternative policies. Eisenhower, however, made it clear in subsequent addresses that he did not propose to go to war to achieve the liberation of the subjugated nations. And Kennan's policy, if one studies his words closely, is not as passive as some of his critics represent. There is a clear recognition of America's political stake in a possible break-up of the Soviet regime.

Containment and liberation should be conceived not as sharp alternatives, but as complementary aims. In some cases holding the line has been the most that could reasonably be hoped for, given the present distribution of military strength, the weakness of many of America's overseas associates and the facts of geography.

But the ultimate goal of liberation of all peoples within the huge Soviet empire should never be lost from view. A passive strategy of waiting for the next Kremlin blow to fall would be an almost certain prescription for defeat. In cold war, as in hot war, initiative is most important.

The policy of containment has been applied most effectively in Europe. Here the demarcation line created by the position of the armies at the end of the war remains the political frontier, with the important exception of Yugoslavia. Tito's defection from Moscow almost immediately began to pay political dividends. The communist uprising in Greece began to languish as soon as aid across the Yugoslav border ceased. It may now be reckoned that the combined military strength of Greece, Turkey and Yugoslavia represents a fair offset to Soviet satellite strength, especially since these countries, setting an example which some older and more mature powers might well follow, have concluded an alliance. Every such development of regional strength diminishes the likelihood of a Soviet military adventure.

For practical reasons containment is probably the only feasible course in Europe until much greater armed power is developed. It would be insane rashness to precipitate an armed clash in Europe under present conditions. Unless political discontent and disaffection behind the iron curtain are far greater than there is any solid reason to believe the immediate result of war in Europe would be a Soviet advance to the Atlantic. What held Stalin back, what deters Stalin's successors from an attempt to add West Germany, France, Italy and the other countries of Western Europe to the number of affiliated Soviet republics is a combination of considerations.

In order of probable importance these may be listed as follows.

Fear of the consequences of a prolonged war with a nation of America's industrial power.

Recognition of the tremendous damage which atomic bombing from bases in Great Britain, Morocco, perhaps Spain and other Mediterranean bases and from aircraft carriers in the Mediterranean could inflict on the large centres of Soviet industrial production.

Belief that the internal contradictions of the capitalist economic system and the conflicts of interest between noncommunist nations will make it possible in the long run to achieve world domination without the risk of a great war.

Uncertainty about the morale of the peoples in the Soviet empire, especially in the satellite states, under the stress of prolonged war.

Preparations which have been made during recent years to create genuine military defense in Western Europe.

This last consideration is probably the least of the deterrents at the present time, and will be until West German rearma-

ment is a reality and not a subject of endless delays and bicker-
ings. But it would be a grave and perhaps a tragic error to stop
or slacken efforts to build, in any way that may be politically
feasible, a strong well balanced European army, with a substantial German contingent. The peace offensive launched from
the Kremlin in the first weeks after Stalin's death is not convincing. It is most probably designed largely to lull the alert-
ness of the noncommunist powers, to disrupt Western defense
preparations.

It would certainly be most unwise to take chances on the
permanence or reliability of Kremlin pacific assurances, which
may well be adjusted to a timetable of Soviet atomic and other
military build-up. The danger of a Soviet invasion of Western
Europe and a Third World War automatically diminishes with
every increase in European defense strength and increases with
every decline in this strength.

Latent discontent in the countries behind the iron curtain
is most likely to break out when genuine military strength is
visible on the other side of the border. Dana Adams Schmidt,
former *New York Times* correspondent in Czechoslovakia, who
hastily left that country after hearing himself denounced as a
"spy" on the official radio, tells a revealing story in this connection. Near the border in his automobile, Mr. Schmidt was
alarmed at meeting a policeman. But the latter merely gave him
road directions and said: "You are leaving the country. I hope
you come back." And then, in a lowered voice: "And when
you come I hope you come with tanks."

There must be many embittered, dissatisfied individuals behind the iron curtain. But their mood is not likely to lead to
action unless and until they see "tanks" in impressive numbers
at the disposal of the free nations.

It was in 1947 that Kennan outlined the policy of containment. How have his assumptions about the effect of this policy
worked out? Most probably containment, accompanied by the
build-up of United States armaments and the assumption by

America of clearcut obligations in the event of attack against any of the NATO powers, against West Germany, Japan, Australia and New Zealand, has imposed on the Soviet Union "a far greater degree of moderation and circumspection." Quite probably the Soviet-inspired aggression in Korea took place because there was no positive affirmation of an American intention to defend Korea. Indeed the withdrawal of American troops, the failure to equip an adequate South Korean army and the ill judged speech of Dean Acheson * had created an opposite impression: that South Korea would be left to its fate.

There is as yet no sign of either "a break-up or a mellowing of the Soviet regime." It is always difficult to calculate political and economic strains and stresses under a dictatorship, which is more secretive in time of peace than a free country is in time of war. But there is no clear indication that the grip of the Soviet regime has been weakened (although the death of Stalin poses a test of which the ultimate outcome cannot be foreseen) or that the cold war has created dangerous tensions inside the Soviet Union.

Since 1947 there has been a steady growth in Soviet industrial output and there has also been a gradual improvement in living conditions. This improvement has been from a fantastically low level, subnormal even for the Soviet Union because of war devastation and dislocation. But successive annual cuts in the prices of foodstuffs and manufactured goods indicate that the supplies have somewhat improved.

Restrictions on trade with the Soviet Union and its satellites have been justified and necessary. Had there been no such restrictions Soviet war potential would certainly be greater than it actually is. But, given the extremely low standard of living which communism always imposes, the communist empire is big enough in area and rich enough in resources to be almost self-sufficient. Before the Second World War, when artificial restrictions on trade did not exist, there was a very small ex-

* See Chapter V.

change of goods between the United States and the Soviet Union. The virtually complete cessation of this trade could not, therefore, be expected to paralyze the Soviet economy. This economy is not dependent on the West for any single commodity so vital as to be indispensable.

What of the policy of "liberation" which is offered as a dynamic substitute for "containment"? To some extent this policy has already gone into effect. It has been realized, somewhat belatedly, that the methods of subversion which the Soviet Government has practiced in foreign countries ever since it came into power call for reprisals in kind.

It is now widely if not universally recognized that it is sheer pedantic absurdity to treat governments which came into power by violence, maintain themselves in power by terror and observe no inhibitions in trying to suborn the allegiance of citizens of noncommunist states as if they possessed any element of legitimacy or were entitled to benefit from normal rules governing intercourse between civilized states. George Kennan deserved well of his country by giving coherent form and logic to the instinctive, more or less haphazard policy of resistance which followed the bankruptcy of appeasement.

But there is a lack of imagination and of logic in the following paragraph in a speech which Mr. Kennan delivered before the Pennsylvania Bar Association on January 16, 1953:

> I would be extremely careful of doing anything at the governmental level that purports to affect directly the governmental system in another country, no matter what the provocation may seem. It is not consistent with our international obligations. It is not consistent with a common membership with other countries in the United Nations. It is not consistent with the maintenance of formal diplomatic relations with another country.

What is overlooked in this type of reasoning, which is not peculiar to Mr. Kennan,* is that obligations, to be valid, must

* In the same speech Kennan used an unfortunate quotation when he cited John Quincy Adams as saying: "America goes not abroad in search

be mutual. Neither the Soviet Union nor any communist state has ever shown the slightest regard for any of the obligations so gravely set forth in this quotation.

The Soviet Government has challenged the West to a competition in the organization of international civil war. Western peoples would prefer that this challenge had never been offered. But, since it has been made, it can be ignored only at serious peril and disadvantage.

The Soviet Government has organized a gigantic international fifth column, devoted to the service of Moscow. The logical and proper response is to endeavor to organize fifth columns of one kind or another in every country behind the iron curtain, including the Soviet Union.

This competition is far from equal and it is not surprising that Moscow is well in the lead in the race for organizing subversion. Communist parties function legally in most Western countries. Even where public opinion has been aroused to the reality of the communist threat, the restrictions and disabilities imposed on communists and communist sympathizers are almost laughably mild, compared with what anticommunists must face behind the iron curtain. There men are regularly shot or sent to concentration camps for actions or attitudes which are not legally punishable at all in free countries. The prospect of a bullet in the back of the head or of an indefinite term at slave labor is a much more formidable deterrent than the possibility of being unfavorably mentioned by some Congressional investigating committee.

Soviet fifth column activity possesses the advantage of long experience, extending over a period of almost forty years. This has created a fund of expert knowledge of such technical details as forging passports, smuggling agents across frontiers, making contacts in foreign countries, etc. International undercover

of monsters to destroy." In Adams's time there was no "monster" comparable with the Soviet regime, intent on the destruction of the United States.

work is a new experience for the United States. It is almost inevitable that there should be blunders as a result of over-zealousness and inexperience. And it is one of the handicaps of a free press that it is not easy to keep diplomatic and intelligence secrets.

Soviet espionage is strong defensively as well as offensively; its operatives are well trained in counter-espionage. And Soviet law (or absence of law) provides no loopholes through which a suspect may escape. The first principle of the communist police state is that a hundred innocent persons should suffer, rather than that one guilty person should elude detection. Opening of letters, wire tapping, torture to extort information, threats to the lives of wives, children, relatives and friends are routine police methods in communist states.

On the other hand, latent discontent is deeper and more bitter behind the iron curtain than it is in the West. About 50,000 Czechs fled from their country in the first years after the communist seizure of power in 1948.* It is doubtful whether as many as fifty Americans and Britons or West Europeans sought political asylum in Czechoslovakia during this same period. Flights from Czechoslovakia, from Poland, from Hungary persist, often by the most daring means, such as the seizing of airplanes or small boats.

Fear and suspicion reach into the highest levels of the communist bureaucracies. The fate of eleven high functionaries in Czechoslovakia, including the Secretary of the Communist Party, Rudolf Slansky, and the Foreign Minister, Vladimir Clementis, hanged after a standard purge trial, shows that men in the highest positions live always in the shadow of the gallows. This situation creates a permanent atmosphere of fear, tension and suspicion which should afford many opportunities for enterprising secret agents of the western powers.

One American response to the Soviet fifth column challenge

* Dana Adams Schmidt, *Anatomy of a Satellite* (Little, Brown), p. 431.

was the organization in 1949 of the Free Europe Committee. A private organization, this Committee enjoys the full sympathy of the State Department and other government agencies. This Committee has aided in various ways the National Councils which have been set up as centers of leadership for political refugees from the satellite countries. Scholars and legal experts have been set to work studying the newspapers and translating the laws of the totalitarian regimes. The most ambitious and aggressive project of the Free Europe Committee was the inauguration of Radio Free Europe in Munich in 1951.

The first principal target of this station was Czechoslovakia, with Hungary also included in the broadcasts and plans for reaching Poland and other iron curtain lands. A very useful type of broadcasting is the exposure of communist informers. The details of every successful escape are promptly beamed back to Czech listeners. The communist government has shown itself very sensitive to this kind of psychological warfare. It has lodged violent diplomatic protests and used up some of the country's limited electronic resources in jamming operations.

Another centre of political warfare is West Berlin. The station RIAS broadcasts to the Soviet Zone. Various German organizations, such as Dr. Rayner Hildebrandt's "League for Fighting Inhumanity," try to keep sparks of resistance alive in the Soviet Zone. Communist secret agents are exposed; escapes are organized for political refugees. With tens of thousands of fugitives arriving every month from the Soviet Zone, West Berlin is a valuable lookout point for the West and a thorn in the side of the Soviet empire.

An attempt to carry political warfare into the heart of this empire was the organization, in the winter of 1950-51, of the Committee for Liberation from Bolshevism. This was the last of several names selected for a group of American citizens who are interested in promoting the liberation of the peoples of the Soviet Union from Soviet tyranny. This organization, now headed by Admiral L. C. Stevens, former naval attaché in the

American Embassy in Moscow, sets for itself goals similar to those of the Free Europe Committee in the satellite countries.

There has been a protracted and difficult effort, which finally achieved partial success, to create in Munich a coordinating centre, with representation for all democratic anticommunist groups among the political emigrants from the Soviet Union. There has been aid to publications and research projects. And radio broadcasting in Russian and other languages of the Soviet Union has been recently inaugurated.

This attempt to drive a wedge between the communist ruling class and the masses of the people in the Soviet Union aims at a very desirable political objective. Obviously the happiest ending to the cold war would be the overthrow from within of the regimes which, by their nature and philosophy, can never be expected to live in sincere peace with their free neighbors.

It would be fantastic to think in terms of the military conquest, subjugation and even temporary occupation of the enormous area, which is now under communist rule. Even if large-scale war should unfortunately prove inevitable, the rational objective would not be a repetition of the Unconditional Surrender fiasco of the late war, but the waging of political along with military warfare, designed to make possible the emergence of governments with which it would be possible to make a genuine peace.

However, the promotion of liberation movements within the Soviet Union poses formidable difficulties, which it would be mere wishful thinking to underestimate. The Soviet Union has lived under communist rule for more than thirty-five years, much longer than the satellite states or the regions which were annexed after the Pact with Hitler. Consequently the sense of contrast in living conditions before and after the coming of communism is less sharp, belief in a feasible alternative to Soviet methods of administration is weaker.

Reliable information is hard to obtain, especially in the Soviet Union, where foreigners for two decades have been debarred from anything remotely resembling normal contacts with the people. But it seems probable that anticommunist feeling is strongest in East Germany, where national oppression and exploitation enter into the situation, somewhat less strong in the satellite countries, a little weaker in the annexed areas (where there have been massive purges of known anticommunists), still weaker in the Soviet Union itself. Almost everyone under fifty in the Soviet Union today has passed the formative years of his life under Soviet influence.

A psychological element to which radio and leaflet propaganda can appeal in the satellite states does not exist, at least in the same intensity, among the peoples who were under Soviet rule from the end of the Russian civil war. This is the sense of being subjected to foreign domination, of being exploited for the benefit of Russia.

Whether and how far this feeling of foreign rule exists among the non-Russian peoples who make up more than half the population of the Soviet Union within its present borders is a hotly disputed question. But a common experience first of Imperial Russian, then of Soviet rule creates certain bonds which do not exist in the case of peoples annexed during and after 1939.

The German invasion of the Soviet Union was a supreme test of the morale of the Soviet peoples. The results of this test are mixed and may be interpreted in different ways. Between half a million and a million Soviet citizens were recruited for the German armed forces. Many Russians fled as the Germans retreated; in this case the Nazis, ironically enough, were "liberators" for some anticommunists. Among millions of Soviet citizens who were taken to Germany and Austria as war prisoners and laborers some two or three hundred thousand refused to go home. This figure, strikingly high in any case, would probably have been larger if repatriation, during the first months after the end of the war, had not been on an enforced basis.

On the other hand, millions of Soviet citizens fought fiercely in the Red Army. And, except in the western Ukraine and the Baltic States, where there were local uprisings as the Red Army retreated in 1941, the reaction of the Soviet population to the Germans was passive, not active. There were no attempts to overthrow the Soviet regime or to put anything in its place. The Germans were accepted, especially in the Ukraine, as a lesser evil by the more anti-Soviet groups in the population. But, apart from a guerrilla movement in the forests and swamps of the Ukraine which pursued the understandable but impractical ideal of fighting both the Nazis and the Communists, there was not much positive anti-Soviet initiative. There might have been more if the German methods of occupation had not been so predatory and so imbued with the Nazi concept of the Slavs as an inferior race.

The most significant anti-Soviet political program which evolved at this time was drawn up by the captured Soviet General Andrei Vlasov, who tried to organize a Russian national army in agreement with the Germans. Vlasov was not a German agent or a traitor to the Russian people. His ideal was a Russia which would not go back to Tsarism, but which would be freed from the oppression of communism.

Hitler suspected that if Vlasov were given an opportunity to form a powerful army among Russian prisoners and Russians in occupied territory, he would turn against Germany. So, although a propaganda legend grew up about a "Vlasov Army," most of the Soviet recruits for the German armed forces had no connection with Vlasov. They were either brigaded with German units in small groups or organized in non-Russian nationality units, Ukrainian, Turcoman, Cossack, etc.*

* Cossacks are not a separate nationality. They are of Russian and Ukrainian origin. But, as they were before the Revolution independent peasant proprietors with above average land allotments and a special obligation and tradition of service as cavalry in the Tsar's army, they were mostly on the anticommunist side in the Russian civil war and suffered much from forced collectivization. It was natural that the Germans should find some of them responsive to anti-Soviet appeals.

Vlasov summed up his political aims in a program known as the Smolensk Manifesto, which still remains probably the best statement of the grievances of the Soviet peoples against their communist rulers. Its more important points * are as follows:

Abolition of forced labor and guaranty to the worker of a real right to labor, leading to material welfare.

Abolition of collective farms and planned transfer of land into private peasant property.

Re-establishment of trade, handicrafts and artisan trades, and the creation of opportunity for private initiative to participate in the economic life of the country.

Opportunity for the intelligentsia to create freely for the welfare of the people.

Guaranty of social justice and the protection of working people from exploitation.

Introduction for working people of a real right to education, to leisure, to a secure old age.

Termination of the reign of terror and violence; introduction of actual freedom of religion, conscience, speech, assembly and press; guaranty of the inviolability of the person and personal residence.

Guaranty of freedom for subject nationalities.

The liberation of the political prisoners of bolshevism, and the return from prisons and camps to the Motherland of all those who suffered detention in the struggle against bolshevism.

Under happier circumstances this might have been a declaration of independence and a draft constitution for the peoples of the Soviet Union. Vlasov was himself the son of a peasant. He grew up under the Soviet regime and knew the grievances of the people at first hand. His proposals coincide closely with

* Cited in George Fischer, *Soviet Opposition to Stalin* (Harvard University Press), pp. 59–60. This is the best available account in English of the complicated relations between the Germans and anti-Soviet Russians during the war.

the feelings and desires of the newer generation of political refugees from the Soviet Union.

Hatred of collective farming, generally regarded as a return to serfdom, is very strong, according to the testimony of these new refugees. Equally strong is the desire for some assurance against arbitrary arrest and exile. And there is a general belief that a loosening of the present system, under which the state controls everything from steel mills to barber shops, would make for more individual comfort and a higher standard of living.

On the other hand, there is a general feeling * that the bigger factories and power plants and similar enterprises, most of which have been built since the Revolution, should remain in public ownership. So much time has passed since the Revolution that there is no longer any sense of private property rights in factories which were nationalized thirty-five years ago. Soviet citizens wish to keep and improve broadened educational opportunities and such social services as free medical treatment and old age and disability compensation.

Vlasov's anti-Soviet movement was almost foredoomed to failure. It fell between two stools: profound Nazi distrust of anything that suggested an independent Russia and undiscriminating western aversion to anyone whom the Soviet Government branded as a collaborator with the Germans. Vlasov was only permitted to organize a small army in the winter of 1944–45 when the German military situation was hopeless and the injection of this force could have no effect. The sole military achievement of the Vlasov forces was the driving of the Germans out of Prague in the last confused days of the war. Then the force dissolved. Vlasov and his principal lieutenants,

* These and other impressions of the moods of Soviet refugees are based partly on individual talks, partly on interrogations of individual Soviet refugees and replies to questions circulated by official and unofficial agencies.

after falling into the hands of the Americans, were handed over to the Soviet authorities for execution.*

The policy of delivering up to the Soviet police Soviet citizens who had fled abroad during the war was worse than a crime. As Talleyrand might have said, it was a blunder. It has been an albatross around the necks of those who tried to carry out America's later policy of trying to rally the forces of freedom among Soviet refugees. It deprived these anti-Soviet refugees of their most popular leader, General Vlasov, and it left an atmosphere of bitterness and disillusionment that is not easy to dispel.

This is only one of the handicaps with which the American Liberation Committee has been obliged to cope. There is no means of reaching the Soviet population. It is only possible to deal with Russians and other Soviet citizens who are living abroad. These fall into two main categories, the million or more who fled during the years of revolution and civil war and the smaller, but substantial number (probably between a quarter of a million and half a million) who escaped abroad during and after the late war.

There is a marked difference between these two categories. They fall, as a rule, into different age groups and the more recent refugees are, of course, in much closer touch with Soviet realities. The American Committee soon learned that there was an embarrassingly large number of emigrant political organizations, deeply divided by questions of ideology and still more, perhaps, by personal rivalries and antagonisms.

Throughout history political exiles of all kinds, living for long periods of time in foreign countries under conditions of frustration and often in circumstances of poverty and hardship,

* The circumstances under which Vlasov fell into Soviet hands are somewhat obscure. There may have been an element of accident in his capture by the Russians. Cf. Fischer, *op. cit.*, pp. 117–18. But in the psychological atmosphere of the time he would almost certainly have been handed over, in any case.

SOVIET CHALLENGE: AMERICAN RESPONSE 309

tend to quarrel and dispute vehemently among themselves. One need only recall the furious prerevolutionary polemics between Lenin and Trotsky, between the Bolsheviki, the Mensheviki and other revolutionary groups.

Both the Free Europe Committee and the American Liberation Committee have experienced much of this tendency of émigré groups to become involved in personal feuds and doctrinal schisms. The Poles are the most numerous of the uprooted ethnic groups and their hatred for Russia and for communism is deeprooted and strong. But it has not yet been possible to form a representative Polish National Council because of disagreements among the Polish exile leaders. These stem partly from pre-war Polish politics, partly from differences of opinion about policies during the war. Factional disputes have affected the efficiency of some of the other National Councils for the satellite states.

Besides trying to reconcile differences among the Russian organizations the Committee for Liberation has been obliged to face the problem of how to deal with the nationalist aspirations of the non-Russian refugees from the Soviet Union. Of these the Ukrainians (of whom there are 35–40 million in the Soviet Union) are the best organized and most articulate abroad. There are a substantial number of naturalized American and Canadian citizens of Ukrainian origin and there were many Ukrainians among the Soviet deportees in Germany who refused to return home after the war.

Many representatives of these non-Russian Soviet peoples are all-out separatists, who believe that the enemy is not communism, but the eternal oppressor, Russia. The Committee has tried to steer a middle course between the position of the extreme Russian nationalists, who are willing to concede little or nothing to the non-Russian minorities and the claims of the extreme separatists. It has sought to find bases of agreement, not of division between the Russian and non-Russian groups. It has refused to adopt any attitude about possible future boundaries or forms of federation among the peoples in the Soviet Union. The Committee has adhered to the position that such matters must be settled in the future, on the spot, by the peoples concerned, that the immediate problem is to organize the widest possible anticommunist front among all the organizations, Russian and non-Russian.

It is not easy to win acceptance of this moderate viewpoint among suspicious, embittered political refugees, to whom argument is the breath of life. The Committee has come under attack from two opposed sources. It has been accused by Russian nationalists of working for the "dismemberment" of Russia. Ukrainian and Caucasian separatists, on their side, reproach the Committee as a tool of "Russian imperialism."

Each side in this dispute is inclined to threaten dire consequences if the Committee and, more important, the American Government does not accept its viewpoint. Say the Russians:

"Any proposal to break up Russia will throw the Russian people into the arms of the Soviet Government."

Reply the non-Russians: "Our peoples will not be interested in the struggle against communism unless their right to separate national existence is recognized."

What is the evidence, historical and modern, on this issue, so vigorously debated between Russians and non-Russians in exile. Unquestionably the Empire of the Tsars was built up in no small degree by the sword; the vast accretions of territory during the four centuries which elapsed between Ivan the Terrible and Stalin were not acquired by peaceful means, or by defensive wars. And throughout this Empire there were smoldering embers of national discontent.

The compact mass of the Russian population is to be found in the northern and central provinces of European Russia, in the area which roughly coincides with the old grand duchy of Muscovy. Russians are scattered out over the whole expanse of the Soviet Union; Siberia was largely colonized by Russians.

In the fertile southern region of European Russia are the

Ukrainians, a Slav people with their own language and literature. Never strong enough to establish a state with secure
boundaries, the Ukraine wavered between Russia, Poland and
Turkey in the seventeenth and early eighteenth centuries and
was finally brought definitely into the Russian Empire as Poland
declined. In the eastern and southeastern parts of European
Russia are a number of peoples and tribes of Mongolian and
Finno-Ugrian origin, Tartars, Bashkirs, Chuvashes, Mordvians,
to mention a few.

The Caucasus Mountain region, between the Black and Cas-
pian Seas, is a museum for the ethnologist and the linguist;
there are few areas in the world where one finds such a mixture
of races and languages. The three largest national groups are
the Armenians, Georgians and Azerbaidjan Tartars. They live
south of the main range of the Caucasus; north of this range
are mountain tribes, mostly of the Moslem faith. In Central
Asia, a region of hot deserts, lush oases, high mountains and
enormous prairies, there are 15 or 20 million Soviet Mohamme-
dans, Uzbeks, Turcomen, Kazakhs, Kirghiz, Tadjiks and others.

The fall of the Tsarist regime and the virtual paralysis of authority under the weak Provisional Government let loose a tidal
wave of centrifugal nationalism. Before the period of political
chaos and civil war came to an end with the definite victory of
the Soviet Government in 1921 almost all the non-Russian peoples had, at least temporarily, set up independent governments.
Five nationalities achieved independence until the Second
World War, the Poles, the Finns, the Letts, Lithuanians and
Estonians.

In words the Soviet Government recognized the right of non-
Russian peoples to self-determination, including secession. But
its armies ruthlessly smashed the noncommunist governments
which were set up for a time in the Ukraine, the Caucasus and
Central Asia. And Stalin took advantage of his pact with Hitler and the Second World War to seize the Baltic Republics,

parts of Poland and Finland, Bessarabia and Northern Bukovina.

While evidence from the test of the German invasion is fragmentary and disputable, it seems that the loyalty of the non-
Russian nationalities to the Soviet regime was shakier than
that of the Russians. Many grievances were common to the entire Soviet population. Russians as well as non-Russians filled
the prisons and concentration camps and suffered from the stern
laws that bound the worker to his factory and the peasant to
his collective farm, like a medieval serf.

But a sense of being different from the Russians in ethnic
origin, history, culture and sometimes (in the case of the Moslems) in religion supplied additional motives for discontent
and defection. It was on five non-Russian peoples (the Volga
Germans, Crimean Tartars, Kalmyks and the Chechen-Ingush
and Kabardo-Balkharian tribesmen of the North Caucasus)
that the Soviet Government inflicted the most ruthless mass
punishments during and after the war. Whole populations were
rounded up and deported to remote parts of Asiatic Russia and
the very names of the offending republics and regions were
blotted off the map of the Soviet Union.*

Before the war, during the war and since the war there has
been a special visible current of anticommunist feeling with
nationalist inspiration. Purges of the Communist Party in the
Ukraine have been especially frequent and sweeping and there
have been repeated complaints in Soviet newspapers of the per-
sistence of what are called "nationalist deviations" in the
Ukraine and other non-Russian areas. Ukrainian guerrilla
forces held sizable regions of the northwestern Ukraine during
the war and continued to fight against Soviet and Polish troops,
at least as late as 1948.

---

* A former German officer whose unit reached the Caucasus Mountains, farthest point of the German advance into Russia, told me that
the attitude of the Caucasian mountaineers was very friendly to the
Germans.

The Ukrainian situation has been complicated by the Soviet annexation, at the expense of Poland and Rumania, of Eastern Galicia and Northern Bukovina, with some 5 million Ukrainian inhabitants. These Ukrainians, Austro-Hungarian subjects before the First World War, have never been under Russian rule and are mostly Roman Catholics of the Uniat rite.

The brutal suppression of the Uniat Church, accompanied by executions and disappearances of its leading prelates, has given these western Ukrainians an additional religious grievance.

It seems reasonable to believe that the Ukraine, especially the western Ukrainian regions which did not know Soviet rule until 1939, the Baltic States, the Caucasus and Central Asia would prove soft spots in the Soviet empire in the event of war. The much advertised Soviet policy of equal treatment for all nationalities has always been a rather unreal façade. To borrow a phrase from George Orwell's *Animal Farm* the Russians, although subjected to the same methods of terrorist control, have been "more equal" than the other nationalities.

Final political and economic controls have been centralized in Moscow. The natives who formally held the highest offices in the non-Russian republics were figureheads who could be deposed and sometimes executed on an order from Moscow.

Freedom in the use of native languages, granted after the Revolution, has been curtailed. The Latin alphabets which were worked out for some of the oriental peoples have been abolished.

It is only Russian national heroes of the past, Alexander Nevsky, Suvorov, Kutuzov, who have been exalted during the cultivation of nationalism in the war and postwar years. Dust still gathers on the memories of Ukrainian, Caucasian and Central Asian historical and legendary figures. Indeed there has been an unfavorable reversal of attitude.

In the first years of the Soviet regime Soviet literature and drama exalted leaders of native peoples who fought what was then called Tsarist imperialism. One of the most famous of these leaders was Shamil, leader of a long struggle of the North Caucasian mountaineers. But now "Shamilism" is officially denounced and discouraged as a reactionary tendency. Russian conquest is depicted as a progressive factor.

It is unlikely that the Soviet Moslems, isolated as they are, have been untouched by the wave of unrest that has swept over the world of Islam, from Pakistan to Morocco. The thought of a new Shamil, leading an insurrection against Soviet rule in the Caucasus or Central Asia, is a nightmare to the Kremlin.

A master race role for the Russians was suggested in a toast which Stalin proposed at a victory celebration on May 24, 1945:

> I drink in the first place to the health of the Russian people because it is the most outstanding nation of all the nations forming the Soviet Union. I drink to the health of the Russian people because it has won in the war recognition as the leading force of the Soviet Union among all the peoples of our country.

So it would be unwise, in propaganda and clandestine warfare, to overlook the divisive possibilities of national discontent in the Soviet empire. But it would be equally unwise to endorse in advance the separatist claims and the often extravagant frontier arrangements demanded by the more extreme non-Russian émigré organizations. Evidence about the feeling of the people in the Soviet Union is too scanty and conflicting to warrant departure from the broad principle of leaving the settlement of the nationality problem to free self-determination after communist rule has been overthrown.

The Ukrainians are much the most numerous of the non-Russian peoples. But the Ukraine itself is not by any means homogeneous. One can take for granted bitter anti-Russian as well as anticommunist feeling among the Ukrainians who were annexed in 1939 and 1940. But as one travels eastward in the Soviet Ukraine (the larger part of the country which has been under continuous Soviet rule since 1920) the population becomes more mixed and the sense of Ukrainian nationality becomes weaker. The most industrialized parts of the Ukraine, the areas around Kharkov and Dniepropetrovsk (formerly Ekaterinoslav) and the Donets Basin, a kind of Russian Ruhr, are heavily Russianized.

There is also a difference between city and country in the Ukraine. The rural districts, especially in the West and in the North, are pretty solidly Ukrainian. But in the cities and towns, before the war, there were many Russians and Jews, although many of the latter perished during the German occupation. The ethnic composition of the Ukrainian population has been changed to some extent by mass deportations. A grim satirical conundrum goes as follows:

"What is the largest country in the world? The Ukraine, because its southern boundary is the Black Sea, its capital is in Moscow and most of its population is in Siberia."

The true will of the Soviet Ukrainian population can be learned only when and if the iron repression of dictatorship is removed. The majority of this population might then desire separate national existence. It might be convinced of the economic advantages of maintaining a close association with a non-communist Russia on a basis of local autonomy and federalism. And it might be that the western part of the Ukraine would show more desire for independence than the eastern part.

It would be a mistake to prejudge the unpredictable answers to these questions. American policy should seek to encourage impartially all groups, Russian and non-Russian which are fighting communism, irrespective of their motives and their ultimate aims. Exception should be made only in the case of fanatics so extreme that they would be a liability, rather than an asset.

There is no group outside the Soviet boundaries that can plausibly claim to speak for the Russians or the other nationalities inside the Soviet Union. The older generation of émigrés is inevitably out of touch with the experience of Soviet life.

Among the more recent refugees there are few outstanding personalities. And Soviet methods of espionage and repression are so far-reaching that no underground organization of any size could conceivably function undetected in the Soviet Union for any length of time. It would be naïve and unrealistic to expect immediate spectacular results from an agreement among a few small groups of exiles to put out a manifesto or establish a common organization.

However, there is a reservoir of disaffection in the Soviet Union that can be tapped. The Vlasov movement, the Ukrainian guerrilla activity, the units which the Germans were able to create among Soviet citizens,—these are historical facts. Vlasov's Smolensk manifesto dealt with real and permanent grievances. And, while material conditions have improved in the Soviet Union from the low wartime level, the fundamental grievance, stifling absence of freedom, remains and can never be removed unless there should be a complete change in communist philosophy and Soviet methods of administration.

This disaffection can be stimulated and kept alive by intelligently framed broadcasts in Russian and other languages of the Soviet Union, delivered by natives of these countries who are familiar with contemporary conditions and whose broadcasts are fitted into a clear pattern of political warfare. Objective verifiable truth is an important condition of success in this kind of activity. Intelligent Soviet citizens are sick of the standardized propagandist distortions and exaggerations of their own press. To broadcast exaggerated or obsolete accounts of Soviet poverty and hardships would have the effect of a boomerang.

There are more limited possibilities for the distribution of leaflets, although it is difficult for individual agents to penetrate into the Soviet Union. But the Red Army soldiers in Germany are more accessible. A vigorous psychological offensive, beamed at these soldiers and promising asylum and a chance to begin life under favorable conditions, might achieve the very desirable purpose of hastening Soviet evacuation of Germany.

In general it is most important that better care be taken of people who escape from the Soviet Union and from the satellite countries. It has happened too often that such individuals, after escaping at the risk of their lives, are first harassed by too numerous interrogations by various information agencies and then cast aside without any interest in what may happen to them. A good deal of money is being spent on psychological warfare operations and one of the best uses of this money would be to set up a refugee direction agency, with a staff well briefed on East European languages and on the background of the refugees, with the job of seeing that no refugee had reason to feel neglected.

It may seem a waste of time, effort and money to try to coordinate the activities of the small, divided Soviet political refugee groups. But this is an inaccurate and superficial view. There are two solid practical reasons why such aid, if intelligently directed, can be very useful to American national interests.

First, the Soviet Government, like every totalitarian regime, is abnormally sensitive to the slightest breath of disaffection. Otherwise it would not devote so much energy to wholesale espionage and to blocking all means of normal contact between Soviet citizens and foreigners. Even a few instances of successful propaganda for freedom among Soviet soldiers and civilians would create repercussions in the Kremlin out of all proportion to their intrinsic importance. This is especially true in the period of internal uncertainty and insecurity among the new rulers that will last for some time after the death of Stalin.

Second, it is most important that as many Russians, Ukrainians, Caucasians and other natives of the empire ruled by the Soviet Government be brought into close political and cultural contact with the West. If the reach of the exile political groups seems very much to exceed their grasp it may be useful to remember how hopelessly futile Lenin and his small band of Bolsheviks, in exile, in hiding and in prison seemed to the few foreign observers who even knew of their existence in January, 1917.

No one knows what the future holds for Russia or whether changing conditions in some future time may make it possible for some of the present-day exiles to return. To assist and in some degree to influence the development of potential political and intellectual leaders who might help to fill a vacuum in the event of a sudden crack-up inside the Soviet Union is a worthwhile political investment, which might pay unexpectedly large dividends.

The challenge of the Soviet Union is to a total conflict between two philosophies of government and life and national power systems. Military preparedness is only part, although an indispensable part, of the response to this challenge. Diplomacy and economic policy, political and psychological warfare must be coordinated and conducted intelligently and flexibly if this challenge is to be met.

What Americans engaged on the various fronts of this war need most is a fighting heart and an understanding mind. All the dollars in the world will not compensate for the lack of these. It is because not all the men in strategic posts possessed these two essential qualities that containment sometimes degenerated into helpless passivity. They will be all the more necessary now, when the prospect after the death of Stalin is that a war of position will be transformed into a war of movement, when the new rulers in the Kremlin may be expected to engage in more surprise maneuvers.

Chapter XIII ~ The Soviet Union After Stalin

The death of Josef Stalin, officially caused by a brain hemorrhage, on March 5, 1953, placed the Soviet Union before its greatest political crisis since the German invasion in 1941 and posed baffling questions of absorbing concern for the entire world. Many issues are bound up with the gradually unfolding picture of the Soviet Union without Stalin and after Stalin: issues of peace or war, of economic welfare or depression, of the continuation, expansion or break-up of the swollen Soviet empire.

So long as Stalin lived in full possession of his faculties there was no doubt as to the ultimate source of authority. He had killed every prominent veteran communist who opposed his will. Those who survived, like Molotov and Voroshilov, lacked the qualities of initiative and leadership which could have made them serious rivals. The abler younger men in the party hierarchy, Malenkov and Zhdanov, were Stalin's creatures, whom he had made and whom he could break at will, so long as he lived.

Two anecdotes, one genuine and one apocryphal, reflect the measure of Stalin's absolute power. An American businessman, Eric Johnston, was granted an interview with Stalin during the war and asked the Soviet dictator for permission for some

American newspapermen to accompany him on a trip to Soviet
Central Asia. After Stalin granted the permission Johnston
turned to Molotov, then Minister of Foreign Affairs, and asked
whether this decision would be agreeable to him, since Molotov
had previously refused this permission. Said Stalin, with a
sneer: "Did you think Molotov would disagree with my decision!"

Molotov hastened to take the edge off the situation by inter-
jecting: "I always agree with the decisions of Marshal Stalin."

This prudent attitude unquestionably explains his survival
of the purges of the thirties.

A Soviet satirical story represents Stalin as arranging successive receptions for two of his chief aides, Molotov and Lazar
Kaganovich, a specialist in industrial administration and one
of the very few Jews in high Soviet positions during and after
the Second World War.

Stalin first asks Molotov: "How do you get along with Kaganovich?" "Splendidly, Comrade Stalin; we are both working for
the build-up of socialism." "But," Stalin continues, "why does
Kaganovich tell everyone that you stutter?" "Well, it is true, I
have a slight speech impediment." "Yes, but Kaganovich talks
about it continually, makes fun of you. He wouldn't do that if
he were a good friend, would he?"

Having dismissed Molotov with seeds of suspicion of Kaganovich planted in his mind, Stalin calls in Kaganovich and puts
the same question: "How do you get along with Molotov?"
"Splendidly, Comrade Stalin." "But why does Molotov tell
everyone you are a Jew?" "Well, it is true I am a Jew." "Yes,
but Molotov is very unpleasant about it. He talks about it all
the time, tells anti-Semitic stories. He wouldn't do that if he
were a good friend, would he?"

Having sent away Kaganovich with the firm conviction that
Molotov is not a good friend, Stalin rubs his hands and says:
"Now I can work in peace." The old maxim, "Divide and

Rule," has served Stalin well in dealing with subordinates and enemies alike.

Knowing that immortality was one gift which even the most abject flatterer could not bestow on him, Stalin seems to have devoted a good deal of thought in his later years to arranging a smooth transition of power after his death. Something of a dress rehearsal was provided by the 19th Congress of the Communist Party, held in October, 1952, after an interval of thirteen years.

Here Malenkov was clearly designated as heir-apparent. He was selected to read the Political Report, a long analysis of foreign and domestic affairs which had hitherto been read by Stalin in his years of power and, still earlier, by Lenin. Stalin at the same time published a kind of political testament in the shape of a long article or short pamphlet, dealing with Soviet foreign and domestic policy. Malenkov's Report was an extremely close copy, almost a replica of the ideas expressed in this article.

Perhaps the most interesting feature of this last substantial published work by Stalin was the emphasis on the possibility that the capitalist world could be destroyed without resorting to the risky expedient of large-scale war. Laying on the shelf, for the moment, his own and Lenin's dogma of inevitable war with the noncommunist world Stalin declared that there is more prospect of wars between capitalist nations than of an attack by these nations on the Soviet Union.

First, he argued, a war with the Soviet Union is more dangerous than a war between individual capitalist states, because such a war "must pose the very question of the existence of capitalism." Second, the capitalist nations know that the Soviet Union itself will not attack.

At the same time Stalin restated another Leninist dogma: that conflicts of interest between the capitalists who are assumed to control all noncommunist states must lead to wars. These conflicts, according to Stalin, must become intensified because the world market of capitalism has contracted very much as a result of two world wars. The Soviet Union fell out of this market after the First World War, and after the second the "people's democracies" of eastern Europe "fell away from the capitalist system." Hence, according to Stalin, there will be an enhanced competition for the high profits of capitalism among the surviving capitalist nations. He paints an alluring prospect of the Soviet enemies destroying each other:

> Capitalist England and, in her footsteps, capitalist France in the end will be forced to tear themselves out from the embrace of the United States, and enter into conflict with them in order to secure themselves an independent situation and, of course, high profits. . . .
>
> One asks what guaranty is there that Germany and Japan will not rise again on their feet, that they will not attempt to break out from American slavery and live their independent lives? I think that there are no such guaranties. But from this it follows that the inevitability of wars between capitalist countries remains in force.

The wish is obviously a very strong stimulus to Stalin's thought. Given the present world distribution of political, military and economic strength, a war between America and Great Britain, France, Germany or Japan seems extremely improbable. And the whole theory of war as a product of capitalist rivalry is the doctrinaire idea of a fanatic, which bears no relation to historical reality.

The two great wars of the twentieth century had political, not economic causes. It is safe to say that, if "capitalists" had possessed any effective voice, neither of these conflicts would have ever started. On the eve of the Second World War the countries which had most completely discarded the free economy, the United States, Great Britain and France, were the least prepared militarily and the most reluctant to take up arms.

Questionable, to put it mildly, is Stalin's bland assumption that American subsidies to ex-allies and ex-enemies alike, running into tens of billions of dollars, represent enslavement, while Soviet pillaging of the occupied zones of Germany and Austria and the satellite states is just good clean proletarian fraternal aid.

What is more important, however, than the logical loopholes in Stalin's argument is the light which it casts on Soviet foreign policy. For, if wars between capitalist powers are inevitable, the Soviet Union has no need to risk a war of conquest itself. What then would be more logical than a peace offensive, bigger and broader than any undertaken in the past and aimed at relaxing the vigilance of the western world and encouraging the growth of antagonisms between the western states.

Heir-apparent Malenkov, now the Soviet Prime Minister, repeated Stalin's arguments with slavish literalness in his "Political Report," delivered at the Communist Party Congress. In judging the sincerity of the Soviet peace offensive some of Malenkov's assertions, in this report, are worth citing:

> By a series of aggressive actions the United States aggravated the international situation and confronted the world with the danger of another war. . . .
> The United States bosses knew, of course, that they stood no chance of imposing their domination over other nations by peaceful means. They knew from the experience of the Hitlerites, who had also tried to impose their domination upon other countries, that it was useless even dreaming of achieving world dominion without resort to force, without unleashing a new war. And so they decided to violate the peace, to prepare another war. . . .
> In pursuit of the same criminal aim the ruling circles of the United States are remilitarizing Western Germany and Japan. . . .
> The American attack on the Korean People's Democratic Republic marked the transition of the U.S.–British bloc from preparation of an aggressive war to direct acts of aggression. . . .

Today American imperialism is acting not only as an aggressor, but also as the world gendarme, striving to strangle freedom wherever it can and to implant fascism.

It is improbable, to say the least, that Malenkov would have changed within a few months the sentiments which he expressed so vigorously and frankly in October, 1952. The peace offensive which developed in the period after Stalin's death must be regarded as a tactical maneuver, counting on the gullibility and short memory of the West, not as a fundamental change of heart and mind.

The death of the dictator who had ruled for a quarter of a century made it easier for a new Soviet administration to launch the offensive, to modify, at least temporarily, some of the more uncompromising attitudes which very much diminished the value of communist peace propaganda in the past. It is much easier for a totalitarian regime, which has no public opinion to reckon with, to shift suddenly from a truculent to an outwardly amiable attitude than it is for the government of a free country where people ask public questions to make the same kind of transition.

The motivation of the shift in Soviet outward attitude is clear. A new administration has taken over a vast empire with complex and delicate problems of adjustment in relations with China and with the satellite regimes in Eastern Europe. It faces a new administration in America, committed to a more vigorous handling of foreign affairs. What would seem more natural than an attempt at disengagement, at softening the sharper edges of antagonism?

The first intimation that a change of tactics was in prospect was Malenkov's declaration, in his speech to the Soviet parliament, that all controversial issues with foreign countries, including the United States, could be solved by peaceful means. Several airplane clashes (the shooting down of an American patrol plane in Germany by a Soviet-manufactured Czechoslovak MIG and of a British training bomber by Soviet MIGs and an exchange of fire between Soviet and American airplanes over the Pacific Ocean near Kamchatka) created uncertainty as to the purposes of the new Soviet administration.

But a series of actions and gestures, some potentially important, some of minor consequence, added up to a general pattern of trying to cultivate a sense of amity. The Chinese and North Korean communists, with Soviet endorsement, intimated willingness to recede from their position that all war prisoners should be sent home and to accept a plan under which prisoners unwilling to return home would be turned over to the custody of a neutral country.

General Vassily Chuikov, Soviet commandant in Germany, expressed regret for the death of seven British aviators (although not for the attack on the plane) and proposed a conference to consider means of avoiding such incidents in the future. He also relaxed the delaying restrictions on traffic on the highway between Berlin and West Germany. A group of American newspaper publishers were admitted to the Soviet Union and hospitably entertained. Comment in the Soviet press on international affairs became less vituperative.

A striking reversal of attitude, with important internal as well as international implications, was the repudiation of the murder and treason charges against the nine prominent Soviet physicians.* It was officially admitted that the confessions of the arrested men had been obtained "through the use of methods of investigation which are inadmissible and most strictly forbidden by Soviet law"—a rather obvious gloss for the use of torture.

In the remarkably frank editorial in *Pravda* which followed the dropping of the case, the release of the accused and the arrest of the investigators there is another highly significant passage. This "fabricated investigation," according to *Pravda,* "attempted to inflame in the Soviet society . . . feelings of

* See page 207.

national antagonism which are profoundly alien to the socialist ideology."

Here is the plainest possible admission of a trumped-up charge, with confessions extorted by torture, and designed to inspire anti-Semitic feeling. This very unusual official admission of secret police wrongdoing * was inspired to some extent, no doubt, by the exigencies of the planned peace offensive. It would have been difficult, to say the least, to go through motions of being friendly with the United States while carrying out a trial representing United States intelligence agencies as inducing Soviet citizens to poison Soviet leaders. The repudiation of anti-Semitism, which, of course, may be revived officially as rapidly as it was temporarily quenched, was also aimed at making a favorable impression on public opinion in the West.

But the significance both of the fabricated charge and of its repudiation goes much deeper. It points to a concealed bitter desperate struggle for power among Stalin's heirs which may lead to a climactic purge and outburst of terrorism that may dwarf everything that has yet been seen in the sanguinary history of the Soviet state.

From the moment when the fantastic charges and the standard "confessions" were announced in January experienced observers of the Soviet Union were inclined to see in the unfortunate doctors innocent pawns in a big and desperate game of Kremlin power politics. Officially, blame for the false charges has been assigned primarily to a "despicable and criminal adventurer," one Ryumin, who was head of the investigating section of the Ministry of State Security and to the Minister of

---

* One sentence in the *Pravda* editorial is an example of the lying hypocrisy that is only possible in a totalitarian state. "Every worker, every collective farmer and every Soviet intellectual can work peacefully and confidently, knowing that his civil rights are under the reliable guard of Soviet socialist law." It has been established by the testimony of scores of independent witnesses that torture is the rule, not the exception, in Soviet investigations of so-called political crimes. See the cases cited in Chapter VIII.

State Security, S. D. Ignatiev, who "displayed political blindness and inattentiveness."

But it is most improbable that such minor figures, without authorization from much higher sources, would have ventured to initiate what was designed to be a public trial with such explosive possibilities, internationally and internally. Had the charges been allowed to stand, Lavrenti Beria, who was responsible for "state security" at the time when Stcherbakov and Zhdanov were allegedly murdered, would have been gravely compromised by apparent inattention to duty.

As is not uncommon with influential members of the top rank of the Soviet hierarchy, Beria had been without a definite ministerial appointment for some time before Stalin's death. He was reported to exercise general supervision over his old field, political police activity, and also to be in charge of Soviet atomic development. Immediately after Stalin's death the two ministries which dealt with police affairs, Internal Affairs and State Security, were merged into a single Ministry of Internal Affairs, with Beria as the Minister.

One of Beria's first acts was evidently to clear his own reputation by reversing the frame-up of the doctors. Most interesting is the question: Who authorized this frame-up in the beginning? Malenkov would have seemed to stand to gain more than anyone else and Ignatiev was considered a Malenkov henchman. Certainly a state of acute political crisis behind the forbidding walls of the Kremlin, which in the times of the old Muscovite Tsardom witnessed so many revolts, massacres and palace conspiracies, is indicated when such reckless charges, with their general effect of discrediting the regime at home and abroad, are publicly tossed about. It is unlikely that Moscow has seen its last, or perhaps its bloodiest purge.

For the problem of succession in a totalitarian dictatorship is inherently insoluble without the use of violence. One of the most impressive symbols of civilized self-government in the United States is the presidential inauguration, especially when there is a change of the party in power. Here is an instrument of enormous power, the executive branch of the United States Government, being transferred in peaceful, friendly fashion, without even the faintest suspicion that the victors will start a ruthless proscription or that the vanquished will resort to conspiracy, assassination and *coup d'état*.

There was also an element of stability in the coronation of a new Tsar, entitled to rule by the recognized law of heredity. But the succession in a totalitarian state has no sanction of legitimacy whatever, either in the verdict of a free popular election or in a recognized principle of hereditary right to rule.

What occurred after Stalin's death, what had probably been arranged in advance expectation of such a contingency, was a sharing out of office and power among his principal lieutenants. The pre-eminence of a triumvirate, Malenkov, Beria and Molotov, apparently in this order of rank, was intimated when these three men, in this order, delivered the addresses at the funeral of the dead dictator.

Malenkov became Prime Minister, with Beria, Molotov, Bulganin and Kaganovich as his deputies. The order of naming of Soviet dignitaries is as important as the medieval table of rank which established precedence among the Muscovite boyars. Beria was given the post of Minister of Internal Affairs; Molotov resumed his old position as Minister of Foreign Affairs; Bulganin retained his post as Minister of the Army, with two well-known Soviet Marshals, A. M. Vasilievsky and G. K. Zhukov, as deputies. Kaganovich, with a background as "troubleshooter" in industrial administration and party organization, remained without portfolio.

All these arrangements, together with certain administrative changes, such as a sharp reduction in the number of Soviet Ministries through fusions and consolidations, were made by agreement among the Soviet leaders, with the purely perfunctory approval of the Supreme Soviet, or Soviet parliament.

This rubber-stamp body met for sixty-seven minutes, approved everything that was proposed unanimously and dispersed.

It is the absence of any kind of legal or constitutional sanction that makes a transfer of power with any assurance of stability so difficult under a dictatorship. There has been only one precedent, the situation after the death of Lenin in 1924. And this precedent is not encouraging for the losers in the struggle for power. Immediately after the death of Lenin power was vested in a Political Bureau of seven members, highest steering committee of the ruling Communist Party. It was a matter of common knowledge that within this Political Bureau three men, Stalin, Zinoviev and Kamenev, wielded the largest share of power.

The Political Bureau was abolished at the time of the Communist Party Congress in October, 1952, and was replaced by a Presidium of the Central Committee, composed of twenty-five members. This was apparently found too large a body to function as a supreme council of state and was reduced immediately after Stalin's death to fourteen, ten members and four alternates. The triumvirate of 1924, Stalin–Zinoviev–Kamenev, is replaced by the triumvirate Malenkov–Beria–Molotov.

Now triumvirates throughout history have a way of disappearing, from Caesar–Pompey–Crassus to Stalin–Zinoviev–Kamenev. And Stalin killed not only the other two members of the triumvirate but all the other members of the Political Bureau before he felt securely established. Fear, jealousy, suspicion, leading to a constant possibility of a terrorist purge, are the inevitable characteristics of a system that has no ultimate sanction but force. Malenkov, titular leader of the new Soviet administration, can feel no confidence that some of his associates may not be intriguing and plotting against him. In like manner, these associates can feel no assurance that Malenkov may not have them on a purge list.

The power relationship between the men at the top of the Soviet pyramid is a subject on which there is a vast amount of speculation outside the Soviet Union, but little if any reliable information. In Stalin's time there was at least no doubt as to who was the absolute ruler. But it seems doubtful whether Malenkov has inherited the full measure of Stalin's power. When a foreign observer considers the question who was powerful enough to initiate and who was powerful enough to call off such a spectacular affair as the proposed trial of the physicians he is faced with an atmosphere of dark, impenetrable mystery, just as if he would try to unravel some of the plots and counterplots which history records in the reigns of such Muscovite Tsars as Ivan the Terrible and Boris Godunov. Up to the time of his accession to power Malenkov had apparently never talked with a noncommunist diplomat or journalist. He is an enormously fat man, ruthless, energetic and cunning, apparently cast very much in the Stalin mold. Born in the town of Orenburg, in the southeastern part of European Russia, Malenkov, according to Stalin's nephew, Budu Svanidze, is of partly Bashkir origin. (The Bashkirs are an oriental people of Mohammedan faith who live between the Volga River and the Ural Mountains.)

Too young to have played any important part in the Revolution, Malenkov is a product of the Soviet system. He was never an underground revolutionary, always a member of a ruling caste,—a point of some psychological importance. His rise to power was in some degree similar to Stalin's. Elected Secretary of the Party Central Committee after 1939, he acquired the immense power and influence that go with ability to manipulate the Party machine of power. During the war he became a member of the State Defense Committee, which Stalin utilized as a kind of inner War Cabinet, and built up a reputation as a driving executive.

In the years after the war the inside history of Soviet communist politics revolves largely around the personal rivalry between two of Stalin's "bright young men," Malenkov and

Andrei Zhdanov. According to the analysis of one of the more erudite foreign students of Soviet affairs, Boris Nicolaevsky,* Zhdanov placed more faith in stimulating revolutionary attempts by foreign communist parties and was mainly responsible for the creation of the Cominform. Although Malenkov acted as a kind of receiver for the dissolved Communist International, taking over direction of the espionage activities of foreign communist parties, he placed a low estimate on the capacity of these parties to bring about revolution by their own efforts.

According to Nicolaevsky's interpretation, Malenkov would be inclined to discourage independent revolutionary action of foreign communist parties, while exploiting them as fifth columns and convenient agencies of propaganda. The rivalry ended with Zhdanov's death in 1948. Whether he died of a heart ailment or whether he was "liquidated" is something that may never be known until the day comes when the Kremlin yields up all the dark secrets of the Stalin era.

Ironically enough, it was Malenkov, who hated Zhdanov and might well have brought about his death, if possible, who probably tried to make capital out of his dead rival by inciting the manufacture of the case against the physicians. What thwarted this project is a mystery which may or may not be cleared up by later developments.

Malenkov does not possess the gift of a brilliant or easily readable style. But his "Report to the Communist Party Congress in 1952" is worth reading and careful study for the possible clues which it offers to future Soviet policy, if Malenkov succeeds in maintaining and strengthening his position as the leader of the Soviet Union after Stalin.

Some of the anti-American passages in this report have been cited. Malenkov's hatred and contempt for the West are obvious. Any statements to the contrary may be dismissed as dic-

* See *The New Leader* for March 23 and March 30.

tated by opportunism. But there are some indications in this report that he may be inclined, as a matter of cold-blooded self-interest, to put off for some years the "last decisive struggle" which every communist regards as inevitable.

For Malenkov is convinced that time is on the Soviet side. He believes that the Soviet Union and its satellite states in Europe and Asia are moving ahead economically and will move ahead economically faster than the nations of the capitalist world. He marshals facts and figures to support this conclusion.

Taking industrial production in 1940 as 100, Russian industry as a whole had reached 202 in 1951, with output in the heavy industries with war potential at 239, in the consumers goods industries at 143. These figures are more impressive because European Russia sustained tremendous devastation during the war. The Soviet Union in 1952, according to Malenkov, produced 35 million tons of steel (90 per cent more than in 1940), 25 million tons of pig iron, 47 million tons of oil, 300 million tons of coal, 117 kilowatt hours of electricity. These figures are considerably behind the United States, as the following table shows:

	USSR (1952)	US (1951)
Pig iron	25 million tons	64 million tons
Steel	35 " "	95.5 " "
Oil	47 " "	307.5 " "
Coal	300 " "	523 " "
Electricity	117 billion kwh	482.3 billion kwh

The contrast would be vastly greater if one should take into consideration items which enter into the everyday standard of living. For the peoples of the Soviet Union have been exploited to the limit in order to build up national industrial and military power. Only in 1951 and 1952, according to Soviet statistics, was Soviet industry, on the average, able to provide one pair of shoes for every Soviet citizen. The Five Year Plan of 1946–50 aimed at producing 65,000 passenger cars, for a population of over 200 million. Small wonder that it is a news item in a Soviet newspaper if a worker buys an automobile. The current five year plan promises that the average meat consumption of the town dweller will rise from about half a pound to a pound a week. Even if this promise should be fulfilled—and gains in agriculture have been much smaller and much harder to achieve than in industry and mining, according to Soviet statistics—consumption will increase to only about a pound a week, about a third of American consumption, in 1955.

The extreme shortage of housing which impresses every foreign resident in the Soviet Union was acknowledged by Malenkov himself in his report: "There is still an acute housing shortage everywhere. Year after year, many Ministries and local Soviets fail to fulfill their housing plans."

He recognized other shortcomings in the Soviet economy. "Quality standards are violated in a number of industries," a point which is often stressed in Soviet newspapers and which anyone with experience of Soviet consumption goods can verify. Inefficient plants live at the expense of efficient ones. Many enterprises work in jerks and crowd much of their production in the last ten days of the month, so as to fulfill the required plan.

However, Malenkov and the high Soviet bureaucrats, who do not feel themselves the tremendous hardships and deprivations of everyday life are quite sincerely convinced that theirs is the winning economic system. They point to the fast rates of growth in the heavy industries, to the absence of unemployment, to the assurance that under a regime of state ownership of the entire economy there will never be periods of slack activity.

What is overlooked in this communist line of argument is the enormous waste and misuse of human energy involved in two permanent aspects of the Soviet economy. There is the vast amount of paper work, of endless checks and controls, due to the absence of the simple and effective individual profit incentive and the attempt to replace this incentive with a network of bureaucratic checks and counterchecks.

And there is the slave labor regime, which, apart from its inhumanity, is far less efficient than the use of the talents and energies of the people affected under conditions of free labor.

There is, however, one element of validity in the communist argument. For political, as well as economic and social reasons, the western world could not afford a repetition of what happened between 1929 and 1933. At that time the Soviet Union was wrestling with the first and most difficult phase of industrialization and collective farming and was breaking resistance by the most savage methods. Even so the dream of the Soviet planned economy possessed a seductive charm for countries suffering from unemployment on a large scale and nonutilization of productive resources. A collapse of the 1929–1933 proportions would be a benefit for the Kremlin that would outweigh its Red Army legions and its auxiliary legions of fifth columnists.

Because they wish to gain time to consolidate their position after Stalin's death, to overhaul their relations with the satellite states of their vast empire, because they believe that time works for them in any case there is reason to expect that the peace offensive launched after Stalin's death may govern Soviet foreign policy for some time. That it will lead to genuine peace is most improbable, unless widespread secession in the empire abates Soviet power or unless some unforeseen, unpredictable forces inside the Soviet Union, coming to the surface in an atmosphere of strife and confusion among the new leaders, creates a type of government which is free from the dream of world domination.

What sort of estate have Stalin's heirs inherited? What are the principal formative forces and influences in the Soviet Union? The Soviet Union has passed through several more or less distinct phases of development; and what was true in one of these phases is often quite untrue as regards another.

Two basic facts of Soviet life have never changed. One is the centralization of absolute, uncontrolled power in the hands of a small group of men, the top leadership of the Communist Party, ruling through the instrumentality of the Party, which is as rigidly disciplined as an army or a strict monastic order. This power has never been under effective popular check or control; repeated promises that the political police would be placed under some kind of normal legal control have never been fulfilled.

The other permanent feature of the Soviet system is the state ownership of the entire economy, the factories, the mines, the railways, stores, banks, etc. Even such small forms of private enterprise as the corner grocery or the twenty-acre peasant farm have been blotted out. Virtually all the peasants, including those in the territories annexed during and since the war, have been organized in collective farms, of which there were 128,000 in 1951. Until 1950 there were 252,000 such farms.

Then there was a drive to combine and amalgamate, on the theory that larger units would be more productive. However, the more ambitious project of moving all the collective farmers into so-called *agrogorodi* (agricultural cities) was dropped, or at least shelved, probably because it made impossible demands on available building resources. The collective farm is completely dependent on the government, and the peasants are obliged to plant what the government requires and to deliver up a large share of their produce as a tax in kind.

Much of the driving appeal of the revolution in its first phase, under Lenin's leadership, was in the ideal of social and economic equality. Although political dictatorship was rigid there was a trend toward bohemian liberty, not to say license, in many fields. Experimental forms were encouraged in the theatre and the arts. Marriage was virtually abolished, divorce being obtainable at the desire of either partner. All disciplinary measures were abolished in schools, along with regular marks and examinations and teaching by subjects. Anything savoring of old Russian nationalism was condemned root and branch.

There was a sharp contrast, in economics and in living conditions, between the first militant years of the Revolution (1917–1921) and the period of the so-called NEP (New Economic Policy), 1921–1928. The first years were a time of fierce civil war and of an economic system known as war communism. The state took over all economic enterprises. Wages were paid mainly in kind and there was an increasing trend toward compulsory labor. The peasants were forced to give up surplus foodstuffs at the point of the bayonet. In theory they were supposed to receive manufactured goods in exchange from the towns, but in practice very few goods were available, because of the collapse of industrial production. Money virtually lost all value.

Although the Soviet Government won the civil war this early communist system broke down from sheer inefficiency and Lenin introduced the NEP in 1921, substituting a fixed tax in kind for wholesale requisitioning of peasant products, permitting freedom of private trade within the country and allowing small factories to start under private ownership. There was gradual improvement in everyday living conditions until 1928, when Stalin threw over the NEP and started a great drive for industrial build-up and collective farming.

Between 1929 and 1933 there was a very sharp fall in the standard of living; there was hunger in the cities and outright starvation in many peasant areas in 1923–33. The welfare of the people was ruthlessly sacrificed to the building up of national military and industrial strength. The well-to-do peasants, or kulaks, and the small businessmen who had emerged during the New Economic Policy were swept out of existence and "liquidated."

In one sense, therefore, the Stalin era was more ruthless than the Lenin era in destroying the last vestiges of private ownership for profit. But in another sense the trend was in the opposite direction. Very sharp inequality of pay for individuals within the framework of a system of all-embracing state ownership and operation became the rule. Soviet books published in 1951 and 1952 * show compensation scales ranging from 6,000 rubles a month for the director of a scientific institute to 250 rubles a month for a rural kindergarten teacher, a spread of more than 20 to one.

Within the ranks of the industrial workers the spread between the pay rates of the most skilled and the least skilled workers in the construction industry was 3.6 to one †; the corresponding spread in the construction industry in New York City was 1.8 to one. Inequality in the Soviet Union is greater if it is borne in mind that intensive speed-up methods are reinforced by piecework payment and that successful industrial managers and engineers are often awarded large bonuses. Moreover the extreme poverty of consumption goods in the Soviet Union makes for much greater inequality in living standards than one finds in the United States. A private soldier in the Red Army cannot buy cigarettes which are available for generals and high officers. The automobile is a luxury which with few exceptions is reserved for the more highly placed bureaucrats. The privileged position of the new Soviet administrative ruling class is emphasized by special summer resorts, special hospitals, special stores, special restaurants—all for "restricted clientele."

So, while one Leninist ideal, the taking over by the state of all means of production, has been realized, another ideal, approximate equality in living standards, has been entirely discarded. This is equally true as regards Lenin's dream that the state would "wither away." Indeed this theory is now considered counterrevolutionary—at least during the period while the Soviet Union is subjected to "capitalist encirclement." An

* See article by Harry Schwartz, in *The New York Times* of April 3, 1952.

† *Ibid.*, in *The New York Times* of September 22, 1952.

enormous apparatus of terrorist repression must, therefore, be maintained and even strengthened until the whole world is conquered for communism. There have been other significant changes, mostly in a conservative social direction, under the rule of Stalin.

Russian nationalism, unreasonably deprecated in the first years of Soviet rule, is now carried to heights of absurd chauvinism. Unknown Russians are now credited with discovering the airplane, the lightning conductor, the incandescent lamp, the Diesel engine, the bicycle, the caterpillar tractor, the automatic oil drill, synthetic rubber, ball bearings and smokeless gunpowder, to mention only a few claims of Russian "firsts."

Educational methods have become extremely severe, with marks, examinations, uniforms for students, disciplinary powers for teachers. The Soviet student now enjoys less freedom of choice of subjects than the average American student and scholarships are given not to the neediest, but to the most capable.

Divorce, once so easy, has been made very difficult and there are premiums for mothers of large families. Experimentalism in the theatre and music, art and architecture is frowned on; composers are required to compose tunes so plain that busy members of the Soviet and Party leadership may whistle them.

Lenin and his associates were not agnostics or sceptics; they were violently dogmatic atheists, convinced of the infallibility of the Marxist materialist interpretation of human life. One of the first acts of the Soviet regime was to put up Marx's saying, "Religion is opium for the people," immediately opposite the Shrine of the Iberian Virgin, one of the most traditionally sacred spots in Moscow.

Despite official denials, there was ruthless persecution of religion, varying in intensity, during the first two decades of Soviet rule. Most of the Orthodox churches were closed; many

bishops and priests were sent to concentration camps, very seldom on any specific charge; people who were actively religious
had to expect to suffer for their faith. Teaching in the schools
was not only nonreligious but actively antireligious; belief in
religion of any kind was cause for expulsion from the Communist Party or its larger junior organization, the Union of
Communist Youth. Antireligious museums, devoted to attacks
on religion, were set up throughout the country and the most
blasphemous mockeries of the sacred rites of Christianity, Mohammedanism and Judaism appeared in the widely circulated
magazine *Bezbozhnik* ("The Godless"). Religious literature and
seminaries for training priests were suppressed.

A somewhat milder attitude toward religion began to prevail during the late thirties and especially during the war, when
the Soviet Government became alarmed over reports of popular response when churches were reopened in German occupied territory. Stalin seems to have decided that a tame, subservient, Soviet-controlled Orthodox Church would be harm-
less at home and useful for show purposes abroad. Antireligious
propaganda was toned down and facilities for educating priests
were restored.

However, it is still impossible for a member of the ruling
party to profess religious faith and a generation of Soviet citizens has grown up under intensive atheistic indoctrination.
In some individual cases no doubt persecution strengthened
religious faith. But it was my impression during twelve years
of residence in the Soviet Union that most of the younger
Soviet citizens were indifferent, if not hostile, to religion.

To some extent communism supplied an alternative faith,
although a faith without God or the promise of immortality.
There was a conscious effort by the Soviet rulers to capitalize
on old Russian religious feeling by preserving the embalmed
body of Lenin as an object of veneration, by the adulation of
Stalin, by the habit, cultivated to some extent, of installing

"Lenin corners," filled with pictures and memorials of Lenin, as a substitute for the old familiar "ikon corners," filled with pictures of the Holy Family and the saints.

The passing of Stalin, who dominated Soviet life more and more openly and completely for thirty years, poses large questions for the new Soviet society. There is the question of whether his heirs will remain in harmonious agreement and of the forces of latent discontent which might be unloosed by open dissension in the Kremlin.

The Soviet order has become more efficient, but less idealistic and egalitarian. The wild, half formed dreams, of universal equality, of revolt against the "old world" have become mocking nightmares in a society of tremendous differences in wages and standards of living and jealously guarded distinctions of rank. The Soviet Government can boast of big new factories, power plants, canals, largely built with slave labor. It has very much increased Soviet military power.

But it has given extremely little to the people, to the workers and peasants, in whose name the revolution was made. The contrast between the big new public buildings, the "industrial giants," the fleets of airplanes and masses of tanks, on one side, and the squalid living conditions of the great majority of the people is one of history's most impressive lessons in the exploitation that is always the accompaniment of concentration of absolute power in the hands of the few.

The Soviet Government publishes no regular statistics of wages, prices and cost-of-living index. This fact alone suggests that the results of any such computation would not be a help to communist propaganda in foreign countries. Using data compiled by the American Department of Labor, Mr. Solomon M. Schwarz, a Russian labor economist living in exile, calculates * that in 1950 the real earnings of the Soviet worker were about

* For estimates of Soviet comparative real wages see Solomon M. Schwarz, *Labor in The Soviet Union* (Praeger), pp. 235–36.

one seventh of the American, less than one fourth of the British, only half of the Austrian.

In terms of the amount of work required to buy a specific item of food, a pound of meat costs the American worker 28 minutes, the Soviet worker 182 minutes. In the case of a dozen eggs the corresponding figures are 22 and 291, a pound of butter 31 and 373. There are similar discrepancies in the cost, and still more, perhaps, in the quality of clothing.

There has been some improvement in Soviet living conditions as a result of annual cuts, averaging about ten per cent, in prices since 1950. But the Soviet living standard, in the fourth decade of the "dictatorship of the proletariat," remains the lowest in Europe.

Stalin's heirs must solve several contradictions. There is the contradiction between the bright promises of communism and the drab everyday realities of Soviet life. There is the contrast, which must sometimes impress even the stupidest Soviet citizen, between the wording of the Soviet Constitution and the arbitrary power of the political police. And there is the contradiction between the revolutionary slogans which are still parroted for use outside of Russia and the frozen bureaucratic system, with sharp differences of rank and pay, which is now established inside the Soviet Union.

Stalin's heirs also confront two problems which did not exist when Stalin was consolidating his own power and carrying the Soviet Union through the first stages of industrialization. At that time the Soviet Union was staying within its original territorial limits. Now it must deal with a subjugated empire. In the twenties and the early thirties the Soviet Union could concentrate on internal development without worrying overmuch about foreign relations. Now the great confrontation between the USA and the USSR compels the Soviet rulers to devote much thought, resources and energy to international issues, all the way from Germany to Indo-China. Stalin's heirs have yet to pass the test of holding the swollen empire. It is by no means certain that they can avoid bitter dissension among themselves, with consequent possibilities of political and social upheaval and perhaps unpredictable change in the Soviet Union itself. In their difficulties lie the free world's opportunities.

Chapter XIV ~ The Cold War: A Balance Sheet

"The existence of the Soviet Republic side by side with imperialist states for a long time is unthinkable. One or the other must triumph in the end. And before that end comes, a series of frightful clashes between the Soviet Republic and the bourgeois states will be inevitable" . . . Vladimir Ilyitch Lenin, in his "Report to the Eighth Congress of the Russian Communist Party," in March, 1919.

"The commies are spreading all over the world and we are there to keep the commies from dominating the entire world." . . . Col. Frank Gabreski, American ace pilot in Korea, in *The Saturday Evening Post,* December 13, 1952.

Forty years ago communism as a form of government and as an international political force did not exist. The dictatorship of the proletariat, the rule of a revolutionary elite, were still untried ideas in the minds of obscure fanatics.

Now almost one third of the population of the world lives under communist rule. A consequence of the First World War was the establishment of the Soviet Government in Russia. The Second World War was followed by the communist seizure of power in China and by the open or veiled absorption into the Soviet empire of nine formerly independent European states: Latvia, Lithuania, Estonia, Poland, Rumania, Czechoslovakia, Hungary, Bulgaria and Albania, together with considerable sections of Germany and Austria.

There are few parallels in history for such rapid expansion of a new creed. It recalls the sweep of Islam in the decades after the death of the Prophet. Is communism an irresistible wave of the future? This is the belief of V. M. Molotov, Foreign Minister in the new Soviet administration. He declared in a speech on the thirtieth anniversary of the Bolshevik Revolution, November 7, 1947:

> The feverish efforts of imperialists, under whom the ground is giving way, will not save capitalism from its approaching doom. We are living in an age in which all roads lead to communism.

This is also the belief of a highly intelligent, passionate and devoted fighter against communism, Whittaker Chambers. When he quit the communist underground, he said to his wife: * "I know that I am leaving the winning side for the losing side, but it is better to die on the losing side than to live under communism."

It would be grave folly, in the light of what has already happened, to understimate the strength of this new power which has conquered so large a part of the vast Eurasian continent.

The principal elements in this strength are:

1. With its scientific up-to-date methods of tyranny, its intensive development of the twin weapons of terror and propaganda, communism is a form of rule very difficult to shake off. There can be no widespread secret organization of resistance when almost everyone is compelled to spy on almost everyone else. Such a system of government numbs the minds and paralyzes the wills even of those who are instinctively opposed to it.

2. Soviet communism in its present form, with its free use of primitive capitalist pressures and incentives, is a workable

* *Witness,* p. 541.

economic system. There can be no assurance that it is predestined to collapse somehow from sheer incompetence. This system is being more or less closely imitated in the satellite countries.

3. This system is singularly well adapted for war and preparation for war. The individual as a producer is speeded up and exploited to the limit of his endurance. And there is no need to take account of the preferences and tastes of the individual as a consumer. The communist economy is a militarist's dream. It makes possible a tremendous concentration of effort on essential military goals and the swift development of heavy industries, serviceable for war purposes.

4. Communism fills a psychological need of some minds. It is a creed which claims with absolute authority to direct all the activities of the individual, and to furnish all the answers to perplexing social and economic problems. Its appeal to the maladjusted, to the spiritually uprooted, to all those who consciously or unconsciously fear freedom, is strong. Hence the explanation of its success in recruiting citizens of foreign countries to perform acts of espionage and treason.

5. There are advantages as well as disadvantages, in the world game of power politics, in the unquestioned authority of the few and the silence, except when mass demonstrations are on command, of the many in the communist empire. There is no need to waste what may be precious time in preparing public opinion for such spectacular shifts of foreign policy as the conclusion of the Stalin–Hitler pact, after years of fierce denunciation of nazism, or the change from the bear's growl to the dove's coo in addressing the United States after Stalin's death. No constitutional court holds up rearmament projects in states associated with the Soviet empire. And if the Kremlin wants some kind of military pact between Poland and Czechoslovakia, designed to increase overall military strength, neither of these countries will hold up the conclusion and implementation of this pact with years of sterile obstruction and bickering.

6. No word of defeatist pessimism is ever uttered behind the iron curtain. For obvious reasons no one in Moscow or Prague or Peiping or Bucharest ever publicly complains that the burden of armament is too heavy to be borne, or that war is so terrible that it makes no difference which side wins. The contrast with the West, where every voice of apathy, neutralism and even procommunist sympathy is allowed to shout itself hoarse is striking and somewhat disturbing.

7. Now in possession of the Heartland of the World Island, the enormous spaces of Northern and Western Asia and Eastern Europe, the communist empire possesses a very strong defense in depth. Large new industrialized areas of this empire in the Urals and Western Siberia are altogether outside the range of seapower and may be outside the effective striking range of air power. It is in these areas that many of the basic munitions and supply centers for future wars have been and are being built.

To keep the picture in perspective, several outstanding weaknesses of the communist empire should be noted.

1. Communism is passionately hated by many of its subjects. There are, of course, no free elections in any communist country. Nor would the citizen of such a country feel free to speak his mind to an inquiring reporter. But there is, on this subject of the true mood of the peoples, the unanswerable evidence of the mass flight from communism, on the part of many hundreds of thousands of individuals, all the way from East Germany and Czechoslovakia to Korea. This is one hard, indisputable fact that does not fit in with the propaganda picture of happy workers, prosperous peasants and general well-being and contentment under the communist dispensation.

It is also noteworthy that alien communists in the United States almost invariably use every trick of "capitalist" legalism to avoid being deported to their communist homelands. A group of convicted communists, offered a choice between possible deportation on probation or serving jail sentences in the United States opted unanimously, and who shall say unwisely, for the American jails.

2. Totalitarian tyranny means extreme insecurity, even for and perhaps especially for members of the ruling class or caste. Short indeed is the step from eminence to execution, from "hero of the revolution" to "traitor and mad dog." After seeing the fate of so many highly placed communists both in the Soviet Union and in the satellite countries of Eastern Europe, the surviving officials in the communist hierarchies must sometimes feel uneasy premonitions that the end for them, also, will be a bullet in the back of the head after nights of sleepless torture. This situation opens wide opportunities for adroit psychological warfare, for the arousing of mutual suspicion and mistrust, for the promotion of defections.

3. Communism demands the immunization of the peoples under its control from contact with the outside world. The Iron Curtain is not a deceptive phrase, but a literal description of the isolation from foreign influence imposed with almost equal rigor on Russians, Chinese, Poles, Hungarians, and other subjects of the communist empire. This is not a mere whim of the ruling group in the Kremlin. It is a practical necessity, if sentiments of discontent and disillusionment are not to be aroused by the spectacle of how much more comfortably people live in noncommunist countries.

But such self-isolation imposes handicaps. The most progressive societies have always maintained the freest contacts with other lands. This has been true ever since Pericles, in his imperishable memorial address for the Athenians who had fallen in battle, boasted of Athens: "We throw open our city to the world and never exclude foreigners from any opportunity of learning or observing, although the eyes of an enemy may occasionally profit by our liberality."

It has been the illusion of Russian despots, from Peter the Great to Stalin, that they could successfully import the technique of the West while excluding from Russia's borders the vital Western gift of freedom. The almost incredible inferiority of the Soviet Union to the West in scores of amenities and comforts and little details of daily life is the product not only of Soviet obsession with grandiose schemes of industrial and military development but of the absence of the stimulus that comes from free, unharassed meetings between peoples, and exchange of ideas and inventions. The intensive reading of foreign scientific publications, an occasional feat of successful espionage, cannot fill the vacuum left by this absence of free contacts.

4. No communist regime anywhere possesses any moral or legal legitimacy. No constitutional traditions soften the fierce rivalry for power among the men at the top of the Soviet pyramid of power. This rivalry may be kept within bounds under the domination of a recognized superior, a Lenin, who ruled by force of personality and revolutionary fervor, or a Stalin, a man of infinite wiles and cunning who built himself up into the image of a demi-god. But the passing of a recognized dictator is likely to usher in a period of more or less well disguised dissension, of mysterious intrigue, of vacillating policies, at home and abroad.

This is a rough balance sheet of the elements of strength and weakness in the communist world after the death of Stalin. What of the corresponding balance sheet for the other camp in the cold war, the camp of which America has become the leader, without conscious will, desire or design, by virtue of superior military power, economic wealth and political stability.

America's greatest strength is not in its atomic weapons, or in its mighty industrial plants and busy laboratories, or in the wealth of its farms and mines. It is in those qualities of individual freedom, opportunity and self-reliance that are more characteristic of America than of any other people.

Without these qualities the material goods of America would rust and decay. With these qualities an America shattered by war or some great natural disaster would rise like a phoenix from its ashes.

Another priceless American asset is a deep underlying sense of national unity that has nothing to do with forced uniformity. Americans are not split uncompromisingly along lines of class and ideology. For almost thirty-five years the Kremlin has been using every subversive means at its disposal to weaken and divide America.

With one exception, the recruiting of individuals for fifth column purposes, the effort has failed. This is an important exception. It calls for measures of legal and psychological national self-defense. But there is happily no parallel in America to the situation in France and Italy, where large minorities of the people are on the side of the enemy.

An intangible force of no mean value on the anticommunist side in the cold war is the heritage of Western civilization. Saints and scholars of all faiths and all nations, every great voice that has been raised for freedom and reason, every soaring medieval cathedral, every memorial that reminds some people of a noble episode in its history—all these are enlisted in the struggle to prevent the transformation of Western man into a soulless robot, living always in the shadow of the concentration camp.

But the noncommunist, like the communist side has weaknesses which should be faced realistically.

A price must be paid for free institutions, especially in a time of high international tension. A dictatorship can maneuver more swiftly and subtly than a constitutional government, affected by public opinion and operating under the klieg lights of an active, powerful and inquisitive press. A free country, unless the peril is very real and visible and immediate, is more vulnerable to fits of apathy and relaxation, more mercurial, less constant in the pursuit of its objectives than is a dictatorship.

A free society, just because it is free, is obliged to tolerate much defeatist and distracting talk, ranging from open support of the enemy's position to fantastic schemes for trying to escape the realities of the cold war in a cloud-cuckoo land of world government and gigantic give-away projects of American substance for the benefit of "underprivileged" areas of the world. Undue pessimism is created because much sweeping, ignorant and poorly informed criticism is uttered without let or hindrance.

It would, of course, be utterly undesirable, and a subtle form of defeat, if the United States and other free nations should imitate the communist pattern of intensive indoctrination and merciless repression of critical thought.

But freedom carries an element of responsibility. Just because he is free to make political choices which are not open to subjects of totalitarian regimes, the American citizen owes it to himself to become familiar with the communist design of world conquest, with communist methods of subversion, with the history and background of the cold war. Equipped with this knowledge, he may be relied on to reject the fallacies and quack remedies of the appeasers and the defeatists. Until this responsibility is generally recognized and fulfilled, American national determination and purpose will not be as firm and resolute for the long pull as the nature of the communist threat demands.

A still more serious weakness on the noncommunist side of the front is the existence of many rifts and fissions that make the building of an effective anti-Soviet coalition, surest guaranty of peace or of victory if the Soviet rulers resort to war, a matter of much delicacy and difficulty. The Franco–German antagonism is grotesquely obsolete, in view of the profound weakening of both countries by the last war and the over-shadowing threat to both of the Soviet empire. Yet this antagonism has seriously delayed the organization of an effective defense of Europe. A glance around the map of the world reveals many other feuds and schisms, between nations and within nations, which are cunningly inflamed and exploited by the right hand and the left hand of the Soviet empire, by Soviet diplomacy and by communist propaganda.

America's immensely high standard of wealth and industrial productivity has disadvantages as well as advantages. It cannot be helped if this standard excites envy and dislike, even in countries which are placed on America's side by overwhelming dictates of national self-interest. Americans would do well to worry less about being liked, more about being respected for firmness and consistency of purpose.

But America's permanently favorable balance of trade and payments with the outside world creates a serious handicap in foreign economic relations. It places the United States in the position of being continually obliged either to export less, to import more or to give away its goods or dollars, in some form. No one of these choices is palatable; and yet it is as plain as the multiplication table that the gap between what America wants from the rest of the world and what the rest of the world wants from America can only be closed by one of these choices, or by a combination of all three.

There is another vulnerable spot in American economic relations. During the war and after the war Uncle Sam played the role of an Uncle Atlas, carrying much of the world on his back by means of lend-lease supplies, Marshall Plan aid and other forms of subsidies to foreign countries. Fair-minded and realistic Europeans appreciate this support. But they are concerned, and not without reason, as to what would happen to the European economies, so dependent on dollar sources of supply for basic raw materials and foodstuffs, if the American giant should falter and stumble over a severe depression. Judging from past experience, American purchases of European goods would then dry up with appalling speed. One of America's greatest contributions to victory in the cold war would be the creation of a depression-proof economy. Apart from the economic and social consequences at home a crisis of 1929–1933 proportions would be a grave, if not an irreparable international political defeat.

America's comparative experience in foreign affairs, a consequence of the comfortably isolated position which America enjoyed before the age of political totalitarianism and air and atomic development, is a handicap in the conduct of the cold war. American attitudes in dealing with foreign countries are often lavish and wasteful in big things and tactless in small things. America's first efforts to strike back in kind at the Soviet world-wide incitation to subversion often gave the impression of amateurs competing with professionals. Americans have yet to learn that often in diplomacy and always in undercover activity silence is golden.

Here, then, are the competing balance sheets in this age of intensely polarized struggle, with the fate of the world as the ultimate stake. On both sides there are political assets and liabilities, points of strength and points of weakness. Probably a historian, writing from the observation point of the year 2,000, can assess these balance sheets more accurately and see more clearly what determined the issue of a struggle that now hangs uncertainly in the balance.

Maybe this issue has already been determined. Perhaps the firm determination of the western powers to stay in Berlin or the secession of Tito will be recognized in the future as the turning point, the passing of the high crest of the Soviet communist tide. There has not yet been time to estimate the consequences of the death of Stalin. It may be that the decisive battles, military or political, are still in the future.

One thing may be said with certainty. There was no course of action, consistent with national security, by which America could have avoided the test of strength that has been generally christened the cold war. Those critics on both sides of the Atlantic who hold America jointly responsible with the Soviet

Union for the cold war should face up squarely to the following questions:

Did the Soviet Union or the United States carry out the more extensive demobilization after the end of the war?

Was it the Soviet Union that blockaded West Berlin or the western powers that blockaded East Berlin?

Was it North Korea, armed and politically controlled from Moscow, that invaded South Korea, or was it the other way around?

What was the Soviet response to specific American proposals for the demilitarization of Germany over a period of twenty-five or forty years?

If these questions are candidly answered, a consistent pattern appears. American actions which have been represented as bellicose—the proclamation of the Truman Doctrine, the building up of air bases in Great Britain and in the Mediterranean area, the rearmament program after the attack in Korea—have been responses to Soviet challenges and would not have taken place, in all probability, without these challenges.

The American conflict with the Soviet communist empire—and it is deep and irreconcilable—does not exist because America wishes to impose on the world its own political and economic institutions or is intolerant of political and economic systems which are different from its own. The cause of the conflict is extremely simple: the existence of an enormous empire, heavily militarized and ruled by men who are convinced that there can never be peace until communism has conquered the entire world. Old Russian imperial ambitions have become fused with the old dream of a Russian messianic mission to save and redeem a sinning western world.

This is why the Soviet Government and the regimes it has organized on a satellite basis have pursued policies which are incompatible with friendly or even normal international relations. They have flooded noncommunist countries with spies and subversive agents, treated noncommunist foreigners as enemies and criminals and intrigued throughout the world to turn discontent into riot and riot into revolution.

Soviet peace offensives are merely a continuation of war by other means, aimed at dividing the noncommunist powers, sowing germs of suspicion among them, relaxing their military effort. While it would be unwise and indeed politically impossible to refuse what purport to be Soviet offers of serious negotiations on disputed subjects, there are a few facts about Soviet and historic Russian tactics which should never be forgotten, either by the men who are directly responsible for conducting American foreign policy or by American public opinion.

A totalitarian state can turn a peace offensive on and off like a faucet. The government of such a state can declare that white is black today and black is white tomorrow without the slightest fear of being publicly charged with inconsistency. There is a very real need to be on guard against taking too seriously the snap judgments of gullible travelers on conducted tours—if and when the Soviet Government resorts again to the "conducted tour" method of propaganda.

So the Soviet Government starts a war which inflicts terrific ravages on Korea and imposes heavy casualties on the United States and tries to pose with the olive branch of the peacemaker when it is apparently inclined, temporarily, to call off this war. Soviet planes in Germany make an unprovoked attack on an unarmed British plane in Germany and shoot it down, killing the seven airmen. And it is represented as a great step toward peace if the Soviet commandant in Berlin expresses regret, not for the attack, but because British aviators perished. Or the Soviet Government, after suspending normal conditions of access to its country, allows a party of American editors to enter the country and treats them with normal courtesy. And some of the dazed editors think the cold war is all off.

Soviet peace offensives should be viewed against the long background of zigzags in the past, with new periods of embittered hostility following delusive professions of desire for peace and friendship. Secretary Dulles, when the outlines of the latest Soviet peace maneuver began to appear on the horizon, set forth three basic facts which, it may be hoped, will set this maneuver in proper perspective:

The Soviet Union is a heavily armed totalitarian state, controlling one third of the people and natural resources of the world.

The leaders of that state are basically deeply hostile to any nation that does not accept communist control.

These leaders do not accept any inhibitions on the use of violence or any moral law.

A voice from the past deserves a hearing on this matter of Russian tactics. The British Foreign Secretary, Lord Palmerston, observed about a century ago:

> It has always been the policy and practice of the Russian Government to expand its frontiers as rapidly as the apathy or timidity of neighboring states would permit, but usually to halt and frequently to recoil when confronted by determined opposition; then to await the next favorable opportunity to spring upon its intended victim.

Another voice of the present that deserves a hearing is that of Tomasz Arciszewski, Prime Minister of the Polish government-in-exile, resistance fighter against the Nazi occupation of Poland, an old man of remarkable vigor of mind and force of personality. As a veteran Polish Socialist, Arciszewski became familiar with the mentality of Lenin and other Bolshevik leaders at socialist conferences before the First World War.

"Remember this above all," he said to me at the end of a long talk in London in 1946. "So long as one free country exists anywhere in the world the communist dictators will never feel safe. No matter how much that country may want peace, Moscow propaganda will always represent it as imperialist and try first to divide it from within, then to destroy it."

The whole course of the cold war confirms the truth of Arciszewski's diagnosis. The men in the Kremlin may not want war—until the balance of political and military strength has tilted more definitely in their favor. But their regime could not stand the shock of real peace, of the establishment of relations with foreign countries as intimate and friendly as those which prevail between the United States and Canada, for instance. Too many official myths would crumble for the captive peoples behind the iron curtain if the light of free contact were permitted to illuminate that vast area.

When one third of the human race has been harnessed to a design of world conquest through force, threat of force and subversion a condition of permanent international high tension has been created. The cold war might go on for decades. It might erupt into a last decisive struggle for military supremacy within a much shorter time. What is certain is that, with aggravations and abatements, twists and zigzags, this struggle will continue until one of two things happens. The communist regimes will be overthrown or transformed beyond recognition by internal evolution or revolution. Or the cause of freedom will be lost forever.

Our political aim in the cold war should not be to go on a crusade for some utopian blueprint of new world organization or to try to convert the whole world, Russians and Chinese included, to American-style democracy. The attempt to use military occupation as a school of democracy in Germany and Japan was naïve and far from successful.

We should seek to organize the broadest possible anti-Kremlin coalition, from Franco to Tito. We should recognize realistically that governments may be useful, perhaps indispensable allies in the fight against the communist empire, even if we may not approve of everything they do in domestic affairs. We should make allowance for the fact that what may appeal to a Spaniard may not appeal to a Norwegian, that a Yugoslav may respond to different motivations than a Turk. We would profit by a study of British policy during the years when Napoleon dominated the continent of Europe. The British statesmen of that time did not promise a new heaven and a new earth as a reward for victory over Napoleon. They simply kept a centre of resistance alive, helped where they could, with an expeditionary force in Spain, with sea power and diplomacy and subsidies in other places, until the overgrown Napoleonic empire became involved in enterprises beyond its strength and came tumbling down.

A main objective should be to divide our enemies and to do everything possible for the disintegration of the communist empire. It would be contrary to all the teachings of history to imagine that some pattern of the past would be restored either in the Soviet Union or in China or in the satellite states. The important thing, from the standpoint of American interest, is to do everything in our power to hinder the consolidation of the communist empire and, if and when the decline and fall of this empire come, to see to it that no power again acquires the predominance in manpower, territory and natural resources, which makes the communist empire, whether its masters may for the moment speak in threats or in lullabies, such a nightmare from the standpoint of American and West European security.

The test of the cold war is supreme. The stakes could not be higher. The ultimate consequences of communist victory are clearly foreshadowed in the fate of every country that has fallen under communist rule. Such a victory would mean the blotting out of every value of our Greco–Roman and Judaeo–Christian civilization. There would be a dark night of the soul. The world would become spiritually a dead planet, functioning like a mechanical ant heap. The cold war is not an oldfashioned gentlemanly power struggle, in which the defeated side loses a bit of territory and pays a moderate indemnity. This is an all-out irrepressible conflict between two irreconcilable conceptions of human life and destiny.

Even if communism should be decisively defeated, the immediate prospective results of a Third World War would be, in all probability, shocking and disillusioning. No responsible civilized statesman would take the initiative in unloosing the terrible destructive possibilities of such a war. Every resource of American and Western statecraft should be employed to remain within the narrow channel between unlimited shooting war and the still more disastrous course of endless retreat and futile appeasement. There is always the chance, which should not be overlooked, that some unforeseen turn of events, some hidden feud within the walls of the Kremlin, some dissension in the enemy camp, will abate or eliminate the "power that fills the world with terror" without the fearful surgery of a war waged with atomic and other modern weapons of mass destruction.

But it is unwarranted pessimism to assume that all-out war, if some new reckless swerve or lurch in Kremlin foreign policy forces a plain choice between fighting or surrendering, would mean the destruction of civilization. The experience of recovery after the last war, notably in Germany, shows that there is more resilience in the human organism than is sometimes imagined. A world rid of the communist nightmare of eternal, scientifically organized tyranny over the souls, minds and bodies of men might realize the age-old dream of a truly free and humane society, rising to new heights of spiritual and cultural achievement and material well-being, with the aid of modern invention and technology, and on the sound basis of individual liberty.

Ever since the shadow of the Soviet Union began to loom so large on the American horizon the question has been put, in hope and in fear: How can we get along with Russia? Many answers have been offered, some sensible, some foolish; some based on reasoned knowledge, others on disingenuous propaganda or dense ignorance. But there is only one realistic answer.

Coexistence with a swollen dictatorship like the Soviet Union is possible only on a basis of equal or superior strength, military, economic, diplomatic, moral. Victory in the cold war will be assured when this lesson is finally and definitely learned by the governments of that greater part of the world which still lies outside the communist orbit, and when and if the peoples who are still free realize that there is no safety in retreat, no security in cowardice and no peace in appeasement. This victory is assured, if only because of the inner weaknesses and contradictions of communist theory and practice, weaknesses and contradictions which will come to the breaking point if the Soviet empire sees everywhere a wall of united opposition.

The winning of this victory may well be long. It may be tragically costly. But the consequences of the alternative, defeat, are too terrible to contemplate, much less to accept. For man, made in the image of his Creator, is destined for something higher than the robot existence of the communist serf state.

Chapter XV — Beyond Containment

Before his election and after his election President Eisenhower committed himself to a policy looking beyond mere passive containment of the vast Soviet empire. "Containment" perhaps reached its height of absurdity in an order which was given at the beginning of the fighting in Korea that American air force units should bomb no targets in North Korea. This order, to be sure, was quickly rescinded. But much of its spirit was reflected in the subsequent failure to take measures which would have made decisive victory possible.

In a speech at the American Legion convention on August 25, 1952, Eisenhower called the roll of the peoples of Eastern Europe, including the Baltic Republics, Latvia, Lithuania and Estonia, which have been forcibly annexed to the Soviet Union, and added:

> The American conscience can never know peace until these people are restored again to being masters of their own fate.
>
> Not only in Eastern Europe has communist barbarism broken forth beyond its own borders. On its Asiatic periphery the Kremlin has made captive China and Tibet, Inner Mongolia, Northern Korea, Northern Japan, the northern half of Indo-China its slaves. It has added five hundred million people to its arsenal manpower. . . .
>
> We can never rest—and we must so inform all the world, in-

cluding the Kremlin—that until the enslaved nations of the world have in the fullness of freedom the right to choose their own path, that then and then only can we say that there is a possible way of living peacefully and permanently with communism in the world.

A similar note was struck in Eisenhower's State of the Union message on February 2. The order to the American Seventh Fleet to prevent Chinese nationalist action against the mainland, as well as communist action against Formosa, was withdrawn. The new President announced his intention to increase United States assistance in the training and arming of South Korean divisions, called for "practical unity" in Western Europe, with the Schuman Plan and the European Army as examples. He also seemed to imply a repudiation of the Yalta and Potsdam Agreements when he declared, in a loudly applauded passage of the speech:

> We shall never acquiesce in the enslavement of any people in order to purchase fancied gain for ourselves. I shall ask the Congress at a later date to join in an appropriate resolution making clear that this government recognizes no kind of commitment contained in secret understandings of the past with foreign governments which permit this kind of enslavement.

The follow-up on this announcement was not happy. The State Department submitted to Congress a resolution which threw all the blame for the consequences of Yalta on Soviet violations of the agreement. This was bad history, bad morals and bad logic. In his State of the Union message and on other occasions Eisenhower had repudiated American acquiescence in the enslavement of foreign peoples.

But the original Yalta Agreement, irrespective of Soviet violations of its provisions, included features which certainly made for enslavement, such as the assignment of Eastern Poland to the Soviet Union and of unspecified German territory to Poland, the consent to repatriate forcibly Soviet political refugees and the sanction of the use of German labor for "reparations."

The State Department resolution was, by implication, an endorsement of the original Yalta Agreement, which had been severely attacked in the Republican Party platform, and its passing in this form would have done more harm than good.

Two arguments were used against outright repudiation of the Yalta and Potsdam Agreements. It was alleged that such repudiation would make it possible for the Soviet Union to expel the western powers from Berlin and Vienna. And it was contended that Democratic loyalty to Roosevelt and Truman would make it impossible to obtain for a resolution condemning their handiwork the large majority which would be necessary to produce a moral effect abroad.

The first argument has no serious validity. It is both humiliating and inaccurate to assume that the United States and the other western powers are in Berlin and Vienna by grace of the Soviet Union. The western powers are in these cities because, as the experience with the blockade of Berlin showed, they can only be put out at the price of starting a Third World War. Their moral right to be there is the desire of the legitimate German and Austrian governments, and of the overwhelming majority of the German and Austrian peoples, that the allies remain until conditions are created for a general evacuation of all foreign troops. The sooner this point is made clear in official statements, the better.

As for the second argument, one wonders how many Democrats, if it came to a showdown, would want to go on record as "men of Yalta." Roosevelt did not go to Yalta as the leader of the Democratic Party. He went there as representative of the entire American people. He failed the American people, Democrats and Republicans alike, by betraying American moral principles and sacrificing American vital national interests. One hopes that some day, somehow, Congress will have an opportunity to express its opinion of the Yalta and Potsdam Agreements. One suspects that this opinion might well be an unqualified and almost unanimous negative.

The Eisenhower Administration missed a most promising opportunity to make its position in favor of a policy that would go beyond containment completely clear by not presenting a resolution calling for lock-stock-and-barrel repudiation of Yalta and Potsdam. As the first of these agreements is naturally and understandably most hateful to Poles and the second to Germans, the propaganda effect of a declaration against them would have been most favorable. And the repudiation could have been placed on the unimpeachable ground that the agreements were null and void anyway because of repeated Soviet violations of those clauses of the agreements which were not in Soviet interest.

Eisenhower's third and probably most important declaration of American policy toward the Soviet Union was contained in his speech of April 16, 1953, a speech clearly inspired by pacific gestures in which the Soviet Government indulged after the death of Josef Stalin on March 5. Eisenhower outlined a package plan for peace, with four main elements.

First, there was a statement of general principles. No people should be regarded as an enemy. The security of every nation depends on cooperation, not isolation. Every nation has a right to a form of government and economic system of its own choosing and no nation should attempt to dictate to other nations their form of government. Any nation's hope of lasting peace cannot be based on an armaments race, but rather on just relations and honest understanding with all other nations.

After declaring that, under present conditions, the alternatives were atomic war or a life of fear and tension, with the burden of armaments preventing the achievement of true abundance, and giving graphic illustration of the wasteful cost of modern armaments, Eisenhower came to the second main element in his address, the terms of a peaceful political settlement.

Here he was firm and uncompromising. There was no suggestion of willingness to settle on the basis of the existing situation. The President definitely set his sights beyond containment of communism and called for the dismantling of the swollen Soviet empire. What he said to the Kremlin, although it was phrased in conciliatory language, might be paraphrased as follows:

> Get out of countries where you have no right to be. Get out of Germany, get out of Austria, get out of Korea, get out of Poland, get out of Rumania, get out of Hungary, get out of Czechoslovakia, get out of Bulgaria, get out of Albania, get out of Lithuania, get out of Latvia, get out of Estonia.

Calling for "honest acts of peace," not "mere rhetoric," the President suggested as first steps the signing of an Austrian peace treaty, the release of "thousands of prisoners still held from World War II" and "the conclusion of an honorable armistice in Korea." Such an armistice should be followed by "political discussions leading to the holding of free elections in a united Korea." There should also be an end to "direct and indirect attacks upon the security of Indo-China and Malaya." Eisenhower also called for

> . . . a broader European community, conducive to the free movement of persons, of trade and ideas.
> This community would include a free and united Germany, with a government based on free and secret ballot.
> This free community and the full independence of the East European nations could mean the end of the present unnatural division of Europe.

As a third point the President suggested that, "concurrently" with the political settlement, there should be international arms reduction, with prohibition of atomic weapons, and enforcement of these limitations and prohibitions "by adequate safeguards, including a practical system of inspection under the United Nations."

Fourth, borrowing an idea suggested by the late Democratic Senator from Connecticut, Mr. Brien McMahon, President Eisenhower proposed that the United States, along with all nations, should devote a substantial percentage of any savings derived from real disarmament to a fund for world aid and reconstruction. The purpose of this fund would be to help other peoples develop the undeveloped areas of the world, to stimulate profitable and fair world trade and to assist all peoples to know the blessings of productive freedom.

"The monuments of this new kind of war," said the President, "would be these: Roads and schools, hospitals and homes, food and health.

"We are ready, in short, to dedicate our strength to serving the needs, not the fears of the world."

No doubt the Eisenhower Administration would have undertaken some initiative for peace on a basis of freedom and justice in any case. But the President's outline of possible peace terms was probably hastened because the Kremlin began to speak in more pacific accents after the death of Stalin. The Soviet peace offensive was inaugurated when the new Soviet Prime Minister, Georgi M. Malenkov, declared before the Soviet Parliament:

> At the present time there is not one disputed or undecided question that cannot be decided by peaceful means on the basis of the mutual understanding of interested countries. This is our attitude toward all states, among them the United States of America.

The language of the Soviet press and radio and of Soviet spokesmen in the United Nations became less truculent and abusive in references to western powers. This was also true as regards the slogans which were displayed in the May First demonstration.

There were also a few pacific actions, although, with one exception, these were all of a kind that cost the Kremlin nothing and were of distinctly minor significance. The one exception (and it is impossible to say whether this was a result of Soviet or Chinese initiative) was the withdrawal from the position of demanding unconditional forcible repatriation of unwilling war prisoners.

Whether there is any serious intention to create conditions for an "honorable armistice" or whether the communists are seeking to get back the prisoners by some means less crude and visibly humiliating to the United States than forcible repatriation would have been is not clear at the time of writing. (May 15, 1953.) Meanwhile the prospect of relaxed tension which was opened up by exchange of some sick and wounded prisoners and the resumption of truce talks was clouded over because of the extension of communist military operations in Indo-China to the remote, primitive, mountainous kingdom of Laos.

The significance and purpose of the communist drive into this area are not clear. But Laos abuts on Thailand and Burma; and penetration of Laos may be the prelude to more ambitious schemes of overrunning southeast Asia. Should this prove to be the case, we may find that the Soviet and Chinese communists have exchanged a war in Korea, which they see no chance of winning decisively, for adventures in a richer and economically and strategically more vital part of the Orient.

Other Soviet actions have been of very minor significance. There has been a temporary easing of harassment on the highway which connects West Berlin with Western Germany. A group of American newspaper publishers was permitted to pay a brief visit to Moscow. Some British, American and French civilians who had been caught by the sudden onrush of the North Korean invasion and had been held in prison camps were belatedly released.

On the other hand, the Soviet official reply to Eisenhower's peace proposals, while moderate in tone, was negative in substance. It took the form of a long article, published in the leading Soviet newspapers *Izvestia* and *Pravda* on April 25, 1953, and broadcast by the Soviet radio. The reply shrewdly emphasized every issue on which disagreement exists between the United States and its West European allies. A conspicuous omission in President Eisenhower's speech had been any reference to China. The Soviet comment emphasized "the restoration of the national rights of China in the United Nations, and also of its lawful territorial rights, including the island of Formosa."

It is just on these issues, diplomatic recognition of Red China and the disposition of Formosa, that American and British public opinion is farthest apart. The Soviet statement also referred to what the French people had suffered from "militaristic Germany" and tried to exploit both French fear of Germany and German desire for national unification against the ideal of West European cooperation.

Eisenhower's two references to independence for the satellite states were brushed off with the bland assertion that "only by a stubborn struggle for their rights did the peoples of Eastern Europe come to the present popular-democratic form of government. . . . It would be strange to expect the Soviet Union to interfere in favor of installing the reactionary regimes overthrown by these peoples."

There was a similar repudiation of any intention on the part of the Soviet Government to use its influence to "retard the liberation movement of the colonial and semi-colonial people in Asia against their centuries-old oppression and enslavement."

The Soviet comment complained that Eisenhower had "tied up his proposals regarding peace with a whole series of preliminary conditions set by him to the Soviet Union, although these claims in his speech have not been reinforced by any corresponding obligations on the part of the USA."

Here one comes close to the heart of a very strong divergence between the American and Soviet viewpoints regarding the basis for peace. It is the American view that the Soviet Union has wantonly provoked a state of chronic high international tension by enormously expanding its power and influence beyond any reasonable Russian ethnic boundaries and by continually stirring up trouble in countries which are beyond the immediate reach of its armies.

Therefore it is the American view, clearly set forth in Eisenhower's speech, that the Soviet Government must change its previous policy and prove this change by "deeds," not mere words, before there can be any basis for stable peace. The Soviet Government disputes this thesis completely. In Moscow's view it is America and the western powers who are "warmongers"; the Soviet Union and its satellites are cooing doves of peace. Not one solid concession to the western viewpoint can be found in the Soviet reply to Eisenhower. There is only an intimation of willingness to discuss disputed issues on a give-and-take basis. The precise Soviet phraseology is as follows:

> Soviet leaders will welcome any step of the United States Government or any other country, if it is directed toward a friendly settlement of contentious questions. This testifies to the readiness of the Soviet side for a serious, businesslike discussion of problems, both by direct negotiations and, when necessary, within the framework of the UN.

A few days after the publication of the Soviet editorial comment Marshal Nikolai Bulganin, Soviet Minister of War, in a May Day address tried to turn Eisenhower's formula, "Deeds, not Words," against the West. Said the Soviet war lord:

> Inasmuch as there are no signs either of the diminution of the arms race by them [the western powers] or of the reduction of the network of military bases distributed on the territory of many states in Europe and Asia, and particularly on territory bordering on the Soviet Union, our government will in the future manifest the necessary concern for the assuring of the defense and security of our country.

So, if the price of peace, from the American standpoint, is the dismantling of the Soviet empire, the unification of Germany and Korea on a basis of freedom, the withdrawal of Soviet troops and secret police and other agencies of compulsion from the satellite states, the Soviet asking price for a settlement is very different. It is the dissolution of the North Atlantic Pact, the reduction or abandonment of the American air and naval bases which have been built up in Great Britain, France, Germany and the Mediterranean area.

Is a reconciliation of viewpoints which are so far removed possible? British Prime Minister Sir Winston Churchill is at least moderately optimistic. He placed the British viewpoint on record in an important foreign policy address in Parliament on May 11.

Churchill advocated "a conference on the highest level between the leading powers without long delay." This conference should be confined to the smallest possible number of powers and of persons and should be held in an atmosphere of informality, privacy and seclusion.

He described as a "supreme event" "the change of attitude and, we all hope, of mind which has taken place in the Soviet domains and particularly in the Kremlin since the death of Stalin." He suggested that it would be a mistake to assume that nothing could be settled with the Soviet Union until all has been settled and remarked that peace in Korea and the conclusion of an Austrian peace treaty might lead to an easement of relations. He spoke of the communist proposal about disposition of war prisoners as requiring "patient and sympathetic consideration."

At the same time the British Prime Minister emphasized the necessity of maintaining solidarity among free nations and keeping up defense. He also asserted that Western Germany would not be sacrificed in the interest of a settlement with the Soviet Union and suggested somewhat vaguely that the western powers might guaranty the Soviet Union against a German attack and Germany against a Soviet attack. The first guaranty would seem highly superfluous, in view of the present distribution of armed strength.

A new secret conference calls up unpleasant memories of Teheran, Yalta and Potsdam and there seem to have been solid grounds for the cool reserve with which Churchill's proposal was first received in Washington. Two obvious objections are uncertainty as to whether and how far Malenkov is master of the internal situation in the Soviet Union and whether and how far the Soviet Union could speak for Red China.

Despite Sir Winston's optimism, the Soviet peace offensive during the first two months after Stalin's death produced few tangible fruits. In many ways it recalled the psychology illustrated in an old Russian folk story.

According to this story a poor peasant, living in a crowded hut, goes to the village wise man to complain of his hard condition. The wise man tells him to take a pig into the hut. When the peasant comes back and complains that conditions are worse than ever he is told to add a goat to the members of his household.

Then, when the peasant has been almost reduced to despair, the sage advises him to take out the goat. The peasant becomes much more cheerful and when he is then told to remove the pig his joy is unbounded. He forgets that he is exactly where he was when he began to complain. *The Economist,* of London, put the same point in a single lapidary sentence:

"What is surprising and alarming is to see how little has to be said from Moscow to obscure the memory of so much that has been done."

Many acts which were hailed as notable Soviet contributions to peace were nothing more than cessation of or abstention from acts which no civilized government would have committed in the first place, such as the release of foreign diplomats in North Korea or the temporary stoppage of airplane incidents along the zonal border lines in Germany.

Cooing from Moscow dovecotes is more dangerous and demoralizing to the West than the rattle of Soviet tanks or the whirr of Soviet airplanes. For many memories are incurably short and there seems to be no ceiling on the qualities of naïveté and gullibility.

Anyone who has been stationed in Moscow as a correspondent will remember with a shudder the know-it-all foreign quick tripper who, immediately after checking in at a Moscow hotel, would announce with finality: "I have been in Moscow twenty-four hours and I *know* that all the stories about hunger and slave labor are lies."

When the Soviet authorities lifted the iron curtain for one very small peep a group of newspaper and radio executives, not one of whom was known as a Russian linguist or a specialist in Soviet politics, displayed a tendency to call off the cold war on the basis of a short stay in Moscow and glimpses of Moscow's much advertised subway and of standard equipment on a Soviet dairy farm. A forthright editor in Wisconsin was not diplomatic when he greeted these tourists to Moscow on their return as "the editorial jackasses of the century for falling for this Soviet peace trickery." But thoughtful Americans will begin to be impressed with a change of heart and attitude in Moscow if and when the Soviet authorities provide facilities for unhampered travel and observation in the scores of centres which have been pinpointed as locations of concentration camps.

At the time of writing it is a matter of speculation how far the Soviet peace offensive may go and what forms it may assume. Quite possibly there has been a change of tactics in the cold war from a war of position to a war of movement. Until Stalin's death the situation was frozen tight on both sides right up to the line of demarcation. It is conceivable, although by no means certain, that there may now be more flexibility of maneuver.

There is no reason to believe that the character or the ultimate purposes of the Soviet regime have changed. But several circumstances may induce Stalin's heirs to employ more subtlety and less brutality in trying to achieve these purposes, the gradual conquest of Europe and Asia and the isolation and final overwhelming of the United States.

The internal balance of power among the Soviet leaders

seems to be precarious and unstable; Malenkov has not given the impression of acquiring the power of another Stalin. The peace offensive may be timed to coincide with the reaching of some special point in Soviet atomic or other armament. There may well be a tendency to see how much can be accomplished in loosening and softening up the western alliance by relatively soft words, unaccompanied by any deeds.

American reaction to this new phase in Kremlin cold war tactics should be wary and vigilant, but not sterile and negative. It would be disastrous in Europe or Asia to be maneuvered into a position of seeming to oppose a genuine Soviet desire for peace. It would be disastrous in Germany to allow communists to pose as champions of German unity.

Eisenhower's speech of April 16, setting forth a concrete program of peace without a word of appeasement, was a move in the right direction. This American peace initiative, and the elements in Soviet philosophy and Soviet foreign policy that obstruct the achievement of peace, should be continually emphasized by every information agency at the disposal of the American Government.

When the Soviet Government offers some essentially meaningless gesture, like a "peace pact among the Big Five" the retort is obvious. Let the Soviet Government honor the non-aggression pacts which it signed with Poland, Finland, Latvia, Lithuania and Estonia by withdrawing its troops and secret police from these countries and restoring their independence and territorial integrity.

An armistice in Korea could have been signed years ago, had it not been for communist insistence on the forcible return of unwilling war prisoners. This is an issue on which honor, humanity and expediency alike would make it most unfortunate to yield an inch. At the time of writing negotiations on this issue seem to be approaching a showdown. While the Chinese and North Korean communists and their Kremlin sponsors have dropped their original uncompromising demand for forced repatriation they are trying to get back the prisoners by subtler methods.

The proposal which they submitted to the UN negotiators early in May was full of dangerous and objectionable features. The prisoners unwilling to go home were to be turned over to a "neutral" commission, composed of Poland, Czechoslovakia, Sweden, Switzerland and India. Such a commission would have been outrageously stacked, two communist states (Russia and Red China might have been proposed just as reasonably), one state which has become a symbol for weak-kneed appeasement and two genuine neutrals.

Red Chinese agents were to work on the prisoners for four months, and it was apparently contemplated that Polish and Czechoslovak troops should take part in guarding them. It is easy to imagine the pressure and intimidation to which this could lead. Those prisoners who resist threats (which, according to communist practice, will be directed against their families) were not to be set free even after the period of four months; their fate was to be left to the uncertain chance of a political conference which might drag on indefinitely or break up without coming to any result.

In retrospect it becomes increasingly clear that one of the worst of many American blunders in Korea was failure to release these anticommunist prisoners promptly and unconditionally. It was suggested that this would adversely affect the fate of our own prisoners. This seems most unlikely. If the communists did not desire an armistice our prisoners would not be freed in any case. If they did wish an armistice they would scarcely prolong hostilities for the obviously impossible objective of obtaining the release of prisoners who would have scattered to the four winds. Indeed the unilateral release of these prisoners might have been a face-saving aid to the communists, who were most reluctant to admit that some fifty thousand of their soldiers were unwilling to go home.

Should there be a final arrangement that compromises in the

slightest degree the right of war prisoners to seek political asylum and resettlement, America will have made itself a partner, as at Yalta, to a crime against national honor and humanity. And it would seem futile to expect that soldiers of communist states will ever trust our promises or surrender voluntarily in the future.

The new Soviet tactics require of American diplomacy flexibility without appeasement. The cold war will not be settled or ended by an armistice in Korea or a peace treaty with Austria. Only the dissolution of the swollen Soviet empire and a profound political, economic and moral transformation of the governing regime in the Soviet Union, with the abandonment of all the basic tenets of communism, could lay the foundation for secure and lasting peace.

But it is barely possible that a kind of truce of disengagement could be arranged, with the Soviet Union withdrawing its armed forces from the heart of Europe, and the United States, as the Soviet withdrawal was clearly demonstrated, cutting down or abandoning some of its military installations near the Soviet borders. Such a prospect is not likely, because there is no recorded case when communism has voluntarily abandoned its grip on a people that has been subjugated.

However, the possibility of some such bargain should not be ruled out, especially as the Soviet Government has intimated willingness to discuss controversial questions. A reasonable American position could be summarized somewhat as follows. The United States has not the slightest imperialist ambition in those parts of Europe and the Mediterranean area where a network of military installations has been created. The reason for the creation of this network was the sweeping aggressive expansion of the Soviet Union beyond its legitimate frontiers of 1939.

We should be willing to relax and diminish our defense efforts if and as the Soviet Government should give convincing tangible proof of renouncing this expansion. Such proof could take only one form: complete unconditional withdrawal of Soviet armed forces, secret police agents and other instruments of compulsion from all the East European satellite states. Such withdrawal would be one of the "deeds" which, as President Eisenhower has said, are to be preferred to Soviet "words," which have so often proved false and perjured. Even if at first the regimes which remained in power in what would then be the former satellite states maintained some communist features the prospect of an ultimate return to freedom would be good, once the shadow of Soviet compulsion was definitely removed.

This proposal should be pressed on the Soviet Government by all possible means. (Against the possibility that Soviet troops might again march into Poland or Rumania, there should be a sanction, under the guaranty of the NATO powers, that any movement of this kind would be treated as an act of war.) Economically and politically the united whole Europe which would become feasible if the tide of Soviet conquest were rolled back would be preferable to the half Europe which is all that can be integrated so long as the iron curtain and the Soviet empire are realities.

There should be imagination and flexibility as well as firmness in America's policy toward Germany. It should be a Number One objective of American diplomacy to cut the ground from under communist and neo-Nazi agitators by removing the last traces of unequal treatment of Germany in all fields, political, economic and military. Should the Soviet Government consent to the holding of genuinely free elections in East Germany, the benefit of reclaiming eighteen million human beings from communist slavery should outweigh the consideration of maintaining every dot and comma of the European Defense Community. After what Germany has suffered from Soviet invasion and occupation the danger that a united Germany would, of its own volition, become a Soviet vassal state is practically nonexistent. This danger is certainly negligible compared with the very real danger of subordinating America's vital interest in a strong rearmed Germany as the shield of Europe and the eastern march of western civilization (at least until the liberation of the Soviet satellite states is complete) to obsolete and harmful emotions of fear and revenge.

If the Soviet peace offensive presents new dangers, notably the possibility of influencing the weak and wavering "neutralist" elements in Europe, it also offers new opportunities of starting the Soviet empire, the greatest threat to our western civilization, on the road to decline and fall. It is only necessary that American spirit and American foreign policy rise to the height of the danger and the opportunity, that Americans be clear as to the nature of the Soviet threat, unyielding in the maintenance of fundamental principles and the pursuit of essential ends, generous and broadminded and flexible in choosing the means best suited to achieve these ends.

Appendix

My friends, before I begin the expression of those thoughts that I deem appropriate to this moment, would you permit me the privilege of uttering a little private prayer of my own. And I ask that you bow your heads.

Almighty God, as we stand here at this moment my future associates in the executive branch of government join me in beseeching that Thou will make full and complete our dedication to the service of the people in this throng, and their fellow citizens everywhere.

Give us, we pray, the power to discern clearly right from wrong, and allow all our words and actions to be governed thereby, and by the laws of this land. Especially we pray that our concern shall be for all the people regardless of station, race, or calling.

May cooperation be permitted and be the mutual aim of those who, under the concepts of our Constitution, hold to differing political faiths; so that all may work for the good of our beloved country and Thy glory. Amen.

My fellow citizens:

The world and we have passed the midway point of a century of continuing challenge. We sense with all our faculties that forces of good and evil are massed and armed and opposed as rarely before in history.

This fact defines the meaning of this day. We are summoned by this honored and historic ceremony to witness more than the act of one citizen swearing his oath of service, in the presence of God. We are called as a people to give testimony in the sight of the world to our faith that the future shall belong to the free.

Since this century's beginning, a time of tempest has seemed to come upon the continents of the earth. Masses of Asia have awakened to strike off shackles of the past. Great nations of Europe have fought their bloodiest wars. Thrones have toppled and their vast empires have disappeared. New nations have been born.

For our own country, it has been a time of recurring trial. We have grown in power and in responsibility. We have passed through the anxieties of depression and of war to a summit unmatched in man's history. Seeking to secure peace in the world, we have had to fight through the forests of the Argonne, to the shores of Iwo Jima, and to the cold mountains of Korea.

In the swift rush of great events, we find ourselves groping to know the full sense and meaning of these times in which we live. In our quest of understanding, we beseech God's guidance. We summon all our knowledge of the past and we scan all signs of the future. We bring all our wit and all our will to meet the question:

How far have we come in man's long pilgrimage from darkness toward light? Are we nearing the light—a day of freedom and of peace for all mankind? Or are the shadows of another night closing in upon us?

Great as are the preoccupations absorbing us at home, concerned as we are with matters that deeply affect our livelihood today and our vision of the future, each of these domestic problems is dwarfed by, and often even created by, this question that involves all human kind.

This trial comes at a moment when man's power to achieve good or to inflict evil surpasses the brightest hopes and the sharpest fears of all ages. We can turn rivers in their courses, level mountains to the plains. Oceans and land and sky are avenues for our colossal commerce. Disease diminishes and life lengthens.

Yet the promise of this life is imperiled by the very genius that has made it possible. Nations amass wealth. Labor sweats to create —and turns out devices to level not only mountains but also cities. Science seems ready to confer upon us, as its final gift, the power to erase human life from this planet.

At such a time in history, we who are free must proclaim anew our faith.

This faith is the abiding creed of our fathers. It is our faith in the deathless dignity of man, governed by eternal moral and natural laws.

This faith defines our full view of life. It establishes, beyond debate, those gifts of the Creator that are man's inalienable rights, and that make all men equal in His sight.

In the light of this equality, we know that the virtues most cherished by free people—love of truth, pride of work, devotion to country—all are treasures equally precious in the lives of the most humble and of the most exalted. The men who mine coal and fire furnaces and balance ledgers and turn lathes and pick cotton and heal the sick and plant corn—all serve as proudly, and as profitably, for America as the statesmen who draft treaties and the legislators who enact laws.

This faith rules our whole way of life. It decrees that we, the people, elect leaders not to rule but to serve. It asserts that we have the right to choice of our own work and to the reward of our own toil. It inspires the initiative that makes our productivity the wonder of the world. And it warns that any man who seeks to deny equality among all his brothers betrays the spirit of the free and invites the mockery of the tyrant.

It is because we, all of us, hold to these principles that the political changes accomplished this day do not imply turbulence, upheaval or disorder. Rather this change expresses a purpose of strengthening our dedication and devotion to the precepts of our founding documents, a conscious renewal of faith in our country and in the watchfulness of a Divine Providence.

The enemies of this faith know no god but force, no devotion but its use. They tutor men in treason. They feed upon the hunger of others. Whatever defies them, they torture, especially the truth.

Here, then, is joined no argument between slightly differing philosophies. This conflict strikes directly at the faith of our fathers and the lives of our sons. No principle or treasure that we hold, from the spiritual knowledge of our free schools and churches to the creative magic of free labor and capital, nothing lies safely beyond the reach of this struggle.

Freedom is pitted against slavery; lightness against the dark.

The faith we hold belongs not to us alone but to the free of all the world. This common bond binds the grower of rice in Burma and the planter of wheat in Iowa, the shepherd in southern Italy and the mountaineer in the Andes. It confers a common dignity upon the French soldier who dies in Indo-China, the British soldier killed in Malaya, the American life given in Korea.

We know, beyond this, that we are linked to all free peoples not merely by a noble idea but by a simple need. No free people can for long cling to any privilege or enjoy any safety in economic solitude. For all our own material might, even we need markets in the world for the surpluses of our farms and our factories. Equally, we need for these same farms and factories vital materials and products of distant lands. This basic law of interdependence, so manifest in the commerce of peace, applies with thousand-fold intensity in the event of war.

So we are persuaded by necessity and by belief that the strength of all free peoples lies in unity; their danger, in discord.

To produce this unity, to meet the challenge of our time, destiny has laid upon our country the responsibility of the free world's leadership.

So it is proper that we assure our friends once again that, in the discharge of this responsibility, we Americans know and we observe the difference between world leadership and imperialism; between firmness and truculence; between a thoughtfully calculated goal and spasmodic reaction to the stimulus of emergencies.

We wish our friends the world over to know this above all: we face the threat—not with dread and confusion—but with confidence and conviction.

We feel this moral strength because we know that we are not helpless prisoners of history. We are free men. We shall remain free, never to be proven guilty of the one capital offense against freedom, a lack of stanch faith.

In pleading our just cause before the bar of history and in pressing our labor for world peace, we shall be guided by certain fixed principles.

These principles are:

(1) Abhorring war as a chosen way to balk the purposes of those who threaten us, we hold it to be the first task of statesmanship to develop the strength that will deter the forces of aggression and promote the conditions of peace. For, as it must be the supreme purpose of all free men, so it must be the dedication of their leaders, to save humanity from preying upon itself.

In the light of this principle, we stand ready to engage with any and all others in joint effort to remove the causes of mutual fear and distrust among nations, so as to make possible drastic reduction of armaments. The sole requisites for undertaking such effort are that—in their purpose—they be aimed logically and honestly toward secure peace for all; and that—in their result—they provide methods by which every participating nation will prove good faith in carrying out its pledge.

(2) Realizing that common sense and common decency alike dictate the futility of appeasement, we shall never try to placate an aggressor by the false and wicked bargain of trading honor for security. Americans, indeed all free men, remember that in the final choice a soldier's pack is not so heavy a burden as a prisoner's chains.

(3) Knowing that only a United States that is strong and immensely productive can help defend freedom in our world, we view our Nation's strength and security as a trust upon which rests the hope of free men everywhere. It is the firm duty of each of our free citizens and of every free citizen everywhere to place the cause of his country before the comfort, the convenience of himself.

(4) Honoring the identity and the special heritage of each nation in the world, we shall never use our strength to try to impress upon another people our own cherished political and economic institutions.

(5) Assessing realistically the needs and capacities of proven friends of freedom, we shall strive to help them to achieve their own security and well-being. Likewise, we shall count upon them to assume, within the limits of their resources, their full and just burdens in the common defense of freedom.

(6) Recognizing economic health as an indispensable basis of military strength and the free world's peace, we shall strive to foster everywhere, and to practice ourselves, policies that encourage productivity and profitable trade. For the impoverishment of any single people in the world means danger to the well-being of all other peoples.

(7) Appreciating that economic need, military security and political wisdom combine to suggest regional groupings of free peoples, we hope, within the framework of the United Nations, to help strengthen such special bonds the world over. The nature of these ties must vary with the different problems of different areas.

In the Western Hemisphere, we enthusiastically join with all our neighbors in the work of perfecting a community of fraternal trust and common purpose.

In Europe, we ask that enlightened and inspired leaders of the Western nations strive with renewed vigor to make the unity of their peoples a reality. Only as free Europe unitedly marshals its strength can it effectively safeguard, even with our help, its spiritual and cultural heritage.

(8) Conceiving the defense of freedom, like freedom itself, to be one and indivisible, we hold all continents and peoples in equal regard and honor. We reject any insinuation that one race or another, one people or another, is in any sense inferior or expendable.

(9) Respecting the United Nations as the living sign of all people's hope for peace, we shall strive to make it not merely an eloquent symbol but an effective force. And in our quest for an honorable peace, we shall neither compromise, nor tire, nor ever cease.

By these rules of conduct, we hope to be known to all peoples.

By their observance, an earth of peace may become not a vision but a fact.

This hope—this supreme aspiration—must rule the way we live.

We must be ready to dare all for our country. For history does not long entrust the care of freedom to the weak or the timid. We must acquire proficiency in defense and display stamina in purpose.

We must be willing, individually and as a Nation, to accept whatever sacrifices may be required of us. A people that values its privileges above its principles soon loses both.

These basic precepts are not lofty abstractions, far removed from matters of daily living. They are laws of spiritual strength that generate and define our material strength. Patriotism means equipped forces and a prepared citizenry. Moral stamina means more energy and more productivity, on the farm and in the factory. Love of liberty means the guarding of every resource that makes freedom possible—from the sanctity of our families and the wealth of our soil to the genius of our scientists.

And so each citizen plays an indispensable role. The productivity of our heads, our hands, and our hearts is the source of all the strength we can command, for both the enrichment of our lives and the winning of the peace.

No person, no home, no community can be beyond the reach of this call. We are summoned to act in wisdom and in conscience, to work with industry, to teach with persuasion, to preach with conviction, to weigh our every deed with care and with compassion. For this truth must be clear before us: whatever America hopes to bring to pass in the world must first come to pass in the heart of America.

The peace we seek, then, is nothing less than the practice and fulfillment of our whole faith among ourselves and in our dealings with others. This signifies more than the stilling of guns, easing the sorrow of war. More than escape from death, it is a way of life. More than a haven for the weary, it is a hope for the brave.

This is the hope that beckons us onward in this century of trial. This is the work that awaits us all, to be done with bravery, with charity, and with prayer to Almighty God.

ADDRESS DELIVERED BY PRESIDENT EISENHOWER AT THE LUNCHEON OF THE AMERICAN SOCIETY OF NEWSPAPER EDITORS IN THE HOTEL STATLER, WASHINGTON, D. C., APRIL 16, 1953.

In this spring of 1953, the free world weighs one question above all others: the chance for a just peace for all peoples.

To weigh this chance is to summon instantly to mind another recent moment of great decision. It came with that yet more hopeful spring of 1945, bright with the promise of victory and of freedom. The hope of all just men in *that* moment, too, was a just and lasting peace.

The eight years that have passed have seen that hope waver, grow dim, and almost die. And the shadow of fear again has darkly lengthened across the world.

Today the hope of free men remains stubborn and brave, but it is sternly disciplined by experience.

It shuns not only all crude counsel of despair, but also the self-deceit of easy illusion.

It weighs the chance for peace with sure, clear knowledge of what happened to the vain hope of 1945.

In that spring of victory, the soldiers of the Western Allies met the soldiers of Russia in the center of Europe. They were triumphant comrades in arms. Their peoples shared the joyous prospect of building, in honor of their dead, the only fitting monument—an age of just peace.

All these war-weary peoples shared, too, this concrete, decent purpose: to guard vigilantly against the domination ever again of any part of the world by a single, unbridled aggressive power.

This common purpose lasted an instant—and perished. The nations of the world divided to follow two distinct roads.

The United States and our valued friends, the other free nations, chose one road.

The leaders of the Soviet Union chose another.

The way chosen by the United States was plainly marked by a few clear precepts which govern its conduct in world affairs.

First: No people on earth can be held—as a *people*—to be an enemy, for all humanity shares the common hunger for peace and fellowship and justice.

Second: No nation's security and well-being can be lastingly achieved in isolation, but only in effective cooperation with fellow-nations.

Third: Any nation's right to a form of government and an economic system of its own choosing is *inalienable*.

Fourth: Any nation's attempt to dictate to other nations their form of government is *indefensible*.

And fifth: A nation's hope of lasting peace cannot be firmly based upon any race in armaments, but rather upon just relations and honest understanding with all other nations.

In the light of these principles, the citizens of the United States defined the way they proposed to follow, through the aftermath of war, toward true peace.

This way was faithful to the spirit that inspired the United Nations: to prohibit strife, to relieve tensions, to banish fears. This way was to control and to reduce armaments. This way was to allow all nations to devote their energies and resources to the great and good tasks of healing the war's wounds, of clothing and feeding and housing the needy, of perfecting a just political life, of enjoying the fruits of their own free toil.

The Soviet government held a vastly different vision of the future.

In the world of *its* design, security was to be found—not in mutual trust and mutual aid—but in *force:* huge armies, subversion, rule of neighbor nations. The goal was power superiority—at all cost. Security was to be sought by denying it to all others.

The result has been tragic for the world and, for the Soviet Union, it has also been ironic.

The amassing of Soviet power alerted free nations to a new danger of aggression. It compelled them in self-defense to spend unprecedented money and energy for armaments. It forced them to develop weapons of war now capable of inflicting instant and terrible punishment upon any aggressor.

It instilled in the free nations—and let none doubt this—the unshakeable conviction that, as long as there persists a threat to freedom, they must, at *any* cost, remain armed, strong and ready for any risk of war.

It inspired them—and let none doubt *this*—to attain a unity of purpose and will beyond the power of propaganda or pressure to break, now or ever.

There remained, however, one thing essentially unchanged and unaffected by Soviet conduct: the readiness of the free nations to welcome sincerely any genuine evidence of peaceful purpose enabling all peoples again to resume their common quest of just peace.

The free nations, most solemnly and repeatedly, have assured the Soviet Union that their firm association has never had any aggressive purpose whatsoever.

Soviet leaders, however, have seemed to persuade themselves—or tried to persuade their people—otherwise.

And so it has come to pass that the Soviet Union *itself* has shared and suffered the very fears it has fostered in the rest of the world.

This has been the way of life forged by eight years of fear and force.

What can the world—or any nation in it—hope for if no turning is found on this dread road?

The worst to be feared and the best to be expected can be simply stated.

The *worst* is atomic war.

The *best* would be this: a life of perpetual fear and tension; a burden or arms draining the wealth and the labor of all peoples; a wasting of strength that defies the American system or the Soviet system or any system to achieve true abundance and happiness for the peoples of this earth.

Every gun that is made, every warship launched, every rocket fired signifies—in the final sense—a *theft* from those who hunger and are not fed, those who are cold and are not clothed.

This world in arms is not spending money alone.

It is spending the sweat of its laborers, the genius of its scientists, the hopes of its children.

The cost of one modern heavy bomber is this: a modern brick school in more than 30 cities.

It is: two electric power plants, each serving a town of 60,000 population.

It is: two fine, fully equipped hospitals.

It is some fifty miles of concrete highway.

We pay for a single fighter plane with a half million bushels of wheat.

We pay for a single destroyer with new homes that could have housed more than 8,000 people.

This—I repeat—is the best way of life to be found on the road the world has been taking.

This is not a way of life at all, in any true sense. Under the cloud of threatening war, it is humanity hanging from a cross of iron.

These plain and cruel truths define the peril and point the hope that come with this spring of 1953.

This is one of those times in the affairs of nations when the gravest choices must be made—if there is to be a turning toward a just and lasting peace.

It is a moment that calls upon the governments of the world to speak their intentions with simplicity and with honesty.

It calls upon them to answer the question that stirs the hearts of all sane men: *is there no other way the world may live?*

The world knows that an era ended with the death of Josef Stalin. The extraordinary 30-year span of his rule saw the Soviet Empire expand to reach from the Baltic Sea to the Sea of Japan, finally to dominate 800 million souls.

The Soviet system shaped by Stalin and his predecessors was born of one World War. It survived with stubborn and often amazing courage a Second World War. It has lived to threaten a third.

Now a new leadership has assumed power in the Soviet Union. Its links to the past, however strong, cannot bind it completely. Its future is, in great part, its own to make.

This new leadership confronts a free world aroused, as rarely in its history, by the will to stay free.

This free world knows—out of the bitter wisdom of experience—that vigilance and sacrifice are the price of liberty.

It knows that the defense of Western Europe imperatively demands the unity of purpose and action made possible by the North Atlantic Treaty Organization, embracing a European Defense Community.

It knows that Western Germany deserves to be a free and equal partner in this community; and that this, for Germany, is the only safe way to full, final unity.

It knows that aggression in Korea and in southeast Asia are threats to the whole free community to be met by united action.

This is the kind of free world which the new Soviet leadership confronts. It is a world that demands and expects the fullest respect of its rights and interests. It is a world that will always accord the same respect to all others.

So the new Soviet leadership now has a precious opportunity to awaken, with the rest of the world, to the point of peril reached, and to help turn the tide of history.

Will it do this?

We do not yet know. Recent statements and gestures of Soviet leaders give some evidence that they may recognize this critical moment.

We welcome every honest act of peace.

We care nothing for mere rhetoric.

We care only for sincerity of peaceful purpose—attested by deeds. The opportunities for such deeds are many. The performance of a great number of them waits upon no complex protocol but upon the simple will to do them. Even a few such clear and specific acts— such as the Soviet Union's signature upon an Austrian treaty, or its release of thousands of prisoners still held from World War II— would be impressive signs of sincere intent. They would carry a power of persuasion not to be matched by any amount of oratory.

This we *do* know: a world that begins to witness the rebirth of trust among nations *can* find its way to a peace that is neither partial nor punitive.

With all who will work in good faith toward such a peace, we are ready—with renewed resolve—to strive to redeem the near-lost hopes of our day.

The first great step along this way must be the conclusion of an honorable armistice in Korea.

This means the immediate cessation of hostilities and the prompt initiation of political discussions leading to the holding of free elections in a united Korea.

It should mean—no less importantly—an end to the direct and indirect attacks upon the security of Indo-China and Malaya. For any armistice in Korea that merely released aggressive armies to attack elsewhere would be a fraud.

We seek, throughout Asia as throughout the world, a peace that is true and total.

Out of this can grow a still wider task—the achieving of just political settlements for the other serious and specific issues between the free world and the Soviet Union.

None of these issues, great or small, is insoluble—given only the will to respect the rights of all nations.

Again we say: the United States is ready to assume its just part.

We have already done all within our power to speed conclusion of a treaty with Austria which will free that country from economic exploitation and from occupation by foreign troops.

We are ready not only to press forward with the present plans for closer unity of the nations of Western Europe but also, upon that foundation, to strive to foster a broader European community, conducive to the free movement of persons, of trade, and of ideas.

This community would include a free and united Germany, with a government based upon free and secret elections.

This free community and the full independence of the East European nations could mean the end of the present unnatural division of Europe.

As progress in all these areas strengthens world trust, we could proceed concurrently with the next great work—the reduction of the burden of armaments now weighing upon the world. To this end, we would welcome and enter into the most solemn agreements. These could properly include:

(1) the limitation, by absolute numbers or by an agreed international ratio, of the sizes of the military and security forces of all nations;

(2) a commitment by all nations to set an agreed limit upon that proportion of total production of certain strategic materials to be devoted to military purposes;

(3) international control of atomic energy to promote its use for peaceful purposes only, and to ensure the prohibition of atomic weapons;

(4) a limitation or prohibition of other categories of weapons of great destructiveness;

(5) the enforcement of all these agreed limitations and prohibitions by adequate safeguards, including a practical system of inspection under the United Nations.

The details of such disarmament programs are manifestly critical and complex. Neither the United States nor any other nation can properly claim to possess a perfect, immutable formula. But the formula matters less than the faith—the good faith without which no formula can work justly and effectively.

The fruit of success in all these tasks would present the world with the greatest task—and the greatest opportunity—of all. It is this: the dedication of the energies, the resources, and the imaginations of all peaceful nations to a *new* kind of war. This would be a declared, total war, not upon any human enemy, but upon the brute forces of poverty and need.

The peace we seek, founded upon decent trust and cooperative effort among nations, can be fortified—not by weapons of war—but by wheat and by cotton; by milk and by wool; by meat and by timber and by rice.

These are words that translate into every language on earth.

These are needs that challenge this world in arms.

This idea of a just and peaceful world is not new or strange to us. It inspired the people of the United States to initiate the European Recovery Program in 1947. That program was prepared to treat, with like and equal concern, the needs of eastern and western Europe.

We are prepared to reaffirm, with the most concrete evidence, our readiness to help build a world in which all peoples can be productive and prosperous.

This government is ready to ask its people to join with all nations in devoting a substantial percentage of the savings achieved by disarmament to a fund for world aid and reconstruction. The purposes of this great work would be: to help other peoples to develop the undeveloped areas of the world, to stimulate profitable and fair world trade, to assist all peoples to know the blessings of productive freedom.

The monuments to this new kind of war would be these: roads and schools, hospitals and homes, food and health.

We are ready, in short, to dedicate our strength to serving the *needs,* rather than the *fears,* of the world.

We are ready, by these and all such actions, to make of the United Nations an institution that can effectively guard the peace and security of all peoples.

I know of nothing I can add to make plainer the sincere purpose of the United States.

I know of no course, other than that marked by these and similar actions, that can be called the highway of peace.

I know of only one question upon which progress waits. It is this: *What is the Soviet Union ready to do?*

Whatever the answer be, let it be plainly spoken.

Again we say: the hunger for peace is too great, the hour in history too late, for any government to mock men's hopes with mere words and promises and gestures.

The test of truth is simple. There can be no persuasion but by deeds.

Is the new leadership of the Soviet Union prepared to use its decisive influence in the Communist world—including control of the flow of arms—to bring not merely an expedient truce in Korea but genuine peace in Asia?

Is it prepared to allow other nations, including those of Eastern Europe, the free choice of their own forms of government and the right to associate freely with other nations in a world-wide community of law?

Is it prepared to act in concert with others upon serious disarmament proposals to be made firmly effective by stringent UN control and inspection?

If not—where then is the concrete evidence of the Soviet Union's concern for peace?

The test is clear.

There is, before all peoples, a precious chance to turn the black tide of events.

If we failed to strive to seize this chance, the judgement of future ages would be harsh and just.

If we strive but fail, and the world remains armed against itself, it at least need be divided no longer in its clear knowledge of who has condemned humankind to this fate.

The purpose of the United States, in stating these proposals, is simple and clear.

These proposals spring—without ulterior purpose or political passion—from our calm conviction that the hunger for just peace is in the hearts of all peoples—those of Russia and of China no less than of our own country.

They conform to our firm faith that God created men to enjoy, not destroy, the fruits of the earth and of their own toil.

They aspire to this: the lifting, from the backs and from the hearts of men, of their burden of arms and of fears, so that they may find before them a golden age of freedom and of peace.

ADDRESS BY THE HONORABLE JOHN FOSTER DULLES, SECRETARY OF STATE, BEFORE THE AMERICAN SOCIETY OF NEWSPAPER EDITORS, HOTEL STATLER, WASHINGTON, D. C., APRIL 18, 1953.

THE FIRST 90 DAYS

President Eisenhower, speaking here last Thursday, opened the door to the mansion of peace. He invited the Soviet Union to come in. That invitation was not mere rhetoric. Its timing was not chosen at hazard. It marked a planned stage in the evolution of Eisenhower foreign policy. The speech really had its beginning when President Eisenhower took office, which was 90 days ago tomorrow.

The words which President Eisenhower uttered might have been uttered at any time during these past 90 days. But these words gained immensely in significance because they came against a background of cohesive, positive action.

When President Eisenhower first took office, a plea for peace such as he made this week might have been interpreted as a sign of weakness or a mere gesture of sentimentality. In order that such a plea should carry maximum impact, it was first necessary to demonstrate to the world, and to Soviet leaders in particular, President Eisenhower's will and capacity to develop foreign policies so firm, so fair, so just, that the Soviet leaders might find it expedient to live with these policies rather than to live against them.

I should like briefly to review this 90-day period, which had as its climax the President's historical address.

THE EUROPEAN DEFENSE COMMUNITY

One of the worries of the free world, and one of the hopes of the Soviet world, has been disunity in Western Europe. For example, it would be particularly disastrous for the West if Franco-German antagonism were revived. That would indeed afford Soviet intrigue a fertile field of operation.

The continental European countries themselves, including France and Germany, had seen the danger and had devised a program to meet it. They had proposed to create a European Defense Community, the members of which would merge their military power into a single force. A treaty to this effect was signed nearly a year ago. It was contemplated by the treaty that it would be ratified and come into force within six months. But, following the signature of the treaty, nothing happened. Last January, it seemed that the project was dying.

The President, out of his own intimate knowledge of European conditions, felt that our Government should indicate its deep concern and point out that failure to realize the European Defense Community could mean collapse of the hopes and efforts that inspired the Marshall Plan, the North Atlantic Treaty and the Mutual Security Program. Therefore, on January 30th, just ten days after the President's inaugural, Mr. Stassen and I, at the President's request, visited the six European Defense Community countries, and also Great Britain. As a result of our visit, and the return visits to Washington of several European leaders, this project has now been revived. It cannot yet be confidently predicted that it will be realized. But it is today the livest single topic before the six parliaments of continental Europe.

The Soviet Union now faces the likelihood that Western Europe will produce a unified military force, including French and Germans. Thus would come to a final end one of the hopes from which Soviet imperialism has taken comfort.

NATO

It was never expected that the European Defense Community, when created, would alone carry the burdens of making Western Europe secure. EDC, a community of six, would stand within the framework of NATO, a partnership of 14. This partnership, however, also presented us with urgent problems. For most of the members had come to feel that the program for NATO represented a type of effort which they could not continue indefinitely to bear.

The United States and its NATO partners had been operating on the assumption that the moment of greatest danger was some early, predictable date. Therefore, it had been reasoned, emergency efforts should be made to meet that date, leaving subsequent years for stabilization and recuperation.

But the Soviet Union did not conveniently relax its threat in order to meet the preconceived time-table of the NATO countries. Accordingly, it was found necessary each year to prolong the extraordinary exertion and to defer the period of stabilization. This spasmodic approach was exhaustive to all concerned. Several of our Allies told us that they could not hold to the present pace without greatly increased help from the United States.

The situation obviously called for a fresh approach.

Because we did not believe that any specific date of peak danger could be reliably forecast; because Soviet Communism itself professes to operate in terms of "an entire historical era"; because new weapons inevitably change the aspect of the military task; because a vigorous and happy society is itself an important ingredient of freedom—for these reasons we decided to find programs which, on the one hand, will provide Europe with substantial insurance against being overrun by Soviet attack, and which, on the other hand, can, if necessary, be sustained for an indefinite period with growing reliance on Western Europe's own strength.

Next week the Secretary of the Treasury, Mr. Humphrey, the Secretary of Defense, Mr. Wilson, the Director for Mutual Security, Mr. Stassen, and I will go to Paris to meet with the other members of the North Atlantic Treaty Organization Council. There we shall listen sympathetically to the point of view of our partners and together with them concert military programs designed to deter attack from without, without undermining inner strength.

All will know, and I am confident that the Soviet leaders know best of all, that what we plan is not greater weakness but greater strength. The productivity of the free world is so prodigious, its inventiveness so phenomenal, that any military aggressor that attacked our free world partnership would be doomed to sure defeat.

What we plan is to dissipate another Soviet hope, the hope expressed by Stalin when he said that "the moment for the decisive blow" would come when the opponents of Communism "have sufficiently weakened themselves in a struggle which is beyond their strength . . . have sufficiently disgraced themselves through their practical bankruptcy so that our victory is assured." We do not intend that that moment of bankruptcy shall come.

Let me add that the policy here expressed was determined upon without regard to any of the recent Soviet moves. We are not dancing to any Russian tune. Nothing that has happened has induced in us a mood of relaxation or any desire to weaken NATO. The purpose and the result will be a NATO more sure to live and to perform its appointed tasks.

THE FAR EAST

In the Far East vigorous policy decisions were also taken since the 90 days began. In Korea we embarked upon a program to change the complexion of that struggle. As President Eisenhower told you, we still welcome an armistice, not merely to end the fighting but on the assumption that it will lead to a peace which accords with the principles of the United Nations—and that means a free and united Korea. Of course we want peace in Korea. But we do not play the role of suppliants.

We have vastly improved our relations with the National Government of China. We now have an Ambassador at Taipei, Formosa, the provisional capital. We are speeding the delivery of military assistance which was woefully in arrears. President Eisenhower has changed the instructions to the Seventh Fleet so that, while it is still instructed to protect Formosa, it is no longer instructed to protect the Chinese Communists on the mainland.

In relation to Indochina, the French Government and the Associated States have been told that we would be favorably disposed to giving increased military and financial assistance to plans realistically designed to suppress the Communist-inspired civil war which for six years has wracked the area and seriously drained the metropolitan resources of France.

We recently announced, in conjunction with the French Government, that should the Chinese Communist régime take advantage of a Korean armistice to pursue aggressive war elsewhere in the Far East, such action would have the most serious consequences and would conflict directly with the understanding on which any armistice in Korea was reached. That decision was taken prior to the recent revival of prospects for a Korean armistice. It was part of our effort to anticipate what may happen rather than to catch up with what has happened.

We negotiated with the Governments of Britain, France and other maritime powers for a tightening of the blockade of Communist China. They are taking important practical measures to restrict the voyages of their own ships to China and to withhold fuel from ships of other nations which are carrying strategic goods to China.

You can see, as others have seen, that a new order of priority and urgency has been given to the Far East. Further, it has been made clear that we consider that our Eastern friends, from Japan, Korea and Formosa, to Indochina and Malaya, face a single hostile front, to be met with a common purpose and growing cooperation as between the component parts of freedom.

This means that the Communists in the Far East can no longer count on winning by shifting their strength and by focusing attack on one or another free world position that is isolated from the others. The Communist strategy, based on a contiguous land mass, is now confronted by a growing free world unity based upon the peninsular positions and offshore island chain now controlled by the free peoples of Asia.

The Middle East and Latin America

The Middle East and Latin America, two areas far apart, have both been the subject of Communist attempts at infiltration. The ground was fertile because these areas have somewhat lacked our attention, and, in the case of the Middle East, there has developed a spirit of nationalism, which has at times grown fanatical in its opposition to the Western powers.

As was announced some weeks ago, Mr. Stassen and I have been invited by the Governments of more than a dozen countries of the Middle East and South Asia to visit them. We have accepted and plan to go next month. That is significant, for no United States Secretary of State has ever visited any of these countries. It will afford us an opportunity to meet at firsthand many of the leaders and, I hope, to dissipate the false impressions which Communist propaganda has fomented.

As President Eisenhower announced last Sunday, the State Department is organizing a goodwill mission to South America which will be headed by the President's brother, Dr. Milton Eisenhower. He will personally carry the President's sentiments of goodwill toward the Republics and peoples to the South of us. Our new Assistant Secretary for this area is already in Central America.

I have had the pleasure of two meetings, one at the United Nations and the other at Washington, with the representatives of all 20 of the American Republics.

What we have done, and what we already plan, mark a determination to develop better understanding, and more fellowship, with peoples whom we know and respect, but whose friendship we have taken too much for granted. Thereby, we may close another possible avenue of Soviet Communist aggression.

CAPTIVE PEOPLES

The free peoples are susceptible to Soviet guile because they so passionately want peace that they can readily be attracted by illusions of peace. One such illusion is a settlement based on the *status quo*. This present status involves the captivity of hundreds of millions of persons of distinctive nationality, race, religion and culture. The hardest task of the Soviet rulers is to beat this disunity into Communist conformity. If that can be done, then the menace of Soviet Communism will be immeasurably increased.

It was of the utmost importance that we should make clear to the captive peoples that we do not accept their captivity as a permanent fact of history. If they thought otherwise and became hopeless, we would unwittingly have become partners to the forging of a hostile power so vast that it could encompass our destruction.

President Eisenhower, anticipating some of the events that have since occurred, acted immediately after his inauguration to propose that our national position should be made clear through a solemn resolution concurred in by Congress and the President. The Congress has yet to act. However, I am persuaded, and I trust that the captive peoples are persuaded, that Congress in fact fully shares the point of view that President Eisenhower expressed. In any event, the Chief Executive has formulated his position on this important matter and by doing so has foreclosed another of the hopes which Soviet rulers had optimistically entertained.

STATE DEPARTMENT ORGANIZATION

While we have been making these policy decisions, we have at the same time been acting to assure that the State Department would be able to make new policies wherever these would seem better than the old and to assure a steadily rising level of performance.

In addition to the new Secretary of State, there are two new Under Secretaries, one of whom specializes in administration and security matters. There are six new Assistant Secretaries. There is a new Legal Adviser, a new Counselor, a new Director of International Information Administration, who has responsibility for the Voice of America. The whole Policy Planning Staff is to go under new direction and be coordinated closely with the revitalized National Security Council.

We are also bringing fresh vision and new vigor into our United Nations Mission and into our Embassies abroad. The Chief of the Permanent Mission to the United Nations, former Senator Austin, retired last January after many years of distinguished service. He has been succeeded by former Senator Henry Cabot Lodge, who now heads the Permanent Mission. His vigor and parliamentary skill already demonstrate that the Soviet leaders cannot look forward to using the United Nations as a sounding board for propaganda but that they will have to deal in the United Nations with a mobilized body of world opinion which is determined that the United Nations shall, in fact, serve its avowed purpose to maintain international peace and security in conformity with the principles of justice.

New Ambassadors are installed or being installed in Great Britain, Ireland, France, Italy, Germany, Russia, Spain, Mexico, Brazil, Japan, Free China, India and Pakistan. Other appointments are in contemplation.

For the first time in State Department history, all of our major appointments are subject to FBI field checks so as to eliminate security risks and possibility of hostile infiltration into high places. So far as is humanly practical, we are seeing to it that Communist agents shall not have access to the State Department.

We are fortunate in having a body of Foreign Service career men and women who can be the main reliance of the President and myself. They are a permanent and non-political part of Government. They became such under the Rogers Act, enacted by a Republican Congress during the Administration of President Coolidge and Secretary Hughes.

There is a tendency in some quarters to feel that confidence cannot be placed in these career officials because in the past, as was their duty, they served under Democrat Presidents and Democrat Secretaries of State. It is, however, easier than most think for our career Foreign Service men and women to adapt themselves to new Republican leadership. Like career soldiers, Foreign Service officers respect and welcome high-level policy direction such as they are getting under President Eisenhower. They are, with rare exceptions, a splendid and patriotic group of men and women, with a fine tradition. They are experts, trained to analyze and interpret foreign conditions and to carry out designated missions, usually of delicacy, sometimes of danger. Just as the nation depends, for defense purposes, on the graduates of our military and naval academies, so the nation, for foreign services, depends on our career diplomats.

Our people here at home, our friends abroad and our enemies abroad can know that we have not only strong foreign policies but that we are rapidly molding an organization which will be secure and which will be efficient in action.

I might add as of particular interest to this distinguished group of American editors that these foreign policies of which I speak are no longer looked upon as state secrets. We are determined that the public shall be as fully informed as possible, and in the clearest and simplest language possible, about what we are doing in the State Department and what our foreign policy is.

I have long felt that, under our form of government, the effectiveness of foreign policy depends in large measure upon public understanding and support of it.

The Soviet Peace Defensive

Our conduct has been calmly strong, never truculent nor blustering. In the face of it, Soviet leaders gave evidence that they were changing their policies. They initiated what presents to you and to me one of the most perplexing problems of our time. It is a problem that I think is largely due to a misnomer. The Kremlin launched what is commonly called a "peace offensive." Whatever it is that the Kremlin has launched—and no one can be sure just yet what it is—it is not a peace *offensive*. It is a peace *defensive*.

It is gratifying that Soviet leaders appear now to have shifted from an offensive to a defensive mood. But we cannot yet tell whether this represents a basic change, or merely a tactical shift. It is prudent, for the present, to assume that we are witnessing a tactical move of the kind which Soviet Communism has often practiced.

Stalin, in his classic treatise on "Strategy and Tactics" taught that, from time to time, "concessions" may have to be made "in order to buy off a powerful enemy and gain a respite." He went on to explain the necessity of maneuvering with a "view to effecting a proper retreat when the enemy is strong . . . The object of this strategy is to gain time and to accumulate forces in order later to assume the offensive."

Is the successor—or should I say, are the successors—following this strategy of the dead Stalin?

Whatever the reason and purpose of present Soviet moves, the fact is that the Communist leaders seem now disposed to grant some things which they formerly denied.

Last February 22nd, in an effort to probe the mood of the enemy in Korea, we quietly proposed an exchange of sick and wounded prisoners of war. Such proposals had frequently been made before, without results. This time a result seems to be in the making.

I should perhaps explain, to end some misunderstanding, that while under the agreement made we will return many more sick and wounded prisoners than we will receive, that is because the total number of prisoners which we hold is many times the number held by the Communists. The ratio of returning sick and wounded to the total prisoners of war held is approximately the same for both sides, with a slight advantage in our favor.

It also now appears that the enemy may now want an armistice in Korea, after having evaded it for nearly two years.

In other respects and in other quarters Communist leadership is making concessions. These are all still minor, but not without significance. They suggested to us that the time had come to launch a true peace offensive. That, President Eisenhower has done. Soviet leadership is now confronted by the Eisenhower tests. Will it meet, one by one, the issues with which President Eisenhower has challenged it? If so, will it abolish and abandon, in fact as well as in name, the Cominform through which it endlessly conspires to overthrow, from within, every genuinely free government in the world? We await the deeds which will give answer to these questions. We profoundly hope that these deeds will, in fact, end a black chapter of distrust and open a bright new chapter of peace and good will.

THE NEW ERA

Some weeks ago when I was at the United Nations, I said that the Stalin era had ended and that the Eisenhower era had begun, bringing with it new hope for all mankind. Already that prediction is in process of confirmation. President Eisenhower's address is a fact which will inevitably influence the course of history. Around the world peoples and governments have universally welcomed that address. In all the capitals of the free world, press and radio have demonstrated an unprecedented spontaneous support for the President's call for a world-wide peace offensive and his challenge to the new Soviet leadership to back up their words with deeds. That response is not merely because of the words the President used, but because what he said had its setting in a ninety-day framework.

I do not attempt to read the future. That must always remain obscure so long as vast power is possessed by men who accept no guidance from the moral law. But surely our duty is clear. Those who represent a nation with the tradition and power of the United States must act boldly and strongly for what they believe to be right. The future is for a higher verdict.

Index